SALVATION
FOR SALE

NEW, UPDATED EDITION

SALVATION FOR SALE

An Insider's View of Pat Robertson

Gerard Thomas Straub

PROMETHEUS BOOKS
700 East Amherst St., Buffalo, New York 14215

90 89 88   5   4   3   2

Library of Congress Cataloging-in-Publication Data

Straub, Gerard Thomas.
    Salvation for sale.

    1. Robertson, Pat. 2. Christian Broadcasting
Network (U.S.). 3. Fundamentalism—Controversial
literature. 4. Straub, Gerard Thomas. 5. Television
in religion—United States—Controversial literature.
1. Title.
BR17525.R62S73   1986   269'.2   86-17000
ISBN 0-87975-436-2

For

Adrienne Frances Straub,
Kathleen Marie Straub,
and
Ronald Joseph Gerhard

Those who believe that they believe in God, but without passion in their hearts, without anguish in mind, without uncertainty, without doubt, without an element of despair even in their consolation, believe only in the God idea, not God Himself.

Miguel de Unamuno
Spanish philosopher and
writer

Doubt is a pain too lonely to know that faith is his twin brother.

Kahlil Gibran
Lebanese philosopher, poet,
and artist

Doubt isn't the opposite of faith; it is an element of faith.

Paul Tillich
German theologian and
historian

Doubt is not a pleasant condition, but certainty is absurd.

Voltaire
French philosopher and
writer

If only God would give me some clear sign! Like making a large deposit in my name at a Swiss bank.

Woody Allen
American comic, writer, and
filmmaker

Contents

Introduction to Updated Edition

> Who can protest and does not is an accomplice to the act.
>
> —The Talmud

"It is finished." Or so I thought on February 4, 1986, at 10:57:34 A.M., when I wrote those words in bold print in my diary. I pushed myself away from my paper-cluttered desk, stood up, and looked down at the typed final draft of my two-and-a-half-inch-thick, 423-page manuscript, which I had just completed proofreading. My sense of accomplishment overshadowed the total physical and emotional exhaustion that I felt from the nearly three-year-long lonely struggle to not only understand but also to tell the dual story of my born-again salvation and my unholy experience of working for the television superstar preacher turned presidential candidate Pat Robertson.

Like a parent proudly holding his newborn child, I cradled the fruit of my labor in my arms, braced myself against the cold, and headed for the post office to mail the manuscript to the publisher. When it was safely on its way, I stood motionless in front of the post office; I took a deep breath of the chilly New York City air and felt the freedom. My obsession to share this frightening story of religious deception and intolerance no longer enslaved me. I was free—but poor. The writing of the book had pushed me to the edge of bankruptcy, and I suddenly realized that I had to get my television career back on track. I quickly put my life as a struggling writer searching for truth and understanding behind me. Within two months, I was working as the supervising producer of the daytime soap opera "Capitol" at CBS Television City in Hollywood.

I thought that *Salvation for Sale* was, for me at least, history; and,

5

while I eagerly awaited the publication date and the moment when I could hold a copy of it in my hands or see it on a shelf in a bookstore, I had no inkling of the storm of controversy that lay ahead of me. It was not finished. The real work—the real suffering—was still to come.

After the book was published, I found myself under the media microscope during numerous radio interviews and television appearances. I was suddenly in demand because of the public's new-found interest in the fundamentalist faith of the televangelists, an interest sparked by the "Pearlygate" scandals involving Oral Roberts and Jim Bakker, and, more important, the surprisingly strong presidential bid by Pat Robertson. The media interrogation and Pat Robertson's vicious, lie-laced assaults combined to make the post-publication period a time of great emotional turmoil. Suddenly I was the focus of hate mail from people who had read the book and of anger from listeners who called the radio station during interviews. Most difficult of all was having to face the hostile television studio audiences. In no time I was transformed from television producer to devil. I had touched a raw nerve and the fundamentalist reaction was explosive. I also received comforting mail from former fundamentalists who thanked me for helping them see that it was okay to doubt. Other former CBNers called with their own horror stories about the Reverend Robertson.

All of this forced me to probe more deeply into the facts about both CBN and the man who conceived and nurtured it into a powerful worldwide religious empire. Gradually I acquired a new occupation, a short-term one, I hoped; namely, correcting as many as possible of Pat Robertson's lies to the press and presenting documentation of some of his more bizarre unpublicized utterances.

The discovery of an audiotape of a January 1, 1980, CBN all-staff prayer meeting revealed a Pat Robertson the public had never seen or heard—a man convinced that God was fed up with most of humanity and was going to unleash a fiery day of judgement in 1982. The prophet was convinced because God had told him so. Obviously, time proved either that the voice Robertson heard was not God's or that Robertson incorrectly heard what was said; the former is my bet.

Driven by a renewed curiosity to understand a man I had once greatly respected and admired, I began reading all of Pat's books published after I left CBN. My reading uncovered many statements about women, the devil, and the government that the vast majority of Americans would consider outrageous, if not downright repulsive. A concerned social psychologist provided me with tapes of the "700 Club" that he had recorded. On one of them Pat Robertson actually claimed that genocide was an acceptable means for eliminating evil. That's just one of a long list of weird and dangerous Bible-based beliefs that Pat Robertson endorses.

The new information I had been gathering made *Salvation for Sale* seem incomplete. I was wrong on that cold February morning: it was not finished. Fortunately, preparing this paperback edition gave me a welcome opportunity to update it with a new chapter, called "Playtime Is Over."

It has become clear to me since the original publication of this book that the fundamentalist faith that is the foundation of Robertson's CBN kingdom is a cult—a fact that I had only hinted at before—and that it takes a long time to recover from the deadly effects of a cult's poison. Pat Robertson, who has won undisputed leadership of the religious right, is more than a threat to the freedoms we enjoy; he is a dangerous man who eagerly looks forward to a God-ignited doomsday, when—as he put it during the abovementioned prayer meeting—"the slain of the Lord will be many." For Pat, politics is purification.

This new edition of *Salvation for Sale* examines the real Pat Robertson —a man on a self-appointed mission to change the world and to usher in the Second Coming of Christ, as well as the faith that has fueled not only his ministry but also his hopes for living in the White House.

I'd like to thank Ed Cohen for helping me to better understand the mind of the Bible-believer and for offering his insightful suggestions during the writing of the final chapter.

Gerard Thomas Straub

Preface

A woman sits alone on her living room sofa. She is motionless. Yet her eyes dance with emotion, while meditatively gazing at the flickering images on her television. She is not caught up in the romantic fantasy of a daytime soap opera, the frenetic activity of a game show, or the action of a feature film. Her eyes are cast upon a real-life religious conversion.

Her attention is held captive by a preacher, one who has moved beyond the ranks of the local church congregation with its half-empty pews. His pulpit stands at the center of a state-of-the-art, technologically sophisticated television studio. His message, along with his personality, is beamed across the nation via satellite: salvation for sale. Television has turned him into a superstar, and the woman's sofa is just one of the many pews in his electronic church.

As she intently watches the drama unfold, she is exhorted to join him in prayer, confess her sinfulness, and invite Jesus into her heart. If she accepts his compelling invitation, she will make Jesus Christ the lord and master of her life.

The camera lens studies the preacher's tightly closed eyes and forehead frown. The woman is entranced by the intensity of his prayer.

"Lord Jesus, I am a sinner," she cries, having engaged his reality.

Having confessed her unworthiness, she petitions Jesus Christ for her salvation. She prays that Jesus will bestow his mercy upon her. The prayer ends with the timeless sound that comprises the word *Amen*. She is born again.

The superstar preacher, neatly attired in a tailored suit, slowly opens his eyes. He flashes a radiant smile that broadcasts a sense of deep satisfaction. Without skipping a beat, he quickly asks his easy-chair-and-sofa congregation to call a counselor (toll-free), who will pray for them and their sins, that they too may project this look of deep satisfaction.

More than 2.6 million people a year respond to this invitation to call the Christian Broadcasting Network. The free booklet offered answers the question "What now?" Undisclosed to the callers is the practice of using their names for a computerized mailing list that will regularly generate "personal" letters from the preacher. The letters will carry one message: Send me your check.

The woman picks up the phone and dials the toll-free number. She has been reached by a very powerful force, but the connection is double-edged: it may be helpful or harmful.

That same force can reach you whether you go to church daily, weekly, monthly, yearly, or never at all. The force reaches you whether you are rich or poor, black or white. The force reaches you whether you believe in God or not. It has no regard for your religious heritage, beliefs, or denominational affiliation. The force can and does affect you and your country.

The force is the electronic church, television's "God Squad," controlled by evangelical Christians out to change the world by changing and controlling your mind. By virtue of owning a television set and tuning in to their programs, you welcome them into your life.

I am a television producer. Two-and-a-half years of my twenty-year television career were spent on one of the nation's largest religious television ministries. This is the story of my abandoning the wide, wild world of network television and joining the backwaters of religious broadcasting. It is also a shocking look inside the electronic church and the experience that drove me out of video evangelism and back into the steamy world of network daytime soap operas as the associate producer of ABC's "General Hospital" and later as the executive producer of NBC's long-running serial "The Doctors."

In the three years that followed my forced exodus from the Reverend Pat Robertson's Christian Broadcasting Network (CBN), which produces "The 700 Club," many questions and doubts plagued me. Sin, Satan, salvation, speaking in tongues, spiritual superiority, religious persecution, biblical interpretation, God's will, fundamentalism, faith, the rapture, church history, and the beliefs of other faiths all became subjects of my investigation. I have reached the understanding that the "spirituality" transmitted by the electronic church contains many deficiencies; but, even more important, it is my conviction that the power of the electronic church, combined with the new Christian political right, poses a threat to peace and freedom. True, in some cases television ministries provide an important service, but they can also be an effective weapon against unity and tolerance.

The lethal mixture of religion, politics, and television has formed a holy terror with the potential to endanger freedoms we take for granted. The 1980 campaign rhetoric and election returns opened many eyes to this religious-political force and its threat to the democratic structure of the country. Religion grabbed a lion's share of the 1984 presidential election headlines; morality and abortion were as intensely debated as the economy and defense. Candidates' Christianity came under scrutiny and was frequently challenged. Ministers openly confronted politicians, and the line between church and state became increasingly blurred. The world of religious television, dominated by fundamentalist Christians, provided live coverage of the national conventions and fanned the flames of a moral uprising by fusing personal salvation with national survival. Fundamentalists claimed to know God's will; yet beneath the hype, healings, praying, preaching, begging, and show-biz glitter of these religious productions, television evangelists were (and are) feeding dogmatic, stifling spiritual pabulum to a spiritually hungry nation as they embellish little truth with many urgent words.

Afterward, as I pondered the period spent inside the fortress of fundamentalism, seeking to resolve lingering questions and doubts, I felt a responsibility to share with the public the dangers I detected in the electronic church. I am not a crusader looking to wage a holy war, and I'm not interested in evangelizing about evangelizing. I am searching, and this book is a result of that search.

The desire to share an insider's experience combined with my lifelong interest in religions and spirituality gave birth to this book. Religion is a very important part of my being. During two periods of my life, I made preparations for ordained ministry in the Roman Catholic church. I subsequently embraced a humanistic philosophy, and then moved toward an evangelical and pentecostal Protestant outlook. My spiritual search took me on a journey that explored many Christian denominations, as well as Judaism, Buddhism, and Hinduism, and led me to embrace television's fundamentalist Christianity and ultimately to reject it.

My initial approach to this book was to give a detailed description of life inside the electronic church, including how money is raised and spent, and to compare what is said in front of the camera with what is done behind it. However, much more is needed to get to the heart of the matter, which is the spiritual experience that motivates all the people who work in the electronic church. How I got there is as important as what I saw. Who was I? What was my world like that it caused me to see answers to old problems at CBN?

CBN is based on a born-again faith that is infused with the power of the Holy Spirit and demands a strict, fundamental, or literal interpretation of the Bible. Understanding that type of faith and how people are led into that belief is vital to comprehending television's role in the evangelists' mission to save the world.

On July 17, 1974, I had a born-again experience that changed my life and turned me into a warrior for Christ. Looking inside my changed heart enhances the look inside the electronic church. Today, I still consider myself a Christian, and a revised idea of God plays an important part in my life; yet I believe the Christian message emanating from the tube is misleading, unchristian, extremely dangerous, and is invading the political system.

The journey of the individual to God is both the oldest journey and the one most laden with changes of belief and personal meaning. The path is neither direct nor clearly marked for those who embark upon it, yet daily the preachings from the electronic pulpit tell us there is only one path to God and salvation, and it is clear-cut and easy. The message is clear: any deviation from their way leads not to salvation but to damnation. Therefore, they must "save" those who fail to subscribe to their beliefs, code of conduct, and method of worship. "Different drummers" are devil-made.

While this book is an exposé of Christian television, in the sense that it exposes the good and the bad that I saw, it is also a story about my spiritual journey. As a television producer, I'm a spinner of tales—and, as is often the case, truth is stranger than fiction. I was not lured out of my executive-level job at CBS by a better deal or more money; I went to CBN out of a sense of mission. Most people who sought employment at this video Vatican of religious television were not just seeking a paying job in a good company; they were responding to what they believed was a divine directive. Everyone who worked there had experienced some kind of deep spiritual conversion that compelled them to forsake anything and everything in order to be part of the ministry. A godly calling led them to CBN, and they were led there to serve. So was I—I thought.

To understand the complexities of this bastion of spirituality, you must understand the born-again phenomenon. This look inside the world of religious television must be seen through my eyes and therefore must include my born-again experience—both the way I saw it at the time and the way I understand it now—because that is a major part of the tale. As is the case with so many others, conditions in my life prior to my conversion left me susceptible to the cultlike influence of fundamentalist Christianity. I got caught up in the web of spirituality that is trying to entangle us all.

Today's video version of God is controlled by a handful of manipulators with similar beliefs, notwithstanding the fact that the fabric of this nation's religious expression is woven into a patchwork of pluralism. Beyond the diversification of the Christian path to God, we have woven into our American culture other major faiths: Judaism, Hinduism, Buddhism, and Islam, and atheism is increasingly tolerated. Along with these traditional forms of religious expression, we also have an ever-growing number of cults and mystical movements. America is a virtual supermarket of spirituality. Everyone who cares about God seems to have a way to God. The problem comes when one group says that its is the only way.

The small segment of fundamentalist and evangelical Christians who control and dominate religious television not only claim to have the "one and only way" to God, but they are also trying to gain political power to legislate "their way" and "their morality" into the law of the land. They are using the most sophisticated means of communication—television. Their aim is to persuade the viewer to action, to move the audience not only to believe but also to live their beliefs—no matter what effect that action has on the nonbeliever or the different believer. They have a simple threefold plan: save 'em, baptize 'em, and register 'em to vote.

Enhanced by the convincing nature of television, the video pulpiteers use all kinds of oratorical tricks to bring their message alive. Day after day I observed Pat Robertson use every ounce of his television showmanship to exhort, rebuke, threaten, cajole, and entice the audience. Most video evangelists are performers who can cry on cue and storm the will of the viewer by the persuasive and moving power of frightening words, similes, metaphors, parables, allegories, paradoxes, hyperboles, and even puns. The odd thing is that the Bible uses these same methods to communicate God's involvement with mankind. Yet the television ministers preach a literal interpretation of the sacred words—a dangerous, literal, our-way-is-right interpretation.

The television preachers are becoming spiritual superstars simply by virtue of having their own shows. You get the feeling from watching them perform that God handpicked these ministers to broadcast his truth—and their fiery words are not going unheard or unheeded.

Television adds a touch of believability and authenticity to their urgent words. The Gospel-according-to-television is showing us, an unsuspecting and unbelieving nation, the "way." They preach a message without compromise, and over the electronic medium they reduce complex beliefs and truth to simplistic questions and answers.

Pat Robertson hopes he can ride his wave of spiritual superstardom straight to the White House. He was featured on the cover of the February 17, 1986, issue of *Time* magazine, which carried the caption "Gospel TV—Religion, Politics and Money." The story revealed that, according to a Nielson survey conducted for CBN, Robertson's daily religious talk show reaches 16.3 million households per month. It focused on the conservative political views and moral principles pushed by the fundamentalist preachers and elaborated on the previously published plans for a possible Pat Robertson run for the 1988 Republican presidential nomination. All three networks covered Robertson's March 1, 1986, appearance before a gathering of southern Republicans in Nashville, Tennessee.

Pat Robertson said in the *Time* interview, "Pacifism is not biblical," and urged America to help defeat the atheistic enemies of the Lord who are endangering freedom in Afghanistan, Nicaragua, and Angola. From a source inside CBN, I learned that Robertson has purchased a quarter-of-a-million-dollar computer dedicated to his political ventures. That and the private jet that he uses to crisscross America seeking support for his presidential aspirations are strong indications of just how serious the minister is about setting up his church inside the White House. In the March 10 issue of *Time,* the letters-to-the-editor section carried eleven letters responding to Pat Robertson and his vision for America, and—much to my surprise—seven of the letter writers supported Pat; that's 64 percent.

While this book is essentially a look inside the most powerful evangelical Christian network in America and may vibrate with vivid images that could only have been seen by an insider, it is important to realize that the stories come straight from the heart of a person who once believed in and approved of the policies and practices of this cultish spiritual kingdom. However, after much struggle, research, torment, prayer, and pain, I have come to understand the folly of my old beliefs. Still, the incidents revealed will not be told out of malice or revenge but from a desire to shed some light on a dark side of religious life.

My purpose in writing this book is not to mount an attack against the fundamentalist spirituality permeating religious television but rather to examine my conversion experience along with the negative side effects I suffered at CBN. This book is about my struggle and the insights I've gained.

Frequently I use the pronoun *he* to refer to God. This is for the sake of expediency only and does not reflect a belief in the maleness of God. The exclusively male God of Judaism, Christianity, and Islam stands in stark contrast to many of the world's religions that abound in female symbolism for the Deity. Some writers, in an attempt to pacify or not offend their readers, use "He/She," but I find that form hinders the flow of the prose. More importantly, I believe that God is neither male nor female, but is pure spirit.

I'd like to take this opportunity to express my heartfelt thanks to: Jane Biteman, Carol Caven, Betsy English, Margaret Farren, Jay Garon, Albert Gorayeb, Stephen Reagan, Tracey Rosenthal, and John Zak. Each, in his or her own special way, helped me find a way to complete this book. Most of all I would like to thank Dennis Robert Foster, without whose constant encouragement, insightful guidance, and faithful friendship my dream to write about my experiences would never have become a reality.

Prologue

There is something blowin' in the wind. A quiet war is being waged by the silent "moral majority" that is in reality a militant minority. Oh, they're making a lot of noise, especially in the political arena, but their real agenda is hidden beneath a shroud of silence. Imbued with the "spirit of truth," they're determined to pound the powers of the flesh into submission. The 1960s poet of protest, singer Bob Dylan, even for a short time added his strong voice to the cause of the self-proclaimed, righteous religious right.

> It's the ways of the flesh
> The war against the spirit
> Twenty-four hours a day
> You can feel it, you can hear it.
>
> —From "Hanging onto a Solid Rock"

In 1979 Dylan walked onto the stage of San Francisco's Warfield Theater and sang seventeen songs; each one carried a fundamentalist Christian message and spoke of the singer's special relationship with Jesus. Dylan had been saved by the Blood of the Lamb—that is, Jesus' death on the cross—and was telling his audience that he was in very sad shape before Jesus came into his life and helped him clean up his act. He saw himself bound for glory while his audience was on a highway to hell. One of his songs claimed that unlike the rest of us he was "gonna stop being influenced by fools."

The untypical Bob Dylan had a very typical born-again conversion response. He suddenly possessed all the truth and was surrounded by fools who couldn't see what he saw because they were blinded by Satan and consequently were doomed to damnation unless they repented and turned to Jesus. He was filled with a passionate desire to make us see what he saw and believe what he believed. Dylan has since dropped his Christian crown of glory and is rediscovering his Jewish roots. He got out; most are held prisoner behind bars of fear.

After ten years of involvement with fundamental Christianity, I can feel and hear the battle between the flesh and the spirit. I began to feel the winds of this spiritual war blowing in 1978 when I joined the staff of the Christian Broadcasting Network. I remember confiding to a friend that I believed that some day Pat Robertson would run for president and that, if he didn't, he would at least play a crucial role in electing a president who would share his political view of the world.

Prior to the 1980 presidential elections, Robertson frequently questioned President Jimmy Carter's competence, and during the 1984 presidential campaign, he fed his faithful followers a constant diet of pro-Reagan rhetoric. Many of Robertson's viewers consider him to be a messenger of God, and the message they were getting indicated that God wanted Ronald Reagan to run his favorite country. But influencing voters was not enough for the power-hungry Robertson; his real desire was to be president of the United States himself. Way back in 1979, during private moments in his dressing room before the taping of "The 700 Club," Pat shared with me his presidential fantasy and his firm belief that he was the one person uniquely qualified to lead this nation. In light-hearted moments, we actually matched up ministry officials with various cabinet-level positions. The staff bully would become the secretary of defense, and the head accountant would be running the Treasury Department in the Robertson administration. Back then the daydreaming was fun; now the possible reality is frightening.

The September 2, 1985, issue of *Time* magazine, which featured Jerry Falwell on the cover under the headline "Thunder on the Right: The Growth of Fundamentalism," contained the news that Pat Robertson, whose ministry received $233 million last year from tuitions, receipts, and donations, was "praying about" whether to run for the Republican presidential nomination in 1988.

Knowing Pat, I have no doubt that he will be seriously praying for God's guidance in his choice to run or not to run; however, his running or not running will have nothing to do with answered prayer or the will of God. If Pat's shrewdness and gut instincts indicate that the odds are against him, then he will not run—he'll wait. If he runs, it will be because of his ego, his self-righteousness, and his lust for political power. Let there be no mistake about it—Pat Robertson is an educated man of great ability, whose brilliance has helped him create a spiritual and political gospel that he can preach with power and effectiveness. More importantly, every fiber of his existence believes totally in his message. He is not a charlatan—not deliberately anyway.

Reverend Robertson's early ministry saw him living in a small parsonage in a slum section of Brooklyn, New York; and, despite the fact that he now lives in regal splendor in a home valued at over $350,000, he still likes to project the image of himself as a humble servant of God whose life is based on prayer and fasting. In reality, Pat is a pompous pope of the video Vatican of Christian broadcasting, and he rules his empire with absolute authority. He does not tolerate debate, discussions, or dissent, because they are considered stepping-stones to doubt. His television followers never get to see the tough-minded, hard-driving, cut-throat leader. There is no room in Pat's mind for any social perspective or political system that differs from his inspired views. While he is a staunch capitalist, Pat's private empire more closely resembles a communist regime. Above all else, Pat Robertson is a master communicator who is blessed with on-camera charm, grace, and wit, and people are buying his message.

W. C. Fields said, "You can't cheat an honest man." Maybe the comedian realized that an honest person doesn't look for shortcuts or for someone else to carry the load. The swindler's biggest ally is the eagerness of so many to believe the unbelievable, to accept dubious shortcuts to love, riches, status, or whatever else they seek. Find a person who can pander to that kind of dream cleverly and shamelessly, and you have a con artist who will go far. Pat Robertson's pentecostal approach to life more than panders to an elusive dream; he convinces people with devastating effectiveness that his understanding of God contains the one-and-only answer to any problem.

The gas that runs Robertson's holiness machine is a blend of a literal interpretation of the Bible, a born-again faith, and a claim to the indwelling presence of the Holy Spirit. The mixture creates a high-octane fuel that can carry Robertson far, perhaps even to the White House. Robertson is quietly and deliberately establishing a secret kingdom of believers whose goal is to make the invisible kingdom of God become a visible kingdom on earth so that the world will see the way God intended his universe and his society to function. The first step is the removal of evil by waging a holy war against the moral sins that threaten America. Like so many other fundamentalist television preachers, Pat believes that God brought this country into existence to fight evil, and for that reason the fundamentalists are fervent in their patriotism. Robertson wants his brand of Christianity to gain control of the nation so that the government can be put back into God's hands and then can properly exercise its responsibility to punish evil-doers—both the evil individuals within the country and entire countries that are considered evil. The government of the fundamentalist would function mainly as God's swift sword of retribution and not as a godly instrument for feeding the hungry, clothing the needy, or educating the public, because those kinds of loving acts of service tend to lead toward the demonic systems of socialism, communism, and humanism. Pat Robertson's goal is to crush evil—and to get a greater share of the evangelical television market in order to broaden his political base.

Two books of the Bible, Ezekiel in the Old Testament and Revelations in the New Testament, provide Robertson with what he regards as the political clues that allow him to predict what events the world can expect to occur in order for the kingdom of God to be established and America to have an anointed role in that process. The fascinating and frightening scenario ends with a major war erupting in the Middle East as Russia invades Israel. The communist force is annihilated, but a catastrophic upheaval results as the oil supplies to Europe and much of the world are cut off. Europe is thrust headlong into economic ruin, and a dictator with great charisma and verve moves swiftly to gain control over all ten nations that comprise the European Common Market, and he manages to establish a new economic order. Remember, two books of the Bible supposedly foretell these events. Even after Pat painstakingly explained all this to me, as we sat together in the back seat of our chauffeur-driven Mercedes Benz limousine during a tour of the Holy Land, I still failed to see how he connected such ancient writings to modern doom.

Pat believes that the dictator—despite his apparent goodness—will be the anti-Christ. While being viewed as benevolent savior, the dictator will be, in reality, evil to the core of his being. Jesus will come back to earth and destroy the leader and set up his kingdom of peace and justice, which will last forever. Of course, during the time preceding the return of Jesus, suffering will reign supreme as a result of nuclear war, famine, economic ruin, and a plethora of natural disasters like earthquakes, volcanic eruptions, hurricanes, and drought. However, the kingdom of Jesus will change all the heartache into eternal bliss for those who have accepted him as their lord and savior.

The idea that the kingdom of God is an actual event in history is a notion that the synoptic gospels of the New Testament most often attributed to Jesus. According to Matthew, Mark, and Luke, Jesus proclaimed a literal coming Kingdom of God, when the diseased shall be healed, the oppressed shall be released, and harmony shall prevail over the whole earth. They mistakenly expected the kingdom to come as a cataclysmic event in their lifetime. However, as the years passed, many Christians came to understand that the "kingdom" of which Jesus spoke merely symbolized a state of transformed consciousness. For almost two thousand years, countless people have taken the words of the gospel writers, which were written without a full understanding of Jesus, to be literally true and have therefore read the signs of the times and deduced that the kingdom of God was at hand. Pat Robertson sees his mission as trying to bring the kingdom of God into existence.

Mark writes in his gospel that Jesus proclaimed "The time has come, the kingdom of God is near." In order to understand what Jesus meant, it is important to comprehend what is meant by time, because it is impossible to grasp the significance of Jesus' words in terms of our modern Western concept of time. For us, time is mostly a measurement—clocks and calendars—and is quantitative. The Hebrews thought of time as a quality. This is clearly expressed in the famous passage from Ecclesiastes (3:1-8):

> There is a time for everything,
> a time for every occupation under heaven:
> a time for giving birth,
> a time for dying;
> a time for planting,
> a time for uprooting what has been planted.
>
> A time for killing,
> a time for healing;
> a time for knocking down,
> a time for building.
> A time for tears,
> a time for laughter;
> a time for mourning,
> a time for dancing.
>
> A time for loving,
> a time for hating;
> a time for war,
> a time for peace.

Time, for the Hebrew, was more than knowing the date; it was a matter of knowing exactly what kind of time it might be, because to misjudge the time in which one lived could prove to be disastrous.

Time was a quality or mood of events. Time was more than a measurement; it was the quality of what was happening. Even today we understand when the time is ripe for something or a relationship has no future. Jesus was announcing a totally new time—a drastically different quality of life.

John the Baptist, the prophet who foretold the coming ministry of Jesus, crystallized the quality or mood of the times before Jesus began to preach: that was a time for gloom, fasting, repentance, and penance. John was a prophet of doom who lived off the prospect of a coming great catastrophe.

Jesus, on the other hand, was a herald of good news who lived off the prospect of a coming great kingdom. The times had changed— God had ordained a new time and was no longer intent on punishing his people; he now wanted to save them. The signs of the times for Jesus were his own successful activities among the poor and the oppressed. The power of faith was liberating and could achieve the impossible. For Jesus the time had come when God was now treating sinners with love, compassion, and care—no matter what God may have done in former times. The kingdom is near, Jesus taught, and is, in fact, among us already; all that is needed to manifest it is love and compassion—and not, as Pat Robertson proclaims, evil-crushing. Those times are gone. Like John the Baptist, Robertson is concerned with the externals, while Jesus was concerned with internals. The times have changed, according to Jesus: God is a forgiving father and no longer a cruel dictator. Pat Robertson clings to the judgmental, wrathful God of the Old Testament, even though he would deny that he does.

Day in and day out, Pat preaches to his massive television audience that we are living in the most chaotic time in man's history: political systems fail, terrorists roam free, war threatens much of the globe, and shortages of food, fuel, and water are spreading. After planting a gloomy picture, Pat flashes a confident smile across his ruggedly handsome face and proclaims that for Christians this is really the most exciting—not chaotic—time in history. Success is yours—just open your eyes and take it; the possibilities for Christians are unlimited. Pat cleverly pitches his "Kingdom Principles" for living to the poor and helpless people who hang on his every word, and of course these "Principles" are available in book form and on audio cassettes. No matter what happens in the world, just practice what he preaches and everything will turn up roses. Of course, the first principle is the law of reciprocity—give, and it will be given to you. You start by giving to Pat.

Guest after guest proudly proclaim how they gave money to CBN and then got something really big in return from God. The message is crystal clear: If you send in your money to help support God's work, God will send a financial miracle your way—the more you give, the more you get. In truth, the viewer stands a better chance of a "miraculous financial windfall" playing a state-run lottery than trusting in the fraudulent claims made on behalf of God by a Christian-run television ministry.

The formula is simple, the style is slick, the execution is professional, and the results are phenomenal. Pat taps his viewer's fears, alienation, anger, outrage, frustrations, and anxieties, and then offers them hope, relief, and a sense of community. In her book *The Bible Vote: Religion and the New Right*, Peggy Shriver writes, "Pat Robertson chats with successful beauties who love Jesus, with congressmen who share his sense of the End Times coming but who also seem unafraid, and he invites those who are troubled to call him and pledge their dollars for God's bountiful multiplication."

The calls pour in by the thousands, and the callers get to chat with a friendly CBN prayer counselor. In a *Harper's* magazine article entitled "God's Own Network," Dick Dabney, who happens to be a Christian, writes:

> Greta and the other smiling counselors were into it now, toiling for Jesus, leaning forward into the two-foot-wide, tiled cockpits, praying and exhorting, as the desperate called out: the suicidal, drunk, drugged, anxious, and the demon-possessed. Their spouses had cheated on them, they were afraid of the bomb, they were full of cancerous lumps. They had been saved, they had been filled with the Holy Spirit, or they hadn't been, and wanted to be. They were looking for love and a better job and they wanted to step out in faith on those Kingdom Principles and send in the rent money, they were afraid to. And these counselors, with Bibles open, and turning through the thumb-indexed CBN Counseling Manuals that gave answers for every situation, were into it with them—advising, pleading, praying in tongues, hands held up to the oppressively low ceiling—and from time to time checking off the appropriate boxes on the forms—Salvation Forms, Answers-to-Prayers Forms, Holy Baptism Forms, Money Gift Forms—that the systems-analysis experts of Virginia Beach had devised for them, and that would later be fed into the computers, along with the caller's name and address. Above them, from the small television set high on the shelf, Efrem Zimbalist, Jr., was explaining urbanely to Robertson how empty his life had been before he'd found Jesus on Christian TV, and been born again, slain in the Spirit, and given the gift of speaking in tongues.

How does one become born-again and spirit filled? How does a seemingly sane person get so hooked by an obscure biblical principle that he or she is practically turned into a new person? Is speaking in tongues a high form of prayer or a psychological joke? How do you learn to speak in tongues? How is a person slowly drawn into a spiritual lifestyle that turns them into a prayer-warrior, a soldier for Christ whose mission is to save the world by defeating Satan and his band of temptors? Does God answer the prayers of Jews? How can someone speak for God? Is it impossible to understand the will of God? Is God a concerned parent who watches over us or an uninterested pure spirit devoid of intellect and will? Is there any connection between the re-cruitment process of either Protestant fundamentalism or Catholic charismatics and some of the unorthodox cults of the day?

How can a fundamentalist Christian consider the Bible to be the literal and inerrant Word of God when it contains hundreds of contra-dictions as well as such cruel regulations that demand, for example (Deut. 22:21), that a girl who is not a virgin when she marries be stoned to death at her father's door? How can a biblical faith cause a mother and father not to bury their ten-year-old daughter for two and a half months while they pray over her lifeless body in hopes of a resurrection of the child? Do fundamentalist Christians want to legislate biblical morality into the law of the land? Why do fundamentalists fear and hate secular humanists? Why do fundamentalists consider the con-sumption of alcohol—even in moderate amounts—to be sinful? Is reli-gious revival dependent on a political revolution? Are Heaven and Hell real places? When did the heavenly Father give fundamentalist tele-vision preachers the franchise on morality and wisdom?

I've struggled for more than ten years with those questions and many, many others dealing with the born-again encounter and the spir-it-filled experience. Insight gained from my leadership in the Catholic charismatic renewal and my life inside of CBN will, I hope, provide provocative answers to those questions. Hold on tight, you are about to take a holy roller-coaster ride through a spiritual amusement park.

The roller-coaster ride starts with problems and a promise of es-cape from them. We are all surrounded by problems, both individual and universal. Most people can talk more about negative things than about positive ones. The dark horizon is crowded with doubt and confusion. We all, whether knowingly or unknowingly, are seeking solutions to the problems that confront us each day. The complex problems of modern life are reflected in our newspapers, magazines, movies, and television shows. Life seems frustratingly futile to many people. Modern technology and material prosperity cannot bring us peace of mind or eliminate the fear and anger that result from living in the midst of increasing violence. While marriages fail, businesses collapse, unemployment rises, the dollar shrinks, cancer spreads, wars rage, and people starve, we are still caught up in the dream that the pursuit of profit will lead us to security. The televangelist reads these signs of the times and prepares for a great harvest of souls who are in need of salvation.

Desperate people look everywhere for solutions to their problems—everywhere except within themselves, where dwell the resources needed to conquer any problem. Many prefer to be led, to be shown the way. There is no end to the list of self-help books on the market. There are expensive seminars teaching us how to meditate, control our minds, grow rich, lose weight, or develop a positive attitude, and these have no problem attracting customers—nor do the fundamentalist preachers. A psychiatrist's couch is rarely empty. People travel halfway around the world to seek the advice of a white-robed, long-bearded guru or enlightened master. Some people claim the Bhagavad Gita, the Hindu scriptures, contain the secret to life. For others Zen Buddhism is the way. The rise of so many cults, like the Moonies, Hare Krishna, and Scientology, is evidence that people will search any available avenue to happiness.

Many people are offering honest and well-intentioned solutions, both religious and humanistic, to the problems of modern mankind. Many different approaches to life have elements of truth contained in their tenets. Each of us must begin to extract the truth for himself. The human race is too complex and diversified to have only one system of belief contain absolute and total truth.

As soon as you think that you have the answers for someone else and that they are lost without your truth, then you are lost. The video evangelists seek to enslave people to their point of view, and the people who idolize these preachers slowly begin to lose their own sense of truth and ability to doubt and search for their own answers.

One needs to continually question. The belief that one has arrived, that the journey is over, that one has found it, can stanch the search for truth. Many people have a material notion of the Kingdom of Heaven, and the televangelists utilize this spiritual immaturity to the greatest advantage. Their audience is not really seeking liberation but merely wants to belong and to be shown the way. The open-hearted viewer who is sincerely looking for answers to the deep questions of life can be seriously damaged by television preachers' fraudulent claims of special gifts from God and a veritable pipeline to the Divinity. Wanting so much to believe that they have found the answer to the mysteries of life, people will suspend their intellect, sound reason, and judgment; overlook discrepancies; and regress into a childlike state of acceptance in which the preacher-turned-authority-figure acts as an intermediary for divine communication. The true teacher or authentic holy person will only point you in one direction—back to yourself. He will not lead you to write out a fat check, chase the devil out of town, convert "heathens," condemn other religions, worship a "Big Daddy" God in the sky, look for Satan in everything that blocks the fulfillment of your childish desires, or vote the way he instructs. A genuine helper will only lead you back to yourself so that you can begin the hard work of self-discovery.

Shortcuts to sainthood and salvation do not work, especially if the shortcut includes the condemnation of much of the human race. Norman Cousins writes, "I cannot affirm God if I fail to affirm man. Therefore I affirm both. Without a belief in human unity I am hungry and incomplete. Human unity is the fulfillment of diversity. It is the harmony of opposites. It is a many-stranded texture, with color and depth."

The world of Pat Robertson is devoid of diversification and color. Guilt and fear are the bookends of his narrow message, whose theme drives us apart by dividing us into camps of saved or lost—and time is running out for the lost. The Robertson doctrine, besides being divisive, gives birth to a form of spiritual bigotry that is as hateful and menacing as anything ignited by the Ku Klux Klan, Hitler, or the Ayatollah Khomeini. Hatred, whether wrapped in white sheets or the scriptures, is still hatred, and fundamentalist hatred speaks a language of condemnation.

In theory they hate only the *sins* of the godless or the unsaved; in reality, many wind up hating the godless themselves. Pat may cleverly articulate how his hate is aimed at the sin and not the sinner; however, his message is not always clearly understood by the masses nor is his directive to hate only the sin uniformly carried out. When one segment of society crusades against the personal sins of the rest of society and consciously uses politics, as Robertson advocates, as its vehicle of vengeance, the game of politics becomes brutally savage—as Anita Bryant's declaration of war against the homosexuals of Florida clearly demonstrated.

The holy men of the cloth know how to play political hardball. Jerry Falwell can spend a few days in South Africa and instantly understand that support for the apartheid government is essential and then label the opposition leader—Nobel Peace Prizewinner Bishop

Desmond Tutu—a phony. Pat Robertson gets on his political soapbox, which is equipped with a satellite, and loudly decries taking the life of an unborn fetus through abortion and at the same time cries out for taking a criminal's life through capital punishment. And he encourages massive killing on a global scale through the arms race.

Pat used to tell me what God's position was on America's selling of the Panama Canal and our relationship with the government of Taiwan. Today he tells his viewers what America's policy should be toward Angola, Afghanistan, El Salvador, and Nicaragua. However, most Christians believe that God's revelation does not cover treaties with foreign nations or political positions divorced from humanitarian considerations. These are purely the works of man and should not be confused with the mind and will of God.

It is ironic how Robertson's message is based on the Bible—or more specifically his literal interpretation of the holy words. Pat taught that the Bible was inerrant in every detail. However, I firmly believe that this dogma, along with a literal reading of Scripture, is not only dangerous and divisive but is also the largest obstacle on the path to understanding between the fundamentalist Christian and mainline Christianity and all the non-Christian population. In *The Parables of Kahlil Gibran*, Anie Salem Otto writes:

> The literal interpretation of the Scriptures has caused man to commit untold cruelties on man with holy sanctions. The declaration "An eye for an eye, tooth for a tooth, hand for a hand, foot for a foot, burning for burning, wound for wound, stripe for stripe" has caused much suffering and agony since its first utterance. Even today, men misunderstand the symbolic meanings of Scriptural words. The meaning of "If thy eye offend thee, pluck it out and cast it from thee," and "If thy right hand offend thee, cut it off and cast it from thee" obviously is not meant to be applied literally. It would be against the teaching of love that the Scriptures are based upon. The verb "offend" means to cause dislike or anger, or to oppose or obstruct in duty. If we assume that "offend" means to oppose or obstruct one's actions, and if we assume further that rather than to the organ called "eye" or to the organ called "hand," the words apply to the action of the eye, that is, what it sees, and the action of the hand, what it does, then we can say that these admonitions can mean: If we see or become aware of something in everyday life which obstructs us in our actions and our knowledge of actions, then we should leave it or cast it away from us for it is better to throw off one thing, no matter if it is as dear to us as an eye or a hand might be, rather than keep it and have it destroy or corrupt our whole body. Likewise, if we perform an action of which we are ashamed, it is better to "cut it off" or forget it completely rather than let the memory

of it disrupt and corrupt our whole body, our entire life. Actions performed are dead actions, and obstacles which cannot be surmounted
should be left alone.

Robertson is too clever to advocate the actual cutting off of a
hand, but his interpretation of the less clear verses of Scripture can still
cause untold cruelty by means of spiritual bigotry. Robertson's real
agenda and feelings are cleverly clothed beneath the acceptable attire
of a Christian minister, and he never shocks the public with overtly
outrageous statements. Calmly and quietly he spreads his simplistic
message and builds his television audience.

C. K. Chesterton makes Father Brown remark, "To downgrade the
human mind is bad theology." The new wave of fundamentalism runs
counter to the traditional Christianity which gave it birth in that fundamentalism is anti-intellectual and simplistic. The church down through
the ages learned that neither life nor faith can be defined in a cut-and-
dried, easy-to-follow formula that can be quickly absorbed. Life is a
process, not a principle, a mystery to be lived, not a problem to be
solved. The main principle in the Pat Robertson school of thought is
that we are sinful and must repent and help crush evil in order to usher
in the return of Jesus. His goal is the uniform acceptance of that creed.

Thomas Jefferson wrote in his "Notes on Virginia" that "difference
of opinion is advantageous in religion. The several sects perform the
office of a common censor morum over each other. Is uniformity
attainable? Millions of innocent men, women, and children, since the
introduction of Christianity, have been burnt, tortured, fined, impris-
oned; yet we have not advanced one inch towards uniformity."

Up until the seventeenth century a person could have been burned
at the stake for questioning the literal truth of the Bible or doubting
that the book had been inspired verbally by the Holy Spirit, almost by
dictation. In the seventeenth and eighteenth centuries, rationalism
questioned such absolutism. Rationalists considered human intelligence
to be as God-given as the Bible and sought to reconcile religious belief
and reason. The process led to the allegorizing, if not the rejection, of
certain scriptural passages. With time, subjective religious experience
was joined with reason as another way of validating or establishing
scriptural meanings. In the nineteenth century came the discovery of
very old biblical manuscripts that differed from modern versions. Bible
scholars began to face the fact that if the original Scriptures had been
dictated by God, they had not been copied all that faithfully.

Today, the oldest of the biblical manuscripts are studied in the
light of history to try to determine the meaning that biblical writers

originally intended in their own times. Of course, to fundamentalists such critical and historical study of the Bible is the work of the Devil.

Pat Robertson's attitude toward evolution is a prime example of his unswerving commitment to what he considers the plain meaning of a book that is utterly sacred to him. The Bible has instructed Pat that a rationale for life apart from God cannot exist. Nothing in life is an accident; rather, all is a part of God's plan. When bad things happened at CBN, it was believed that sin had invaded the camp, and God was chastising us. If projects failed, it meant that God had closed the door on mere human plans. Good things are the blessings of God. God is always good, but his goodness is sometimes rather terrible.

There is something blowin' in the wind. It's not easy to see. It feels like a gentle, harmless breeze, yet it packs the wallop of a killer hurricane. For a while Bob Dylan bought the message the wind carries, and so have countless other unlikely converts.

My personal story of conversion contains a subplot with an ironic twist, involving a woman who could never pick up her cross and follow Jesus. Her Bible was the *New York Times.* She subscribed to *Time* and *Psychology Today.* She had worked for CBS-TV as well as a number of major publishing houses. She was a liberal Democrat who contributed her time and money to the 1968 presidential campaign of Eugene McCarthy. Eating out at fashionable East Side cafes and going to see foreign films were her favorite pastimes. Urban and sophisticated, she was a born cynic and a woman's libber. She found worshiping someone who was nailed to a cross barbaric and incomprehensible. Her heritage was Jewish, her faith agnostic. She was my wife when I started working at CBN. Working at CBN, I thought, was going to make my life complete: it made it completely different. My ex-wife is now a cameraperson on "The 700 Club," and her skill captures Robertson's every word and smile. She bought the message the wind carries and now helps to spread it. I once tried to cram the Bible down her throat; now she clobbers me with the book.

Don't for a second think that if you are an orthodox Jew, a Hindu monk, a transcendental meditation teacher, a movie star, a college professor, a corporate executive, or even an astronaut that you are immune to the lure of the hucksters of holiness and their army of dedicated followers that dominate Christian television. Given half a chance, today's television preachers can attract and hook anybody. The most ruthless con artist is the scoundrel who doesn't realize he is cheating his prey and believes he has God on his side. Pat Robertson believes beyond any trace of doubt that God is on his side—and, more important, that the Almighty is really talking to him. In their arrogance, the self-appointed world saviors of video Christianity act as if they alone have a direct line to God, when in fact we all must have the same possibility of connecting with the divine.

Knowing what God wants and believing you are in a privileged position to speak for God are vital steps to be taken in order to actually become God. Most of the television ministers act as if they are God, and in their respective ministries they wield unchecked, God-like powers over their staff and television followers. Their ministries are run more like a cult than a church. They hear God's voice clearly, they know God's law, and they are intent on enforcing it.

For the fundamentalist, the laws of God are absolute, while Jesus himself claimed it was, under some circumstances, all right to break the Sabbath or even sit with women who were considered immoral. Many of God's laws found in the New Testament seem to come not from Jesus, but from the overzealous Christians who followed him. For example, Paul told the church at Corinth that if a woman prayed without her head covered, she might as well have her head shaved. Was that what God wanted Paul to write, or was Paul just reflecting his rabbinical training that taught him that a woman's head covering was a symbol of her subservience to men, just as men are subservient to God? It's no wonder that Pat Robertson loved reading the writings of Paul; they are fellow zealots separated only by time, not dogma.

I recently spotted a bumper sticker that summed up the fundamentalist's closed-mindedness: "God said it, it's in the Bible, and that's that." Radical and totally Bible-based Christianity that dominates religious television considers compromise to be the language of the Devil. The Bible compels them to convert the world. Armed with satellite technology, they believe they can reach the world, and they will not settle for anything less. Your television set has become a twentieth-century bully-pulpit for the "God Squad," which offers salvation for sale and preaches and promises a quick and easy shortcut to sainthood.

Word of the publication of this book reached CBN while I was in the process of proofreading the galleys. I was told by a source inside CBN that many staffers are anxious to read my account of life at CBN because they know that the organization is plagued by many problems. However, the more common reaction is that "anyone who attacks the anointed of God will lose his life." In other words, God is going to get me, and I will be severely punished for doubting and questioning the Reverend Pat Robertson.

1

The Lie

Tick, tick, tick, tick. The steady beat of a stopwatch tells that portion of America tuned to CBS-TV that it's time for another edition of "60 Minutes." The sight and sound of the ticking watch means trouble for anyone trying to dupe the public. And trouble was on its way to the Christian Broadcasting Network in Virginia Beach. The pending arrival in 1978 of the CBS newsmagazine show sent shock waves of worry through the halls of CBN. However, trouble to the powerful CBN had a different definition: the Devil in sheep's clothing was coming to twist reality and distort the truth, God's truth. After all, no members of the liberal East Coast news media were interested in seeking the truth; they only sought to destroy it.

A collective sigh of relief was breathed when it was learned that mean Mike Wallace would not be the reporter looking inside CBN. Surely the pleasant and sophisticated Morley Safer would be softer and safer. Not that there was anything to hide; it was just a matter of their blindness. What we had they could not see. How could unholy and unsaved men see spiritual truth through their worldly eyes?

Pat Robertson thought it would be a good idea to capitalize on my fourteen and a half years at CBS in New York and assigned me the task of escorting Morley Safer around, acting as his official tour guide. My attitude about meeting Mr. Safer stood in sharp contrast to that of my colleagues: I was thrilled and considered him a certifiable television star whom I respected, not a person who needed to be rescued from the snares of Satan.

I greeted him enthusiastically and quickly blurted out that I used to work down the hall from him at CBS, and that, even though we never formally met, we had frequently passed each other in the hall. His summer suit was crumpled, and he looked somewhat disheveled and nothing like his dapper on-camera appearance. Despite his discomfort with the southern sun, our mutual CBS heritage made him comfortable with me. We exchanged humorous stories about the coffee wagon that parked between our offices, better-known as the "roach coach" by its patrons. I got the feeling, as we strolled around the exterior of the massive new broadcast center which was nearing completion, that he was relieved to find someone from the worldly side, the more familiar side. His own built-in bias might have led him to have doubts about the type of people he would encounter. He may have expected to find religious fanatics but certainly not someone who had stood behind him in the coffee line at CBS.

He seemed genuinely interested in why I would leave CBS for CBN and felt free enough to ask me probing, off-the-record questions about my faith experience. I recall talking freely about spirituality and healing. My approach was not one of a hardline minister but a more personal, soft sell. The typical self-righteous arrogance one frequently encounters in fundamentalist circles would have turned him off. It certainly turned me off; my nature much preferred gentleness. As I described my conversion experience, my words said indirectly that it was very good for me and more than likely would be good for many others. I tried not to make him uncomfortable or defensive. The company line preached that there was only one way to God. I claimed that it was a possible way because I traveled it and it worked for me; come try it and it may also work for you. There is a world of difference beween the two approaches. Mr. Safer listened intently, although he soon tried to turn the conversation from the spiritual to the fiscal.

Even though his visit predated Wendy's "Where's the Beef?" commercials by six years, he seemed adamant about "Where's the Money?" He knew our yearly budget was around sixty million dollars, which meant at least a million a week flowed into the ministry, and he wanted to see the flow. Television is a visual medium, and he knew that a shot of a conveyor belt carrying stacks of green stuff would speak louder than any of his well-crafted words about the mammoth monies spent for God.

We had a small, unmarked, guarded warehouse near our headquarters that received the daily donations that poured into Virginia Beach from all over the world. The volume of mail was so overwhelming that the post office had assigned us our own zip code. The bags of money, both cash and checks, were dumped onto a conveyor belt that carried its payload past dozens of people who opened every letter. The conveyor belt transported its bounty six days a week, and the thought of about $200,000 a day piled high was an image Mr. Safer wanted to capture. I refused him access for security reasons.

Morley Safer was impressed by the size and design of the building and the studios, the sincerity of the workers, but most of all by the polished sophistication of the founder and president—Reverend Pat Robertson. As the "60 Minutes" correspondent and "The 700 Club" host shook hands and exchanged smiles and laughs following a taped interview in front of the CBS camera, I felt that both men seemed charmed by each other. The interview had not taken on the tone of dueling adversaries; rather, it looked more like a pleasant conversation between two civilized gentlemen who happened to have divergent points of view.

The piece that aired on November 19, 1978, was puff—and fair. It was not vicious, nor did it attack us or distort our mission. There were no scandals uncovered, and the statements recorded were not edited in such a way as to alter their meaning. It was an honest, unbiased impression reported by a man who was sincere in his attempt to understand the phenomenon of the electronic church. It is impossible during a one-day visit to understand the complexity of a born-again experience, which is the focal point of the electronic church, let alone describe it in a fifteen-minute news piece. So the born-again experience was ignored, along with the theological, sociological, and psychological impact the message has on a diverse society, as well as the powerful effect a collective fundamentalist audience could have on the political arena. The Devil had come and gone with no real harm done, and all the saints rejoiced.

A Not-So-Miraculous Miracle

It could have been very different had the cameras of "60 Minutes" visited this capital of video Christianity a few years later when, following the taping of "The 700 Club," Pat Robertson was shaking hands with members of the studio audience as he worked his way toward his dressing room. He stopped when he reached a man sitting in a wheelchair. The elderly man looked as if he were moments away from death's door. Emaciated and jaundiced, his head and hands shook constantly. I felt sick just looking at him. Someone pushing his wheelchair whispered to Pat about the man's condition and that he wanted to see the show in person before he died. The man hadn't walked in months. Pat leaned over and spoke compassionately with the man and then laid hands on him as everyone prayed for a healing. As we prayed, you could see the yellowish tone fade from his skin. A staff member ordered the cameras turned on because they sensed God was going to work a miracle. At Pat's urging the man stood up. The people cheered as the old man took a couple of very shaky, small steps. While everyone applauded God, I feared the man might fall. The next day we showed the nation the miracle.

Cynicism comes easily to lots of people, but I always tried to avoid it. Yet I wondered if the man's cure wasn't the result of an emotional upheaval. While convinced beyond any doubt that God has the ability to heal, I also believed that our own expectations can create our health and that we each have some power over our own conditions. Norman Cousins, author of *Anatomy of an Illness* and *The Healing Heart*, tells a story of an eighty-four-year-old man who felt fine but went to his doctor for a checkup. The doctor sent him to a cardiologist, who told the old man, "You have a badly enlarged aorta and need surgery. You have a time bomb ticking inside you, and you're a candidate for sudden cardiac arrest." The man went home and that night developed chest pain, swollen ankles, nausea, a rash, and shortness of breath. He then consulted a second cardiologist, who told him, "Your enlarged aorta is just right for you. Not every abnormality is bad for every person. I am asking you to go home and have a good time." Within twenty-four hours, the man's symptoms disappeared. I simply wanted to know if the old man in the wheelchair was permanently healed by God or if he temporarily thought that he was healed. A few weeks later I had an assistant track down the man's family in order to see if the cure had lasted. He had died ten days after his visit to CBN. We reported his "healing" but not his death. During my two and a half years at CBN, I never saw one clear-cut, "beyond a shadow of a doubt" type of healing; however, I did see a tremendous amount of faith in healing—cleverly created, I believe, by Pat Robertson.

The incident would have made mild Morley Safer mad. He might have claimed that the healing power of faith was aided by "smoke and mirrors" because we gave God the glory for a miracle that could easily be explained in psychological terms. The prophet-turned-healer could have been described as prophet-turned-fake for the sake of a profit.

It's a Miracle

Is Pat Robertson a fake? In the sense that a fake is out deliberately to dupe the public by distorting spiritual facts in order to reap some financial harvest for himself, the answer is no. I observed on many occasions facts and situations stretched beyond reason to make a point, but the actual manufacturing of miracles for the express purpose of deception was not part of his method of operation. Everyone working at CBN was simply predisposed to believe in miracles—so much so that the supernatural became natural. God was the master magician who was happy to perform, but only if you believed. There was no room for doubt or skepticism about his powers or about those who experienced his miracle-making wonders. Employees freely spoke of how God gave them clear-cut direction for their personal and professional lives.

A perfect example of what passed at CBN for godly direction involves a meek, mild-mannered man who held a middle-management job. He was a model Christian, who made a sincere effort to live a holy life. His on-the-job performance was not dynamic or innovative; nonetheless, he was effective and always strived to improve himself and his management skills. Inspirational he was not, but he was extremely dependable and a team player who had served the ministry faithfully for more than ten years.

One day this man was abruptly fired. This married man, who had two teenage daughters, could not be given any logical reason for his dismissal because nothing in his performance warranted such a severe action. Unfortunately, he had a boss who loved reading about management theory and had a passion for making his division a well-run operation, because God demanded nothing less. He claimed that God told him to terminate the man. I could not believe that the heartless, almost un-Christian, action had anything to do with God but rather reflected the head honcho's obsession with management principles which dictated that a more forceful person was better suited for the job. It's bad enough to be fired by an insensitive boss, but imagine being fired by God!

My Buddy Jesus

God played such an active part in the personal and corporate events of the day that there was little room to doubt supernatural intervention or help. The fact that we believed in miracles and even expected them is apparent in any random sampling of "The 700 Club." Guest after guest, flown into Virginia Beach from all over the nation, was trotted out on the stage to tell of dramatic conversions, healings, and personal relationships with Jesus. Former gangsters and murderers told how Jesus reformed them. Former beauty queens and football players told how Jesus filled the emptiness inside them that glamour, fame, and fortune could not. People who suffered almost intolerable abuse or torture at the hands of foreign dictators or rotten fathers told how Jesus healed the scars and made them whole. Successful business people told how their stumbling enterprises had turned around after putting Jesus in charge.

No matter who the guest was, he or she placed extreme emphasis on the personal aspect of a relationship with Jesus. A typical studio interview would include some variation of the question, "Have you known him long?" *Him* refers to the Lord. The guests' answers would feature the exact date they met Jesus. Jesus was very, very real to both the host and the guest. He was not a historical figure or concept that embodied God in a human form. Jesus was as real as your wife or boss or the guy who delivers your mail. The viewer got the feeling that the people they were watching not only really knew Jesus but actually loved him in a way that was more spectacular than romantic love.

This was no theoretical or theological Jesus that literally took their breath away. These people were talking about their superbuddy savior in extremely affectionate terms. Listening to the questions and answers, one got the feeling that the people you were watching on your television could touch, feel, see, hear, and even smell Jesus. Their love and excitement were caught by the camera; and, judging from the phone response, many viewers were moved. As I watched from my catbird seat in the control room, I felt that Jesus was real for me—that is, in a way beyond some vague concept, I could sense the existence of his consciousness. I believed his spirit existed—yet the testimonies of these Christians made their relationship with him unnaturally familiar—and mine inferior. I could hardly express my disconcertedness to my colleagues because they always appeared uplifted and inspired by the guests, and they considered the guests' experience to be very normal.

I wondered what effect our technique of parading people who had become successful after turning to God had on the public. Back then, I figured it was all harmless; however, today I see the approach as superficial—but ultimately harmful. Dr. William Fore, a minister in the United Methodist Church and the assistant general secretary for communication of the National Council of the Churches of Christ, wrote in an article on the electronic church published in the July 7, 1981, issue of the *Christian Century* magazine, "The message is simple: believe in God and all will be wonderful for you too. But when hopeful converts begin to realize that they are not becoming especially healthy or wealthy, are not getting what they want, they can't blame God; they blame themselves and sink deeper into the spiral of self-doubt."

Reaching In

During my early days at CBN, what puzzled me the most about my new friends' faith was that their relationship with God resulted in a big smile of peace and joy that was always on public display. They had reached out to God, and he touched them with heavenly bliss. My experience was different and not always blissful. I found a sense of comfort that bordered on peace in my faith experience; however, I also encountered anguish and confusion in my relation with God. When compared to the always-positive faith of my friends, that uncertain side of my belief gave rise to the feeling that my faith was lacking. My doubt wore a frown; their faith wore a smile. Time would reveal, however, that their public certitude often hid private darkness and doubt. But they were taught to see that dark side of their faith as demonic, yet nothing could be further from the truth.

Christianity is not some kind of wonder drug that miraculously helps you get your life together; it is not an instant cure for suffering. The two-thousand-year history of Christianity teaches that it is a religion of struggle, not assurance. A simple sentence from the writings of an eighteenth-century Jesuit priest named Jean-Pierre de Caussade sums up the life of struggle that was common to all the saints who devoted themselves to following Christ: "So we follow our wandering paths, and the very darkness acts as our guide and our doubts serve to reassure us." That sentiment, which is harmonious with authentic Christianity, would be considered heretical by CBN—where the path to God is believed to be clear and straight, where Pat Robertson is considered to be the guide, and where doubts are thought to be destructive.

The Dutch Roman Catholic theologian Henri Nouwen writes in his book *Reaching Out*, ". . . it would be just another illusion to believe that reaching out to God will free us from pain and suffering. Often, indeed, it will take us where we rather would not go. But we know that without going there we will not find our life." My reaching out took me to places I did not want to go—years of wandering about Hollywood and a year of self-imposed exile in upstate New York—and it has caused me much suffering. Yet I did discover my life, a life that was almost lost in the cult-Christianity of CBN. I've learned since leaving CBN that reaching out to God is really reaching in—and *not* listening to some self-proclaimed prophet of God.

Do You Need a Friend?

After the guest interviews, which usually were sprinkled with reports of miracles, Pat would look into the cameras and ask if you, too, would really like to know Jesus as your personal savior. He let you know that you were not alone and that thousands of people were responding and reaching out to God. To back up his claim that Jesus was touching and changing lives, he might begin to tell how a viewer just like you was recently and dramatically healed of some serious ailment while watching "The 700 Club." These words served as an introduction to a prerecorded and edited videotape that the producer had ready to roll on Pat's prearranged cue.

Up on your screen would then pop a three- or four-minute feature that was taped on location at someone's home, where the miracle was reenacted. The scripted and staged report would describe the person's physical problems and present some medical evidence of its existence. Then the typical man or woman next door would describe with great emotion how God had healed him or her. A dumbfounded doctor would testify that somehow the problem disappeared. The combination of a reporter (who happens to be a born-again CBN staffer concerned not with testing the truth but in presenting a strong case for the acceptance of miracles) and a doctor help make this unbelievable event seem very believable.

The clip ends, we cut back to the studio, and a beaming Pat Robertson gets you to nod in agreement that what you just witnessed was wonderful. He lets his audience know that this healing is not an isolated miracle but just one of thousands of dramatic answers to prayer. He might then hold up a letter, as he did on February 4, 1985, that told how a fifty-one-year-old Hispanic woman from New York City was cured of a case of insatiable lust. She was a new woman: pure and freed from the powers that held her captive.

The studio guest, videotaped testimonial, and the letter built a powerful case that God was not only a personal God but also a wonder-worker who can help you avail yourself of his help. You don't even have to leave your living room. "Close your eyes and pray with me" is an invitation to share in the wonders of God. Pat would join hands with the cohost, tightly close his eyes, and begin to pray. He then might indicate that God was healing someone of cancer of the womb, alleviating the need for a scheduled operation, or that a painful problem with a jawbone causing severe headaches was being healed, or a young man was being freed from a lifelong grip of fear, or an eye infection was clearing up, or a kidney problem was being corrected.

Pat's awareness that God was healing special medical problems afflicting particular chosen people was known as a "word of knowledge." God was giving Reverend Robertson a message containing important information that he wanted Pat to relay to some viewer watching. God was healing some viewers of these illnesses, and he was telling Pat so that the people would recognize and claim the miracle. God knew whether the person being healed was watching the show live via satellite or on a two-week tape delay in some small city. To doubt the authenticity of a "word of knowledge" was unthinkable. For the CBN staff, doubt was a devil; however, I saw doubt as an angel whose wings flew to the truth.

Time Is Up, God

The show builds to the miraculous climax described above, and as Pat received the messages of healings from God and relayed them to the people being healed, he would still be able to hear when the musical theme of the show began to play, which was the producer's way of telling Pat and God that time had run out. Pat would open his eyes and tell those who had been touched to call a counselor and let CBN know what God had done. Who knows, in a couple of weeks a camera crew might come to your house to videotape your miraculous testimony.

These tales of conversions and miracles happen constantly, daily, year after year: the supernatural became natural. God is no longer a mystery that we live within, because he has given us an answer to all our questions and a solution to all our problems. It's easy—close your eyes, pray with Pat, and Jesus will become your buddy. He'll be as real to you as he is to the people you see on your televison. Real peace will soon be yours. Call and catch the excitement; we'll even send you a little booklet that answers the question: What now?

God Knows Who's Watching and Who's Not

I used to muse that if this healing and "word of knowledge" was really happening, why was it relegated to the last few minutes of the show? If God was in the middle of working such wonders, then how could he be cut off by a music cue? If God knew who was watching, either live or on a tape delay, wouldn't he also know how long the show was? Beyond that, if this activity was legitimate, I would think we'd want to fill the entire show with it, but instead we chattered about politics, the economy, or the Supreme Court for most of the show and let God do his healing during the last few minutes. Although, as the producer, I did write this miraculous exchange into every format, I never really understood this aspect of the production. But not a soul in the place ever questioned what was happening. I just assumed that someday I would understand. I was wrong.

There was nothing "mystical" to understand; it was simply "statistical." Robertson's little faith-healing procedure is a charade—he simply "calls out" an illness and predicts its cure, and with millions of viewers the statistical probabilities are that *someone* will have the disease named and that they will naturally recover. People put their faith in the belief that God speaks to Pat: H. L. Mencken wrote, "Faith may be defined briefly as an illogical belief in the occurrence of the improbable," which is exactly what the viewers do while watching Pat Robertson deliver a "word of knowledge."

Psychiatrist Thomas Szasz has observed that if you talk and pray to God, you are religious; if God talks to you, you are crazy. Unless, of course, I would add, you happen to be a televangelist—then you are not crazy, you are rich. I am convinced that if Pat Robertson—or any of television's faith-healers—were proven to be pranksters and frauds, the vast majority of their staffs and viewers would not drop their belief in the ministers' healing power or weaken their faith in God.

The Confession

Different insights into this spiritual kingdom could have been captured in the autumn of 1980 if the sometimes-hidden cameras of "60 Minutes" had caught Pat Robertson when he asked the question, "Brother—did you sleep with her?"

The question stands frozen in time. The answer altered many lives. It's the type of question you would expect to hear during a conversation between a couple of guys sitting at a bar, sipping beer, and exchanging boastful stories of their "sexploits."

The words were not uttered in a bar. They were spoken in the office of one of the most influential religious leaders in the United States. The probing question was directed at one of his most favored employees. Me.

We had been talking for about an hour before the question was popped. This was to be a time of confession, repentance, and, I hoped, spiritual healing. Growing up Catholic, I was used to going into a darkened confessional box and kneeling in front of a concealed screen. I would nervously rehearse in my mind all the things that I'd done wrong. Suddenly the slide partition covering the screen would be pushed aside by the priest, revealing his shadowy figure as he leaned forward in order to better hear my offenses against God's law.

My heart would quicken as I would nervously blurt out the standard opening line, "Bless me, Father, it has been one week since my last confession. During that time I disobeyed my mother twice. . . ." Once you got past the first sin, you were on a roll.

This was different; the sin and the stakes were bigger. I anxiously walked into the office of the founder, president, and chairman of the board of the Christian Broadcasting Network. I wish it could have been a little dark box instead of his elegant office.

The room was huge and the furnishings magnificent. Expensive antique chairs, sofas, serving tables, and a huge desk, as well as a rare Oriental rug, highlighted the minister's inner sanctum. There was a simplicity to the elegance of the room, which contained many valuable appointments yet still maintained an uncluttered look. Like the man who occupied the office, the room had style, grace, and a touch of class. The walls were covered with dark, decorative mahogany paneling and bookshelves containing neatly stacked books, precious vases, and numerous mementos of a lifetime of serving God. There was even a secret back door that allowed the chief executive to slip out without going through his outer office, which might have been holding unwanted guests. The fireplace and the deluxe bathroom that included a shower made the office fit for a king.

Who said that the rewards of working for the kingdom of God are in the next life?

The Reverend Marion Gordon (Pat) Robertson extended a warm greeting and motioned me to sit down on the couch. He lowered his large frame into the chair directly across from me. As we exchanged preliminary pleasantries and a passing comment about that morning's edition of "The 700 Club," one of the women from his staff entered the room through the door that led to the boardroom and adjacent full-sized kitchen. She asked if we would care for any tea. Pat said yes to his usual cup of herbal tea, and I opted for the more tempting caffeine fix of coffee. She left, and we returned to our small talk.

Pat looked tired. Some days the immense burden of hosting a daily ninety-minute talk show along with almost single-handedly running this multidimensional corporation that included four television stations, one radio station, a university, and a twenty-four-hour cable programming package, seemed to take its toll on the charismatic leader. Ruling his empire, which consisted of more than 1,300 employees, was a gigantic responsibility he rarely delegated. Nothing happened without his approval.

The young woman reappeared moments later. She politely placed the delicate, tiny china cups on the serving table between Pat and me. Her silent manner spoke loudly of Pat's attitude toward women. The biblical image of man being the head of his house as Christ is the head of the Church illustrated the husband's authoritarian headship over his wife. The principle is extended at CBN to include all male-female relationships and was an unwritten law. Women always played subservient roles in the organization. In the New Testament, Paul recommends that women keep silence in the churches, and it seemed almost as if that recommendation had been extended to include CBN. I had raised more than just eyebrows when I attempted to promote women who were more qualified and talented than their male counterparts.

Pat always seemed ill at ease around women, as if they were only temptations to be avoided. And it's no wonder—after all, the paradise myth in the Old Testament clearly states that Adam was first formed, then Eve; and Adam was not deceived, but the woman was led into transgression. It leaves no doubt that a man is not of woman, but the woman is of man. The lessons learned in the Garden of Eden were clear: Man is naturally superior and favored by God. A noted second-century Christian writer, Tertullian, wrote, "And do you not think that each of you women is an Eve? The judgment of God upon your sex endures today; and with it invariably endures your position of criminal at the bar of justice." Just being a woman was a crime. Can you imagine living in a time when half of humanity was considered not only inferior but also criminal by the men who led religious movements?

The image of Eve as sexually tempting and a God-defying seductress still lives today, and many men at CBN figure that with the right perfume a woman can still cause the fall of a man. By 1985 women's liberation was beginning to infiltrate CBN, and some women were starting to get responsible positions; yet, listening to Pat on the air, it's still clear that he is obsessed with the sins of the flesh.

With the china cups resting on the table, Pat nodded his approval to the secretary-turned-servant and began to sip his tea as she left the room. The dainty cup looked incongruous in his massive hands, into which I was about to place my trust and hope.

I had used the short serving time to quickly decide how best to begin my confession. I was concerned that I might get cut short by the constant flow of people who urgently needed to see the master. At CBN the important was seldom urgent, and the urgent was seldom important. But my confession was important because gossip and rumors were spreading quickly through this Christian kingdom, and Pat had to hear about my problem from me and not from one of his soldiers.

I told him that partially due to an affair I had with one of his most-liked female employees, I was no longer living with my wife. He was stunned. He buzzed his secretary and informed her that he did not want to be disturbed under any circumstances. This was an encouraging sign.

We spoke at great length about the problems of my marriage that went all the way back to the wedding day and that ultimately led to my falling in love with a married woman. I assured him of my repentance over the unfortunate affair and guaranteed that it had stopped.

I spoke openly. He listened intently. We prayed together. He offered tender advice. I felt great about the entire meeting, with the possible exception of his directive that I must go to the woman's husband and seek his forgiveness.

That seemed like an odd request, and I wasn't thrilled with the prospect of facing my former lover's husband. But the order was in perfect harmony with Pat's male-macho spirituality. As my counselor (a man I agreed to meet with regularly for marriage counseling) later explained to me, I had stolen the heart of another man's wife. At the time I had accepted that notion, but eventually realized it only reflected their view of a woman as a possession. I had taken something that didn't belong to me. The theory that the husband is the head of the home fosters a misguided belief that a man owns his wife.

In addition to being an adulterer, I was also a thief, and that indictment only compounded my guilt. The entire responsibility for the affair was given to me, ignoring the reality that the husband's chronic habit of putting his career ahead of his wife had driven them apart and had caused her restless and adventuresome spirit to seek attention and affection long before I appeared on the scene. I had no intention of stealing her heart; she simply gave it to me because her husband didn't seem to want it, and my miserable marital situation made it easy for me to accept. Four people contributed to an affair planted in our discontentment and watered by our physical love. It had nothing to do with stealing—or lustful temptations by a woman.

My meeting with Pat concluded with a big hug. Turning and heading for the door, I felt as though a tremendous burden had been lifted from me: Pat understood my situation, forgave me my failures, and wanted to help me try to put my marriage back together.

My fleeting thoughts of relief were punctuated when, with my back to him, came the word, "Brother." As he paused, I turned and looked right at him. He seemed almost embarrassed or hesitant as he glanced down at the floor and continued, "Did you sleep with her?"

I froze. It was as if he wanted to ask, "Did you have sexual intercourse" or "Did you make love to her," but couldn't form those words and settled for the less passionate "sleep" euphemism instead.

For a split second, I felt as though I were standing before my father.

Flashback: My Father

"You've broken your mother's heart, and your hurting her has made me very angry with you. I've removed that filth she found in your closet, and you'd better never defile this house with sick crap like that again. I'm too disgusted to talk with you."

My father turned and left the room, leaving me standing alone, scared, and shattered. I stood frozen in fear as my heart pounded with anxiety for a few minutes before I ran to my room and entered the cult of guilt that would entangle me until years after my departure from CBN.

The "sick crap" that my father removed from my closet was a few issues of *Playboy* magazine. I was fifteen years old at the time. I had spent the first nine months of high school away from home in a minor seminary located in New Jersey as I pursued my dream of becoming a missionary priest. The death of that dream will be discussed later, but a few months before my father's discovery, I left the seminary and transferred to an all-male Catholic high school in Brooklyn, New York.

I knew virtually nothing about sex, but my new classmates were all experts.

My sex education was about to begin. I initially went to daily mass, but I slacked off because the kids who engaged in this holy and pious ritual tended to be the biggest wimps in the school. Looking for acceptance in this social sphere caused me to not want to be associated with the outcasts of school society. The "in" crowd skipped morning chapel for the delights of the corner hamburger joint. All the cool guys could be seen crowded around the dingy tables in the dirty backroom of the store.

The school was located smack in the middle of the slum section of Brooklyn known as Bedford-Stuyvesant, and this favorite school hangout reflected all the decay and poverty of the neighborhood. You needed an oxygen mask to breathe in this smoke-filled hideout where the morning orange juice was spiked with gin or vodka.

Smoking and drinking weren't the main attractions to this morning alternative to the sacrifice of the Mass, because just down the block was a complex of buildings that housed a home for wayward girls, mostly of Puerto Rican descent. Somehow the mystical Body of Christ offered in the chapel ran a distant second to the well-shaped living bodies offered for free handling at the hang-out. The homeless girls served everything from food to sex—take out to put out—to the early morning crowd.

I was a fat and shy kid who normally wasn't attracted to a dive like this, but curiosity drew me into the den of iniquity. This place was a hot-bed for dirty jokes, which I usually laughed at even though I rarely understood the punch lines. In this hoodlum-populated, prehistoric McDonalds, I learned much about life and sex. The sexual portion of my storefront education was all theoretical without any practical experience. It wasn't until after high school that I even got to kiss a girl. I was interested, very interested, but shy, very shy.

Readings from *Playboy* magazine during the breakfast hour at the hang-out replaced readings from the lives of the saints during the postliturgical breakfast at the seminary. My shy nature made the skin mags an obvious choice for some sort of sexual stimulation, and I began to take much comfort from their lifeless pages. At first I was too embarrassed to buy them myself, so for a long time I had to be content with stolen peeks from magazines bought by my more unashamed classmates. But I craved more than just short looks. I wanted to linger over the naked female forms and prolong my enjoyment. I began to steal the magazines.

My larcenous career ended when one observant store owner spotted my adolescent caper. He issued me a stern warning and let me go. Getting caught in the act shook me up enough that I was able to overcome my shyness and shamefulness. I finally purchased all the magazines I needed to feed my growing lust. I hid my pleasure-giving treasure in my closet.

My early childhood "religious" training and my parents' sexually repressive attitudes forced my youthful and natural curiosity about sex not to be expressed and, even worse, caused me to have feelings of guilt, unworthiness, and inadequacy. These things contributed to my "cult ripeness." My father must have had an inkling that there was more to my involvement with the hidden magazines than just looking at the pictures. If only we could have talked about my sexual awakening and curiosity in an open and honest way. But talk was a scarce commodity.

My father loved to debate. He had been known as "Battling Bill" on his school debating team and could speak eloquently on either side of any issue. What he considered a discussion, I viewed as an argument. The more he drank, the faster a debate would evolve into a verbal fight.

As a teenager, I realized that to engage him in one of his ludicrous debates was not only a waste of energy but also a no-win situation. Any simple statement shimmering forth from my mouth could ignite a vicious counterattack. He was a fighter looking for a ring. "Gee, Dad, Mickey Mantle had a great game today. He's the best player in all of baseball." The first half of the quote may have been a fact, and the second half a simple enthusiastic observation of a fan. Yet, even if my dad agreed he would counter with, "That weak-kneed bum couldn't carry Willie Mays's bat, let alone his glove." Why bother talking to him?

I avoided all arguments the way a six-year-old avoids a bath and bed. No matter what kind of outrageous statement my father would make I would just nod my head in silent agreement even though every fiber of my being ran counter to his words. I would not follow my father's lead and wanted no part of his ideas or the place he lived. No hostility. No animosity. We just had nothing to say to each other. He must have thought I was mute.

Years later we spoke on a fairly regular basis, but I just said what he wanted to hear and rarely shared my views of life. For so very long, life for me was like wearing a Halloween mask in June. The real me was hidden from all. Nobody got to see my masked emotions and attractions. Like an actor, I created an alter-reality by denying my natural sexuality. I believed I had to replace my sinful urges for a girl with a biblical reaction that was pleasing to God. But how?

My father's angered response and his reluctance to discuss the "filth" he found did not help the situation or eliminate my "problem." Right up until their deaths, I felt that my parents never forgot this episode, and that no matter what good I did it would never undo the harm my sexual curiosity had done them. I felt that in their eyes I had a tragic flaw that I would never overcome. And so did I, for a long, long time.

CBN caters to countless masses of guilt-ridden, "holy" fanatics, who were also trapped by early childhood training. My fundamentalist lifestyle viewed my youthful foray into pornography as the work of Satan, who was clever enough to lure me into sin and eventual eternal damnation. If Satan led me into anything, it was confusion and stagnation. The pictures glossily displayed in my hidden magazines weren't the real problem—my unnatural and unhealthy attachment to them was.

The fundamentalist dichotomizing of the world into camps of good and evil as interpreted by their understanding of the Bible results in the loss of a middle ground. Compromise is a trick of Satan and therefore is anathema. The fundamentalist doesn't deal honestly with the shades of gray in which we live; he only offers a schizophrenic break from the world at large. My father, unintentionally, helped set me up for my fundamentalist fall by drowning me in an undeserved guilt instead of teaching me to swim through my natural curiosity.

As I stood in front of Pat Robertson when he asked, "Brother, did you sleep with her?" he suddenly became symbolic of my father. I didn't want to argue his right to ask that question, nor did I want my answer to hurt him.

Back to the Confession

Why was Pat so interested in the unspoken details of the terminated affair? Scripture says that if you commit adultery even in your heart, you've already offended God, so the degree of the physical manifestation of my desire should not have been important to him. Besides, was he so naive as to think that an affair didn't include lovemaking? Even an affair of the heart includes other major organs. What difference did it make if I was truly repentant? And was I so naive as to believe I could confess my "sins" to another person?

There was no good answer to a question that should not have been asked.

I wanted to say yes, but I also wanted to protect the woman's reputation and job.

"No," was my response.

As I walked toward my office, I was tormented by the fact that following an honest discussion I had lied. I turned and walked slowly back to the outer office and asked his secretary if I could have a few more minutes with Pat. She looked at me as if I were crazy. While she was saying "Someone else is in with Pat, and it might be a while," I sensed she was thinking, "Look, big shot, you already had more than an hour, and you screwed up his entire schedule." I recognized a dead end when I saw one and left, planning to reverse my faulty answer the following morning in the dressing room before we taped the show.

By morning my need to set the record straight was less intense, and Pat and I had only a few precious seconds alone. It seemed my "no" to his question wouldn't pose any real problem. I let the whole episode slip away.

Thanks to a covert spy operation and my guidance counselor's sharing with Pat the secrets of our confidential conversations, Pat discovered the correct answer to his intrusive question. He knew that, in the awkward moment that followed our talk and prayer, I had lied.

Within two months I had to eat the rotten fruit of that lie—more on that later.

There were no hidden cameras from "60 Minutes" capturing my confession and lie, nor was a reporter assigned to investigate the spirituality and reality of the ministry. I began my own investigation, a study that would take six years to complete. I started by asking two questions: What led me into a born-again experience? Why did I go to work for CBN? The answers to those and many more questions will provide insight into the world of religious television—which, strangely enough, began for CBN in a dream almost four centuries ago—long before television was even invented!

Holy Roots

It was the spring of 1607, and the beach was peaceful and still. The constant breeze blowing in from the Atlantic Ocean had, over a long period of time, arranged the sand into gentle hills and small dunes. The untouched splendid beauty of the white, virgin sands was suddenly penetrated by a large wooden cross. This isolated moment in time—planting the cross—was the culmination of a dream that would live for more than three hundred and seventy-five years.

Some fifty years earlier, the seeds of the dream were sown in the heart and mind of a young boy named Richard Hakluyt. Growing up during the middle of the sixteenth century in England, young Richard was intrigued by the bold and courageous men who crossed the ocean and explored the new world. Curiosity led him to visit his cousin frequently, who was a London-based lawyer and geographer, to hear stories about this vast and unknown region. He stored up a treasure of information, maps, and artifacts dealing with the portion of the new world that is today Virginia.

But Master Hakluyt grew up to be known as the Reverend Hakluyt, an Anglican priest, and his interest in the new land had little to do with adventure on the high seas or the thrill of exploring new frontiers. He saw the land as populated with ignorant savages who knew nothing of his Christian faith and were in dire need of salvation. The preacher's hallowed vision was to establish a permanent English settlement consisting of godly men who shared his commitment and sense of divine destiny to spread the Gospel and save the souls of the savages. The settlement would be a base from which the word of God could issue forth, a beacon in the darkness.

He formed the Virginia Company. In April of 1606, King James I granted this company a charter and with it the duty of settling the land in order to propagate the Christian religion to all the people who they believed were living in darkness and miserable ignorance of the true knowledge and worship of God. With the charter in his hand, the Reverend Richard Hakluyt's dream became a reality.

On December 20, 1606, as England prepared to celebrate the birth of the Messiah, a small group of 105 settlers and 40 seamen set sail for the new world in order to give birth to the Christian faith and thereby snatch from the arms of the Devil savage souls doomed to eternal death.

Ironically, Hakluyt was in poor health and watched from the shore as the ship embarked on its holy mission. The mantle of spiritual leadership was given to the Reverend Robert Hunt. The crossing was difficult and took more than four months. They landed on the Virginia shores on April 26, 1607, but Hunt would not allow anyone to leave the ship until they had spent time in prayer and personal examination before God. It was three days before they left the ship and planted a wooden cross on the beach. Presumably, after four grueling months at sea in small, cramped quarters with hunger and sickness as fellow travelers, the three days of prayer passed quickly.

The spot was named Cape Henry in honor of the King's son.

During the first formal, land-based prayer meeting they made a covenant with God: "From these very shores the Gospel shall go forth to not only this new world but to the entire world." After the prayers and dedication, the visionary Christians reboarded their ships and headed for the Chesapeake Bay and on up the James River. In fulfillment of the dream, they constructed the first permanent English settlement in the new world at Jamestown, and the task of conquering the wilderness and Christianizing the Indians began. The years that followed were filled with death from disease, famine, massacres, and cruel conversion practices as well as uneasy relations with the native Indians; yet their courage and determination, fueled by religious zeal and Christian piety, overcame all obstacles.

Destiny With History

On April 15, 1978, just before the 396th anniversary of the cross raising on Cape Henry, I found myself heading for the same beach for the same reason: spreading the Gospel of Jesus. Since I was ignorant of the site's historic importance, I was unaware of my role in the continuation of Hakluyt's goal.

My goal was far less ambitious and rigorous: simply to start work for the Christian Broadcasting Network located in Virginia Beach. Following what I considered the leading of the Lord, I had just resigned from CBS-TV in New York in order to use my God-given skills in broadcasting to spread the Gospel worldwide via television. Unlike the first settlers of Virginia, I did not need to escape religious persecution, nor would I persecute in the name of religion. Rather, I had a new job with a total change in lifestyle. How total the change would become was completely unpredictable.

The decision to abandon a successful career looked impetuous and ridiculous to my family and friends; yet the choice was the result of four years of personal spiritual renewal and increasing religious fervor that followed my born-again experience, which will be examined in detail in later.

My journey didn't require a cruel, four-month trip in a stuffed ship; however, the trip was tough. Despite the relative luxury of a non-airconditioned, six-year-old Datsun station wagon, the eight-hour drive from New York through the eastern shores of Maryland and Virginia was unseasonably hot and seemed to drag on forever. My daughter and I made the trip together, and my wife, after tending to some final details, would travel alone in our other car in a day or so. My car was packed with odds and ends that didn't fit in the moving van. My four-year-old daughter, bored and restless, climbed about the car while annoying the cat, which was also seeking to escape the heat plus the reach of the child. After six hours the climbing gave way to sleeping.

I glanced down at my daughter, whose head was resting in my lap. She looked calm and angelic. I loved her very much; yet, within two and a half years and partly because of my decision to join CBN, I would be living alone as an outcast three thousand miles from her.

As she slept, my mind was free to wander. Even though the land I was looking at as I drove was rich, fertile farmland, the area seemed to me a godforsaken wasteland. A city kid needs tall buildings and crowds to feel at home. I began to doubt the sanity of what I was doing: leaving a large house in suburban New Jersey and a good job. Yet, I believed God wanted me to turn my back on that upwardly mobile secular lifestyle, that he was leading me into a life of service to him. I cried out, "God, why me? Where are you taking me?" I felt very alone in this spartan section of Virginia wilderness that was dominated by old, rundown buildings, shanty-type houses, and small dusty towns that broke up farmlands, and I thought that God had abandoned me and led me astray. As a tear worked its way down my face, my daughter sat up and asked where we were. I had no idea.

With my daughter awake and the Chesapeake Bay Bridge-Tunnel quickly approaching, my time of inner reflection ended. The bridge-tunnel combination is so long that when you reach the midpoint you can't see either shore. The middle section of the bridge hovers just above the water, and that, combined with the tremendous distance from the shore, helps create the illusion that you're crossing an ocean, almost driving on water.

My daughter pointed excitedly to the sea gulls that sat on the guardrail and to those that flew alongside the car as if they were extending a warm welcome to us. Even the cat seemed to enjoy being at sea, as she watched the bright sun dancing on the choppy waters. The desert of doubt I had experienced just moments ago was replaced by an ocean of hope. My heart pumped with new excitement: tomorrow a new house, the next day a new job.

Holy Nightmare

Our first night in Virginia Beach was spent in a Holiday Inn. The sterile cleanliness of a uniformly decorated hotel room somehow manages to capture the heart of a child. Freed from the confines of the car, my daughter burst into the room. There were beds to test with leaping jumps and a television set to challenge with rapid channel changes. A bathroom with a heat lamp and a bed with a coin-operated massage added to her fun. After letting her explore her new surroundings, I tucked the travel-weary child in bed, and after a short prayer thanking God for the day and safe trip, she fell quickly asleep.

I was too wound up to sleep, so I turned on the television set and tuned in WYAH, the CBN-owned station. The station carries many religious programs that are produced by other ministries, and I had not been exposed to much of the material not produced by CBN, since my job had nothing to do with the local station. The images beaming forth from the set into the darkened room horrified me. I slumped into a stiff chair in the corner of the room, my eyes glued to the set in utter disbelief. The lunacy I was watching frightened me and sent me into a state of panic.

I wasn't watching a monster movie, nor did I understand what I was watching. WYAH—owned by the people with whom I was about to work—was broadcasting a faith-healing show featuring an evangelist named Ernest Angley. Frantically roaming up and down a large stage cluttered with excited people wildly waving their arms toward Heaven, he would place his hand on the forehead of the physically or emotionally sick and command the demons to come out of the person's body. He yelled, "Heal," but in a twang that pronounced the word "Heeeal-aaa!" When someone would collapse and fall to the floor, he would shout, "Praise God—they've been slain in the spirit—thank you, Jesus!" Some people mumbled strange sounds, presumably speaking in tongues, an unknown language inspired presumably by the Holy Ghost. When the camera cut to a wide shot of the auditorium, it looked like a raging sea of emotionalism—and very far removed from the healing power of God.

Maybe it was due to some unrecognized northeastern prejudice, but this short, stubby man in a white suit and dark shirt with a large red flower in his lapel looked ridiculous to me. He even wore a toupee that looked homemade. He strutted about the stage, commanding the enraptured audience to "give God a big hand." He also informed the television audience that he saw angels. I thought I was seeing things or perhaps having some kind of twisted and bizarre nightmare.

(Years later, Angley's traveling healing circus turned into his own nightmare. In July 1984, Angley and his entourage, consisting of almost two hundred people, including public relations men, guards, and attendants, toured Western Europe. In Germany, a full-page ad proclaimed him as *Wunderheiler*. On July 8, a woman died of a heart attack at one of his healing crusades. Three days later, Angley was charged with practicing medicine without a license at a public gathering and with promising "sure cures." He was thrown into a Munich jail and held on suspicion of fraud. He was released on bond and quickly returned to the United States, where taking an evangelist to court would be political suicide.)

I turned off the set; and, as I lay on the bed, I was in a state of shock. Wait until my wife sees this! She wasn't thrilled about moving to this cultural wasteland. As an agnostic Jew, she didn't understand why my Christian faith had to invade my career, thereby dragging the family to Virginia.

My work at CBS was nothing exceptional, but compared with the CBN staff I had a wealth of training and expertise, and my new coworkers heralded my arrival as a major step forward for the cause of television evangelism. Pat Robertson was pleased and excited to welcome me to CBN. Little did he know that I was a nervous wreck—perhaps needing to belong to something more than I admitted to myself.

The Man and the Myth

Pat Robertson isn't some country-bumpkin, Bible-totin', give 'em hell preacher. Fortunately for me he was the antithesis of Ernest Angley. While much of Pat's staff was of minor-league quality when it came to television production skills—largely due to the low pay and the religious convictions required to work there—nonetheless, Pat was a shrewd and sophisticated media maverick who singlehandedly (and, according to him, with God's help) changed the face of religious television. He didn't grow up in the choir of some church, nor was his rise to television fame some miraculous rags-to-riches story.

His father was a United States senator and, as befit a senator's son, Pat received a first-class education. In fact, Robertson is the most educated of the video pulpiteers, holding a degree in law from Yale. (Surprisingly, the other superstars pitching salvation via television have little formal theological training. Jim Bakker of "The PTL Club" is a Bible-school dropout; Rex Humbard was ordained a minsister by his father without benefiting from any theological schooling; Oral Roberts attended a few college courses but did not study theology; Jimmy Swaggart is a high-school drop out; and James Robison didn't finish college. Even Dr. Billy Graham never earned a graduate degree. He attended three Bible colleges and earned a bachelor's degree in anthropology; only his fame brought him honorary doctorates. Apparantly, when God talks to you directly there is little need for formal education.)

Following God's lead, Pat went from riches to rags when he turned his back on a promising law career in order to study for the ministry and wound up working in the slums of Brooklyn after he earned a degree from the New York Theological Seminary.

Having read his book, *Shout It From the Housetops*, I was familiar with Pat's story of conversion and how he started CBN with virtually no money, and I was impressed by his faith and dedication. However, when I began working at CBN, I knew little of the real man and the myth that surrounded him. To some he was a god. To others he was a prophet. To still others he was a holy man. To me he was a television personality with limited appeal and range. But many thought of him as an anointed leader chosen by God. To all of us he was unmistakably the boss.

I was overwhelmed with the warmth of my reception. I was led to every corner of the building and enthusiastically introduced as a fourteen-year alumnus of CBS. I was almost smothered in hugs and promised prayers for God's blessing upon my work. Everyone was so nice and amiable. "This place must be heaven" was my most predominant thought during the first day. It was one big happy family, and Pat was the father.

Everyone from the staff to visitors worshiped the ground on which Pat walked. My first in-the-flesh view of him came just as he finished a broadcast and was mingling with the studio audience. His adoring fans treated him with the same wide-eyed awe that is given to any television star. But there was something extra. Their starry eyes had a gleam in them. Pat was more than a television personality. He didn't just entertain his audience. Presumably, he gave his viewers hope and, for many, a new life. This man who fed them spiritual food came across on the screen as a gentle friend, caring father, and a sage who really knew God.

Television fans are intense in their loyalty to their favorite stars. To the people who watched "The 700 Club," Pat Robertson was a genuine star; his fans were fanatical in their loyalty. God was real to Pat, and Pat was real to the people. There was a spiritual connection that transcended the normal celebrity-inspired idolatry. They hung on his every word as if God himself were speaking.

Pat's opinions on politics and economics are so entwined with the

Bible that they become a new gospel that cannot be rejected by his easily-swayed fans. This is raw power. People come from all over this vast nation just to sit in the audience. They long to touch him and to be one with him. A smile from this spiritual superstar makes a fan feel loved.

During my early days at CBN, the impact of the cultish way people perceived Pat had not yet struck me. In time I began to see that his having endless legions of supporters who believed that he was chosen by God to lead them through a modern maze of false teachings into the eternal truth of the Almighty was an awesome burden for this mere man to carry. They believed God spoke to him and that he spoke for God. This, too, is raw power. I may have wanted to laugh at Ernest Angley; however, to do so would be a serious mistake. Those who dismiss fundamentalist television preachers as a lunatic but harmless fringe of Christianity do not understand this type of fanatical power. An Islamic soldier fighting the Russians in Afghanistan believes that if he dies fighting for Allah, his soul will go straight to heaven. The power of that belief has trapped the Soviet Union in a bloody six-year war it thought it could easily win. *(Yeah, that, and American military equipment.)*

Beyond the reality of Robertson's power is the question of who judges whether he is misusing or abusing that power. I wasn't concerned with these thoughts or questions back then, and I'm sure if I had been, I would have dismissed them as a satanic trick played to push me into doubt. There was no room for doubt at CBN; everyone was comfortable in the security of his dogmatic belief, which ruled out the possibility of any error. That kind of security is dangerous and even destructive.

The nineteeth-century philosopher Immanuel Kant claimed that "the death of dogma is the birth of reality." The staff of CBN lived in the illusion that they were the sole possessors of the truth. Dr. Rollo May wrote: "People who claim to be absolutely convinced that their stand is the only right one are dangerous. Such conviction is the essence not only of dogmatism, but of its more destructive cousin, fanaticism. It blocks off the user from learning new truth, and it is a dead give-away of unconscious doubt. The person then has to double his or her protests in order to quiet not only the opposition but his or her own doubts as well."

Those four sentences perfectly express the spiritual condition of the staff at CBN; they are closed-minded fanatics who possess the truth and suppress their own doubts and those who doubt their truth. Perhaps the German philosopher Friedrich Nietzsche was correct when

→ he wrote: "Faith means not wanting to know what is true," and "One's belief in truth begins with doubt of all truths one has believed hitherto." I slowly began to learn that truth lives in the shadow of doubt and that only madmen live without doubts.

Within six months of my arrival at CBN, doubt began to knock gently on the door of my CBN-style faith. The knocking grew increasingly loud as time passed.

Seek and You Shall Find

To seek the truth is no satanic trick. I looked at CBN's ministry and saw how real power grows. As Pat expands his viewership to more and more markets, his audience builds. He builds bigger buildings; an empire builder is born. Short of reaching and converting the world, all this building and expanding has no limits because it is based on a vision of divine proportions and urgency. The heart of Pat's belief is that Jesus is coming back, *soon*. The return of the Son of God will be preceded by a period of great tribulation and will be marked by the "rapture"—a strange word that describes the theory that all true believers (that is, followers of Jesus) will be lifted up—both living and dead, body and all—from the earth and into Heaven to reign with Christ. If you don't make that heavenly blast-off, you'll get a chance to repent before being flung into the fiery furnace of Hell. This was all news to me—and not good news either.

As a Catholic I had been taught that Jesus was coming back. During Mass, after the consecration of the bread and wine, the people and the priest say aloud together, "We remember His death, we proclaim His resurrection, we await His coming in glory." Earlier in the Mass the congregation stands and repeats the words of the Nicene Creed, which in four tight paragraphs summarizes the Christian faith, and it boldly proclaims that "He [Jesus] will come again to judge the living and the dead." After a lifetime of hearing those statements, I believed, in a vague kind of way, that Jesus was coming back, but this rapture stuff was a whole new story, a very strange one to my ears. Despite the fact that some of the people debated whether or not the rapture would happen before or after a period of terrible tribulation, they believed it would happen—and very soon! So for Robertson and his rapture-bound staff there was an urgent need to use what time and resources they had to reach all those lost souls headed for ages and ages of agony.

The Chosen One

Pat Robertson sees his mission as bigger than saving the souls of doomed sinners. In the spring of 1968, during a luncheon that was part of the festivities celebrating the dedication of a renovated and expanded building, a member of CBN's board of directors (and a long-time friend of Pat's) delivered this prophetic word that Pat knew to be from God, "The days of your beginning seem small in your eyes in light of where I have taken you, but, yea, this day shall seem small in light of where I am going to take you . . . for I have chosen you to usher in the coming of my son." It was clear to all who heard those words that God had spoken. It's one thing to believe that God has healed you or spoken to you or answered your prayer or blessed you in some special way, but to believe that God has selected you to usher in the biggest event in the course of human history is heady, to say the least.

The doubts I began to feel had nothing to do with my belief in the existence of God or my faith in God; rather the doubts confronted this new expression of faith that featured a preoccupation with sinfulness, damnation, salvation, the second coming of Christ, evangelism, and the Bible. It became easy for me to understand how otherwise normal, main-line Christians became outraged at the pleasant people at CBN and felt that they were a collection of "crazies" who only wanted to "save" them. My Catholic version of being born-again seemed to stress personal spiritual renewal flamed by a sincere desire for holiness. Of course this awakened spirituality did lead charismatic-pentacostal Catholics into a zeal for sharing Jesus with others; but, basically, praising God and giving thanks for all things were higher priorities than converting lost souls. Joy was the catchword for my pre-CBN Christianity. After joining CBN, that joyful spirit soon gave way to a doom-and-gloom outlook.

Years before joining CBN, I read a simple sentence written by Mahatma Gandhi. The words rang true to me. "I am endeavoring to see God through service to humanity, for I know that God is neither in heaven, nor down below, but in everyone." Whenever I would discuss Gandhi with my new friends they would simply dismiss the efforts of his life because they considered him to be misguided.

Television evangelist Jimmy Swaggart claimed on his June 23, 1985, broadcast that "Gandhi was one of the most noble men ever to live, yet as we know he died without God." What a strange statement, considering Gandhi died with the word *Ram,* which means God, on his lips. Swaggart, who, with his wife, earns an annual income of over one hundred thousand dollars from his ministry, had just finished telling his vast television audience that as a young man in South Africa, Gandhi had gone to a Christian church but was unmoved by the experience. The Reverend Jimmy declared that was because "Gandhi went to a Christian church that did not know the glory of God" and therefore did not get a chance to hear the truth. In other words, that great man of faith had not gone to a spirit-filled church that taught Swaggart's brand of truth, and now the evangelist was lamenting that the Mahatma "led his people but not to God."

Ignoring Gandhi's tremendous respect for Jesus, Swaggart turned on the tears of remorse not only for Gandhi's lost soul but also for the millions of unsaved that the Indian leader could have led to Jesus—had he only heard the Gospel preached in power and might. Swaggart speculated that the ministers of the Christian church Gandhi briefly attended would be judged harshly by God for preaching watered-down gospel that could not be fully embraced by the Hindu holy man. In his heated fervor, Swaggart stated that Hinduism was atheistic and that Clarence Darrow was an atheistic simpleton.

I was surrounded by people who were always seeing evil in others and believed they would see God in some glorious setting beyond the sky and stars. They were bound for gloryland. Once inside CBN, I was stunned by some of the narrow-minded spirituality and beliefs, but I was a captive audience who began to fear they might be right. I soon got on the stage and became a part of God's play written by a family of fundamentalists. But there was tension in my performance.

A Dream Come True

On my first day, as I was introduced to Pat Robertson, I couldn't help feeling overwhelmed. Nervously, I called him "Father," momentarily slipping back to my Catholic background. An embarrassed and faint smile came across his face; however, the irony of the verbal slip was that it became prophetic. Pat Robertson evolved into a father figure for me, and our relationship became almost father and son in nature.

During my first week at CBN, preparations were underway for the annual commemoration of the April 29th erection of the cross at Cape Henry. Pat Robertson viewed CBN as the modern-day fulfill-ment of the settlers' vision and prayer that "from these very shores the Gospel shall go forth to not only this new world but to the entire world." Consequently, every year on that date, CBN televised a prayer service from that location, which today is marked by a large concrete cross.

Armed with satellite technology, Pat Robertson and CBN have the capability to reach the entire world. A dream—nearly four centuries old—was going to play a real part in the return of Jesus. Richard Hakluyt and Pat Robertson may be separated in time, space, culture, and even understanding of faith, yet the people at CBN believed God would unite their prayers into a beacon of hope for the future. CBN stood on sacred ground. I wasn't sure I understood the prophetic connection between the first settlers and "The 700 Club," but my Catholic background made me feel uncomfortable with lots of things I saw and heard at CBN.

My love for the visual artistry of television production combined with my hectic work schedule outweighed and quieted the many questions and doubts about the spirituality being transmitted, thus making it possible for me to last thirty months inside this fortress of evangelical Protestantism. I not only lasted, I thrived and became a key member—until the lie.

2

Assorted Snapshots
from Behind the Scenes

Before examining the gospel according to CBN and how information
and events are manipulated and broadcast to shape CBN's view of the
world, politics, morality, creation, and sin, it is important to set the
stage with some snapshots and stories of daily life at CBN. These
assorted snapshots will reflect the people behind the scenes, their
routine, and the rules that govern them. If the studio cameras that
capture Pat Robertson's every word could be turned around and
focused on the people whose hard work and dedication keep Pat on
the air, a completely different image would emerge. These snapshots
reveal that the staff may not be picture-perfect examples of what
Robertson advocates. Pat Robertson sells a "salvation" that will transform the viewer's life, and a flood of benefits will flow from heaven
following salvation: Restored health, healed relationships, career success, monetary rewards, and an improved lifestyle can all be yours if
you just say "yes" to Jesus. Yet these almost secular and very earthly
rewards are only an illusion for most of the staff.

   The first snapshot is of a building. Buildings aren't personal, yet
the CBN headquarters building is not only the personification of a
leader's vision but is also a visible manifestation of God's blessing on
his ministry. It is also seen as a fulfillment of the first half of the
prophecy concerning Pat Robertson being chosen to usher in the
second coming of Jesus. This building, dedicated in 1979, dwarfed the
building in which the 1968 prophesy was uttered. In a word, the
building is magnificent. It rests on 145 tree-lined acres of prime Virginia
Beach real estate.

Cottage Cheese and Prophecy

Long before the first architectural plans were drawn and the first brick laid, God gave Pat Robertson the inspiration for the building during a solitary moment of prayer. As the lofty legend goes, Pat was alone in his room at the Disneyland Grand Hotel in Anaheim, California. For some weeks he had been moderating an internal debate about the merits of buying five acres of land in order to build larger facilities to house his ever-expanding ministries. Room service had just delivered his spartan, meatless lunch, and, as he paused to silently thank God for the food, he suddenly sensed that God was about to speak to him. Thus saith the Lord: "Don't just buy five acres, buy all 200 acres, and build an international communications center and school to take the message of Jesus to the world." The minister had his marching orders— the debate was over. The seeds for the building as well as a university were planted during a blessing of cantaloupe and cottage cheese.

Did God, the designer of the universe and the source of all life plant that seed and inspire that vision? It's dangerous to judge another's faith, but I wonder what effect Pat Robertson's being at that moment in the Magic Kingdom of Walt Disney had on his subconscious mind. If Mr. Disney's playful fantasy could be turned into such an exciting empire, could not Reverend Robertson's godly dream succeed on an even larger level than the Magic Kingdom? Did Disneyland's flair for the exaggerated fuel Robertson's expansionist desires? This wasn't a topic of debate for Robertson. He had come to know God's voice. There was no doubt about it. His motto might have been: "God said it, I'll buy it, and we'll build it."

Building for the Lord

Apparently God is into colonial-American style buildings that are cross-shaped. Actually one can't tell that this massive structure is the shape of a cross unless one happens to be looking down from a plane—or from Heaven. The red brick building features three-story-tall white columns that sit atop a short flight of marble-like steps that lead to the front entrance. Not just any old red bricks either. They are special hand-crafted, expensive bricks made from a deep-red clay and were manu-factured to look aged—nothing but the best for God. The building was crowned with a cute cupola that is surrounded by a white, wooden fence. The lobby is palatial. Dual winding staircases, marble floors,

Persian rugs, a huge crystal chandelier, and a marble sculpture that depicts the apostles at Pentecost all join together to form an image of style and grace. At the center of the cross is a circular chapel with a large wooden cross suspended from the domed ceiling.

The building contains four studios that are crammed with the latest state-of-the-art technical equipment. Beyond a doubt, the television facilities are the best in the world and are the envy of every television operations manager in the country. Two of the studios are bigger than anything I ever worked in at all three networks. The equipment is extremely expensive. Just one camera cost one hundred thousand dollars, and they have at least a dozen of them. The control rooms for the studios and satellite transmission center are the most sophisticated and best designed I've ever seen. The place is a technological marvel, with a not-so-modest twenty million dollar price tag.

In an October 1985 letter to CBN partners, Pat Robertson recalled how, after the major portion of his construction goals were completed, he began to waver in his belief that God wanted the center to be bigger and better. Once again, Pat heard, clearly and unmistakably, God speak to him. Pat wrote in the letter, "Much more remained to be built. But now I was hesitating. But the Lord's voice seemed insistent: 'Why are you so timid? Finish the CBN Center!' There was no room for doubt. There was only one option—move forward." The letter suggests that God honored Pat's faith in following his command to keep building by providing the finances needed to finish CBN University, including a huge library building, and a World Outreach Support Center. God had little to do with the flood of money that poured into CBN: effective direct-mail marketing should get the credit, not God.

When I started working at CBN, the building was just a collection of steel girders, a lifeless skeleton pointing skyward. I was part of a group of people who had responsibility for breathing life into the building by designing the internal guts of this communication center and also picking out and purchasing the equipment that would allow it to communicate effectively the gospel of salvation; the cost per soul saved was not a factor. As I watched huge amounts of money being poured into the construction and the technical outfitting of this broadcasting palace, I had two thoughts that ran counter to the unrestricted enthusiasm of the staff.

One thought can best be articulated by telling a short story told by William Paley, founder and former chairman of the board of CBS. One day during the early 1930s he was walking down Broadway in New York City. He noticed a fancy theater with a dazzling marquee.

It was playing a B-grade flick to only a few patrons. In sharp contrast, directly across the street was a rundown theater that featured no ornamentation or sparkling lights, yet it was housing a feature movie starring two big-name actors. It had long lines of people clamoring to get in to see the film. The lesson was clear to the visionary Paley. Spend your money on talent, not buildings. The people don't care where you broadcast from—just what you broadcast.

Today, CBS broadcasts from what once was a dilapidated dairy plant; the cows gave way to cameras. I thought our emphasis on the building itself was overrated but told this Paley parable to no avail. Our needs did not require the expensive technical eloquence they sought to aquire. Slowly, I began to see that historically during the ministry's twenty years of existence, its tremendous growth was marked more by the acquisition of large buildings stuffed with impressive technical equipment than by drawing into their ranks the creative people needed to develop the programs that might change the world. The strict religious atmosphere had a tendency to squelch creativity. Machines don't question or sin. Consequently, we were overequipped and understaffed. As the building was taking form, I was truly concerned with why we were underpaying and overworking such dedicated people in order to build a monument. Perhaps it had something to do with the sin of pride.

The other thought that hounded me also had to do with money—not the spending, but the receiving. There were lots of people who gave as much as one thousand dollars a month to the ministry. Even one-time gifts of one hundred thousand dollars were not uncommon. Special seminars tailored to wealthy supporters were periodically given in order to harvest even more money from this rich field of Robertson believers. The affluent were brought together from all over the nation for a weekend retreat in a swanky hotel in order to attend lavish banquets and listen to several inspirational messages from Robertson. Special tours, Christian entertainment, and audio cassettes of Robertson sermons were provided along with an opportunity for a private chat with Pat. A small fortune was spent to orchestrate an event that would deliver a symphony of large donations that would be music to Robertson's ear.

I wan't concerned so much with these megabuck donors, but the image of a poor, elderly widow parting with a portion of her pension demanded strict fiscal responsibility on our part. She stuffed her own much-needed ten dollars into an envelope each month, and we spent the collective sum of thousands upon thousands from such trusting people on fancy business lunches, high-priced consultants, expensive research trips to check out the New York and Hollywood operations of three networks, studios and equipment that would lie idle or be under-utilized, a university to train a handful of students, long retreats at a Virginia resort that caters to and pampers the wealthy, furniture that would be too fine for most people's homes, company cars for executives, a luxurious home for Robertson, and a landscaping bill that would choke a goat.

Once, during the preparatory stages of a dramatic series launched by CBN, I made a research trip to London in order to visit and study the drama department at the British Broadcasting Corporation. I wonder how many widows it took to pay for that unnecessary trip? Most of the staff looked at the building and marvelled at the marvelous handiwork of God while I wondered about the madness of one man. Yet, I grew to respect him—and I think even to love him. I went from doubter to a follower.

Servants of the Lord

Robertson is both heart and head, and the building merely the body, but the people behind the scenes are the soul of the ministry. Snapshots of the people form a picture-perfect, people-version of a bar of Ivory Soap. 99 and 44/100 percent pure and squeaky clean! With their bows in place and smiles on their faces, the women are clothed in whole-someness. They don't "dress to kill or give a guy a thrill." Tight-fitting, designer jeans would never be seen; after all, they're for women with loose-fitting morals. The men are well-groomed. Vitalis lives. Long hair or untrimmed beards would be out of place with their polyester-preppie taste. The men are men, and the women are women; unisex is a dirty word.

You can feel and see their piety. In every purse, in every briefcase, and on every desk you will find a Bible. Big ones, little ones, leather-bound ones, hardcover ones, paperback ones, and ones with pictures. The King James version is by far the most popular; in fact, the vast majority of people consider it the only authentic translation despite the fact that most biblical scholars believe it is the one most laden with translation inaccuracies. I don't know why they need them; most people seem to have the entire book memorized by chapter and verse. Conversations are sprinkled with Scripture quotes. And these Bibles aren't just decorative. They are opened frequently during the day.

They are read, reread, underlined, highlighted, discussed, digested, and turned to as a source of guidance for almost any situation.

The Final Word

No picture of the people or the ministry is complete if the Bible is not included. The building is built on the promises of the Bible, and the lives of the staff are based on a literal interpretation of the book, which they claim to be the inerrant and complete word of God. The Bible is the final word on everything. If the Bible is at odds with history, science, theology, or psychology, then those fields of study are wrong. End of discussion.

The Bible was always important to me, but the people I met at CBN seemed to worship the book. They acted as if the Bible fell from heaven or at least as if God dictated it word for word to holy men who were merely passive instruments, human pens. It seemed to me that all words are human words, and the words of the Bible contain all the marks of the men who wrote them as well as of the time and culture in which they were written. The lyrical poetry of the Psalms, written over the course of several centuries, expresses vivid human passion and revenge. According to the writers of these inspired poems, the virtuous, protected by his God, will "smite his enemies on the cheek" and "break the teeth of the wicked." Somehow that doesn't sound like God talking.

Despite the humanness of the Bible, Christians can still find the self-revelation of God and come to true knowledge of him in and through the symbolic words of the men who wrote it. I felt that the symbolic language of the Bible merely points the way to God; however, for the people at CBN it is *the way.* Years after leaving CBN, I began to better understand that a literal interpretation of Scripture is dangerous because much of the writing is simply an anthology of fictions that speak about outward manifestations of an inner reality. By means of the imagination, the writers send messages and images in the symbolic language of their times to our conscious minds. The Scriptures contain numerous contradictions, inaccuracies, and absurdities, and there are varying portrayals of the relationship between humanity and the Divine. The books attributed to Moses differ from the later prophets; Job is special; Paul's epistles are very different from the Synoptic Gospels. Yet, overall, the book portrays a supreme being who wants to have a loving relationship with each of his creations.

Claiming that Scripture contains contradictions and absurdities would cause most people at CBN to fly into a defensive rage, but here are a few examples which support that claim. According to Genesis 1:20-22 and 26-27, birds were created before man, but Genesis 2:7 and 19 inform us that man was created before birds. Genesis 1:31 claims that God thought everything he made was very good, yet Genesis 6:6 tells us that God was sorry he made man on earth. God dwells in thick darkness according to 1 Kings 8:12, and 1 Timothy 6:16 claims that God dwells in unapproachable light. (Maybe he moved.) Psalm 78:69 states that the earth was established forever, but according to 2 Peter 3:10 the earth will perish. Jesus was a descendant of David's son, Solomon, according to Matthew 1:6-7; however, Luke 3:31 claims that Jesus was a descendant of David's son, Nathan. Matthew 5:22 teaches that anger by itself is a sin, yet Ephesians 4:26 states that anger is not always a sin. Matthew 7:7-8 leads us to believe that if we seek, we will find; Luke 13:24 warns that many seek, but only a few will find. Both Romans 3:23 and Ephesians 2:8 preach that we are justified by faith alone; yet James 2:24 maintains that good works are also required for justification.

Paul's conversion from persecutor of Christians to a believer is a major event in the growth of Christianity, and his writings form a large part of the New Testament; nonetheless, the details of what happened on the road to Damascus contain a major contradiction. In the ninth chapter of the Acts of the Apostles, verse 7 states, "The men traveling with Saul stood there speechless, for though they heard the voice they could see no one." That account is contradicted in the twenty-second chapter of the Acts of the Apostles where verse 9 claims, "The people with me saw the light but did not hear his voice as he spoke to me."

Even the chronicles of the most significant event in Christ's life— the resurrection—are laden with contradictions. Without the resurrection, Jesus' death on the cross would be pointless, yet reading the various accounts of the resurrection and the ascension of Jesus, one is confronted with the conflict of details and the meagerness of enthusiasm. There is no agreement in the four gospels concerning the time of the resurrection, those who came to the tomb, or the presence of angels.

Those are just a few examples of contradictions; another hundred could easily be listed. The Bible also abounds with seeming absurdities like the story in Numbers 22:21-30 which tells how a donkey sees an angel, recognizes it as such, and then is able to speak in order to relay a message to his master. Joshua 10:12-14 asserts that God made the sun and the moon stand still so that Joshua could finish his vengeful battle in daylight. Genesis 3:1-5 presents a serpent who speaks fluently. I think it is possible to believe in God without believing in a talking donkey or snake.

Beyond the numerous absurdities, there are countless atrocities. According to Exodus 21:7-11 God allows a father to sell his daughter into slavery in order to pay a debt. 2 Kings 19:35 indicates that during the course of one night, one angel killed 185,000 Assyrians in order to defend Jerusalem. The Old Testament is sprinkled with stories of mass killings ordered, committed, or approved by God. Numbers 16:41-49 describes how 14,700 Jews died in a plague because they rebelled against Moses. Numbers 14:37 gives an account of how eleven rulers of Israel were killed by a plague because they refused to invade the Promised Land. Numbers 25:4 and 9 records the beheading of 24,000 Israelites who cohabited with Moabite women and worshipped Baal. 1 Samuel 6:19 recounts how 50,070 innocent people of Bethshemesh were struck dead by God because a few of them who were working a field violated a no-peeking rule and happened to glance into the Ark. 2 Kings 2:23-24 tells how 42 children were eaten by two bears after Elisha cursed them in the name of the Lord for making fun of his bald head. 2 Chronicles 28 indicates that 120,000 Judeans were massacred in one day by King Pekah of Isreal because they had forsaken the Lord. Vengeance wreaked by God is really drastic. Leviticus 26 contains 33 verses of descriptions in God's own words of unbelievably dreadful consequences that will result if the Jews incur his displeasure. These stories make the violence on television seem like kindergarten pranks.

The contradictions, inaccuracies, absurdities, and even atrocities don't mean that the Bible was not inspired by God. Obviously, an omnipotent God did not dictate the book word for word. The Bible simply records the apparent seeking and the yearning of God for his people, and it tells of humanity's journey in response to God's supposed call to follow, to grow, and to become one with him. It is a story of movement, a living word that cannot be frozen in time. God cannot be trapped in a book of metaphysical fiction from a time and place not our own. The Bible records some of humanity's spiritual experiences in order to help guide people, but our lives cannot be shaped by another's words about God but only by our own experience—or nonexperience—of the Supreme Being.

For my new friends at CBN the Bible was God's last word on everything, and nothing could be added to it or removed. Rather than critical examination, the Bible was treated with cultish fascination. What should have been a word of life was twisted at CBN to a word of judgment, a judgment whose verdict was "guilty" for all who did not listen. But I could not understand how a biblical quotation could solve a moral problem or be the final word in a discussion. I was faced with a spiritual dilemma that would take years to resolve.

Today my understanding of Scripture runs contrary to CBN doctrine. I believe that the Christian community can find comfort, help,
guidance, enlightenment, and may even be strengthened by some of
the Scripture; but only God, who dwells within a person, can help him
or her discover the appropriate response to new situations and needs.
The Bible alone can't give anyone God's revealed solution to a moral
problem. The prophets of the Old Testament could summon the people of God to a holy war to exterminate enemies, including women
and children. Should a self-appointed prophet of today, like Jerry
Falwell or Jimmy Swaggart, be permitted to wage a holy war against
those they consider the enemies of the Gospel?

The apostle Paul would be stunned at our modern-day abhorrence
of slavery. Why quote Paul's first Letter to the Corinthians to the effect
that homosexuals are excluded from the Kingdom of Heaven, and
ignore what the Bible says in Deuteronomy 21: "Women are not to
wear men's clothing"? God's word cannot be locked in time; a con-
tinual revelation is needed. It doesn't make sense to take those words
from a holy book as a reason to reject a fellow human being. God
doesn't throw stones, bolts of lightning, or AIDS at homosexuals. He
accepts them as they are and exerts no pressure to change them into
anything else. Scripture doesn't compel us to do otherwise and should
only lead us to love.

Calling AIDS a "gay plague" is not only hateful but, even worse,
paints a picture of a "just" God waging germ warfare against a selected
group of "sinners" without serving similar stiff sentences on warmakers,
polluters, slum landlords, and drug dealers—"sinners" whose actions
affect society so much more profoundly. Fundamentalism distorts and
deserts authentic Christianity.

The Scriptures are one of the means that God uses to make his act
of love, as epitomized in Jesus, real to each person in each generation.
They are words of love from a God who reveals himself in a human
language that speaks a wisdom hidden in mystery in an effort to draw
our attention and affection to him. (Even referring to God in masculine
terms—*him* and *Father*—is limiting God because God is neither male
nor female but pure spirit.)

By using images of material things which we know about, the
Scriptures lead us to the unknown and invisible things of God. It starts
us on our own inward journey to the Almighty. The Bible is a scriptural
stepping-stone to the sacred; and the notion that it's all in the book and
nothing else can be added is putting a limit on God, who is limitless.
Why would God render the mind useless by making it so rigid and

unacceptable as to depend on one book for all answers? But that kind of evolving enlightenment is threatening to those Christians who need a cut-and-dried biblical approach to the moral dilemmas of life. I would have been stoned for expressing these thoughts at CBN, because doubt and criticism have no place in a cult.

What the Camera Can't Catch

The collective picture of the people at CBN may lead the casual observer to think they were all frozen in some past, innocent time and unaffected by the changing world around them. It is the nature of cults that members feel saved, protected, "chosen," and cut off from the world at large.

The people at CBN do not see themselves as trying to live a form of piety from the past; they believe they are the future. Far from being frozen in the past, they think they have been chosen for all time. They are special, and working for CBN isn't just a job—it's a divine calling, and they feel privileged to be part of the ministry. In this multiracial world, they are the new Chosen People of God, and they possess the *found truth* to which we all must bow. They are modern-day missionaries, who transmit the Word of God by satellite around the world, instead of carrying it by foot to remote regions.

By many standards, they would seem one-dimensional, downright dull, rather nonintellectual, naive, and close-minded. Yet these same traits make them hard-working, easily motivated, highly dedicated, and extremely enthusiastic—an employer's dream. And no wonder! After all, God is the employer. Through Pat Robertson, God tends to hire family-centered people who are morally righteous and have a tendency to look at everything through religious eyes and more than likely to vote conservatively.

During my two and a half years, no matter what I thought of the collective power and impact of my coworkers for Christ, individually I found them to be among the nicest people with whom I've ever worked. Still, beneath the snapshot of their picture-perfect piety there is a sea of emotional turmoil that the camera fails to catch. They may have been holy, but they were also human. Like workers anywhere, they have a tendency to gossip about fellow employees and complain about their bosses. Professional and personal discontentment is frequently felt, but rarely expressed. Pressure to conform to the spiritual norm forces a suppression of many feelings and emotions—and ev' worse, the burial of any doubts.

Sexuality is also buried, despite the fact that it is far from dead. Adoration of the Almighty did not prevent adultery, because sex is such a dynamic impulse in human nature that most efforts to repress it or entirely eradicate it usually result in failure and aggravation. At CBN sex was thought of as the diabolic element in our being (which of course flies in the face of the benevolent character of the Creator), and therefore had to be repressed because without sex repression there could only be sex obsession. The middle road was ignored, and the emphasis was put on the body, not the mind, as self-torture dictated by fear was preferred to self-control ruled by a controlled mind that understands the sacred nature of the body and the wisdom of restraint and moderation. I think many single men at CBN rushed into marriage simply to fulfill a sex urge. The funeral service CBN tried to hold for sexuality as well as doubt was premature.

Among such a large staff, many personality conflicts naturally existed, and they tended to be covered up by some unnatural, ersatz form of Christian love and false forgiveness. Being born-again may give a person a new lease on life and even make someone a new person, but it does not change a person's personality. At CBN, every problem from gossip to sex to doubt is seen as a satanic weapon employed by the Prince of Darkness to destroy their ministry. This failure to accept the "dark side" of personality results in a schizophrenic reaction to life. The in-group's darkness is projected out onto out-groups, who are then attacked. Neither having a new opinion of yourself nor attacking "wicked" others is a mark of mature spirituality. In fact, in indicates a blockage in growth.

Bull's Eye for Satan

I was at CBN about four months when I received a promotion. An executive invited me into his office for a prayer; at CBS the same situation would have called for a victory drink. I sat down in a comfortable chair in front of his uncluttered desk. He stood next to me, gently placed his hands upon my head, and began to earnestly pray that God protect me in my new job.

At first I was warmed by the experience. The personal attention, concern felt good; however, the actual prayer seemed understand his imploring God to guide me in my new ut why would I need God's protection in a job that held no elements of danger? I wasn't exactly smuggling Bibles into Russia or blasting off to convert the man in the moon. When he finished praying, he put his arms around me in a fatherly fashion; and, with a big sigh, he began to share what he considered to be a pearl of wisdom. He told me that I was now in a very, very important job, and because of that I was a prime target for the enemy. In effect, he was saying, in nuclear parlance, that I was a "first-strike site." He advised me to picture myself with a large bull's eye on my back, because that's how Satan saw me, and he wouldn't rest until he hit his mark by driving me into sin and out of CBN, thereby depriving God of my creative talents. Not exactly positive imaging. Two years later that man would become more instrumental in my ouster than the Devil.

The Picture Fades

My first reaction to the staff I met left me with the impression that I was surrounded by people who were true followers of Jesus. Actually that is not strong enough. I was so overwhelmed by a "goodness" so real I could almost touch it, that I honestly thought the people were more than just followers of Christ—they were actually like Christ. That was only a surface and temporary impression.

What is a Christian, a follower of Christ? The 1984 presidential campaign actually tried to examine how good a Christian each of the candidates was, and during the first debate the ticket-toppers were asked about their faith commitments. Who is the judge of a heart, which is the home of faith? Despite the diversity of the Christian faith, it seems to me that a Christian's life reaches the apex of its fulfillment when his or her life resembles the life of Jesus, and perfection resides in the assimilation of the likeness of Christ. The resemblance must be more than skin deep, and the assimilation needs to be internal as well as external. Christianity rises above a pedestrian expression of itself when Jesus Christ is not just a moral example outside a Christian: Christ is living in him or her. The likeness of most CBN staffers to Christ seemed only skin deep. They may have been on the road to holiness, but they acted as if they had already reached that destination. I initially saw the external manifestation of their faith and believed it was an expression of real Christianity. The inner turmoil was hidden for some time.

Headlines from Heaven

One of my first encounters with the mingling of this apparent authentic Christianity with the reality of business began to open my eyes. For years Pat Robertson was peeved at the news media's liberal bias. He harbored a secret desire to present the news through a different prism, one which would refract a conservative, Christian point of view. He wanted to beat them at their own bias game.

One of the members of the board of directors was a former newspaper journalist. Together they believed they could put on a nightly news show of network quality, but they didn't want to be smothered with the details of how they would do this. In his typically impetuous fashion, Pat boldly announced on the air that by the fall of 1978, CBN would begin airing a half-hour nightly news program. Press conferences were held and articles started appearing proclaiming that CBN was moving from spreading the Good News to gathering world news.

Visionary leaders frequently march far in front of their followers, who are left with the tough task of implementing the vision—ready or not. CBN was not ready to produce a news show—not from *any* point of view. The writer-journalist-turned-television-producer held a meeting, the purpose of which was to plot the steps to be taken in order to turn the news vision into television news. The man had no idea what he was doing. The people present at the meeting had to put together the physical and technical operations required, and they soon realized that the road ahead was going to be very, very rocky.

Sitting next to the board member was a recent graduate of some school of journalism, who also knew nothing about television, and together they formed the News Department. This terrible twosome faced a group of people who needed specific answers, and they tried to feed them generalities. They came without plans, armed only with a mandate from God. Tensions grew. Tempers flared. Pressure mounted from a timetable publicly announced before it was privately determined if the goal could be reached. Time and inexperience were the enemy, and the task was so overwhelming that it was doubtful that even God could help. A meeting that started in prayer looked as though it was going to end in war. Reflections of the Prince of Peace were nowhere to be seen. I was stunned by the snide remarks and personal jabs. Until this meeting I had thought I was in the Promised Land. Now the heavenly bubble was burst, the illusion shattered. After going around in circles for a few dizzying hours, the meeting was mercifully adjourned.

Then something truly amazing, almost miraculous, happened. Each of us pushed our chairs away from the large, wooden conference table that had turned into a battlefield. We stood facing each other. There was a long pause during which some of the men began to bow their heads. It was common knowledge that all meetings began and ended with a word of prayer. We began as brothers and ended as battlers. Prayer seemed wrong or at least unwanted. However, the man who knew nothing knew enough to ask us to join hands and pray. We did. It could have been a simple almost ritualistic "thank you, God, guide us, God, help us, God" type of prayer. Zip, zip, zip—over and out. But no. Someone asked for forgiveness from the news department by saying that he was sorry that he insinuated that one of the two members was a jerk. The floodgates opened. Teary-eyed confessions of disunity abounded. We tightly grasped hands and sang songs of praise to the Lord. I was almost crushed by a wave of hugs. We were brothers again. This *was* the Promised Land.

The image of men standing around a conference table holding hands and prayerfully asking for forgiveness was haunting. I couldn't imagine differences of opinion at CBS being downplayed by prayer and brotherhood. I concluded that this really was the greatest place in the world to work, and I thanked God for my being there.

The euphoria of the postbattle forgiveness bath soon lost its cleansing effect as the real problem surfaced again and still was not recognized. The fact was that the news department duo clearly wasn't equipped to handle the difficult task entrusted to them by the prophet of God whose judgment went unquestioned. We needed to be forgiven our back-stabbing; however, that didn't mean our opinions and questions should be ignored. From a business point of view, these two men were not qualified. From a religious point of view, they were looked at as being ordained and anointed by God to perform their jobs. It was as if we had two minds about them. To me, the problems grew out of our being both a church and a company. Each needs to be run differently. Some days we acted like a church concerned with a high calling. Some days we acted like a business concerned with the bottom line. To add to the confusion, some of the staff liked the church model of operation and others preferred the business model. Plastic Christianity turned real business problems into satanic tricks aimed at dividing and destroying us. We wanted to do the right thing in our dealing with others; however, the reality of Jesus was not so internalized that it came easily.

What follows is a postscript of CBN's heralded entrance into the news business. I was plagued with deep doubts about how these two very nice men could develop a full-fledged news operation in a few months. I couldn't sit back and wait for a miracle. God might feed the birds, but he doesn't put the food into their nests.

I called a friend at CBS News, and he helped me gather some inside facts and figures. Besides the studio broadcast that features the anchorperson (who is backed up by a team of writers, researchers, editors, and all the technicians needed to operate the cameras, video-tape machines, audio and video controls), we needed news bureaus around the country and around the world. These bureaus needed administrators, writers, producers, reporters, and technicians. We needed a method of transmitting their stories to our control point in Virginia. I presented these facts and the associated financial figures to Pat. He was overwhelmed at the budget for the CBS Evening News. The commercial revenue on the evening news doesn't even come close to covering the cost. And we didn't even have commercials. Yet Pat was undaunted by the cold hard facts. God would supply our needs. God wanted the news.

Within a few months, the writer-journalist stepped down. The task was impossible. The stench of defeat filled the air. Pat was crushed. His being let down bothered me in human terms, because I didn't like seeing him suffer the pain of public defeat. Even though I didn't see the need for our doing a news show, I prepared a simple alternative that would enable us to save face in the eyes of the press, the public, and our supporters. While I intended it as a serious solution to the problem, this is where the story turns comical, unintentionally so.

My plan for the salvation of CBN News started with a bit of broadcasting history. I told Pat how during 1976 CBS News produced the "Bicentennial Minute," which aired following the first prime-time show each evening. Those historic reflections of two-hundred-year-old headlines were a critical and financial success. Of unseen importance was the fact that CBS News had wrestled one minute of precious pro-gramming time from CBS Entertainment. Those were seven money-making minutes a week. As 1976 drew to a close, the news division didn't want to give up the time they had captured. Necessity became the mother of invention. They developed a concept for a one-minute update type of news format that consisted of a series of quick head-lines. The brief, capsulized version of the news was born. The mini-news even contained a quicky commercial, only ten seconds long, that grabbed a maxi-profit of over six million dollars annually. The simple production cost virtually nothing. The information, staff, and tech-nicians were all left over from the evening news.

I suggested to Pat that we could easily produce a headline type of newscast. The only additional staff we would need were an anchorperson and maybe a research writer. If we aired the show at the end of "The 700 Club" crew's regular eight-hour day, not only would the technical manpower cost of the newscast not be an additional burden on the ministry, but we also would have a more cost-effective utilization of the workers. Once we got a UPI wireservice teletype machine that would provide us with up-to-date news and a graphic house to supply us with generic slides to spruce up the production, we would be in the news business. We would start out by doing just one little minute of news a day and every few months we would attempt to add additional minutes to the schedule. During this period of moderate and cheap expansion, we would slowly bring on board the types of qualified people needed to do a full-fledged nightly newscast. He bought it hook, line, and sinker. The funny part is that I was suddenly a news producer.

After designing a set, I found and hired a former television newsman whose radical Christianity had forced him out of his journalism job and into a career as a used-car salesman. I figured no serious journalist could sit floating among a sea of Christians just waiting to deliver one minute of headlines each day. This young man looked good on camera and could read a cue card with conviction. Those two qualities, along with his strong religious belief and extreme right-wing political views, made him perfect for the job as the first anchorman at CBN News. Besides, all he did was read the Bible most of the day.

Pat watched the first broadcast from home, and the next day he ordered me to fire the former used-car salesman because he wasn't authoritative enough. Reading between the lines of Pat's ranting, I realized he had expected an older, more mature man, who could capture Walter Cronkite's father-figure image without the master's substance. I pointed out that Walter Cronkite didn't do Update News. This young man, I insisted, was fine for our purposes at this time, and we could hire a more authoritative person later for the nightly news. Pat nearly choked a few months later when I added a research writer who functioned as a back-up anchor, because the person was not only young but also a woman.

The really comical part of all this is that Pat proudly proclaimed we were in the news business, yet our news operation consisted of only a producer (whose interest was more in drama than news and who at the end of a hectic day scribbled out a newscast using as his source a wireservice machine and a local newspaper) and an anchorman (who was really a used-car salesman). Smoke and mirrors! It was fortunate that Morley Safer didn't look into this part of the operation. The anchorman's salary and that of the researcher who took over my writing chores, the UPI wireservice contract, the graphics, set construction, and associated technical cost added up to over $150,000 during the first year. Was this a valuable service? Hardly. Did our cable viewers need it or benefit from it? Not likely. Did it justify spending money that had been sent in to spread the Gospel on a news service that could only be seen by a handful of people? Doubtful.

Today, Update News airs more than a dozen times a day and even has its own night shift. CBN News now has bureaus in Washington and Jerusalem, the only centers of news that interest Robertson, and they feed their slanted reports to Virginia for broadcast in the supposedly religious "700 Club." CBN calls it journalism with a different spirit. A veiled attempt is made at suggesting that the Holy Spirit is the news director. CBN News has even sent a crew to Turkey to report on the search for Noah's Ark.

During the 1984 Republican and Democratic conventions, CBN News traveled to San Francisco and Dallas and fed daily live reports to "The 700 Club." In fact, the board member who was appointed to breathe CBN News into existence but ran out of breath was the on-air correspondent reporting from the conventions. He was terrible, and many insiders quietly considered his performance an embarrassment. He was so nervous that he shook. I guess Pat thought he would come across as authoritative. (Clearly not an on-the-air journalist, he now serves as president of CBN University.) His reports might have been a bit incoherent, but they were definitely pro-Reagan. CBN News is playing the bias game with the big boys. It is a joke I wish I hadn't help create.

End of the Road

A personal portrait of many CBN people includes another trait that can't be seen in a picture: a preoccupation with salvation—not just their own, but everyone's. One weekend I was strolling through a large shopping mall in Virginia Beach, when I ran into a fellow CBN employee. Both of our wives were shopping, so with some time to kill we leaned against the second-floor guardrail and talked as we gazed down on the throngs of people crisscrossing the main shopping plaza below.

He began to slowly shake his head back and forth over and over. He said, "Isn't it sad?" I didn't know exactly what he was talking about and figured he might be referring to our consumer-crazed society that scurries all over trying to fulfill desires that are stirred up by advertisers, television, and movies. I said nothing. "It's sad that they are all going to Hell." I stood in stunned disbelief at his judgmental pronouncement.

Prior to my arrival at CBN, I considered my Catholic version of being born-again as an awakening of a true faith that was asleep. My new state of spiritual alertness prompted me to want first of all to change those things in myself that needed some long-neglected improvement and secondly to try to be a mirror of God's love that would reflect happiness and kindness to all I met. The idealism of these twin aspirations might take a lifetime to perfect, but my daily goal was to work at changing myself, with God's help, one day at a time.

The nineteenth-century Catholic theologian John Henry Newman wrote, "In a higher world it is otherwise, but here below to live is to change, and to grow perfect is to have changed often." I knew I had a lifetime of change ahead of me, and my conversion signaled the beginning of a lifelong struggle. The important point about my awakening or conversion was that I had a new way of looking at life. This revised vision looked for a change in my old way of living and loving. The apostle Paul wrote, "Let your behavior change, modeled by your new mind" (Rom. 12:2). The conversion experience is putting on the mind of Jesus, and this change of mind is supposed to convert the person into a more loving being. The moment of conversion is only the beginning of a transformation—a stage we pass through. When that change has penetrated into the depths of a person's heart, he or she can reach out to others in an attempt to share the secrets of that change in an act of pure love, not persuasion.

It's been more than ten years since my moment of conversion, my born-again experience, and I have achieved nothing near a love so pure that I can preach a message of Jesus, which is a message of love. However, the teachings of Jesus have become more and more real to me, and that growing reality has made a small difference in my behavior. The theological concerns of whether Jesus is really God made flesh or the most God-filled human ever to live is irrelevant to his inspiring change in me. Theologians could argue; I had to live. And Jesus set the standard for living.

The Divine Commission

The simple yet beautiful idea that conversion is the beginning of a life of personal change that will eventually manifest itself on a societal level in the form of social justice (which is a concrete way of loving your neighbor) is in stark contrast to the pentecostal fixation with evil that makes up CBN's infatuation with "salvation." For them, conversion is the goal; it is the end of the road, not the beginning. Conversion is salvation, not a road that leads to unity with God.

This spirituality emphasizes the fall of man during the Creation at the expense of the blessings of Creation, and it concentrates on salvation as deliverance from some impending doom rather than a sharing in the creative love of God. For the people at CBN, salvation is simply the state or fact of being saved or delivered. Saved or delivered from what? Separation from God, or more bluntly put—sin and eternal damnation. Salvation, from a fundamentalist point of view, is attained only by accepting Jesus as God and savior. Christ's birth, death, resurrection, ascension, and return are the only elements of God's plan of salvation. They believe that to be saved is to join in the victory of Jesus, a victory of life over death.

The fact that a person's cultural experience or the faith of his or her parents may make such a pro-Jesus choice repugnant or impossible is ignored by television evangelists. I do not think that God rejects any of his creations just because they are unable to believe in their head or heart in Jesus as God.

However, for the fundamentalist, the only truth that matters is that those who are and were saved will participate in the fruits of that victory during the Rapture. They think that God wants every man and woman to hear this good news and have the opportunity to say "yes" to Jesus. To refuse or say "no" to the saving message is to turn your back on salvation and to be lost forever. It somehow seems unjust that "sins" committed in time will be punished for all time. Moreover, what crime committed by a finite human being against his or her infinite God could warrant an eternity's worth of suffering in hell?

Spain's most influential philosopher, Miguel de Unamuno, wrote in his masterpiece *The Tragic Sense of Life:*

> For to assert that since God is infinite, an offence committed against Him is infinite also and therefore demands an eternal punishment, is apart from the inconceivability of an infinite offence, to be unaware that, in human ethics, offence, if not in the human police system, the

gravity of the offence is measured not by the dignity of the injured person but by the intention of the injurer, and that to speak of an infinite culpable intention is sheer nonsense, and nothing else.

The extremeness of fundamental Christianity is that it claims a person can't be saved by the quality of his or her life and ethics, the fidelity of his or her religious observation, or the merit of the sacrifices he or she offers. Your morally uprightheous neighbor, who is a good, kind, honest, and caring person but does not go to a spirit-filled, Bible-based church, will be marching straight to Hell along with legions of Jewish rabbis, Buddhist monks, Hindus, Muslims, and any polytheistic worshipers. Salvation only comes from the savior-god Jesus. This is why evangelical television ministers are obsessed with telling the world about Jesus.

God compels them to give everybody the opportunity to be saved. It is a divine commission they execute vigorously. Their method is simple: promote unbearable guilt and promise the blood of the Lamb. Their reaching out is simply a compulsive and persuasive act of prose-lytizing that happens to pay very well; it is not an act of pure, God-like love. Their message of redemption by the blood of Jesus is urgent because the sooner everyone gets a chance at accepting it or rejecting it, the sooner the Savior will return.

A desire to save part of the world was never a part of my con-version picture, although I did try to convert some friends and family. While I tended to look for the good contained in each new day, my friends at CBN seemed bent on searching out evil. You see, evil is Satan's way of persuading you to say "no" to Jesus, which, of course, is a twisted way of saying "yes" to a lifetime burning in Hell with Satan. What follows are a series of short stories that illustrate the CBN staffers' obsession with saving the world, not loving it.

Salvation Mania

It was mid-morning. I was slipping out the back of the building with a coworker. We were fleeing the office hustle-bustle and the ever-in-trusive phone calls. We were heading for the tranquility of the study in my home. We were in the process of creating the first Christian soap opera and needed a quiet atmosphere to concoct all the turbulent situ-ations our characters were going to endure. As my writing partner drove us onto the highway and sailed toward Virginia Beach, the glo-rious sunshine, deep blue sky, and crisp ocean breezes created a mighty urge to drive straight to the oceanfront, skip the work, and simply enjoy our freedom from the confines of the office. My mood was very upbeat and as sunny as the day. Yet my writing partner was able to spot storm clouds where none existed. He was ever alert to seize an opportunity to spread the news of the Son of God. Even on a sunny day, Jesus was the only sunshine he could see. As we approached the toll booth, he began to rummage through his briefcase which rested between us. "Here, I got a quarter," I chirped, figuring he was searching for some change. "No, no, I got it," he replied as he continued shifting around the contents of his briefcase. The toll booth was quickly approaching, but his attention was increasingly focused on finding something in the briefcase. I was relieved to hear him exclaim, "Got it," and see him look ahead in time to stop before we crashed into the tollgate.

The object of his frantic search was a small pamphlet. As he stretched out his arm to hand the toll to the toll-taker, he began to say what must have been frequently-heard words for the attendant, "Do you know the way——?" During the few seconds it took to stretch and speak those five words, I guess the toll-booth tender thought he had another lost tourist to save. My friend knew the way to my home, so his words were a puzzle to me. The next words were "to Heaven?"

The exasperated attendant must have thought his hearing was going, for there is a Lynnheaven in Virginia Beach. I was embarrassed at being in the car. Before the attendant could respond, my crusading Christian companion blurted out, "Jesus is the way to heaven—the only way. Are you saved?" And along with the quarter toll, he handed him the pamphlet that proclaimed the message of John 3:16: "For God so loved the world, that He gave His only begotten Son, that whosoever believeth in Him should not perish but have everlasting life," along with the suggestion that Blue Cross, Blue Shield, Medicare, Medicaid, life insurance, social security, and retirement plans only take care of this life; so, "why not try God's Old Rugged Cross plan? It gives you Life Assurance now and for all Eternity."

What did he know about that toll collector? Nothing at all. But he was convinced that the man needed to be saved. The possibility that the man might have been a Christian made no difference. Nor did it matter that his mixing pamphlet-pushing, proselytizing, and paying the toll might have been insulting to the attendant. Feelings are not important; only the revealed truth of God is important. What impact could a pamphlet have on any person on whom it is forced? Absolutely none, would be my guess. But the odds for success are not considered. The only consideration is the "divine mandate" to spread the word and save the world. Working for God was taking its toll.

Littering for the Lord

A few years later, Pat Robertson and I traveled through Egypt, Israel, Lebanon, and Jordan. During our time in Jerusalem, I saw the art of pushing pamphlets on unsuspecting people reach an insulting high, or rather low. In a certain section of the Jewish quarter of the holy city there lives a small sect of very orthodox Jews. Their lives are deeply dedicated to God in a most extreme fashion. When the men must venture out in public and walk through the marketplace, they walk bent over toward the ground, their eyes riveted to the passing pavement. The reason for this posture is that they fear seeing evil or being tempted by things their wayward eye might observe—like a woman.

A Christian with a compulsion to save these pious and reverent men whose lives are dedicated to following very strict religious observances, is met with the problem of establishing eye contact in order to hand them a pamphlet. The solution is very creative: Go to a corner where the men must stop for traffic, and place the pamphlet on the pavement. They'll have to see the words, "God so loved the world that He gave His only Son. . . ." These devout Jews will be forced to read the Christian message of salvation. Could a Jewish person who is so dedicated to the faithful following of his religion that he doesn't even allow himself to look straight ahead when walking because he fears he'll be distracted from holy thoughts be persuaded by a piece of paper on the street to change his mind about his faith and accept Jesus as his lord and savior? The possibility is nil. The act of scattering pamphlets has more to do with littering and insulting another faith than with loving; it also indicates that, for the fundamentalist, scripture has some magical power to instantly convert a person. Authentic transformation comes from inside a person, not from the outside; lasting transformation occurs through love, not fear, because, as Gandhi exclaimed, "What is gained through fear lasts only while fear lasts."

The aggressive and offensive act of dispersing pamphlets eventually turns into a thoughtless habit. If Art Linkletter were to examine the contents of a CBN female staffer's purse, he would more than likely find an assortment of pamphlets extolling the eternal benefits of Christianity. In a male employee's jacket pocket, the pamphlet is as at home as a pen. Handing them out or leaving them behind along with the tip at a restaurant becomes as natural as a reflex action. But the insensitivity of the procedure has a tendency to cause an adverse reaction that does more harm than good.

A Soap with Hope.

In my early CBN days, pamphlet-pushing may not have been my style; nonetheless I still wanted to proclaim the message of salvation and occasionally even thought that God lent me a helping hand in those efforts at spreading the word. Stemming from a personal concern that not everybody could tune into "The 700 Club" and be turned on to God caused me to seek alternative ways of presenting the saving message of Jesus. Out of my belief that many people are put off by television preachers trying to lead them into prayer, a dramatic alternative was born—a Christian soap opera. People love dramas, and in the late 1970s soap operas had reached the apex of their popularity.

The idea was to present real people struggling with real problems. Our leading Christian character would be confronted with such overwhelming difficulties that he would abandon his Christianity for the comfort of a bottle. The character—consumed with problems—would have enough personal appeal so that the audience would not only like him but also root for him to triumph over his troubles. After hooking the audience, he would have a true born-again experience. Viewers would observe the transformation and draw their own conclusions. Hopefully they might see that Jesus was the answer to their beloved character's problems and that perhaps he could also be a solution to theirs.

But for all this to work, the show had to attract an audience. It had to be believable, yet dramatic and interesting. Mixing soap emotions and spiritual resolutions would be no easy task, and I realized that I needed help in mastering the basic soap-opera writing and production skills required to make this revolutionary concept work. That help had to come from professional experts with proven track records, regardless of their religious beliefs. But who would want to help if he or she weren't a believer? Here's where what I thought to be help from the hand of God came into the picture.

In response to an ad I placed in a trade magazine, I received a letter from a man who was a former network vice president of daytime programming, who had helped put on the air many daytime serials. His resume was overwhelming. As a successful independent producer, only curiosity, not need, led him to contact us. He had no idea what CBN was all about. I called him, and we had a lengthy conversation. He seemed impressed with our efforts; and, over the course of the next few weeks, we spoke on a regular basis. I grew to admire him very much. He was a devout Catholic who had missed Sunday Mass only once in his entire life, and that was when he had been caught behind enemy lines in France during World War II. Sounded like a good excuse to me. I could recall a few snowflakes being a good excuse for skipping Mass. His Catholicism was not superficial and meant more than going to church once a week. He carried his faith as a light, not a sword, into the workplace and into his home. He was moral, decent, bright, a family man of deep integrity and honesty. His friends saw him as a faithful husband and fantastic father.

This Harvard graduate, with a sincere love of God and a wealth of high level network experience, seemed like an answer to a prayer, yet others at CBN viewed him as being in need of prayer. He had only one problem for my friends at CBN: He wasn't born-again. Pat Robertson struggled for a long time before hiring this man of God, a struggle rooted in the spiritual flaw Pat found in this almost flawless human being. If televangelist Jimmy Swaggart can believe that Mother Teresa of India, a saintly woman whose care for the dying and homeless creatures of the curbs of Calcutta truly reflects the living compassion of Jesus, is going to hell because she is not born-again, it is no wonder that Pat Robertson, who shares the same fundamentalist faith as Swaggart, felt that my network find was also headed for the same fiery fate as the saint from India. At least the former network executive is in good company. The spiritual snobbery, insensitivity, and ignorance of fundamentalism form a mighty alliance whose bond is rarely broken.

Joy to the World

We'll return to the soap opera story after a message about cheerfulness and condemnation. Fundamentalism wears a frown because it is consumed with the deadly serious work of eradicating the sin of others. They see in a person sin and not the God contained within. Much of their piety is little more than pure projection and opposes the essential message of Jesus, who taught people to heal themselves and others and to be instruments of peace. Instead of healing, they bring condemnation. By judging another's conduct, they try to exile the accused from the human family as well as to divert attention away from their own failures.

The worship services of fundamentalists seem to be upbeat and happy, but only because they focus on praising God with shouts of joy that flow from the fact that their friend Jesus has saved them from eternal damnation. It's rejoicing without any lasting joy. Julian of Norwich, the English Christian mystic, understood that "the fullness of joy is to behold God in everything," and Meister Eckhart, the German Christian mystic who exulted at the exultation of all creation, believed, "This then is salvation: to marvel at the beauty of created things and praise the beautiful providence of their Creator." At CBN we saw sin everywhere and beauty nowhere; we had lots of bubbly enthusiasm, but not much real joy.

St. Theresa of Avila, whose mystical writings have inspired people of all faiths, wrote, "From frowning saints, good Lord, deliver us!" For her, Christianity should wear a smiling countenance that reflected the inward joy of being at one with God. Mother Teresa of Calcutta looks for and finds the bright side of things. She is able to extract sunshine from the darkest corner. She walks through life with a smile and a cheerful song even though she is surrounded by death. Jimmy Swaggart frowns because his passion for converting lost souls fills him with gloom, doom, and strife. According to the Bible, "The servant of Christ must not engage in strife, but be gentle to all men" (2 Tim. 2:24). Swaggart's use of national television to say that an authentically holy woman who serves the least of God's people is going to Hell because she doesn't believe the same things as he does is not being gentle or a gentleman. Jesus treated prostitutes better. It seems apparent that truly spiritual persons, regardless of their particular religion or faith, simply and humbly revere others and see beauty in all of creation. Paul wrote in the Bible, "In humility count others better than yourselves" (Phil. 2:3). Joy, gentleness, and humility form a triptych whose separate qualities are joined to create an accurate picture of Christianity.

Much of the wisdom of the early church grew out of the barren deserts that proved to be fertile grounds for the seeds of monasticism. An early fifth-century monk of the desert, St. Mark the Ascetic, wrote, "He who seeks forgiveness of his sins loves humility, but if he condemns another he seals his own wickedness." Much of the condemnation and judging I encountered in fundamentalist circles stemmed from a feeling of spiritual superiority. In his book *Behold the Spirit*, Alan Watts writes, "If Christianity cannot be Christianity without pushing the claim to be the best of all possible religions, the world will breathe more freely when it dissolves." During my post-CBN days a spiritual search led me to see a tremendous amount of holiness in other faiths, and oddly enough this new vision led me to a deeper appreciation of my Christian faith.

Christians who can resist the temptation to view their faith as superior learn much from the great Eastern religions. With a proper respect and love for each other flowing from humility, people of different faiths can help each other to become more God-like. My understanding and appreciating the convictions of other faiths actually helped purify and deepen my own religious experience.

Today, my Christianity is more mystical and has freed me from the guilt complexes I received from fundamentalism, which has only the Bible as its basis for truth and understanding. As we will see later, much more than the Bible is needed. I came to see this form of biblical idolatry (as preached by the television ministers) as depressing and oppressive. With as much joy, humility, and gentleness as we can muster, we all must strive to see not the doubt or the sin of another, but only the spirit of God within.

St. Theresa of Avila knew from practical experience that God was within her, and she saw God within all others. That is real joy, and this joy is within the heart of Mother Teresa and is reflected on her smiling face. Her words themselves stand in stark contrast to Rev. Swaggart's:

> Be kind and merciful, let no one ever come to you without coming away better and happier. Be the living expression of God's kindness, kindness in your face, kindness in your eyes, kindness in your warm greeting. In the slums we are the light of God's kindness to the poor. To children, to the poor, to all who suffer and are lonely, give always a happy smile—give them not only your care, but also your heart.

It is much easier to give people hell than your heart. Jimmy Swaggart's give 'em Hell rhetoric has nothing to do with kindness. His pentecostal pulp is perfectly packaged for television and is reaching millions. According to the May 1983 Arbitron ratings, his show reaches 1,800,000 households. His record albums have sold more than twelve million copies, and his monthly magazine, *The Evangelist*, reaches eight hundred thousand readers. In January 1983 that magazine carried a very strong anti-Catholic article written by Swaggart. The following excerpt will show where his negative comments regarding Mother Teresa's salvation come from:

> Catholicism is a false cult. The mark of a false cult is that it has some authority other than or besides the Bible. The Roman Catholic Church forms its doctrines and methods from human pronouncements and labels them as "traditions," totally ignoring the Word of God and adding to or taking away from it as they see fit. This means it can not be the true church representing the Lord Jesus Christ. Wherever Catholicism has had broad authority over people, the people have been led into ignorance, superstition and sin. When the Catholic Church teaches peo-

ple to offer Masses for the dead and to pray them out of Purgatory, when they teach people that they are free to confess their sins to a man who is an unmarried priest and then expect divine forgiveness, when they teach people to pray to Mary, saying she will intervene with God for them—they are teaching heresy, error and total contradiction of the Word of God. I don't see how a nun, a priest or a Catholic layman can remain in this tradition as they become familiar with the Bible and realize that the Catholic tradition is in complete contradiction to the Word of God.

Such are the rantings and ravings of an authoritarian personality. On May 30, 1983, *Newsweek* published a not very complimentary article on Swaggart, which he described in a newsletter to his supporters as a "spurious piece of liberal journalistic trash." The letter was written in response to the story and was seeking a vote of confidence from the ministry's backers. Swaggart suggested that the *Newsweek* attack was an orchestrated backlash by Catholics offended by his preaching the truth about Catholicism. Swaggart claimed that he had expected this kind of persecution of his ministry because of the following prophetic words given him by the Holy Spirit: "You have angered the powers of Satan much. He will in turn rise up against you in great ways; but if you trust me, victory will be yours because I will keep you in the palm of my hands."

It's amazing how messages from heaven always indicate that God is on the minister's side and that he must continue to preach the word no matter what obstacles are placed before him; and even more amazing is that millions of naive people believe that God really sent such a self-serving message. The Reverend Jimmy told his followers they must prepare for battle and continue to save people by the blood of Jesus. He urges them to band together and fight alcoholism, secular humanism, abortion on demand, homosexuality, and liberal politics. While Brother Jimmy passionately bangs his piano for Jesus, Mother Teresa quietly touches the dying with the kindness of Christ.

Is This Any Way to Say Thanks?

Back to the story about the "soap" meant to cleanse viewers' souls. I sent my Harvard-bred, heavenly-helping-hand a copy of our outlines along with background information on the characters. He read the material and felt we were in big trouble—dramatically dead! Without any prospect that he would work with us on the project, he offered to give us some free advice. He invited me and one of my writers to spend a weekend at his home near New York City. He would arrange an evening meeting with a man who had created three network serials and was considered by many television historians to be the father of daytime drama. He was now retired and a good friend of the former network executive. The plan was for the four of us to sit down and have a little rap session about soap operas in general and my show in particular. These pros would give us neophytes a lesson in soaps and a detailed critical analysis of our writing.

The session was more than informative; it was enlightening. Many valuable insights were gained. Critical analysis can come across as ridicule, but when these gentlemen had some devastating comments about our style or story they couched their remarks in a respectful and caring fashion as well as presenting possible alternatives. It was a very fruitful meeting, and I was grateful to have had the opportunity to learn from their combined wisdom. Our host also gave us dinner and provided bedtime snacks before showing us to our rooms. This man had opened his heart and home in an effort to help us launch our show successfully. How did my CBN partner respond to this kind man's generosity? With typical insensitivity and ruthless religious zealotry.

The next morning after feasting on a scrumptious home-cooked breakfast, we shared some final thoughts with our host before heading back to Virginia. Unknown to me, my partner was more preoccupied with our host's spiritual blindness, caused by the satanic Catholic Church, than he was responsive to his advice and thankful for his hospitality. His natural response was to reach into his pocket and pull out a pamphlet. Unnoticed by either the host or me, he placed on the dining room table a message of salvation claiming that unless a person were born-again in Jesus he could not enter the kingdom of God. The pamphlet also proclaimed that Catholicism was a false religion. Can you imagine the reaction of our host, who after showing us out the front door turns back and finds a document—left by someone he just tried to help—that insults and ridicules his religious beliefs. I heard his response in an angry phone call the next day. Our host was discomfited by my friend's callous action while my sanctimonius friend took comfort in the belief he had done what God had wanted him to do.

Ticket to Eternity

It is comforting to know that you are saved and a member of a select group going to heaven, and the fear of being rejected by the cult can drive you to do strange things. Despite today's problems, for you, eternity is going to be forever blissful because you have full assurance of salvation. That's a nice concept. And it has appeal, especially to the American who struggles with loneliness and feels like an oppressed segment of society who just can't get ahead or even get "out from under." This effortless, just-say-yes-to-Jesus salvation is very attractive to our fast-paced, instant gratification world. But the truth is that changing into more God-like creatures takes tremendous effort.

Any honest post-conversion "you" will more than likely reveal a lot of stuff that isn't so heavenly. The more you look, the more you know you have to change. Facing your own shortcomings doesn't leave much room for a religious elitist attitude. The television preacher's proclamations of "I've got it, you don't," is more of a turn-off than a turn-on.

Salvation must be more than just saying "yes" to God; it must also be saying "yes" to God-inspired changes in your behavior. People will notice that change and might be receptive to your message of how you started on the road to change; but people will never respond to empty words and pamphlets left at toll booths, on street corners, or on dining room tables. Passing out pamphlets is a lot easier than changing yourself into a loving, joyful person. The former requires only a little time, the latter takes time and effort. There are no shortcuts to sainthood and salvation—or life.

Plastic God

The summer of 1984 saw America riding a new wave of patriotism on a surfboard called the Olympics. The "gold rush" was on, and the nation caught the fever. Once again flag-waving became as American as apple pie. Athletes of such obscure sports as Greco-Roman wrestling were thrown from inglorious training to stardom in hamburger commercials. In unathletic fashion, we sat comfortably in front of our television sets and acted as expert judges in diving and gymnastics even though the vast majority of viewers had never stood on a diving board or balance beam. We turned the cream of the world's athletic crop into winners or losers. Winning a silver medal was seen as losing the gold medal. Participation meant little, and perfection was the only prize to be cherished.

The real story of the Olympics lies not in the pursuit of perfection and excellence but rather in the value of participation and struggle. Behind all the hoopla and hype, the personal portraits of each participant, regardless of his or her country or sport, revealed the same quality—determination. From javelin thrower to scull rower, you could see a single-mindedness at work that allowed each young man or woman to dedicate every fiber of his or her existence to the pursuit of the gold. Long, lonely hours of hard work and sweat marked the uphill road to the Olympics. Families, careers, and pleasures took a back seat.

As the torch was extinguished and the games became history, one clear, timeless message still glowed: The search for excellence takes dedication, hard work, constant training. In a word—effort. What separated the living-room spectator from the on-field participator was not so much ability as effort. The enemy of effort is laziness. You must strive to arrive at the finish line. The Olympian, even though he or she is primarily interested in physical development, has much to teach the person who is interested in spiritual development. Seeking Olympic gold and searching for the true reality of God both require the same key ingredient of determined effort. There are no easy victories in the Olympics, and there are no easy answers or shortcuts along the spiritual journey. If your gold is to seek God, then the road will be hard. Going to church once a week for an hour or so is closer to spiritual entropy than to spiritual evolution. Faith must be exercised daily. If you found God without any effort, then you found a fraudulent and plastic god . . . and perhaps a cult. Cults allow easy entrance. Invariably, they are hard to leave.

To Pray or Not to Pray

One of the rules at CBN that surprised me the most seemed totally unnecessary for such a group of religious people: mandatory prayer. That's right, we *had* to pray—together and at the same time each day. Prayer has always been an important part, an essential part, of any faith experience, no matter what the particular religion. After all, most people think of prayer as basically a form of conversation with God. Talking and listening, but usually more talking. Communication is vital to the nurturing and growth of any relationship, even a relationship with God. Prayer is a primary means of communication with God. For some people it can be formal, and for others prayer is informal. Prayer can be communal or private. It can be expressed or internalized. It can be jubilant or reflective. It can be active or passive. But prayer can never be compulsory.

I do not dispute the fact that a group of religious people involved in religious work should make prayer part of the daily agenda. The intriguing aspect of a forced daily prayer is that the leaders do not trust the people to pray voluntarily each day. Yet the New Testament instructs Christians "to pray at all times" (1 Thess. 5:17). Luke informs us that Jesus was "praying always" (Luke 18:1). I've always thought of prayer as a conversation with God, and that is a common understanding of prayer at CBN. However, the Gospels do not promote the claim that prayer is a form of talking with God. How could Jesus be praying always when we read that he was busy feeding the multitudes, changing water into wine, teaching in the temples, healing the sick, raising the dead, angrily chasing the money-changers out of the Temple, and even going for a boat ride with his followers? We even know that he slept and wept. If the definition of prayer is simply talking and listening to God, then Jesus couldn't have been praying always. But the Bible says he did.

Great religious thinkers throughout history did not believe that prayer's primary means was conversation with God. Origen taught that life is "one great continuous prayer." Augustine informed us that "there is an interior prayer without ceasing." Prayer is also a living response to life, and that response is dictated by the indwelling presence of the spirit of God. Prayer should breathe new life into a person. Prayer should help steady the mind in all circumstances—victory and defeat, praise and blame, love and hatred. Prayer should free people from the grip of fear and the attachments, possessions, habits, and desires that are harmful; it should allow persons to gain mastery over themselves, not others. How can prayer do all that? The reality of God in Jesus' life allowed him to make godly responses to the everyday situations he encountered. His constant prayerfulness was an ever-present reality of God. Jesus gave flesh and form to a highly evolved understanding of God, and by doing so he revealed new heights of spiritual awareness for humanity; prayer is a tool that allows us to dig deep into our subconscious being where we can discover that same reality.

Prayer might be more a way of finding God than of communicating with God. For some, the tool of prayer is the study of Scripture, for some it is meditation, and for others it can be the silent and constant repetition of God's name.

At CBN, prayer most frequently took the form of petitions. We were always asking God for something: good weather, a healing, financial help, the salvation of a family member, a new car—as if God were some kind of cosmic bellhop or big daddy eager to respond to our every desire and wish. Gimme, gimme, gimme was the core of most of the prayers during our prayer meetings. We never tired of asking God to change his plans to suit our personal or corporate best interests. I now see these prayers of petition as misdirected and that the aim of prayer should not be to ask for something for our comfort or well-being but rather should be about transformation. Through prayer we implore God's help in making us more loving, more godlike. The prayer of St. Francis seems almost perfect: "Lord, make me an instrument of your peace; where there is hate let me sow love."

The "gimme" prayers that deal primarily with our safety and success are childish. Surely, God is not concerned with our external situations; these are our own business, and we can create our own wealth and health. God is only concerned with our hearts. In fact, even the notion that God calls us into some form of ministry (like working at CBN) or that he gives us some mission to carry out on earth is ridiculous. You can be a Wall Street executive, a police officer, or a monk— it really doesn't make any difference to God what you do with your life, as long as your heart beats with divine love. Striving for the constant prayerfulness that Jesus exemplified mysteriously creates within us a new heart. Imagine Jesus praying for a new donkey or a sunny day.

My point here is not to embark on a discourse on prayer but simply to state that the very nature of prayer is a mystery, and the solution to or understanding of that mystery cannot be legislated through forced times of prayer because we are not living a monastic life, in which regularly scheduled periods of communal prayer help to create a sense of discipline and a spirit of unity.

Symbolically, the center of CBN's day was given to the Lord. At noon all work came to a halt, and everyone headed for the chapel. In the beginning of my time at CBN, attendance at the noonday prayer meeting was strongly suggested although not formally required. I didn't need to be pushed into going. I loved going. It was one of my favorite times and a very pleasant aspect of working there. It felt great to put aside the pressures and problems of the job for a refreshing break that gave me a boost of energy and enthusiasm. I met people I didn't work with, and it reminded me why I was there—to serve God. I thought it promoted unity among the staff; after all, you couldn't gossip about someone's work habits during a coffee break and then a few hours later hold their hand during a prayer meeting. Soon the novelty of being paid to pray (a religious fanatic's dream) started to fade, and I began to see that this time of communal communion with the Lord was not all it was claimed to be.

Each day different people, usually male managers or division heads, led the meeting, which lasted half an hour. This usually consisted of a period of united prayer of praise to God, the singing of standard Protestant hymns, requests for prayers, reports of answers to prayers, Scripture readings, speaking in tongues, personal testimonies of God's help in some matter, and a short teaching by the leader. Some days the tone was upbeat, some days quiet. It all looked very harmonious.

Soon, however, I realized that not everybody loved this period of fellowship. The reason was that we were humans—vastly different humans at that; we had frailties and failures. This time of worship had a nasty habit of illuminating our faults—often before we were ready to deal with them or let them go. We remembered we were forgiven but forgot we were not perfect. You must stumble before you walk. Some of us still had very human prejudices. Maybe we didn't personally like the man leading the meeting, or maybe we didn't like his theological view of things. We came from a wide range of religious backgrounds, and consequently we brought with us a lot of theological baggage that didn't conform to the corporate view of the mystery of God.

These splits in understanding involved nothing as basic as salvation. They centered on minor articles of faith where there was room for personal speculation. For instance, there were many interpretations about the Rapture and the tribulation. Occasionally I would cringe when someone's Baptist background showed through in a biting anti-Catholic comment. The problem was that detachment from personal opinions does not come easy and not everyone could make graceful concessions on nonessential concepts. Many lacked the forbearance not to force their opinions on others, and many also got rattled when they were contradicted by others. Rigidity was rampant and flexibility absent.

Attendance was difficult for others because they deplored hypocrisy. The reality that was eventually revealed to everyone was that sin did exist among the saints. Big sins. My initial feeling that I had found "heaven" when I started work at CBN is a very common reaction for new employees. Just being there was a dream come true. Most had stories detailing events they believed that only God could have arranged in order for them to work in this ministry. They had a God-ordained purpose and were riding a spiritual wave of enthusiasm. Spiritual significance was read into the most simple and mundane events of the day. Everything seemed perfect. The lustre of perfection soon wears off, and we started to spot the tarnished reality—and we didn't like it.

My first encounter with the imperfect side of life at CBN involved an extremely attractive woman in her early twenties who worked in my division. Her sultry style of dress was far more fashionable than that of any of the other females. She had flair in personality too. I always thought she appeared more sensual than spiritual, but I suppressed those thoughts and ignored her almost flirtatious behavior. Whenever I caught a glimpse of her during the prayer meeting, I thought of her as angelic—she seemed too good to be true. Rumors that this young woman was sexually involved with a married coworker with two children eventually reached management's ear. The rumors turned out to be true. But a double standard prevailed. She was fired for leading the man astray, and he was offered counseling in order to help him avoid any future temptations. For people who knew of the pair's involvement, it must have been very disconcerting to see them sitting in the chapel with hands and eyes lifted heavenward while singing songs of praise and worship. Jesus' plea to love the sinner and hate the sin is not easily carried out. Those who are aware of the sinful side of others saw their attendance as living hypocrisy, forgetting that the fallen need worship more than the righteous and that saints are only people who, no matter how many times they fall, always get up and never give up striving for perfection. If saints were the only ones who could attend church—the churches would be out of business.

The psychological make-up of some people contributed to attendance problems. Not everyone could shift easily from work to prayer. Our minds are not like machines that instantly respond to start and stop commands. Some people arrive at work half an hour early so that they can slowly sip some coffee and read a newspaper before they begin the work day. Others can storm in at the last second and dive right into the task before them. We are not cookie-cutter copies. There were days that the prayer meeting ended just as I became emotionally involved. Some people could leave the concerns of the job at the chapel door, and some could not. For others, the concerns of the job kept them from even going to the chapel door. Many believed that without the chapel, one couldn't handle the concerns of the job. These different views required flexibility and understanding from management. These qualities were usually in short supply. Also, Pat Robertson's frequent absence provided others with a psychological block to going. If it wasn't important enough for him to attend, or if he had something better to do, then why should anyone else bother? A radical and ancient concept like work being a form of prayer was viewed as heretical here, even though karma yoga, the religious way through action, is known in the East.

For some people, skipping the noon prayer meeting had nothing to do with prejudices, hypocrisy, or psychological factors. It was simply the lure of a longer lunch break that tempted them. Shopping and restaurants are normal midday instincts that are hard to ignore. For others, sitting alone in a shady spot on the grounds was a very effective method of prayer.

As the company began to grow, it grew tired of merely *suggesting* that people attend the noon prayer. Managers felt compelled to set a good example, and if they didn't they were reprimanded. It was decided that the voluntary system of prayer didn't work. Officials were bothered by the fluctuating attendance. They were annoyed when they spotted people in their offices talking on the phones at 12:05 P.M. Why weren't they praying? was their only response. But, they never seriously tried to seek the answer. Instead, attendance at the noon prayer meeting was no longer optional and became mandatory. I resented this tactic and sought ways to test the rule, but eventually I had to conform. You could lead them to chapel, but you couldn't make them pray.

In many ways CBN's attempt to legislate prayer is similar to the Moral Majority's efforts to legislate morality. It just doesn't work. No matter what the laws of our nation say, it is impossible to lock God out of the classroom if the student carries him within his or her heart, and God cannot be brought into a classroom by a mandated moment of prayer.

Unholy Spirits

Another rule, enforced by undercover-spy operations, also seems unnecessary for the people who worked at CBN. There is a total prohibition of alcoholic beverages. This booze-banning rule extends beyond the confines of the office building and reaches into the home of each employee. It includes wine and beer. The rule is at the same time understandable and distressing.

The banning of alcohol at work is understandable and did not cause a problem for anyone. The ban's extension to include the exclusion of drinking at a public restaurant is somewhat understandable in light of the apostle Paul's admonition to the early Christians that they should not do anything that causes another to stumble. In other words, don't set any bad examples.

CBN plays a very visible role in Virginia Beach. They employ many people and attract a tidal wave of tourists to the area. Their moral and political position on everything from movies to abortion is well-documented by the local press. If staff members were to be recognized at a restaurant and spotted sipping a cocktail during a meal, they would not only send out a message that is contradictory to company policy but also foster the idea that, if it's okay for these Christians to drink, then it must be okay for everybody.

Consumption of alcohol may not be okay for everyone and can cause someone to stumble, both literally and figuratively. According to Paul's warning, you share the guilt if you lead someone into sin. The logic that a person who sees a Christian enjoy a drink could be led down the road to alcoholism is weak; however, CBN policy instills the employees with fear that their actions may cause someone to stumble. The policy uses the Bible to impose a guilty sentence on the employees if someone should stumble as a result of their behavior. Fear and guilt: a marriage made not in heaven but in cultic fanaticism.

The prohibition rule reaching into the home is dangerous. Invasion of privacy and enforcement procedures are two of the problems it presents. The issue is simple: Is alcohol consumption a sin? Most people would say no and still might think of excessive consumption of alcohol as sinful, or at least harmful. As Scripture so rightly points out: all things in moderation. Others may hold the opinion that at certain times in a person's life drinking could be perfectly acceptable and at another period it could be unacceptable; this paradox is based on the level of a person's spiritual awareness. The rule banning drinking at CBN was born out of a belief that it is sinful—always and everywhere sinful—and if you break the rule you will be punished.

My study of Buddhist spirituality gave me a helpful insight into the nature of sin: We are not punished *for* our sins; we are punished *by* our sins. The people at CBN will say that God is just and merciful, but their most predominant image of God does not support that belief. They envision God as a combination of a police detective and a stern, law-and-order judge who is ever ready to catch us in any act that violates the law and then slap us with a stiff sentence. Is mass paranoia the way to God? Every move we make, every step we take is being watched. If that wasn't bad enough, there is a "sting operation" always going on that uses the Devil as an undercover agent to trick us into breaking the law. Abscam according to God. What makes this picture of Godly retribution even more repulsive is the concept that even those who don't subscribe to the laws of God and even those who don't know about the laws are nonetheless going to suffer the same harsh punishment as the Christian for nonconformity to the regulations.

Buddha's teaching—and also Christ's—was far more compassionate because, instead of stressing strict judgment, it spoke in terms of mistakes and consequences, or, more basically, of personal responsibility. Drink and you can get drunk. Smoke and you can get cancer. Use a knife carelessly and you can cut yourself. In the same way, if you give in to greed and lust you'll reap their sour fruit. God doesn't punish us for our failures; we punish ourselves. He only stands ready to help, although he is hidden behind or beneath our own self-centeredness. He allows us the freedom to choose to become angry, and that anger becomes its own form of punishment, since it damages our health and hurts our relationships with others. Sin becomes choosing our uneducated way instead of God's enlightened way.

By losing ourselves in a sincere effort to dig for the God within, we will slowly learn how not to make mistakes and how to become a little more loving and Godlike in our behavior. People need more than a rule to curb drinking and smoking. They need to learn how to be freed from the attachment to those things and to grow into an awareness that the body is an instrument of loving service. We must be tolerant in understanding that not everyone is going to reach the same level of awareness at the same time. For some a glass or two of wine will be no problem; they believe they can handle the mild euphoric or depressive results of the drink. And so they may. For others no wine is needed, for they have come to see that alcohol is only an inferior method of altering consciousness and they, therefore, want no part of alcohol consumption. In either case we can not be judgmental or force our understanding on others. We are all on individual journeys, and for some the road to enlightenment may take them to the point of radical moderation where they can respond to Mahatma Gandhi's advice, "Eat only what you need, only when you are hungry, and only when you have done at least a little work for others." A life that reflects such wisdom does not need rules of prohibition.

The alcohol ban at CBN is not based on wisdom; it is based on a literal understanding of Scripture which considers alcoholism a sin. While developing "Another Life," the title of the soap opera I created for CBN, I learned for the first time that alcoholism is not considered a disease by the fundamentalist. I had hired a prominent writer, who was not a born-again Christian, as story consultant, and in a memo he wrote, "Alcoholism is a prevalent disease. We should study it as a disease, not morally. . . ." One of my staff writers read that and fired off this heated response:

From a scriptural point of view, alcoholism is not a disease. It is flat out sin, and referred to as drunkenness. The Scriptures declare that everywhere Jesus went He healed diseases, but nowhere does it mention healing a disease of drunkenness. Rather there are strong warnings against this sin. If it were a disease, it would be the first case in Scripture where God would condemn a man to hell because of a disease. Know ye not that the unrighteous shall not inherit the Kingdom of God? Be not deceived; neither fornicators, nor idolaters, nor adulterers, nor effeminate, nor abusers of themselves with mankind, nor thieves, nor covetous, nor drunkards, nor revilers, nor extortioners shall inherit the Kingdom of God. (1 Cor. 6:9).

End of story for this crusading Christian writer.

In like manner, Pat Robertson condemns government policies that treat the alcoholic or the homosexual as special or a privileged minority that deserves special treatment and rights. According to Pat, the government has no right to pander to or to protect individuals whose "sinful" behavior can be changed by simply acknowledging their problem and asking God to correct it for them. Robertson believes the government should not be in the business of protecting the rights of homosexuals or treating the alcoholic as a sick person because those who have those conditions can help themselves. To reinforce that belief, Pat airs slickly produced "news features" about homosexuals who have turned to a "straight" lifestyle and chronic drunks who have turned sober by simply calling a "sin a sin" and crying out for help from Jesus and no longer making excuses for their excessive drinking or sexual preferences.

Government programs that create an atmosphere of understanding and tolerance toward the "sins" of alcoholism and homosexuality tend to—according to Robertson—make excuses for those tendencies and thereby prevent the alcoholic and the homosexual from accepting responsibility for their conditions—whether the "sins" are rooted in a chemical imbalance or genetics. The underlying message is that Satan is in league with the government and tricks people into accepting the way they are and not becoming what God wants them to be. On the December 2, 1985, broadcast of "The 700 Club," Pat claimed that each year twenty thousand homosexuals and fifty thousand alcoholics respond to his message and call CBN. With Robertson in the White House, the Devil will be kicked out of the government.

I never encountered any alcoholic problems at CBN. Many people did enjoy a glass of wine at dinner or even an occasional bottle of beer. Those who did consume moderate amounts of beer and wine felt compelled to hide the evidence. Wine bottles were hidden and beer cans buried way in the back of the refrigerator. If a fellow employee visited your home for the first time, you might not know whether your guest was a teetotaler who backed the CBN policy completely or was a person who had no problem with moderate consumption. Usually after a few hesitant and uncertain moments your guest's position would become clear. The rule made you feel guilty in your own home for doing something that was not even a crime, and yet you feared that your guest might turn you in at CBN.

The Law of Dominion

The tension created by the alcohol ban was for Pat Robertson a healthy situation. The Book of Genesis claimed that during creation God let man have dominion over the earth, and Pat looks at life today and is left with the impression that people have no authority over their environment. In fact, he thinks that Christians are a defeated people: sick, depressed, needy, confused. Pat reads Jesus' words that "I will build my church; and the gates of Hell shall not prevail against it," and believes that Hell seems to be prevailing and, therefore, that God wants Christians to recapture the dominion over the earth that men had held in the beginning until Eve faltered and failed to exercise her authority over Satan.

(One of Pat's tricks is to join—under the guidance of God, of course—quotations from the Old Testament and quotations from the New Testament that together form a new message for today's Christian. He frequently began staff teachings by saying something like, "I was praying and fasting when I heard His voice, level and conversational. . ." and everyone accepted the teaching as if it came from God.)

Since the "fall," Satan has been exercising a kind of dominion over humans by deceiving and destroying us. Pat believes that Satan has stripped Christians of their God-given authority and dominion and replaced it with a spirit of timidity. For example, people will openly walk down the street carrying a copy of *Playboy* or *Penthouse* or a bottle of whiskey or a carton of cigarettes, and Christians are too intimidated to say anything or take authority over the situation by stomping out the obvious evil. Pat loathes ministers who preach without power and dislikes Christians who are too timid to hold up the word of God for all the world to see. Pat sees flowers, vegetables, and fruit as having dominion over man, as the tobacco plant kills people, and corn, barley, rye, and grapes hold many in alcoholic bondage. Pat teaches that God has given Christians the authority to destroy evil. Pat's hidden agenda has more to do with crushing Satan than with saving souls. The tension created by prohibition rules and the concerns about brother spying on brother are the first steps in reestablishing dominion over the earth; the sooner Christians assume their rightful authority, the quicker the Kingdom of Jesus will come.

Video Vampires

Pat Robertson is leading a moral uprising in the name of Christ that is devoid of compassion; however, without compassion all religious crusades, practices, and beliefs are useless and empty. In compassion, justice and love embrace. The fullness of God is seen only in compassion. Pat Robertson's religious superiority is not so much a matter of pride as an inability to share God's compassion for mankind. This is not the stuff of sainthood. Thomas Merton writes in his book *New Seeds of Contemplation* that:

> The saints are what they are, not because their sanctity makes them admirable to others, but because the gift of sainthood makes it possible for them to admire everybody else. It delivers them from the burden of judging others, condemning other men. It teaches them to bring the good out of others by compassion, mercy and pardon. A man becomes a saint not by conviction that he is better than sinners but by the realization that he is one of them, and that all together need the mercy of God.

No sainthood for me. I was criticized at CBN for having a desk calendar that featured quotations from the writings of Thomas Merton along with some of his sketches. This gentle monk who lived in isolation and whose writings have touched so many people—both Christians and non-Christians—was not considered an authentic Christian by CBN standards; therefore, not only was he not respected, but also his thoughts and ideas, no matter how well thought out and eloquently expressed, had no value at all. In fact, Merton angered them. In his book, *No Man Is an Island,* Merton claimed:

> The arguments of religious men are so often insincere, and their insincerity is proportionate to their anger. Why do we get angry about what we believe? Because we do not really believe it ourselves. Or else

what we pretend to be defending as "truth" is really our own self-esteem. A man of sincerity is less interested in defending truth than in stating it clearly, for he thinks that if truth is clearly seen, it can very well take care of itself.

That statement rang very true to me the first time that I read it. My mind flashed back to the early days of my conversion, and I remembered how angry I got when, out of honesty, my wife asked probing questions about my new beliefs, and I couldn't find adequate answers. I became very angry because I knew that Jesus was Lord, and I could not tolerate or respect her doubt. She was more secure in her disbelief than I was in my belief, and that is what caused my anger. Like Pat Robertson, my newfound spiritual superiority lacked compassion and was full of anger and intolerance.

The Kingdom that Jesus wanted his followers to believe in was a kingdom of love and service, a society of brotherhood built on respect. Belief in this kind of kingdom is impossible unless a person is first moved by compassion for his fellowman. True compassion does not grow out of pity and grows beyond mere forgiveness.

In the time of Jesus, the basic causes of oppression, discrimination, and suffering were the loveless religions of the powerful Romans and of the Pharisees, Sadducees, and Zealots; today, the venom from the Jerry Falwells, the Jimmy Swaggarts, and the Pat Robertsons will also cause increased hatred as they gain more and more political and economic control. They want to bring back the so-called good old-time religion and earnestly pray for a religious revival in America. But Jesus was not interested in revival; he wanted a revolution, a revolution of love. These video vampires are righteous men whose righteousness and bank accounts are fed by the blood of "sinners" who can't be trusted to find the truth for themselves. They earn their lucrative livings by cleverly creating a sense of sin and guilt in the viewer's mind and then selling them salvation. They are not leading a revolution of love; they are living off a repulsive form of hate.

Big Brother is Watching

Recently I was told a story about a young woman on "The 700 Club" production team who had invited her friends to a backyard cookout. Most of those gathered were single and under thirty years of age. The young hostess lived at home with her parents, and a member of her family had a couple of six packs of beer in the refrigerator. They were spotted, and the adventuresome group decided it was safe to indulge in a beer. After all, a cold beer goes down great with hot dogs, especially on a simmering summer afternoon. It seems that one of the guests apparently didn't think gulping down a beer was such a great idea. A rule is a rule. He kept his mouth shut during the barbecue as he made a mental list of those who drank the brew, and the next day he informed the girl's boss about the insurrection. All who consumed the beer were put on probation and threatened with termination. In attendance, along with the girl's parents, were some of the finest and brightest young adults you could ever meet. They loved God and lived good Christian lives, yet they were treated like delinquents who had staged a wild, drunken orgy and needed to be punished, when the crime they had committed was sipping a few beers during a backyard barbecue.

Like some kind of Christian KGB, the no-drinking rule uses brother-against-brother as the main method of enforcement. This is the distressing part of the rule. If the young woman had known her Bible better, she could have opened her boss's holy book to Ecclesiastes 11:70, which advises, "Go ahead, eat your food and be happy; drink your wine and be cheerful." I guess that, if she had, she would have been canned; however, if the Bible is the word of God, how can you selectively ignore the words you don't like?

The Grapes of Wrath

During a Middle East trip with Pat Robertson, I saw just how strongly he feels about total alcohol abstinence. While in Jerusalem, we broadcast live via satellite a communion service from the Upper Room, allegedly where Jesus celebrated the last supper on the day before his crucifixion. During that meal, Jesus instructed his disciples to drink from a cup of wine as a commemoration of him. In the middle of my frantic effort to get the cameras in position, establish phone communication with the switching center in New York and our studios in Virginia, check out all the technical equipment in our rented Israeli mobile unit, brief the freelance Israeli crew, and assure the monks who cared for the sacred shrine that we wouldn't damage anything, Pat came storming up to me holding an unopened, cheap bottle of red wine. "What's this?" he asked in a demanding voice.

"A bottle of wine," I wryly replied, feigning innocence, even though I fully realized what was bothering him.

He offered a weak smile and said, with a touch of exasperation, "I know. And what am I supposed to do with it?"

I explained how earlier that morning I had gone shopping for the elements needed for the communion service, namely bread and grape juice. Most Christian denominations, especially Anglican and Catholic, use wine during the celebration of the eucharist, or holy communion. At CBN and in most fundamental and Baptist churches, grape juice is used instead of wine. That morning I had no problem locating some bread, but a thorough scouring of the nearby markets produced no grape juice. Time was running short, and I had to get to the location and begin setting up the equipment. I spotted a bottle of wine and figured that would just have to do for this occasion. Pat responded to my explanation in total disbelief and shock. He wanted no part of my failed efforts to locate grape juice.

I wanted no part of his unreasonableness. Precious time was ticking away, and I told him just to think of it as a prop. He had only to drink but a sip. But the thought of even a drop of wine touching his lips was repulsive and sinful.

Tiring of his whining, I said in aggravation, "Jesus at the wedding feast turned water into wine, not grape juice. And right here in this room he gave his followers wine to drink. Come on, what's the big deal? We're going on the air in a few minutes, and there is no time to go shopping." He turned and walked away. I don't know how he did it, but he found a bottle of grape juice. Rumor has it that a Christian woman who happened to be touring the shrine had some in her backpack. For Pat, I'm sure he felt that was God's way of saying he was right in refusing to drink the wine I had purchased.

The total prohibition of alcoholic beverages at CBN reflects Robertson's paranoia more than the will of God. If you applied for a job at CBN and it was discovered during the interview that you drank, even if only wine at a meal, then it would be curtains for you. Most people must lie to get the job and live a lie to keep it.

No Butts

The next rule of prohibition is a tough one: no smoking. Once again, this means anywhere, even in the bathroom at home. I think this rule is more a Baptist policy than a Christian concern. Robertson is a Baptist minister. In 1984, the Southern Baptist Convention condemned both unsanctified growing and smoking of tobacco. One of my pamphlet-pushing friends at CBN used to pass out a pamphlet to smokers that insisted that Jesus would never smoke. "Would you want a savior with a butt in his mouth?" Many Baptists believe that you can't be a witness for the Lord through the defilement of tobacco spittle or smoke. The Convention condemnation stirred up a great debate, because many fine Southern Baptists live in North Carolina, the nation's largest tobacco-producing and manufacturing state. Profit from the evil tobacco crop has financed the building of many Baptist churches.

Now some Baptists are being forced to choose between the way they make a living and the way they worship. The issue of smoking is very sensitive not only for Baptists but also for all smokers and non-smokers. A person's right to smoke is butting up against a person's right to breathe clean air. As the evidence indicating that smoking is hazardous to your health begins to mount and the protests from non-smokers grow louder, the banning or limiting of public smoking is becoming more in vogue. In that light, the CBN policy is not that bad or offensive—at least when confined to the workplace. CBN considers the body to be the temple of the Holy Spirit, not to be defiled with the impurities of smoke and nicotine—whether at work or at home. (Maybe coffee and red meat will be banned next.)

But smoking is an addiction a simple rule cannot stop. Behavior modification programs are proving effective. While smoking is obnoxious to the nonsmoker and ungodly to the fundamentalist Christian, we should be tolerant and understanding of the smoker. Condemnation cannot help. CBN smokers were made to feel guilty and like little children who had to hide and sneak a drag on their beloved cigarette. The few smokers at CBN soon found each other out and puffed away together in secret. It annoyed me to see fine people fired because they got caught smoking. The penalty was extreme and failed to care about the person and his or her habit.

The rule creates a mindset that encourages a witchhunt. Evil must be stamped out. It would be no problem to locate legions of people who would agree that smoking is harmful, even lots of smokers agree on that, but not many people would consider it evil. Yet the gospel-according-to-religious-television does.

Warning: Fundamentalism May Be Dangerous To Your Freedom

Are we as a nation ready for a group of people with such a fundamentalist point of view—a militant minority that claims to be a moral majority—to set the standards of morality for all of us? If they can't get new legislation that will reflect their view of morality, then they will try to repeal current laws they don't favor. Reverend Jerry Falwell claims that, "One day Jesus is going to come and strike down all the Supreme Court rulings in one fell swoop." And in the meantime, the far right will help Jesus by mounting a crusade to pack the federal judiciary with judges who share their narrow, extremist ideology. With their men on the bench, they'll know how a case will be decided before the facts are even presented, and the decision handed down will be one Jesus will like because it will reflect the standards of this "moral majority." Enforcement of those standards seems more injurious to a nation that needs trust in its makeup than do the standards themselves. One of the ministers who gave a benediction during a morning session of the 1984 Republican Convention is a fundamentalist and proud of it. He advocates—on Christian television—that homosexuals should be put in jail. If our government becomes a Holy Government, watch our America!

The Gay Wrongs Movement

Just as there are smokers, drinkers, and adulterers among the Christians at CBN, there are also homosexuals. How and why a homosexual could or would work at CBN is a subject for an entire book; however, the reasons are not pertinent to the point I'd like to make. The simple fact is that homosexuals do work there, and they are forced to lock their true sexual identity in a closet that they may never open. Their holy, heterosexual mask must never be removed. I never imagined that a homosexual would work in such an openly hostile, anti-gay environment, so I was stunned when I spotted a CBN staffer emerge from a gay bar in Norfolk. Stunned, but not disgusted. The thought of turning him in to the law-enforcement agents at CBN never entered my mind. My thoughts wandered in the direction of imagining what life must be like for this man. How did he respond internally to Pat's constant harangue against homosexuality?

I also wondered if he had ever spotted a document one of the secretaries received from Jerry Falwell that was proudly pinned up on her wall. She must have made a donation to "The Old Time Gospel Hour," which is Falwell's electronic bully-pulpit; and they, in appreciation of her gift, sent her a piece of paper that was suitable for framing and resembled a diploma or official declaration. The words atop the parchmentlike paper boldly stated: "Declaration of War." The fine print revealed that war has been declared on the evils threatening America, and as a supporter of "The Old Time Gospel Hour" the displayer of the document is a soldier fighting in God's army against abortion, secular humanism, pornography, homosexuality, socialism, and the deterioration of the home and family.

How did this man feel about being lumped with such "evil" and having open warfare declared on his hidden lifestyle? I knew that I certainly didn't understand homosexuality; however, I also knew that I couldn't join the army that sought to eliminate this man.

Give Me That Old-Time Religion

Jerry Falwell desperately wants America to return to the old-time religion—a religion of certainty, a religion based on the clear-cut truth of the Bible—exactly as it was written. Numerous legends, gathered from all over the globe, of virgins giving birth to heroes who die and are resurrected are being condemned by preachers who find them dangerous to the faith of their flocks. Mythologically based taboos and symbols upon which much of the Bible is based are being challenged and discredited by modern science and biblical scholarship, thereby stripping religious persons of the life-giving illusions they believe and need. For many modern-day believers this causes uncertainty and confusion—leaving them little in the way of security onto which to hold.

Seeing the rise in crime, vice, violence, and despair, the fundamentalist preacher cries out for a return to the old-time religion and tries to put a stop to the search for disturbing truths. The simplicity of human disobedience and divine punishment that teaches dependency, fear, and devotion is preferred to facing the challenge of truth.

In the year 1616 Galileo was condemned by the Office of the Inquisition—the Moral Majority of his day—for holding and teaching a doctrine contrary to Holy Scripture: namely, that the sun is the center of our planetary system. Today—armed with the Bible—the fundamentalists believe that they are favored by God in some special way and that they are in direct contact with the Almighty. Jailing homosexuals is what God wants. But their absolutism in a pluralistic society is dangerous and divisive.

The Death Penalty

The roots of today's holy war against homosexuals goes all the way back to the third book of the Bible. Chapters 17, 18, 19, and 20 of Leviticus lay down the rules of holiness, along with the penalties for their violation. It clearly states that a man must not lie with a man as with a woman; and, if two men lie together as a man and a woman, then they both must die. The Book of Leviticus also demands the death penalty for anyone who curses his father or mother, for a man who commits adultery with a married woman, for a man who lies with his daughter-in-law, for a man who lies with an animal, and for a woman who has intercourse with an animal. This legislative book of the Bible is equally clear in its disdain for both homosexuals and adulterers. It forbids a man to uncover the nakedness of his father's sister and son's daughter. 20:18 speaks for itself: "The man who lies with a woman during her monthly periods and uncovers her nakedness: he has laid bare the source of her blood, and she has uncovered the source of her blood; both of them must be outlawed from their people." Leviticus also forbids the practice of magic, getting a haircut, and trimming a beard!

My inner feeling was that homosexuality was not good. That negative feeling may have stemmed from a simple lack of understanding about what makes a gay person choose a homosexual lifestyle, or it could have sprung from some Bible-based belief that God was opposed to such unnatural activity. But how natural was my fellow CBNer's dual identity—crusading Christian by day, cruising queen by night? Tension existed in my mind. I found the thought of men kissing and hugging each other repugnant, yet I wanted to be compassionate and tolerant of the way they chose to live. Beyond that I wasn't sure they even had a choice, because some studies indicated that their sexual tendencies might have been there from birth. (Of course, such studies were considered satanic by CBN.) I would not rush to judgment of this man. Besides, his presence at a gay bar did not automatically indicate that he was gay. Maybe he was using the phone, simply having a beer with a gay friend, or maybe he was handing out pamphlets. Jesus' words as recorded in Matthew 7 seem very appropriate when the temptation to be critical of a person's sexuality arises: "Why do you observe the splinter in your brother's eye and never notice the plank in your own?" I needed a loving heart and an open mind. Minds, like parachutes, only work when they are open.

More than homosexuality, I despised close-minded bigotry. The benefits of attempting to understand homosexuality rather than to exterminate homosexuals became clear to me before I began work at CBN.

During my last few years at CBS, people who knew me were aware of my newfound Christianity. The Bible in my briefcase was a dead giveaway. One morning I was watching the "CBS Morning News," and sitting next to me was one of the department clerks. We were glued to a report on Anita Bryant, who at the time was waging a vicious campaign against homosexuals in Florida. Miss Sunshine claimed that the destruction of the Florida citrus crop by a devastating freeze was the result of God's judgment and wrath for the State of Florida's tolerance of homosexuality. She was quoted in the *Washington Sun* as saying, "The reason homosexuals are called 'fruits' is because God says in the Bible that men are trees, and new life is the fruit of the womb. You are forbidden to eat new life—the sperm." That commentary probably passed for insightful biblical exegesis for many fundamentalists. Anita was in the news this day because a member of the persecuted gay community threw a pie in her face during a press conference. As I watched the pie splatter all over her, I yelled a cheer of approval, "Great!"

The clerk, who was Jewish and male, looked at me and asked, "Aren't you a born-again Christian?" The question made me pause for a second, but I responded, "Yea, why?"

He said with sincerity, "Don't you like Anita Bryant? After all, aren't born-again Christians opposed to homosexuality?"

I explained that it was impossible for members of any group to be in total agreement on everything, and I said that, while I could understand many Christians' concern about homosexuality, it was necessary to temper that concern with caring and understanding and that simpleminded persecution was wrong. I could dislike homosexuality, but somehow I must still show love or at least concern to the homosexual. I told him that I certainly didn't know enough to sit in judgment of anyone and that I was very uncomfortable with Anita Bryant's methods. Later in the day, I found on my desk a brochure from the clerk's synagogue. He penned a note on it saying he thought I might be interested in it. As I read it, I couldn't imagine why he thought I'd be interested until I realized, much to my surprise, that it came from a gay Temple.

Following our talk after watching the report, he felt confident enough to tell me about his secret lifestyle. I couldn't believe he trusted me enough to confide in me that he was gay. No one knew or even suspected.

During the next few months, we had many wonderful discussions about homosexuality, Judaism, and Christianity. We shared our religious beliefs and practices. As he grew in appreciation of Christianity, his hostility toward my faith shrank. We weren't trying to convert each other, just respect each other: two people breaking down the walls of ignorance and bigotry that were built to make us enemies by not allowing us to become friends. For us, understanding led not just to tolerance but to mutual respect.

That trend toward tolerance has led me to many friendships with gay men. Out of those friendships has grown an understanding of their pain, confusion, doubts, and struggle for acceptance. Not only is it impossible for me to condemn them, but I support their right to be who and what they are.

Gay Undercover Spy

A troubled young man at CBN who had a hidden history of homosexuality and drug abuse once worked for me. It's a mystery how he ever got hired, but the fact that he dated a division head's daughter helped prevent anyone from discovering his secret. I subtly let him know that I saw through his masquerade and let him know that the truth didn't bother me. Once I gained his confidence, I spent many hours helping him deal with his guilt and confusion and made sure he steered clear of drugs.

He once told me how a vice president summoned him to his office and confided to him his suspicion of homosexual activity at CBN. The nervous twitching in the young man's stomach ceased when he realized he wasn't the subject of the suspicion. The vice-president-turned-detective told the young man the names of two people he thought were gay. He wanted my friend to act as an undercover cop and gather the incriminating evidence needed to rid the place of these two sinners. Fortunately, the young man was a good actor and was able to keep a "straight" face during the entire meeting. My young friend used to wonder whether if you were gay but celibate, were you still a sinner? He eventually quit CBN and is now living in Hollywood with his male lover.

These various prohibitions and witchhunts demonstrate that any behavior that deviates from CBN's highly moralistic Bible-based views were simply not tolerated. In short, they're bigots.

Holy Rollers, Not Rockers

One CBN official believed that rock and roll was demonic. While no policy banned listening to rock music, it was strongly recommended that we listen only to Christian music. In fact, CBN owned an AM radio station in the area that spun only Christian discs. Many parents at CBN destroyed any rock records their kids brought home. Their children were even banned from owning Sony "Walkmans" because the parents would be unable to know if the child was tuned to a rock station. I believe that parents need to be aware that some of the lyrics sung by popular rock stars carry messages they might consider inappropriate for teenagers: promoting free sex, glorifying drugs, exhorting rebellion against all authority—to name just a few. Guidance and discussion can soften the impact of the music on a teenager, but a total prohibition is not an effective solution.

The CBN official couldn't fire anyone for listening to rock and roll music; however, he did take a group of guys who were "hooked" on rock music to Chicago for a visit to a fundamentalist minister who specialized in exorcising the devil of rock and roll.

A rock exorcism—sounds like it would make a great music video for Michael Jackson! I wondered whether, if the exorcism were successful, the evil spirit would exit the body screaming, "I wanna hold your hand. Yea, yea, yea." It really isn't funny—it vividly illustrates how at CBN everything that is perceived as ungodly must be under the influence and control of Satan, and he must be defeated. Because a person happens to enjoy the beat and sound of rock and roll does not mean he or she is possessed by a devil who drives them to listen to the music. I was very curious to know what happened in Chicago; however, no one wanted to talk about the trip.

During the 1984 Michael Jackson Victory Tour, students at a Christian school in Dade County, Florida, were prohibited from attending the concerts. Strong disciplinary action was promised for those who ignored the ban. Not only did the school despise anything connected with rock music, but worse than that was the fact that Michael Jackson is a Jehovah's Witness, and the children could not be exposed to a person who espoused such a heretical faith.

While I was producing "The 700 Club," I liked to occasionally break up all the talk with some musical entertainment, and more often than not the music I chose was rock and roll. The following excerpt from a letter I received from an irate viewer clearly illustrates the fundamentalist mind at work:

Dear Friends,

We are writing to let you know that we were led to reduce our giving to CBN by a considerable amount as of the first of the year, and why. After several months of prayer and exercise of patience and understanding, the program this morning was the last straw. Our soul is sick of "Jesus (or gospel) Rock." In our opinion, it is most unacceptable and destructive to a total and deep commitment to our living LORD, and should not be "puffed." We find it regrettable and sad that such a fine network as has been established by the LORD is used as a sounding stage for the presentation of counterfeit Christianity. The many excellent teachings and testimonies that have been presented via this medium of communication are all nullified by the "leaven" that is also introduced. It is a sad commentary that many Christian teenagers have become hooked on the rock beat generated by some gospel groups in the name of Christ. Our continued giving to CBN is being re-evaluated as we wait on the LORD for His direction in this matter.

The letter writer believed that God established CBN, and she was waiting for a word from him about her continued support of a network that presented music that made her soul sick. The entertainers I booked on the show were Christians who believed that God wanted them to reach out to lost souls through rock and roll, while the letter writer believed that God thought that rock and roll was causing teenagers to lose their souls. Somehow God was sending out contradictory messages. I think that neither was really in tune with God.

Satan Sings the Blues

Is rock and roll music sinful? Absolutely not; but that does not mean it is good. The simple truth is that excessive noise dulls not only our sense of hearing but also our sense of smell and sight. Modern man is out of tune with his surroundings and his lifestyle differs vastly from that of the people who lived during Jesus' lifetime. The apostles were fishermen, and early Christianity reflected the rhythm of that lifestyle.

With the coming and spreading of urbanization and industrialization, we must deal not only with pollution of all varieties and overcrowding but also with the rival rhythm that comes from Van Halen and The Who. The fast-paced beat of today's lifestyle and rock music both penetrate and dull the deeper levels of our psychic life. Silence is unheard. Zen stresses becoming attuned to the profound rhythm of life and teaches that through meditation and breathing exercises we can reach deeper levels of consciousness. Silence teaches us how to speak.

Zen has much it can show today's Christians without threatening their faith. For example, it teaches the connection between breath and the psychic life. Did you ever notice that when you become angry or excited your breathing becomes intensified and is short and fast? Conversely, when you are at ease and calm, your breathing is also relaxed and much slower. During a Zen meditation, breathing almost stops, and you can hear the beating of your heart. Music that is loud, driving, and frantic deadens the sense of the deeper rhythm of life that is within us; however, banning it is not the answer. The answer lies in understanding, education, and moderation. We need to grow in an awareness of how everything that touches us affects us. If you believe the Bible's claim that you can reach God through stillness, then listening to a constant barrage of rock music would simply be undesirable and inappropriate—not evil. Growth and change come from inner enlightenment, not outward pressure.

Not Picture Perfect

These "snapshots" of CBN show that the employees may not be perfect examples of what they advocate. They have problems, all kinds of problems; nonetheless, they all are really trying to live good, decent, and Christ-centered lives. However, that is not enough—perfection is demanded, and problems are not tolerated by management. Problems do not dissolve into thin air, and salvation is not a sanctified pill that can cure all that spiritually ails one. The CBN staff believed they were saved; however, they were still held captive by their own fears and frailties. If prior to "salvation," Satan had possessed a person and kept him or her bound up in the shackles made of their own sins, then their "yes" to Jesus should have given them their freedom—a freedom to choose a new alternative lifestyle that was reflective of their new value system.

The people I came to know and love at CBN were not free. They were forced into action as gladiators of light and truth who struggled, in a daily, worldwide morality play, against the evil forces of darkness.

These soldiers served Pat Robertson and God with a respect that was based on fear. They were constantly reminded of the divine-satanic struggle of good and evil. This spiritual warfare is a paradox: hard to believe and hard to ignore. It either makes perfect sense or is perfect nonsense. It is either strikingly simple or confoundingly complex. It can either be a transcendent truth or a lethal lie.

For the staff at CBN there is no either-or; the reality of the unseen battle between God and Satan is the simple, factual truth that makes perfect sense to them. It can be no other way, and this emphatic conviction converts the staff into a collection of extremely opinionated zealots. They have compulsive likes and dislikes, habits and opinions that grow out of their supposed spiritual insight and maturity.

While working at CBN, it began to occur to me that those likes, habits, and opinions were the children of spiritual blindness and immaturity. Jesus gave people their freedom. CBN held people captive. We were not free to give a spontaneous and compassionate response to life. Spontaneity was considered repulsive because in any situation there can be only one godly response. Pat Robertson knew what that godly response was for everything from politics to ethics. And so did the fundamentalist pastors of the three local churches that claimed 90 percent of the CBN staff as members. There was only one way to heaven: their way. For them life was a one-way street of spiritual fundamentalism, and for two and a half years, I found myself traveling down that very same one-way street—but for me it led to Hollywood, not heaven.

3

Life on a One-Way Street

CBN knows the way to God. For the staff, there is only one way. Clutching the Bible, they can offer answers to anything. They see God clearly; they hear God distinctly; there is no mystery. The highway to heaven ran right through CBN and was bordered by the communities that comprised the local fundamentalist churches.

Shortly after joining CBN, I began attending such a church. The services were emotionally charged. People actually jumped up and down with excitement. I could feel the balcony section of the church quiver from all the joyfully jumping congregants. They enthusiastically yelled out praises of God. Shouting, jumping, dancing, crying, and waving of hands lifted heavenward were things I had never experienced in church. Sleeping I knew about. This was more like a college football rally without the beer than a church service. I kept coming, at first because the church was equipped with a small television control room and three cameras that turned the church into a large stage. Thousands of wonderful images and excitement were captured on videotape, and I was given an opportunity to direct the television coverage of the Sunday service, which was later broadcast around the nation via CBN satellite. I loved the challenge of catching the spirit of the service through my use of the cameras. After a few weeks of watching the services through the eyes of those cameras—observing and capturing the excitement without participating—I began to see how in comparison the people quietly, stiffly kneeling in the pews of the Catholic church seemed dead whenever they passively spoke aloud the structured words of the liturgy. I had mistaken enthusiasm and emotionalism for holiness.

Every new member of that church must attend a comprehensive course that met once a week for thirty-two weeks and gave a complete indoctrination into the beliefs and teachings of the church. When one completed the course, no doubt existed: this was the real church of Jesus Christ. They had all the answers.

Shades of Gray

Pastor John Gimenez of the Rock Church, a Puerto Rican and former gang member who turned from a life of crime and debauchery to a shepherd of souls, knew the godly response to my marital problems. One day we were sitting in the air-conditioned comfort of his parked luxury car in order to spend some uninterrupted time together. This overweight, undereducated, boisterous, fire-and-brimstone type of preacher was a busy man, who, besides leading a large nondenominational, charismatic church whose Sunday services were broadcast across the nation, was also the coordinator for the Washington for Jesus rally that attracted over two hundred thousand born-again Christians to the nation's capital on April 29, 1980.

As director of his weekly television church service and one of the producers of the massive rally, I warranted this special uninterrupted counseling session in his car. After a lengthy discussion of my rather complex marital situation, he simply said in his thick, New York, staccato accent, "Gerry, I know how this whole situation will turn out."

I hadn't the foggiest notion of what the eventual resolution to my domestic struggle would be, so I was curious as to what prophetic insight he might have that could clear up my vision; so I said, "Really, well, please tell me."

"If you love God you will stay married. If you don't love God, you will leave your wife," was his prediction.

It was that simple. There were no shades of gray, no doubt. No use for psychiatry. No room for compassion. No need for understanding. No tolerance for mistakes. No examination of the motives and emotions behind the actions. No possibility of misjudgment. Could I say or admit that I did not love God? Of course not. Did I want to stay married? Definitely not. Was the future of my marriage and my present love for God connected in some mystical fashion? Could my choice be reduced to terms of good and evil? According to Gimenez and CBN theology, the answer to both questions was "yes."

Yes, the people at CBN had many problems, not all of which were visible, but the solution to all the varied problems, whether hidden or manifested, was found in the Bible, and the answer always boiled down to a choice between good and evil. We either follow God or we follow Satan. Surprisingly, the marital relationship was a personal battlefield for many CBN staffers, especially for those whose spouses were not saved or supportive of CBN's mission.

I knew women whose husbands were not believers; but, because the Bible stated that a woman must be obedient to her husband, who is the head of the household, they endured psychological or physical abuse because they believed the suffering to be the will of God. For those tormented ladies, their faith had to overcome their pain and unhappiness, regardless of the fact that their very faith was forcing them further into their terrible situations. No matter how intolerable marriage became, divorce was hardly ever an option. If you were divorced before you had been saved and started working at CBN, it was not a problem from a company point of view. Once working there, though, a divorce became a job-threatening problem.

A Light to the Nations

Besides all the individual spiritual skirmishes, we were collectively under corporate attack from the prince of darkness, and like any soldier or army we would rather be on the attack. Each of us, as individual soldiers, stayed on the offensive in searching for souls to save, abortion clinics to picket, and books and movies to ban. Together as an army, CBN was always ready to launch a major offensive assault.

In a pitch for funds to support an effort to produce programs to change the world, Pat wrote in a widely distributed brochure, "This is not just another skirmish with the enemy. This is a major confrontation, perhaps one of the last, great strategic battles on the earth for the souls and minds of men." The power of darkness could not stop us from becoming a light to the nations. Our leader was a daring commander-in-chief who planned to invade Japan, China, the Middle East, and Latin America by bombarding them with the message of Jesus, and he would use the biggest and most effective weapon in his arsenal: broadcasting.

With a broad base of support built by his broadcasting efforts, it came as no surprise to me to read the AP and UPI news releases of August 7, 1985, which reported that Pat Robertson was praying about running for president of the United States in 1988. After all, the Oval Office would be the best place in the world from which to preach the message of salvation.

Broadcasting can be used as a balm or a bomb. As a balm it

attempts to communicate information and ideas in a soothing fashion that facilitates a free exchange of thought. As a bomb it distorts, twists, and bends the facts in order to form a heavy-handed, highly suggestive thesis that resembles propaganda more than a presentation of ideas or beliefs. For CBN, broadcasting meant bombing. And our broadcasting army was made up of troops of saved sinners out to destroy the sinful.

The heavy emphasis on sin is central to the spread of fundamentalist Christianity. I think it is fair to say that the subject of sin makes most people a bit itchy and uncomfortable. Some people can dismiss sin as a silly and antiquated religious idea, some people can deny that sin exists, and some people see sin everywhere. There are probably more different understandings of sin than there are sins. Nobody wants to think of themselves as sinful, yet almost everybody feels—at least occasionally—some degree of moral or ethical shortcoming that borders on the violation of a higher law.

Sin is a very small word that has had a huge impact on the lives of thousands upon thousands of people who have bought the message of the electronic church. A great deal of my energy in attempting to understand all I saw and did as a card-carrying, fundamentalist Christian was directed at dissecting the notion of sin. The results of that autopsy provide clues to how the cult of the electronic church works.

The Wages of Sin

St. Paul tells us that sinning is missing the mark and falling short of the glory of God. God made us in his image and longs for us to be as perfect as he is. Sin is our failed attempt at perfection. Even if we love God and have accepted Jesus as our lord and savior, we still fail to do the best we can in every situation because it is virtually impossible to be continually perfect. Who among us is perfect and without sin? Perfection is the mark we miss, and our failure does not make us evil; rather it gives us an opportunity to grow toward perfection.

Developing a habit of constant sinning may very well transform one into an evil person, but the fact that we do sometimes stumble and even take big tumbles does not mean we are evil. The people at CBN did not consider their mission to be an act of kindness—lending a helping hand to a person who out of human weakness had stumbled; rather they saw their mission as one of converting or exterminating the stumbler—because all the fallen were evil-doers bent on attacking God. Together we formed a "God Squad" that broadcast a shortcut to sainthood and salvation. We saw God, not as a loving father, but as a military leader who had appointed Pat commander-in-chief of his earthly forces. Pat led us into battle, and, as good soldiers, we followed.

Under Pat's leadership we were assured of more than salvation. We were constantly reminded that, no matter how difficult the battle may become, no matter how overwhelming the odds of winning the war with evil may seem, in the Book of Revelation, which is the last book of the Bible, we were guaranteed victory. The devil is a loser. A spiritual song, entitled "Victory in Jesus," was our battle hymn. The only thing that could rob us of our promise of victory was sin.

The day before the 1984 Reagan landslide victory, Jerry Falwell implored saved Christians to join in a day of prayer and fasting for a spiritual revival that would sweep the nation and sink sin. The country needed to be awakened to its spiritual sinfulness that blinded them to the political truth of the gospel according to Ronald Reagan.

Whenever CBN encountered rocky periods—like contributions running low—it was assumed that sin had snaked its way into paradise, and therefore we needed an individual and corporate cleansing of the soul. This was not a good time to get caught smoking or drinking because you might be considered the reason for God's displeasure and his subsequent withholding of blessings. Evil must be eradicated. Pat would summon the troops for a time of prayer so that we could refocus our vision on Jesus and turn from our sinfulness. And one had better turn quickly, because time is running out. All the signs point to the fact that God is getting ready to vent his anger and shake the earth to its foundation.

Trying to avoid sin out of the fear of the everlasting torments of Hell or even for the promise of eternal bliss in Heaven is a waste of time, which is why we had to refocus our effort constantly. Avoidance of sin is only possible through the stillness of mind and purity of heart.

No matter what CBN might preach about salvation, Jesus had only one message: We are loved by God. We can choose to open our hearts to that love, or we can reject it, and in his infinite respect and love for his creation, God allows us full freedom of choice. He no doubt yearns for us to make our hearts his home, but he will not force us. Pressure—like possessiveness—degrades love and therefore cannot be found in God. Sin simply is a vain form of self-exaltation and our doomed attempt at creating our own happiness instead of allowing it to flow from God. To portray the ravages of sin, Scripture paints the image of a hardening heart that causes mankind to become calloused and stubborn. Without God, we are enshrined in our own self, and it becomes impossible to relate to others in a godly fashion.

Only when I know that I am loved can I love others without fear, but when—without the reality of God's love—my heart has turned cold and lonely, people are threatening. Seeing sin as merely the evil breaking of rules is short-sighted; what we need to see is the lack of love in our hearts. Sin is eradicated internally by love, and not externally by fear. Erich Fromm has written, "The fear of pain is the way of a slave and the desire of reward is the way of a mercenary, but God desires that we come to Him by the way of sons who lived well and honestly for the love of Him and desire to serve Him and take pleasure in a saving union with Him in soul and heart."

Even those who do not believe in God would be able to at least tolerate the possible existence of the God that Jesus proclaimed; however, the God that is worshiped by the fundamentalist Christian is not worthy of any recognition and, in fact, deserves to be despised.

Missing the Mark

Did sin rob mankind of its salvation and douse the flickering flame of promised victory? Pat Robertson preached over the airways and during mandatory prayer meetings that we should not lean on our own understanding or even have a mind of our own in the matter of sin and evil. My problem was having a mind and using it to understand the frightening concept of sin. The CBN staff saw sin everywhere, even in the violation of their own house rules against smoking and drinking. Guilt cluttered everyone's mind. These irrational guilt feelings were produced by an infantile conscience. This kind of guilt inflicts deep spiritual scars and makes a person feel totally useless and rotten.

"Backsliders," a wonderfully colorful term that identifies Christians who have fallen back into the world, tend to weaken their concept of sin in order to lessen the burden of guilt. Real guilt in a morally mature person who has acted against his conscience is healthy because it helps him become what he can be by pointing out his deficiencies and curing them with acknowledgment, repentance, and atonement.

Having been put through the "sin-wringer" for so many years, I now see sin as not just a matter of breaking a bunch of biblical or man-made rules. In fact, there was no specific Hebrew word that expressed the theological concept of sin. The apostle Paul, who was a Jew, knew that the Old Testament used a word that meant "to miss the mark," which indicated, not a mistake or bad judgment, but rather a failure to reach a goal. The Old Testament notion of sin was not the mere transgression of a law but a break in the relationship between God and his people.

The New Testament added a new twist to the idea of sin by claiming that sin is not only an individual act but is also a condition and a power that is at work in the world, finally overcome by Jesus. John writes in his gospel that he who sins is from the devil and becomes the slave of sin. For him sin is the lust of the flesh and the lust of the eyes.

The tradition of seeing evil in a person who has not allowed Jesus to overcome sin lives on today. I had a friend at CBN who talked of his neighbor who was "under sin" in the same way a child is under its parents. The image of a demonic despot lording it over a man mowing his lawn was repulsive to me. I couldn't understand how my friend could look at his neighbor and consider him to be in the grip of evil because he had not turned his life over to Jesus. My mind continually struggled with the concept of a monumental spiritual battle being waged between the forces of darkness and the Prince of Light.

While the idea of good and bad angels fighting for my salvation made little sense, I have come to realize that there *is* an unseen battle being fought, although it is very different in nature from the holy war of the fundamentalist. A war rages within each one of us, and the two armies in conflict are all that is selfish in us pitted against all that is selfless in us. For Christianity rooted in Western culture this is a lifetime symbolic battle between the demonic and the Divine. Instead of demonic and Divine, the terms *higher* and *lower* are used in the East, especially among non-Christian faiths. It is interesting to note that the lower is not demonic, just material.

In the Beginning

Either way, it's a very old war. The first words in the book of Genesis, the first book of the Bible, are "In the beginning. . . ." In fact, it tells us nothing of what happened at the beginning of time. However, it does tell us the spiritual meaning of what is happening at all times. The Bible begins with this account of creation:

> In the beginning God created the heavens and the earth. Now the earth was a formless void, there was darknes over the water. God said, "Let there be light," and there was light. God saw that the light was good; God divided light from darkness. God called the light "day" and the darkness "night." Evening came and morning came: the first day.

Obviously, this isn't an eyewitness account, so either God told the writer—verbatim—exactly what happened or the writer used the power of his imagination to express a divinely inspired concept concerning God's relationship with humanity. Three things strike me as curious about this short passage which my friends at CBN considered to be a literally true and dependable account of the origin of the universe. Since God presumably lives in Heaven, then the heavens referred to in the opening line mean the skies. Regarding the earth, why would God use his infinite creative power to create a formless void? Second, after speaking light into existence, he looked at it and thought it was good. It sounds like a painter who upon completion of a painting stands back and looks at it and decides whether or not he likes it. Was God not sure when he created light whether or not he would like it? Third, if there was nobody around but him to even see his creation, why bother giving it a name? Consider the idea that maybe this dark, formless void might be symbolic of the state of confusion that exists within man until he is enlightened by the reality of God. God brings order, hope, and purpose to mankind. The writer is telling us that there is a higher reality than ourselves and that there is more to life than aimlessly roaming about seeking self-satisfaction.

A little later in Genesis we read how a serpent tempted Eve into eating of the fruit of knowledge of good and evil. It always seemed a little strange to me that Satan would take the form of a snake in order to talk to Eve. At the least it is an odd disguise, but solid research has uncovered a good reason why the writer used a snake in the creation story. Genesis was written around five hundred years before Christ and long after the beginning of the universe; and, at the time it was written, the Jews had a bad habit of being led easily into false beliefs. Just like today, there were many concepts of and ways to God, and some Jews frequently got involved with the religious practices of their so-called "pagan" neighbors. One group believed God resides in snakes, and Jews were beginning to accept that belief. The writer cleverly wove a secondary meaning into the creation episode by having the snake represent evil and also suggested that people who follow strange new teachings wind up in trouble. So, the snake was merely a symbol for pagan practices, and the writer was trying to make the point that Jews need only to listen to their god, Yahweh.

The creation story told in Genesis is not intended to be the basis of an argument against the theory of evolution, as the Christian fundamentalist believes, because it has little to do with historical concerns. Rather, it attempts to describe God's plan for man. According to Genesis, God created us and wishes to treat us like friends. Whether he did it in one day, seven days, or over a million years was not important to the Old Testament writers. What was important was conveying the idea that we are not content in receiving God's goodness; we want more. We want to be gods ourselves and determine our own selfish destinies and decide for ourselves what is right or wrong. For the religious person it should not be a story about gardens, snakes, ribs, women, apples, and punishment.

The tale portrays the essence of mankind's earliest understanding of sin, which is simply to put ourselves before God, to want what is not ours, and to want it with such a passion that we are blinded to its effect on us and others. Its truth has stood the test of time because selfishness still strips us of our true divine identity and potential and leaves us naked and hiding from God and each other. Our punishment is our becoming disenfranchised from our surroundings and at odds with our neighbor. Sin divides us and cuts us off from our true selves, from others, from the world we live in, and from God, because we fail to reach out in love. We create our own Hell, and it is here and now. Sartre's words, "Hell is other people," is truly understood by the selfish person who no longer lingers in God's intended paradise of selfless love.

The history contained in the Bible, on which Judaism and Christianity have been founded, is in reality little more than a compendium of manufactured fables. These holy tales are only attempting to tell us about essential principles that we need to know; they were not composed in order to be accepted as dependable accounts of the origin of the planet and subsequent prehistoric events.

Joseph Campbell, in his book *Myths to Live By*, writes:

> Taken as referring not to any geographical scene, but to a landscape of the soul, that Garden of Eden would have to be within us. Yet our conscious minds are unable to enter it and enjoy there the taste of eternal life, since we have already tasted of the knowledge of good and evil. That, in fact, must then be the knowledge that has thrown us out of the garden, pitched us away from our own center, so that we now judge things in those terms and experience only good and evil instead of eternal life—which, since the enclosed garden is within us, must already be ours, even though unknown to our conscious personalities. That would seem to be the meaning of the myth when read, not as prehistory, but as referring to man's inward spiritual state.

Heaven isn't a reward for living a good life, and "salvation" doesn't spare us from Hell. Salvation is the discovery of the unity of life. We are all in this together, and there is no room for divisiveness. We each have a touch of heaven every time we forget ourselves and bring joy to others, and we have a dose of hell every time we think or act unkindly. The reality of heaven begins here in this life as soon as we begin to increase our capacity to love and decrease our need to put ourselves first. Peace is not found in accepting Jesus—like CBN claimed—but in loving, like Jesus.

Despite their claims, the video evangelists spread not the good news of salvation but the fear of Hell. They claim that God is love, yet portray him as brutally judgmental. They preach that God is compassionate, yet they condemn adulterers, homosexuals, and leftwing liberals. Pat Robertson likens God to a military leader whom we must fear. He tells us we must "do" certain things in order to obtain God's guidance. He tells us that God rewards our goodness and generosity by providing us with material success; yet, in reality, worldly success and failure are irrelevant to God and should be to us. The Bengali philosopher and Nobel Prize winner Rabindranath Tagore wrote, "God is ashamed when the prosperous boast of his special favor." Televised religion plays on infantile guilt, self-rejection, feelings of unworthiness, fear of God, original sin, a hatred of the body, and an idolatrous worship of the Bible. It's all based on retribution and punishment.

The Sin of Adam and Eve

Why should we be punished for the disobedience of Adam and Eve, two fictional characters? Maybe we don't need to be punished but healed. Erich Fromm presents in his book, *To Have or To Be,* some healing insights into the myth of man's prehistoric "fall":

> God had put Man into the Garden of Eden and warned him not to eat either from the Tree of Life or from the Tree of Knowledge of Good and Evil. Seeing that "it was not good for Man to be alone," God created Woman. Man and Woman should become one. Both were naked, and they "were not ashamed." This statement is usually interpreted in terms of conventional sexual mores, which assume that, naturally, a man and a woman should be ashamed if their genitals were uncovered. But this seems hardly all the text has to say. On a deeper level, this statement could imply that although Man and Woman faced each other totally, they did not, and they even could not, feel ashamed, for they did not experience each other as strangers, as separated individuals, but as one. This prehuman situation changes radically after the

Fall, when Man and Woman become fully human, i.e., endowed with reason, with awareness of good and evil, with awareness of each other as separate beings, with awareness that their original oneness is broken and that they have become strangers to one another. They are close to each other, and yet they feel separate and distant. They feel the deepest shame there is: the shame of facing a fellow being nakedly and simultaneously experiencing the mutual estrangement, the unspeakable abyss that separates each from the other. "They make themselves aprons," thus trying to avoid the full human encounter, the nakedness in which they see each other. But the shame, as well as the guilt, cannot be removed by concealment. They did not reach out to each other in love; perhaps they desired each other physically, but physical union does not heal human estrangement. That they did not love each other is indicated in their attitude toward each other; Eve does not try to protect Adam, and Adam avoids punishment by denouncing Eve as the culprit rather than defending her. What is the sin they have committed? To face each other as separated, isolated, selfish human beings who cannot overcome their separation in the act of loving union. This sin is rooted in our human existence. Being deprived of the original harmony with nature, characteristic of the animal whose life is determined by built-in instincts, being endowed with reason and self-awareness, we cannot help experiencing our utter separateness from every other being. In Catholic theology this state of existence, complete separateness and estrangement from each other, not bridged by love, is the definition of hell. It is unbearable for us. We must overcome the torture of absolute separateness in some way: by submission or by domination or by trying to silence reason or awareness. Yet all these ways succeed only for the moment, and block the road to a true solution. There is but one way to save ourselves from this hell: to leave the prison of our egocentricity, to reach out and to *one* ourselves with the world. If egocentric separateness is the cardinal sin, then the sin is atoned in the act of loving. The very word atonement expresses this concept, for it etymologically derives from "at-*one*ment," the Middle-English expression for union. Since the sin of separateness is not an act of disobedience, it does not need to be forgiven. But it does need to be healed; and love, not acceptance of punishment, is the healing factor.

There is so much more to the creation story than just a simple explanation of how the world began. It is a story of love and unity; not disobedience and punishment. It is a study in human consciousness.

The Death of Joy

Most video evangelists attempt to drive us apart. They make Christianity an elitist religious experience, and those who don't embrace it are considered unsaved and sinful even if they are devout Jews, Muslims, or Hindus. These video spiritual seers think they are endowed with a prophetic vision so clear that everyone else appears blind. They hear God's voice so distinctly that everyone else seems deaf to them. They mistakenly believe that God's word resounds within them, and they must shout it from the housetops.

While the world is asleep, they continue to scream their warnings and point the way. They are bent on straightening out man's crooked ways. They become unbearable extremists who despise the "middle of the road."

God is compassion, not compromise. Pat Robertson and Jimmy Swaggart seem to live in a constant state of emergency, as if we are only an instant away from a cataclysmic event. Their relentless message is that both doom and redemption are at hand, so we have to get ready. Yet the words ring empty.

The way a person lives his or her life may compel others, by example, to change their lifestyles, but empty words—especially those that sound like commands—alone will have no effect. Say it with silence—that would be effective.

I became completely disillusioned with people at CBN who tried to bring Christ to others through quoting biblical passages and demanding repentance. I would have loved to have met someone in this hotbed of born-again Christianity who was truly like Jesus. It seemed to me the meaning of a true Christian's life should be found in imitating Jesus, not "saving" the world.

If the Hebrew idea of sin is missing the mark, then the goal remains perfection—and with perfection will come the ability to live together in peace and harmony. We can find lasting fulfillment only by contributing to the joy and fulfillment of others, in which our own joy is included. Joy could not be seen in the soldiers under Pat's command. Their search for evil had destroyed their sense of joy and humor. Humor and self-righteousness are incompatible.

Imagine

Pat Robertson preaches and believes that God is loving and forgiving. This concept is manifested in the image of God as a father who always stands ready to love, forgive, help, nourish, and guide his children. He is the kind of father we all wish we had—faultless and perfect. Despite this soothing and paternalistic picture of God, Reverend Robertson

still clings to the conception of God as a military leader. These conflicting images—tender daddy and tough commander-in-chief—gave
birth to much tension for me.

During my post-CBN days, I looked at many different faiths, as
well as the many factions within each faith, and wondered how anyone
could determine which one was correct—or at least contained the most
truth. Imagine that they are all right on target, the best way for
whomever is following them at any given moment in time. It is possible.

During different times in history and within different cultures
throughout history, the concept of the Deity has changed greatly. From
childhood I learned that God is unchangeable—the same yesterday,
today, and tomorrow. I believe that is true. Therefore, what *does*
change is man's concept and understanding of the Almighty.

Is a jungle-dwelling aborigine, whose spiritual acts of worship seem
crude, guilty of a crime of incorrect or false belief and consequently
bound for Hell? Can salvation or the incarnation of God or the indwelling presence of the life-giving Trinity make any sense to a primitive mind? Translating the Bible into their language is going to be of
little help. Are they to be pitied, saved, or loved? The aborigine can
only be loved and should be seen as worshiping the highest concept of
God possible to his underdeveloped mind. If he is loved then he won't
be seen as a heathen or an unbeliever in dire need of salvation. The
god of the savage appears to be a reprehensible villain to many people.
The aborigine's idea of a deity reflects the reality of his life, and his
god is only just a little bit better then he is. His enemies become his
god's enemies, and he may believe that his god welcomes and needs
barbarous sacrificial blood offerings. Less developed groups of people
cannot form the Christian concept of one god (let alone the notion of
one god who consists of three distinct persons), and so they create
many gods that together portray all the attributes of God.

These many gods are given human attributes, and they do what the
people would do if they had the power to reward or punish. The god
of the electronic church is obviously a conservative Republican who
advocates school prayer and a big military budget in order to support
a strong defense system.

Some religions of the East view God as an impersonal force that is
a part of each of us. The aim of our lives is to become detached from
the things of this world—our bodies, our thoughts, our hopes, our fears,
or anything else that has to do with our bodies or our egos—and to be
awakened to the transcendent reality of the Absolute that is within our
consciousness and to identify with the majesty of the Self that is All

and in all. The body is a vehicle for reincarnation, and the things of the body are illusory; individuality must be dropped—along with free will—into a sea of sameness and unity with all.

The religions of the West do not stress *identity* with a Supreme Being, whose substance is contained in each person; rather, the emphasis is on man entering into a *relationship* with God, who is a distinctly different person, man's creator, and reigns in a faraway place known as Heaven. Obedience to the will and laws of God, which were divulged in revelations to the Chosen People and recorded in books that are above criticism, is essential. God and man have been separated by man's disobedience, and redemption and repentance are required for a reunion and eternal life. From one point of view, we are a-wakened to our true identity, and from another point of view we are saved from our sinful nature. Today many people are becoming spiritual eclectics—picking bits and pieces from both East and West and mixing them together into the creation of what I regard as an even more confusing point of view: I call it "Christzen mysticism," in which the words of Jesus and Buddha mingle to form a belief that features detachment, atonement, asceticism, meditation, materialism, yoga, altered states of consciousness, visions, divine revelations, health-food stores, and, of course, spiritual superiority.

A Looking-Glass God

The God of the Old Testament appears vengeful, bloody, and savage and is a far different God from the caring God of the New Testament. The difference comes from the growth and development of the mind of mankind. Mankind's understanding of God is constantly changing—sometimes very slowly—as the human race makes evolutionary changes. But this growth and accompanying changes are not universal or uniform.

During our country's Civil War period, some people believed their God gave them the right and privilege to own slaves. The Bible even supported that point of view. At the same time, many of their fellow countrymen worshiped a God who hated slavery and wanted to kill those who favored it. Each saw God through his own eyes as if looking into a mirror.

History abounds with stories of people persecuting others in fulfillment of God's will, while others heroically shed their blood for God's holy cause. The Puritans were forced to flee to America because of their unique understanding of God; and, once here, they proceeded to punish the peaceful Quakers, because their idea of God annoyed them. The Quakers believed in the inherent goodness in men and women and that the power of evil was overemphasized; and, if that wasn't disturbing enough, they taught that the Kingdom of God is now and that questions about an afterlife appear unnecessary, inappropriate, and a fruitlessly speculative basis for religious belief .

Pat Robertson spoke of how God slowly revealed himself to humanity through the Jewish people and how this revelation reached its completeness in the New Testament. This gradual self-disclosure by the Almighty accounts for the difference between the God of the Old and New Testaments.

One day Pat explained that a father would treat a two-year-old son differently from the way he would treat the same son at the age of ten and again vastly different from the way he would respond to the child at age twenty. The father was the same, but the child grew in his ability to understand the father. In the same manner, it took God almost two thousand years of Old Testament history before humanity was ready to fully understand and appreciate his godliness. For the fundamentalist, God's slow revealing of himself to us ended with the life of Jesus on earth. They believe God still speaks to us through the Holy Spirit; nonetheless, nothing new is going to be said, because all we need to know is the Bible—a book that was written in times, places, and cultures vastly different from ours and whose message is open to a wide range of interpretations. The video evangelists want us to ignore the last twenty centuries of intellectual growth in the human race.

Grow Not

While submerged in the "sea of fundamentalism," I felt that any form of intellectual growth was damnable, though it didn't overly concern me; I certainly didn't see myself as an intellectual. I was, however, reasonable, and soon enough even that became a problem. Reason made me squirm one day as the preacher in a large, charismatic church breathed fear into his congregation. He was ranting and raving about how God's wrath would soon be upon us—the Tribulation was coming. According to this minister of God, God is holy and righteous and therefore can't condone sin in any degree. Although the Almighty is long-suffering, God must ultimately pour out his wrath against sinners.

I squirmed because to me that sounded not godly but human because, after all, humans have limitations regarding patience, understanding, and forgiveness. Theoretically God should have none. But this sermon made it sound as though God also had his limits—divine justice and retaliation might even eventually triumph over divine love and mercy. There is great contrast between God's love and his wrath. The Apostle John clearly stated that contrast when he wrote, "He that believeth on the Son hath everlasting life; and he that believeth not on the Son shall not see life; but the wrath of God abideth on him" (3:36). It's very simple: choose life or wrath.

The Book of Revelation is loaded with vivid images of just how deadly God's wrath is going to be. The pulpit-pounding preacher proudly pointed out that, according to this final book of Scripture, there will be plenty of warning before the Final Judgment, and everyone will be given a chance to repent and accept Jesus as his or her personal savior. Plagues, natural disasters, and war will usher in the world's big day in court. The preacher proclaimed that people will ignore these God-given signs—like the earthquake in Mexico and the volcanic eruption in Chile—because, given time to think about the numerous and ominous warnings, people will begin explaining away the events on a natural basis and conclude there is "no reason for alarm."

This argument rests on the belief that the devil of modern science can explain almost anything in natural terms so that people will be deceived, not see the hand of God, not repent, and hence soon find themselves in the midst of the great judgment by a vengeful God. After painting such a frightening picture, the pastor told his glory-bound followers they should rejoice in the fact that they will be ready and will have a good defense before the awesome judgment seat of God. Yes, people were converted by his well-crafted message: converted into hypocrites who were sermonized into shame, guilt, and fear, which compelled them to act as if they were loving and morally righteous people.

Sin Scoreboard

God must have one hell of a computer in order to keep lifelong records on each of us and a running total of our sins. Just imagine the billions of people living today—each one of us with an active file of faults, failures, and petty performances to compare against God's holy standards. Who among us can measure up? We are all sinners. To those who acknowledged their sinfulness, Jesus always gave every assurance of love and forgiveness. The message of Jesus in the Gospels actually undermines the sin-scoreboard-in-the-sky image of an authoritarian God. God's response to us is governed only by love.

At CBN I began to believe that God cannot get angry at our "sins" because they don't hurt him and, in fact, are only damaging to ourselves. I believe that God sees our "sins" as our blind and confused following of our own self-will instead of searching for peace in Him. God would feel, metaphorically speaking of course, only sadness and never anger at our sinful tendencies. God isn't preoccupied with counting our sins but only with revealing the true nature of his divine love. Most of the people who sit listening to fiery preachers are only concerned with conforming to a set of behavioral responses imposed upon them by a superior being and rendering them holy. I don't think it has anything to do with holiness.

Jesus saw sin as a bondage that entangled people, and he was more concerned with freeing them from the shackles that crippled them than judging them for their failures—liberation, not blame, was his style. Jesus did not create a religion for a small group of chosen people who somehow were blessed with an ability to hear and understand his message; he hung out with the sinners, not the saved!

The Big Clock in the Sky

Besides deprecating reason and knowledge, the minister explicated one of the strangest lines in Scripture, Revelation 8:1: "There was a silence in heaven for about half an hour." Apparently before the Tribulation begins, God is going to give those in Heaven a glance at what is coming, and what those inhabitants of Heaven will see is so frightening that the suspense and horror of it will fill them with awe-inspired silence. I couldn't imagine a half-hour sneak preview of ultimate terror. Does that mean that there are clocks in heaven, and when the period of silence is over the people will go back to singing? After the preacher's highly animated talk, many people came forth for prayers of salvation, and the congregation sang songs of praise, rejoicing over all the people who had chosen to be born again.

Seeing the throngs of people coming forward for "salvation," the preacher passionately cried out:

Praise God! By coming forward you have found the answer to all your problems and the answer is sin. Alleluia, praise God! The sinner has no place in the Kingdom of God—we have all sinned; but, praise God, he does not wish us to perish, so my brothers and sisters, despite our tendency to embrace sin, he has sent his beloved son to take our punishment and clothe us with his holiness. Praise God! At this moment, as you accept Jesus as your lord and savior, you have accepted his blood sacrifice as atonement for your sins, and the old "you" will disappear from the face of the earth. Praise God!

Thanks to the highly charged emotion of the moment and the experience of being bathed in a sea of hugs and tears of joy as the angels in the congregation sang heavenly songs of praise, you did disappear from the face of the earth. But you'll be back. However, you will never forget the high of that moment of surrender. You have been hooked, and the preacher has scared you out of Hell. And thanks to the miracle of videotape, this same message will be able to scare people all across the nation when it is broadcast on the CBN Cable Network.

Who Invented Heaven and Hell?

During the course of human history, man's worship has moved from sticks and stones forming crude symbols of God to thunder and lightning, the sun, the moon, the stars, the wind, and eventually reached the point where God has become a supernatural being living somewhere in outer space, unseen but seeing.

In April 1985, evangelist Percy Collett rented the five-thousand seat Felt Forum in New York City in order to talk about his five-and-a-half-day trip to Heaven, which he claims is really a planet located two trillion miles from earth. It has never been discovered by astronomers because God moves it away if they get close. Collett's voyage to the distant Planet Heaven took only six hours, and during the trip his body remained on earth in a coma. According to Collett, God is twice the size of a man and sits atop a two-thousand-mile-high throne overlooking millions of diamond-studded mansions on more than three million miles of streets. Around the outer perimeter of the kingdom of Heaven dwell souls, including President Kennedy and an unnamed religious figure, who have not yet learned how to worship God.

For the people at CBN, God is a very personal God with whom we must develop a personal relationship. To them Jesus is flesh and blood, here and now. Their Heaven is a place they invented to bribe people to follow God's way, and their Hell is designed to coerce people into being good in case the bribe failed. Hell has become the psychological sledgehammer that fundamentalist preachers use to pound their congregations into fearful submission. Is it comprehensible that, while the lost are experiencing unending suffering, God and the saved are dancing in Heaven because the unjust are finally receiving their due? To believe that God's justice demands that he despise sinners and turn his back on them is to make a mockery of the God Jesus revealed to us in the Gospels.

It is true that Jesus did preach of a Hell of fire and punishment. As a preacher, he used imagery prevalent among the Jews of his day and drawn from apocalyptic literature taught by the Pharisees. It was a metaphorical language that resonated in the conscience of his listeners and led them into a mystery, not a literal preview.

Through the ages, and even today, preachers have used this imagery that had its origin in pagan practices and have pictured a Hell that is in direct conflict with and opposition to the rest of Jesus' teaching. George Maloney, a Jesuit priest, wrote in his book, *The Everlasting Now:*

> God does not create a "place" where he punishes us with material fire, but that the meaning which Jesus meant to convey was even greater self-punishment from within, according to our own human choices. God does not send us to hell. If we continue to make choices based on selfishness rather than self-sacrificing love, we will evolve to a state of "Aloneness," a state that is destuction of God's true life shared through authentic love of others. Hell must be found in a man's heart and not in some "place" below the earth. God can never go against his nature to always love us, yet we can continuously make choices that form a state of consciousness that separates us from God and our world.

The fundamentalist firmly believes in the myth of Hell—a fiery pit where the evil will be thrust—and when that belief is challenged, and the reality of Hell is questioned, they embrace the myth more tenaciously. Very few people trapped in a fundamentalist belief system ever change their minds.

The Chosen Ones

For the fundamentalist, God is a personal God who resides in Heaven and elects to speak directly and clearly to a few chosen high priests of faith. Many televangelists claim to be so chosen. The writer Norman Corwin clearly illustrates this point in his excellent book, *Trivializing America:*

Oftener than not, American evangelists profess to know God very well and have inside tracks to Jesus, but the one who knows God the best, would appear to be Morris Cerrullo, self-proclaimed "prophet of God," whose Third World Crusade appearances have attracted more than 100,000 congregants to a single service. He claims in his autobiography *From Judaism to Christianity* that he met God face to face in Paterson, N.J., and was lifted into heaven, where he encountered "the Presence of God" in the form of a six-foot-high flaming ball.

[Cerrullo said] "My eyes were drawn to the place where the glory of God was standing in the heavens, and right where He had been standing, there was a hole in the sky in the form of two footprints. It was as if someone had taken a knife and cut a hole in a great big cake of cheese and one could see right through it. I knew what I had to do. I put my feet in the indentations that had been made by the presence of God, and to my utter amazement my feet fit perfectly into those footprints. They were the same size."

This trumps the story of Cinderella's shoe, and for the first time reveals that God has the foot size of a short, stocky man.

Morris Cerrullo was a guest on "The 700 Club," and I found him to be very peculiar. I thought he had an unnatural quality about him. He was stiff and wooden. His face had an insincere smile glued on it, but not a trace of real joy could be seen. He seemed ill at ease around people. I had this feeling that he was hiding some big secret or was afraid that people wouldn't believe his vision. He spoke of his hard work for God, yet his impeccable tailoring and well-groomed appearance hardly presented an image of a struggling servant of the Lord, but rather a wealthy celebrity.

I could not shake the feeling that Morris was a fake, but everyone else thought he was fantastic. I was suspicious of this "holy" man's impatient desire to reform other men, especially Jews and Communists. Maybe my uneasiness with Cerrullo grew out of the impression he gave that he was more interested in politics than spirituality. He was dedicated to converting Israel and fighting communism, and his zeal was draped in anger and frustration at Satan's power around the world. Cerrullo's mission is international evangelization, and his overzealous methods of proselytizing have been condemned by several Israeli groups that resent strong-armed missionary tactics aimed at undermining and discrediting their faith. Cerrullo wanted to counterattack the work of the devil in Nicaragua, but that government denied him entry into the country. But Morris was always welcome on "The 700 Club," where his views and visions were accepted as godly and not unusual.

Another, more well-known evangelist, Oral Roberts, claims that a five-hundred-foot-tall Jesus told him in a dream to build a hospital on the campus of Oral Roberts University. He did—despite the fact that the area of Oklahoma surrounding the new three-building medical complex featuring praying physicians didn't really need another hospital. The new healing center proved to be a financial drain on his ministry, and when funding began to lag behind expectations, Jesus impatiently spoke to Oral, "When, when are you and your partners going to obey me? When?" Previously, Jesus had instructed Roberts to ask people to become his partners in the medical venture by donating $240. In return, these partners would receive forty-eight audio tapes of Roberts' commentaries on the New Testament plus fourteen special blessings that included money and success. Following Jesus' chastisement, Roberts sent out a new twelve-page, fundraising letter in which Jesus was quoted verbatim: "Tell them this is not Oral Roberts asking [for the $240], but their Lord."

Jesus and the Bible have become trivialized: reduced to fairy tales, slogans, pins, pamphlets, and bumper stickers. Pop in an audio cassette, and the truth of the Bible is yours. Salvation is quick and easy. Harvey Cox, a professor at the Harvard Divinity School and a noted theologian, has written, "No deity however terrible, no devotion however deep, no ritual however splendid is exempt from the voracious process of trivialization."

Mail Fraud

The master at trivializing the message of Jesus is a California-based television preacher named Peter Popoff. His show closely resembles that of Ernest Angley—the minister who nearly scared me to death my first night in Virginia. People are crammed into auditoriums, and for the better part of the show Popoff frantically zig-zags his way through the emotionally highstrung crowd and pauses only long enough to lay hands on people, to claim miraculous healings, and to cast out devils. The show is sprinkled with close-ups of people crying and praising God. The only thing that interrupts the miracles are commercials that feature Popoff calmly sitting behind his office desk. He tells the viewers about members of his family who are trapped in Russia and about his deep burden to smuggle the Gospel of Jesus into Russia. He pleads for his viewers' financial support for his plan to airlift Bibles behind the Iron Curtain. I considered this man to be a harmless charlatan until I started receiving mail from his ministry after I wrote to him requesting a free booklet he offered to his television audience, entitled *Predictions for 1985 and 1986.*

From August 2, 1985, to December 28, 1985, I received eleven pieces of mail, and those letters led me to the conclusion that this man is an extremely dangerous fraud who is literally stealing money from the viewers who write to him.

To prove my point, what follows is a brief summary and excerpts from the material that he mailed to me.

The booklet I requested was only twelve pages long, but it was not short on outrageous predictions. This minister of God predicted that God was ready to unleash revival or chaos—it was up to the reader to pray and work for revival in order to prevent chaos. The booklet claimed that Gorbachev's charisma came from Satan, and that Finland's economy would grow because an army of Christians from that country have been preparing to help in a great exodus of God's people from the Soviet Union. He predicts that food prices will sky-rocket, and food riots will erupt everywhere. A coming ice age will devastate the earth's economy. The Soviet Union will start a revolution in Mexico. Violent, senseless crime will become more rampant, more brutal, and more random. A Soviet invasion of Israel will be stopped in the mountains of Israel, and only one-sixth of the Red Army will survive. The American stockmarket may go haywire. There will be an attack of Satanic forces as never before in history, and armies of demons will focus their mission on the ministers of the Gospel. After painting a gloomy picture, Popoff states that Christians do not have to worry as long as they obey God and hold on to Him.

And now, excerpts from the letters:

Postmarked August 2, 1985:

Dear Brother Straub,
This is what the Holy Spirit spoke into my heart as I was praying for you today. As I was holding you up in my prayers, God gave me the most glorious word of promise: "Yea, you will see definite divine guidance in your affairs. I will lead you by my spirit from victory to victory and from glory to glory. I will lead you to do certain things that will cause new money and new blessings to come to you. From a material viewpoint those around you who are carnally minded will not understand at all, because they will not comprehend my work. But you will see not just one miracle take place, but many miracles will come to you. In unexpected ways I shall pour out upon thee a blessing that you will not even be able to contain. You will see that I will bless you not only in expected ways, but also in completely unexpected ways for my servant has touched the hem of my garment for thee. The time has come for you and your house to rejoice, saith the Lord of Hosts." Gerard, I feel a very unusual anointing flowing through me to you as I

write. I feel guidance to do something special for you now to help you receive what God has for you. The Lord is directing me to put this picture of myself with my hand outstretched toward you inside this letter. Hold this picture in your left hand and say out loud, "Oh Lord, I receive all that you have in store for me! I receive it now!" As you say these words out loud (saying it helps it to take place) touch my outstretched hand with your right finger in faith. As you do this, I believe you will see a release in the spirit.

Postmarked August 15, 1985:

Dear Brother Straub,

I lovingly write you to let you know Jesus has clearly and directly spoken to me again about you. He has given these words telling you how God is leading me to help you get the complete victory that the devil has stolen from you. As I sat down to write you the Holy Spirit whispered in my soul to tell you two powerful things: "(1) Yea, you are on the very edge of the miraculous now, saith the Lord of Hosts. The miracle you have been believing for, is now ready to be released unto thee. Hear the word I have put in the mouth of my servant for thee. (2) Behold, my spirit is even now preparing the ground so that as you sow your most sacrificial special seed it shall be burst forth into a special miracle harvest that shall be more than enough to meet your every need. Miracle harvest is coming to you, saith the Lord, as you sow in faith now!"

Now, Gerard, God has laid on my heart what I must do to help you. In the nearly 25 years of this ministry I have never felt His power like I feel it today. As I write these words, wave after wave of God's healing power is flooding through me. Both my hands are burning with a supernatural heat. My entire body is tingling with a powerful new anointing. From deep in my spirit I felt the Holy Spirit welling up within me. I heard the familiar voice I have heard often before telling me exactly what to do for you. You may wonder how it felt to hear God's voice. Well, His voice seemed to fill my head, my whole body and spirit. It blotted out all sounds, and all I could hear was His voice. I heard Him, oh, so clearly, "You are to tell Gerard how he is to use this very special point of contact to receive my miracle." Through God's special anointing upon my life, I'm willing to do anything he tells me to help you get your miracle from him. I love you in the Lord and it's no accident God has me send you this special point of contact. I am bold in enclosing this WHITE FAITH SOCK that I have been praying over for a very special reason—for a point of contact to help you release your faith in God. Now I feel led to ask you to wear this faith sock overnight on your right foot. While you are wearing it ask God to anoint your mind to think of your most special needs. When you know from the Lord what to write—and He will show you—quickly grab a pen and start writing your needs to me on the last page of this letter. Then wrap up the sock you have worn overnight inside this letter, and rush it back to me. Gerard, when I receive this letter back with your special requests

I will send you the instructions God gave me for you to get your special miracle. Please do not keep this faith sock, I must have it back so I can obey God and send you the instructions He has given me for you. Brother Straub, this letter is confidential between you and me and God. Please don't discuss it with anyone else because satan will try to steal your blessing. Ask God to show you while you are praying about what you are to give to His work at this very urgent hour.

Postmarked August 23, 1985:

Dear Brother Straub,
    Most of last night I was in a deep spirit of prayer, asking God to move in your life with a real miracle . . . a miracle of peace, healing, finance and most of all a miracle of victory. Yes, God is giving me something very special for you. I feel now is the right time for you to claim a special miracle from God. Gerard, as I was praying about your needs, the Lord gave me this word for you: "Gerard, knowest thou not that you shall have the strength of the Lord thy God, for angels are around about thee this day and the thing you have cried out for in thy soul shall come to pass as the Lord doth change minds and doth make a new way. Others do not understand thee but I have laid my hand upon thee and cut all fetters. You shall now move forward in real power and victory for a new day hath dawned for thee. I have placed thee by my spirit with my servant and as you agree and touch him, nothing shall be impossible." Oh, thank you, Jesus! Isn't God good? I have asked our Heavenly Father to impress your heart, Gerard, to give a love gift of $33.00 (Jesus was 33 years old when he said, "Now I send you. . . .") The needs are so urgent now. This is God's time. Don't miss it. Your $33.00 obedient offering of love or your $66.00 double portion blessing gift of love is so needed.

Postmarked September 6, 1985:

Dear Brother Straub,
    Early this morning, it was just about 7:00 A.M., I was making a pot of coffee and the spirit of the Lord began to deal with me about your family. I felt such a burden for every member of your family. Is some member of your family having trouble? Are they sick or discouraged right now? I feel this so strongly that I had to drop everything and rush this to you. The Lord dealt with me about setting aside a special day to pray for the victory of every member of your family. In this busy day and age sometimes we need to make time to do the things that are really important. That's what I feel led to do for you. Set aside a day to pray for each member of your family individually. Would you do something right now that the Lord has definitely put upon my heart? I felt led by the Holy Spirit to ask you to send me a picture of each member of your close family along with their names. I will anoint each of them with oil on September 23rd and pray a special prayer for each of them as I hold their picture in my hand. I will anoint their picture with Holy oil and continue to pray exactly as the Holy Spirit leads and directs.

Postmarked September 30, 1985:

Something very bad is about to happen to this ministry; and this ministry is our life. We are facing a very, very serious situation. It must be stopped and a miracle simply must happen to stop it. And time is running out for us. God spoke to my heart that He has several people who need a miracle themselves. And they are going to get in on being a part of this miracle. When they get in on this miracle, God will send them the miracle they need. And you, Brother Straub, are one of these blessed ones.

Postmarked October 15, 1985:

In the last few weeks over thirty thousand dollars worth of checks have been returned by our bank (one for $10,000). This is money I was counting on, in fact, it's already been spent overseas to bring God's word to underground Christians. Another $30,000 in pledges simply have not come in. This is so serious! Our entire gospel invasion is at stake. My back is to the wall! At first I was devastated. I shut the door to my room, closed myself in and everything else out. Then right in the middle of my deep hurting I began to hear the Lord saying something to me. "Peter, I will double back everything the devil has stolen." God gave me guidance to write you Gerard, and tell you "God will double back what satan has stolen from you." I am enclosing a copy of some of the returned checks along with some special anointing oil. Will you anoint these checks with this special oil? Will you claim this miracle of restoration with me for the sake of millions who don't have God's word? When you answer this letter telling me what the devil has stolen from you or what you desire from God, obey the Lord as He speaks to your heart about the size of the seed you are to sow. Pray about this! The Lord may lead you to make good one of these returned checks!

Postmarked October 26, 1985:

I've read it in the Bible. I re-read it and I prayed about it and I've heard the voice of the Lord speaking to my heart concerning you and a need that you have in your life. The Lord is leading me to loan you my "Faith Handkerchief" in Jesus, to start a miracle in your life. Brother Straub, you must listen. I have been on my knees in prayer for you. I am burdened about you. Brother Straub, the Holy Spirit of God spoke to my heart and mind and gave me this message. He said, "My son, if you really want Gerard Straub to be blessed by God's power in a special, miraculous way, mail one of your blessed handkerchiefs (red for the blood of Jesus) like Paul did in Acts 19:11-12. For I did it for the apostle Paul and I love you just as much as I loved him."

Right now, I am asking you to get out your largest bill. God sees your sacrifice, and it will be a sacrifice. God sees. It may be a $100.00

bill or a $50.00 bill. It may be a check. But step out in faith and give it to the work of Jesus Christ as a seed. The Holy Spirit is in this letter and is speaking to you now while you read these words. Please obey the Holy Spirit. The greater your sacrifice, the greater your blessings. I am waiting on this powerful red "faith handkerchief" back from you.

Postmarked December 23, 1985:

I hope that you will accept this letter personally for yourself. God told me to write only certain ones like yourself who are very special to Him and His work as we enter 1986. Gerard, the Lord definitely impressed me to send this to you! Yes, it is for you! Will you accept it? Only five times in my ministry has God released me to say the things I am about to say to you! This is glorious! Get ready. Just before dawn, this word came to me and I know it is for you: "I am ready now, saith the Lord, to pour out upon thee the greatest blessings of thine entire life. The next 30 days will be the greatest days of thine entire life if you will move in obedience unto me. I have a golden prosperity blessing that is ready to be released unto thee, even this very week. Hast thou not needed new strength and also thy finances increased? Yea, right now the glory and power of my divine life is breathing upon thee. The very windows of heaven are ready to be opened unto thee as thou dost move in the realm of proving the Lord thy God. For I am breaking the bondage of the enemy, as my servant is praying for thee even at this very moment. Yea, saith the Lord, even as my servant is holding thee up in travail before me this special blessing is flowing from the golden throne of thy God. Don't hold back but turn loose and praise me now in thy giving and a door that has been closed a long, long time shall be opened. I am stirring the gifts of my spirit within thy innermost being and the new ministry that I promised unto thee shall blossom forth like a rose. I am touching you with my divine power, my angels are encamped around thee. I am also moving upon that loved one that is upon thy heart. I have my hand upon them and shall touch them. January shall be a month of golden prosperity blessing that shall begin a whole new move of my power in your life and home in 1986."

A beautiful divine golden light has filled my prayer room. Just now God spoke to me to place this GOLDEN MANTLE [fabric] inside this letter for you. I have been praying over it all night. You are to cut it in half and put half of it in your billfold for the next seven days for the Lord has something unexpected coming your way. Then if you will move in the power of God with me and take your very best offering unto the Lord and lay it on this golden mantle. I feel led to prove God and borrow a hundred dollars for reaching over ten thousand souls for Christ. I believe God will impress you to do the same. Pray sincerely about what He wants you to give and do. It may be a great sacrifice, I realize this, it is for us, but do the best for God at this time and on the 10th of January God told me to lay the golden mantle you return to me on my prayer altar. I will leave it on the altar until you write me and let me know your miracle has started in your body, financially and also for your loved one. Yes, a three-fold miracle is what I believe God is going to do for you. Don't you dare lay this golden mantle aside, but cut it in half and with your best offering just as I have instructed you now, and move with God. I will be going to Box 641 each day to look for your letter and offering.

This goes beyond trivialization of Christianity and approaches outright deception. The minister uses his expensive television pulpit to get inside your living room and he presents an emotionally charged picture of people finding instant cures and happiness. During his commercial messages, the faith-healer demonstrates the communication skills of a consummate actor—his sincerity about caring for the suffering souls in the Soviet Union is very convincing. In order for him to survive and continue to have access to living rooms across America, he needs massive amounts of money, and in order to get that money he requires a mailing list. The solution is simple: offer a free booklet that looks interesting. The viewer has only a 22-cent stamp to lose. It is interesting to note that before conversion, doubt is very helpful . . . just maybe this guy on TV is right, I'll write him and try to find out.

The computer-generated letters were cleverly disguised to look very personal. The paper the letters were printed on looked as if it came from a drawer of the minister's desk: simple three-hole loose leaf paper or inexpensive scraps of note paper. The simplicity and individuality of the paper conveyed the feeling that the minister personally typed the letter himself. The sprinkling of the viewer's name throughout the letter further fueled the impression that the busy man of God took time to write a personal letter.

He sets the tone by proclaiming that you are very special—to him and his buddy, God. You can't help but get the feeling that you are always on his mind—even when he is making coffee in the morning. One letter even claimed that he was writing to me after midnight. He constantly reminds the letter-reader how much time he spends in prayer for him . . . and that God hears his prayers. This "you are special and I think about you and really care about you" approach has great appeal to a lonely or disenfranchised person. Popoff is a friend they can count on.

I believe this approach, whether sincere or a con job, becomes deceptive, unethical, and highly immoral when the minister begins to quote God. God's direct words are in quotations or are capitalized, and are never preceded by any cautionary statements—like, "I feel or think that God may have given me a message for you." Popoff makes it crystal clear that he irrefutably hears God's voice and that God is distinctly directing him to write and is giving him specific promises to send the reader. His conversations with God reveal that God speaks Old English.

Almost every letter contains something that must be returned to the minister—handkerchiefs, socks, packets of spices and herbs from the Holy Land, cheap gold fabric. The point is simple. If you accept his message and obey God in returning the items he has loaned you, then it would be difficult to return the stuff without including some money for your thoughtful friend who cares so much for you. These materials—he calls them points of contact—help make the relationship between the minister and his viewers more tangible. You even exchange family pictures.

Every letter has the same tone: Victory is at hand—don't give up— God thinks you are special and He has something special for you. Send me money and God will reward you—the more you send, the bigger the reward.

The more letters Popoff sends out, the more positive responses he will receive. It's a matter of mathematics . . . not faith. I believe many people are tricked into responding. They think they are helping God— as if God needs their help—and they like the "personal" attention they receive . . . besides, what do they have to lose—maybe there is some truth to it all and mailing some money is an easy way to find out. It's almost like betting on a long shot at the race track.

If God really spoke to this minister, it seems highly unlikely that he would have him send material to a person who was writing a book on the abuses of the electronic church. Furthermore, Popoff and his computer-generated letters always expressed concern for my household members and indicated he was praying for my wife, children, and grandchildren. Well, I live alone! The letters must be automatically generated by a computer, because I never responded to any of his urgent appeals for money nor followed any of his instructions to return any items or fill out prayer request forms. Yet each letter sounded as though I was a special friend of the minister and a faithful supporter of his ministry. Only a computer could make such a ridiculous assumption.

I honestly believe that, in the name of God, Popoff is duping his naive yet well-intentioned viewers. Whether this mail fraud is intentional on his part or whether he really believes that God is talking to him is really unimportant. What is important is that he is selling false hope; what is distressing is that nobody seems to care.

The Committee for the Scientific Investigation of Religion sent a task force of eighteen volunteers armed with sophisticated electronic surveillance equipment to a number of Popoff crusades and uncovered the secret of how Popoff was able to call out the names of members of the audience, tell them about their afflictions, and ask them to come forward to receive a miraculous healing. While the audience and the home viewers are led to believe that the Holy Spirit is speaking to Popoff, in fact, his wife is feeding him the information via a radio signal picked up on a small audio receiver hidden in his ear. This is flat out deception and as a result this "Man of God," whose ministry has an average gross income of $550,000 a month, is endangering the health of the hopeful faithful who come to his crusades expecting a miracle and may leave thinking they have been healed when they have not and who, in some cases, may give up needed medicine.

Blind Faith

In an age when man's concept of God appears to be growing greater, grander, and kinder, and when instances of ecumenical brotherhood and sharing are becoming more commonplace, the kind of spirituality in which a personal God speaks directly to maverick ministers seems oddly out of place.

Good things are happening today. People are learning to love God and not just to fear him. Old creeds that once filled a need in the religious evolution of mankind are being questioned and frequently dropped. But not without pain. The governing General Synod of the Church of England brings together bishops, priests, and laymen three times a year to legislate church business, and the February 1985 gathering turned into a battle over the nature of belief and the bishop's responsibility as guardian of church doctrine. The cause of distress was a liberal theologian who a few months earlier was consecrated as a bishop and then angered many church members by publicly and repeatedly questioning whether the virgin birth, the resurrection of Jesus Christ, and certain miracles described in the Bible had to be interpreted literally. While the Anglican Church prides itself on a tolerant attitude toward a wide range of views and religious practices, the feeling was that this bishop had gone too far. Upon their consecration, bishops solemnly agree to "teach and uphold sound and wholesome doctrine, and to banish and drive away all erroneous and strange opinions." The theological heavyweights assembled at the Synod debated what constitutes soundness and error.

At CBN the subject of the Virgin Mary stirred conflicting feelings. For most staffers, she was an almost forgotten biblical figure, respected but not held in as high esteem as by the Catholic church; yet many considered her to be the Mother of God and, consequently, worthy of prayer and praise. But nobody doubted the virgin birth. Yet a very strong case for the denial of the virgin birth of Jesus (based on biblical evidence) can be built. The story of divine conception—a miraculous act of God whereby a child is conceived of a woman without a human father—is found among the traditions, legends, and beliefs of many pagan peoples, both before and after the birth of Christ. Nearly all of the Eastern religions, in existence long before Jesus, contain tales about prophets being born of a virgin. Evidence exists to support the notion that early Christianity did not claim or teach that Jesus was born of a virgin but that this belief was injected into the teachings about one hundred years into the Christian era when the infant religion spread to pagan nations, and the story was born out of evangelistic zeal.

The New Testament barely mentions the idea. Only two Gospels—Luke and Matthew—tell of the virgin birth. Paul was utterly silent on the subject, which is out of character for him. The Gospel according to Matthew was more than likely not written by the apostle—at least not in its present canonical form—but by one or more of his disciples, who wrote the text in Greek during the latter part of the first century, and it was an enlargement and elaboration of the Aramaic writings entitled "Sayings of Jesus," which is thought to have been written by Matthew. The disciples of Matthew may have "fit" in the legend of the virgin birth that was being spread by converted pagans.

The idea of a virgin birth was obnoxious to the Jews because it downgraded the notion of family, which they held in high regard. Many scholars consider it remarkable that the virgin-birth account should be included in the Gospel of Luke, because Luke was an ardent student of Paul, and Paul seems never to have heard of the idea. If he had, he certainly would have had something to say about such a wonderful event. Luke was not a Jew and was converted to Christianity after the death of Jesus. His Gospel was written after the death of Paul for the benefit and teaching of an official living in Antioch. It appears from textual and form criticism of the writing that the virgin-birth legend was inserted into the Gospel narrative *after* it was written by Luke, who, by the way, was a very obscure figure in early Christianity; very little is known about him.

Is the virgin birth historically accurate or a myth turned into a fact? In reality it does not matter; in fact many of the great Christian writers of the first four centuries—such as Irenaeus, Clement of Alexandria, Origen, Athanasius, Cyril, Basil, and Gregory of Nazianzen—seemed to think that it was not a very important issue, and they each explained it in slightly different ways. Mary's biological virginity was not an issue; of far greater importance was her virginal consciousness. Mary is the mother of Jesus and, as the Eastern Christian churches call her, the Theotokos—Birthgiver of God. George Maloney writes in his book, *Mary the Womb of God:*

> The virginial womb of Mary, St. Augustine asks, is it not Mother of the Church? Grace mediated through Mary or the Church is always participation in the incarnational, free-will act of Mary which is both maternal and spousal. Mary is the perfect type of regenerated humanity, the Church, in attaining its supreme fruit, through the feminine, maternal act of receiving Divine Life through the Holy Spirit. Mary, in deep contemplative prayer, long before she received physically the Word as enfleshed in her womb, had received Him in her consciousness and in the deepest recesses of her unconscious. She was able to be God's mother because she had allowed in utter active receptivity that God's Word would dominate completely in every facet of her being. Because Mary was totally woman, in her virginal faith and complete surrender to the Holy Spirit working within her from the first moment of her existence, she is the prototype of what every Christian must become. The womb of Mary is a dynamic archetypal symbol drawn from the Greek fathers to express to us beyond a clear and distinct idea, even into the farthest reaches of our unconscious, the primeval urge that God has implanted into all of us when He fashioned us according to His image and likeness. Deep within us is an unquenchable hunger to surround, enfold, possess, hold, embrace, as a mother does her child in her womb, God's very own life-giving Word. From that inner possession of God's life, we give birth to Jesus Christ in the events of our daily lives. Virginally by total surrender in faith, hope and love, we conceive by the Holy Spirit and then maternally we give birth to God's word and give that Word to others by our love and humble service shown to them.

Again, it really does not matter whether the virgin birth of Jesus is fact or fiction; however, what it symbolizes does matter. Thomas Merton wrote: "The true symbol does not merely point to something else. It contains in itself the structure which awakens our consciousness to a new awareness of the inner meaning of life and of reality itself. A true symbol takes us to the center of the circle, not to another point on the circumference. It is by symbolism that man enters affectively and consciously into contact with his own deepest self, with other men, and with God."

Mary became an important part of my faith experience after I left CBN. Before that could happen, however, I encountered the suffering of doubt, disbelief, confusion, rejection, questioning, and searching before returning her to the same place of honor that she held in my childhood—only now with adult insights and faith.

There are no shortcuts in seeking the truth. It is an arduous task that few want to undertake. The Episcopal bishop was a troublemaker because he threatened people's childlike beliefs and caused them the painful problem of reflecting and then reaffirming or denying the truths they held. For many people a Jesus conceived and born of human parents without the direct intervention of God somehow seems less divine or at least less special; and for Mary to have conceived a child in her womb without the aid of sex with her husband makes her more pure, as if sex were dirty or at least not holy. It is difficult to struggle with such possibilities and far easier to blindly accept the childish myths we were taught in our youth. The public forum might be the wrong place for personal reflections—especially for the shepherd of the flock. Spiritual leaders are supposed to give life to those in their spiritual charge; many no longer can.

According to the mythology expert Joseph Campbell, "In their intimate role of giving spiritual advice, the clergy have now been overtaken by the scientific psychiatrists—and indeed to such a degree that many clergymen are themselves turning to psychologists to be taught how best to serve their pastoral function. The magic of their own traditional symbols works no longer to heal but only confuse."

Confusion is the child of today's spiritual movement from the West to the East. In the Eastern religions God is sought beyond all thought and feeling and is not "out there" but within—and when a person from the West begins to see the symbols he has valued point to a God that can be forgiving or damning, that chooses one select group of people over all others and listens attentively to those who pray or annihilates those who do not, then suddenly these very human traits of God, who is a mystery beyond thought, makes the seeker's Western religion seem very childish: that realization is very painful. He or she has nothing to hold on to, and confusion exists everywhere; its symbols are shattered, and life loses its structure.

The problem was not the Anglican bishop's raising some difficult questions but rather his reciting a creed in his cathedral affirming the virgin birth and then saying on television or during lectures that he really believes something else. The common man in the pew finds that dichotomy difficult and confusing.

Changes in belief don't necessarily mean that people are turning away from God but in fact can indicate movement toward God. These changes in belief frequently cause bitterness. As we outgrow old conceptions or our childhood faith matures into a more adult manifestation, we are tempted to become impatient with—or even scornful of—those who don't seem to change. Those who are stagnant spiritually often display disdain for those who seek new meaning or understanding. Those who reach out for change and those who are happy with their beliefs frequently fail to recognize that members of the other camp are in the best place for them at the time being. There are many people today, especially in non-Christian, Eastern faiths, who are disturbed by the idea of a "personal" God because for them God is devoid of personality; he goes beyond personality, not contrary to it. Which is better or more truthful—a personal God or impersonal God—is immaterial; the answer can be different and correct for each individual. No matter which way you go, there is no room for spiritual superiority. God isn't finished with anyone, and each of us has room to grow—each of us has a long way to go in order to become more God-like. Until then confusion and doubt are natural. The fundamentalist wants to eliminate all confusion and doubt; however, those conditions are healthy and helpful because they lead a person to genuine examination of their religious beliefs. Blind faith is folly.

After the Bite

For the fundamentalist Christian, the road to gaining the ability to choose good over evil is paved with the firm belief that mankind can respond only to the promise of a reward or the threat of punishment. The unsaved are like puppies who need to be paper-trained. Ignored is the fact that man is an ethical animal. Man does not reach his full potential for ethical judgment through a desire for a reward or a fear of punishment. According to Dr. Rollo May, in *Man's Search for Himself*, man's capacity for ethical judgment:

> is based upon his consciousness of himself. Ethical awareness is gained only at the price of inner conflict and anxiety. This conflict is portrayed in that fascinating myth of the first man, the Biblical story of Adam. This ancient Babylonian tale, rewritten and carried over into the Old Testament about 850 B.C., pictures how ethical insight and self-awareness are born at the same time. Like the story of Prometheus and other myths, this tale of Adam speaks a classic truth to generation after gen-

eration of people not because it refers to a particular historical event, but because it portrays some deep inward experience shared by all men.

Life for Adam and Eve in the Garden was delightful. They had everything they needed and didn't have to work to meet those needs. There was no anxiety and no guilt. Theirs was a life without conflict. This dreamlike state could only be threatened by breaking God's command not to eat of the tree of knowledge of good and evil because if they did they would become like God.

They ate the fruit and, according to Dr. May, "the first evidence of their knowing good and evil was in their experiencing anxiety and guilt. They were 'aware of their nakedness,' and when at noon God walked through the garden for his daily airing, as the author says in his child-like and charming style, Adam and Eve hid from his sight among the trees." God was mad as hell at his human creations, so he created a stiff penalty: Eve craved sex with Adam, and Adam had to work. Dr. May believes that the Garden of Eden represents innocence—a state where neither shame nor guilt exists. Before their choice to bite the apple, Adam and Eve symbolized a human being's period of infancy— a time when all our needs are met by our parents. Life for Adam and Eve after the bite represents the sudden emergence of self-awareness that each of us experiences by our third birthday.

Dr. May writes:

This eating of the tree of knowledge and the learning of right and wrong represent the birth of the psychological and spiritual person. But what is amazing is that all this is pictured as happening against God's will and commandments. Are we to believe that this God did not wish man to have knowledge and ethical sensitivity—this God who, we are told just the chapter before in the book of Genesis, created man in his own image, which, if it means anything at all, means likeness to God in respects of freedom, creativity and ethical choice? Are we to suppose that God wished to keep man in the state of innocence and psychological and ethical blindness? It is understandable that primitive story-tellers would be unable to distinguish between constructive self-consciousness and rebellion, considering the fact that many people even today find it very hard to make that distinction. The Greek myth closest to the story of Adam is that of Prometheus who stole fire from the gods and gave it to human beings for their warmth and productivity. The enraged Zeus, noting one night from a glow on earth that the mortals had fire, seized Prometheus, bore him off to Caucasus, and chained him to a mountain peak. The torture devised by Zeus' skillful imagination was to have a vulture feast by day on Prometheus' liver, and then, when the liver had grown back during the night, the vulture would tear at it again the next day, thus ensuring perpetual torment for the hapless Prometheus. So far as punishment goes, Zeus had the edge over Yahweh in cruelty. For the Greek god, smoldering in anger that man should now have fire, crammed all the diseases, sorrows and vices into a box in the form of mothlike creatures, and had Mercury take the box to the earthly paradise (very much like the Garden of Eden) in which Pandora and Epimetheus lived in untroubled happiness. When the curious woman opened it, out flew the creatures, and mankind was visited with these never-ending afflictions. These demonic elements in the gods' dealing with man certainly do not represent a pretty picture. As the Adam story is the myth of self-consciousness, Prometheus is the symbol of crea- tivity—the bringing of new ways of life to mankind. Prometheus' torture represents the inner conflict which comes with creativity—symbolizes the anxiety and guilt to which the man who dares to bring mankind new forms of life is subject. But again, as in the Adam myth, Zeus is jealous of man's upward strivings and vindictive in punishment. To be sure, there is rebellion against the gods in both the actions of both Adam and Prometheus. This is an angle from which the myths as they stand make sense. For the Greeks and Hebrews knew that when a man tries to leap over his human limitations, when he commits the sin of overreaching himself or arrogates to himself universal power or holds that his limited knowledge is the final truth, then he becomes dangerous. The myths are sound in their warnings against false pride. But the rebellion these myths portray is clearly good and constructive at the same time; and hence they cannot be dismissed merely as pictures of man's struggle against his finiteness and pride. They portray the psycho- logical truth that the child's "opening his eyes," and gaining self-aware- ness, always involves potential conflict with those in power. In these myths there speaks the age-old conflict between entrenched authority, as represented by jealous gods, and the upsurging of new life and creativity. The emergence of new vitality always to some extent breaks customs and beliefs, and is thus threatening and anxiety-provoking to those in power as well as to the growing person himself.

The authoritarian nature of fundamentalist Christianity wars a- gainst new ethical insights. For them, to be good means to obey the laws of God.

Fast-Food God

The 1970s and 1980s have focused much attention on relationship. Encounter groups have explored better ways for husband and wife, parents and children, employers and employees, live-in couples and singles to relate better to each other. A close, strong, and loving rela- tionship with a personal savior seems very much in tune with the times. We are no longer willing to settle for a poor relationship. Besides a longing for the ideal relationship, our society wants things now. Buy now, pay later. We are all in a hurry.

The born-again experience is today's religious response to the instant gratification syndrome of a fast-paced society. It's a spiritual quick fix; and that is a judgment not rendered out of spiritual elitism but out of experience. Throughout history, the road to God has taken a lifetime to travel. In some religions, the trip takes many lifetimes. But the space-age seeker can find God in a twinkling of an eye. For the Hebrews of the Old Testament, God often shrouded himself in a cloud. They had so much reverence for God, they wouldn't use his name in ordinary conversation. *Shekinah* is a Hebrew word that means "cloud," and they frequently used the word as a substitute name for God.

Today, the born-again believers see God clearly. There is no cloud, no doubt. They have a personal relationship with God and are assured salvation. Reverence is replaced with familiarity in daily conversation. "God told me to call you" or "God is leading me in a new direction" are the types of statements frequently heard from today's chosen believers.

Pat Robertson once received in the mail a book entitled *Friendship with Jesus*, and the inside of the jacket cover contained this handwritten inscription:

Dear Pat,

This book has been sent to you at the request of Our Lord.

His Obedient Sender,
Joyce F.

The book was coauthored by a Catholic priest, and more than likely the woman who mailed it was a Catholic who wanted Pat to see that a Catholic priest had been saved. Pat never read the book. The woman was responding to her own desire for Pat to read a book she enjoyed and not to God's need for Pat to read material contained in the book.

One day Pat Robertson related "on the air" how God had told him that his horse was going to be the mother of champions. I was shocked by Pat's sharing this personal divine revelation because it sounded like pure projection of wishful thinking. Horses are Pat's main pleasure in life, and for God to reward him with a championship horse would undoubtedly be a dream come true. One of the biggest dangers of the pentecostal movement is that people begin to confuse their personal thoughts, desires, and emotions with the inspiration of the Holy Spirit.

Chosen One?

I used to speak about God with the same degree of familiarity; however it bothered me a bit. If one is discussing a spiritual point with another believer who indicates that God has revealed something new to him or her, then it becomes hard to debate the point. After all, God has the last word, especially if that word is spoken to Pat or a company vice president.

People at CBN believed I was anointed by God to do my job and that he had chosen me to write and produce programs that would spread his word and change society by bringing this country back to biblical principles. There was even a prophecy spoken along those lines during an actual "700 Club" program. I never became comfortable with the idea that God specifically chose me to perform a particular function within CBN's role in his overall scheme of salvation. My discomfort did not grow out of humility but more from a downright sense of improbability. The fact is that I did some of my best creative and productive work during a period when I was living the life of a double agent—adulterer and video crusader for Christ.

The "Execution"

The assorted snapshots of the troops and the rules that govern CBN begin to form a larger picture of the spirituality of the people behind the preacher. Before describing how I found myself in that picture, let's go back to the day I got to bear the fruit of my lie to Pat Robertson.

On September 12, 1980, as I sat quietly at my desk engaged in a little late afternoon daydreaming, I was totally unaware that in another part of the cross-shaped building a group of crusaders was coming together in order to expedite their God-ordained plan to terminate me. This seemingly uneventful, yet peaceful, moment would soon be replaced by a moment of spiritual violence that would alter the course of my life.

My afternoon daydream was triggered by the walls of my office. They were cluttered with memorabilia from my two and a half years at CBN. I loved pinning stuff up on the walls. The look of my office was distinctly out of character compared with all the other offices in the building. I often took refuge in the memories or ideas pinned on the wall, but today's flight into fantasy was shattered by the annoying intercom buzz from my secretary. She informed me that the vice-president of personnel wanted to see me in his office right away.

My heart began to thump erratically. This man came across as a cold-hearted, tough-minded, hard-nosed general. Fun he was not, nor was he a member of my fan club, and in fact I think my flamboyant style deeply annoyed him. He once tried to build a case for my dismissal that was based on faulty and circumstantial evidence by claiming that, on a business trip to Los Angeles, I was guilty of lewd and licentious behavior, smoking and drinking. The truth was far less interesting than the fictional accusations.

Miss X-Rated

The lewd and licentious behavior consisted of the following: During a casting session for the Christian soap opera that I had created, I spent the day auditioning scores of actors and actresses who were fervent Christians but lousy thespians. As one bland, pious performer after another droned on before me, I questioned the wisdom of the directive which clearly stated that I could cast only born-again Christians.

Near the end of the dreary day, a buxom blonde strutted into the basement of the Presbyterian church where we were conducting the auditions. This vivacious bundle of bouncing sexuality looked more like a hooker than a holy actress. God only knows why this girl was there or what she thought she was trying out for. She handed me her resume, along with a series of photos. One photo revealed her ample charms through a sexy, sheer negligee. I couldn't believe that I had been handed an "X-rated" picture. Sitting next to me was my friend from CBS who was helping me with the auditions, although he did not work for CBN and was not a born-again Christian. I slyly slipped him the picture and he practically burst out in laughter. When "Miss Hot Stuff" left, we proceeded to laugh and joke about the entire episode. The laughter felt good. However, one of my Christian assistants failed to see the humor in the situation and was appalled by my jesting comment that "I wouldn't mind laying hands on that number."

It's Not What It Looks Like

As for the smoking accusation, it was founded on circumstantial evidence. Later that night, during a staff meeting in my hotel room, the same serious assistant spotted a cigar in my briefcase. For him this indicated that I smoked and thereby clearly violated the no-smoking mandate that is strictly enforced at CBN. I was not a smoker at the time. During a luncheon the previous day with an NBC executive, he tossed a cigar into my opened briefcase after I declined his offer to join him in a post-meal puff.

Regarding the drinking charge, I was guilty. The next night, while waiting for a table in a crowded Mexican restaurant, my Christian assistant saw me sitting at the bar. I was with my friend from CBS, and we were also waiting for a table. Neither of us are drinkers, but we elected to sit at the bar and nurse a beer rather than stand during the half-hour wait for a table, but we weren't exactly leading anyone astray with un-Christian behavior.

All these un-Christian activities were dutifully noted by my assistant-turned-informant, and he reported them to the vice-president. He called me into his office for the express purpose of firing me. I convinced him that appearances don't always reflect the truth; and, after he delivered a lengthy sermon and strict warning, he dropped the charges. My assistant seemed surprised to see me emerge from the office still employed; he had envisioned a promotion following my dismissal, and now he had to explain to me how he felt led by the Lord to share what he saw in Los Angeles with the vice-president.

This Way Out

Now, almost two years later, as I once again entered the vice-president's well-appointed office, I scanned the room and saw that he had with him the director of operations, the director of programming, and the executive producer of "The 700 Club." I knew that this gathering meant trouble. This group of four men were my jury and judge. Within minutes I was convicted of adultery and lying. My sentence was to clear out my desk immediately and vacate the premises. This sunny afternoon had suddenly turned into the bleakest day of my life.

Actually, "bleakest day" is a worried understatement. I was devastated. In an emotional appeal before leaving the office, I told the men that I did not blame them for that they were doing; I also said that I understood the reason for letting me go. Still, I pleaded with them for mercy, asking them to consider my spiritual well-being and any possible future my marriage might have. I needed to be among a group of supportive Christians for spiritual survival. I asked them to take back my title and power but allow me to work out my problems from within CBN. I wondered aloud how they could forgive me my adulterous affair and accept my repentance as being sincere and could still fire me because the lie to Pat Robertson indicated that I could not be trusted. Was not that lie understandable?

The vice-president asked me if I was still in contact with the woman. I told him no—that I had not seen her since two weeks before my "confession" to Pat and that I had absolutely no plans of seeing her again—whether they fired me or not. He said they could not believe that; they had tapped my office phone and they knew that we had spoken. Even though I was angered at the thought of them spying on me, I nonetheless explained that our relationship was not based on some physical desire, but that I really loved her. I carefully described how I now realized Satan had tricked me into this notion of love, but that nonetheless I still cared about the woman, who, due to her termination, was suffering. Yes, I'd spoken to her on the phone but only to console her and help her understand all that had happened. No one else seemed to care anymore about this once highly regarded woman.

I really believed in my heart—then and now—that my involvement with a married woman while I was still married was wrong, although today I don't blame my actions on the Devil. I did not want to leave CBN, yet I could see through my tears that these men were unmoved by my appeal for clemency. I stood up, looked each of them in the eye and told them that I loved them. I gave each one a hug, and then I turned and walked out of the office.

And my search for God began—again.

Incompleted Pass Play

Tapping my office phone and following me weren't the only methods used to gain evidence for my dismissal. One member of my staff was an extremely attractive young woman who had the kind of figure that could make male heads turn when she passed them in the hall. Because she was my lover's friend, she was one of the few people who knew of our affair. She even thought it was wonderful and very romantic.

One day the vice-president of personnel called her into his office and bluntly inquired if I had ever tried to seduce her. He must have assumed that I would have made a pass at such a lovely lady. She told him, much to his disappointment I'm sure, that not only had I not made a play for her affections but that I was a perfect gentleman with all the female staff.

This vice-president was a great judge of character. What he didn't know was that this married woman was having a hot affair with a staff member—and, worse than that, when she learned that I had terminated my relationship with her friend, she knocked on the door of my apartment one evening claiming that she was lonely and wanted to watch television with me. Well, I didn't get to watch much television because it didn't take her long to slip out of her clothes and into my arms. She literally attacked me. We did not make love; in fact I insisted that she leave.

It is really funny to think that the dirty-minded executive just assumed that I would try to lead this "pious" young woman into sin when in reality she offered herself to almost every guy in the place. Today, she is divorced, remarried, and miraculously still working at CBN, doing her part in saving sinners.

Starting Over

I was truly alone for the first time in my life—no wife, no family, no job, no home. I sat, stunned, in my small, rented, furnished room in a dreary, slum section of Norfolk. After many weeks, I went to the unemployment office, for the area offered no hope for a job, and I was broke. The woman who reviewed my case at the unemployment office could not believe that I was fired for having an affair. She suggested that I sue them. I understood why they thought they had to fire me, and I had no stomach for suing them, so I sat. After weeks of bathing in a sea of guilt and seeing myself as very sinful, I got on a plane and headed for Tinsel Town—Hollywood, California—to live among the heathens.

Heading west in order to escape my role as an evil outcast and to try to start a new life for myself was not easy. Deeply torn, I thought of myself as a failure, yet not a failure either. On the one hand, because I could not make my marriage work in the past and no longer had the desire to make it work in the future, I saw heading for the coast as running away from the problem and turning my back on God—after all, I had been brainwashed into thinking that a marriage could not be dissolved and that it was God's will that I must try to make it work. On the other hand, I believed that God really knew the inner secrets of my heart and ultimately did not concern himself with my staying or going. But what if I were wrong and they were right? Did it follow that Hell was the ultimate destination, no matter where this damn plane was headed?

As I sat high above the clouds, flying into a very uncertain future, I kept replaying in my mind the words of the three men who joined with the vice-president to sit in judgment of me, words spoken before and during the brief meeting. I had had many conversations with these three men prior to that dreadful day, and each had offered me guidance and insight on Christian marriage. Each was convinced that I was wrong for not living with my wife. The ironic part is that within four years, two of those three men would be divorced and gone from CBN.

One of those two gentlemen was not only the most responsible for my ousting but also had the greatest influence on me. He had hired me, and for the longest time I truly admired him. He was a large and forceful man. Every fiber of his existence seemed dedicated to serving God. "Determination" was his middle name. He gave 100 percent of himself to everything he did. He pushed CBN into far greater technical growth than they needed, because for him God deserved and got nothing but the best. His knowledge of television operations was vast. His technical skills could easily have landed him a job at any network. His diligent study and research made him an expert on everything from satellites to lighting equipment. He designed and gave management and leadership courses based on material he obtained from a wide range of scholarly books, as well as the Bible. These lengthy Christian leadership seminars sprinkled standard management techniques with Scripture quotes. He taught his troops God's idea of leadership, God's way of resolving problems, and the traits of godly leadership. He was an overwhelming force in the growth of CBN. He left no stone unturned in his efforts to make CBN as technically efficient and effective as any network. I thought I could learn a lot, both professionally and spiritually, from this dynamic man.

You Think You Got Problems

As we became friends, I confided to him some of my marital problems, both past and present. After listening to my tale of woe, he told me about his disaster of a marriage. His words formed a classic "you can't top this" tale. Before being saved and joining CBN, he had worked at a modeling agency, which provided not only his livelihood but also lots of opportunities to indulge his lust for women. His marriage before being saved was a shambles; after becoming saved, it was a sham. His wife had some severe psychological problems. She was physically repulsive. Not only was she overweight but also poorly groomed and sloppily dressed—in all, a disheveled wreck. She frequently flew into fits of anger and rage. They had not slept together for years. She constantly tried to embarrass him in public and was very open about her disdain for him. She would often call and interrupt him at work in order to nag him about some insignificant thing. His story brought tears to my eyes. His home life was beyond being miserable; it was a constant state of torture.

Compared to him, my marriage was paradise, and my problems were trivial. Why did he tolerate such a deplorable situation? God told him to. His extramarital affairs prior to salvation must have contributed to his wife's jealousy and lack of trust in him, and despite his new-found Christianity and pious behavior she seemed obsessed with making him suffer. He was determined to turn the situation around, and he was convinced that by the grace of God his home would be healed, no matter how long it took. He prayed frequently and intensely. No matter what she threw at him, he tried only to love her in return. His tolerance and patience were without limits, and so was his demand for holy perfection within himself and others. It was a noble effort, and to me he seemed very courageous—and even saintly.

I started to tell him about my problems at home because I wanted to know what the official reaction would be if I got a divorce. His response was that I hadn't even begun to work hard enough at saving the marriage and therefore was not in a position to think about ending it. He led me to dismiss as meaningless the deep psychological problem that existed from the first day of my marriage and was a major factor in its failure; however, ignoring the problem did not solve the problem. He gave me the strength, encouragement, and inspiration to try to work out my domestic plight. Forgetting that he was my boss and that I had better try to resolve those problems, I truly admired his determination to love and serve God. I still had a very immature understanding of God and was overpowered by his apparent spiritual maturity. It was quite a while before I began to consider his spirituality to be sick.

Like most fundamentalists, his zeal for the Lord made him unbending; and that rigidity robbed him of his vitality and freedom and made changing his likes, dislikes, and opinions virtually impossible. He was not content to be just intolerant of sin where he found it among his troops; he had to also search for it. He began to suspect that my determination to deal with the problems of my marriage had begun to wane. I think he was tormented by the demands of his own lust, so he must have figured that I was also. He looked for an opportunity to catch me.

It was funny how he was blinded to the fact that one of his favorite employees, a married man and a member of the crew of "The 700 Club," was having an affair with a married secretary and was also fond of telling dirty jokes and trying to fondle the young women who were under his authority. People were too timid to point out his indiscretions even though they were well-documented and legendary, perhaps because Pat Robertson was totally charmed by his country-style, down-home humor. I was the big fish the executive wanted to catch, and on May 5, 1980, he thought he had his chance.

Me and My Shadow

Late that afternoon I received a phone call from Pat Robertson. Pat told me that the next morning he was going to be a guest on the "Today Show" in New York. Apologizing for informing me so late, he asked if I would fly to New York that night with him. I would never turn down a trip to New York. I think the last-minute request grew out of Pat's nervousness, because all that week Tom Brokaw had been doing a series of reports on the electronic church, and most of the evangelists didn't fare too well under Brokaw's tough questioning. Pat wanted some moral support.

Much to my surprise, on the same flight were Pat's wife and the head-hunting executive. They were going to New York to meet with an interior designer to review his plans for remodeling our linguistics studio used for dubbing "The 700 Club" into Spanish and Portuguese for distribution to South America. The three of them were staying at a swanky midtown hotel, but because of my last-minute inclusion on this trip, there was no room at the inn for me, and I had to stay at a nearby stable of a hotel. As they dropped me off at my hotel, Pat suggested I register and then join them for dinner. I told him that sounded fine; however, by the time I got to the restaurant, I decided I'd rather spend my one night in the Big Apple with some friends at CBS.

One of my good friends was working the night shift, and I told him I would drop in for a visit. When I met Pat, I asked him if he would mind my skipping dinner because I wanted to run over to CBS. He had no problems with that, and we made plans to meet at NBC in the morning.

I zipped out the door of the restaurant; not spotting a cab, I elected to walk across town to CBS. I did not notice my executive-friend-turned-spy following me, convinced I was up to no good. I walked up 44th Street, and when I reached 8th Avenue, instead of walking north toward CBS, I turned south and proceeded in the direction of 42nd Street. Eighth Avenue between 42nd Street and 44th Street is one of the most notorious red-light districts in the city. Dope pushers, pimps, prostitutes, massage parlors, topless bars, peep-show joints, and theaters that feature live sex, bondage films, and gay flicks, are the star attractions along this two-block stretch. Porn is king in this rotten part of the Big Apple.

Why was I walking right into the middle of all this trash? Because there is one lonely break in the decadence. A small, unmarked storefront that is the home of Covenant House and Under 21. Run by a Franciscan priest, it is a refuge for the throwaway kids who litter the streets. It is a place that cares for the homeless teenage hookers and junkies. I worked there as a volunteer before joining CBN, and I thought I'd stop in for a quick look and see if I spotted anyone I knew. My double-agent shadow had lost me in the crowd and did not notice where I disappeared and just assumed that I ducked into a massage parlor or topless bar. He must have gloated in his now-confirmed suspicions.

I stayed at Under 21 a few minutes and then walked north along 8th Avenue to 57th Street and CBS. The friend I visited was the ranking executive on the night shift. I called him from the lobby and asked him to get me past the guard station. Instead of calling the guard to clear me, he just walked down the hall and waved me past the guard, who simply nodded his approval and never asked me to sign the guest book. My CBS buddy had to work until midnight, and we sat in the control room and talked and laughed our way through his shift. He then drove me to the hotel, because I had to be up early in the morning, and he made the long drive home to Connecticut. The next day the CBN executive managed to have that guest sign-in book from the CBS lobby checked by a lighting director friend of his who just happened to work at CBS. It was then discovered that my name was not on the list of visitors, so it was assumed I never went to CBS. Case closed.

Thou Shalt Steal

It infuriated this overzealous executive that Pat liked me so much, and the events of Pat's appearance on the "Today Show" fueled his contempt for me. I got to NBC about 5:00 A.M.—a full hour before Pat was due to arrive. I just wandered around the studio observing the frantic efforts of the staff and crew to get ready for the 7:00 A.M. start of the show. Around 6:15 A.M. the technical crew was given a five-minute break. I walked into the empty control room, and my eyes zoomed to some papers on the production team's table. Right before me was the format sheet that gave a detailed rundown of the show along with all the questions Brokaw was going to ask Robertson. My heart pounded with anticipation. With these questions in hand, Pat could breeze through the interview—there would be no surprises.

Should I scoop up the papers before anyone could spot me? Go for it, was my reaction, and I quickly stuffed the papers in my jacket pocket and swiftly scurried away from the scene of the crime. I was proud as the NBC peacock as I strutted up and down the corridor by the elevator in anticipation of sharing the stolen questions with Pat. At 7:00 A.M. he walked off the elevator. In contrast to his solemn and apprehensive look, I was beaming from ear to ear. "What are you so happy about? Don't you realize I'm about to walk through the valley of death?" was his gloomy greeting.

"No sweat, Boss. You're going to skip through the valley and come out triumphant," was my upbeat response. He wanted to know why I was so confident, and I smugly patted my breast pocket which contained the questions.

"What are you doing?" he snapped.

I whispered, "You have nothing to worry about. I managed to procure some papers that contain all the questions Brokaw is going to ask you." His face lit up as brightly as the Rockefeller Center Christmas tree. We hurriedly stepped into an empty room provided for the show's guests. Huddled in the corner, we read each of the questions, and he wrote notes on how best to answer them. You could see his confidence grow. He knew he had nothing to fear because he would be well-prepared, and his answers wouldn't provide any good opportunities for ad-libbed follow-up questions from Brokaw.

Panic hit when one of the producers burst into the room to greet him. We stuffed the papers under the chair. We both thought we were caught, but our clumsy cover-up attempt succeeded. During the actual on-air interview, I managed to slip past the stage manager and stood next to the camera into which Pat looked and spoke. He delivered his well-thought-out answers to my smiling and supportive face. He was a hit! We had walked through the valley of death! He was so thrilled that afterward he treated me to a hearty and expensive breakfast.

During the next day's prayer meeting at CBN, he proudly told the assembled staff how brother Gerry boldly invaded the enemy camp and clipped the questions. He was still excited. No one questioned the ethics or morality of my actions—after all, I did steal the papers. I guess all is fair in religion, as well as in love and war.

But the spying executive had plenty of questions and confronted me about my immoral and sexual misbehavior during the trip. Once again, I had to prove that circumstantial evidence had made me look guilty. He couldn't prove that I went into a massage parlor; and, even after his investigation of my version of the night proved factual, he never really believed me. He wasn't finished, and he never gave up trying to catch me in some evil slip-up. During my final months, I was followed almost everywhere I went by staff members he appointed to tail me. His spirituality was a form of Big Brother religion that fostered mistrust and encouraged entrapment. He could not trust that a person's dignity, worth, and sense of personal responsibility could lead them to do the right thing and to be obedient to the laws of God. His position of leadership did not guarantee freedom for those under his authority, but he thought it gave him the right to control his subjects and provide them with spiritual protection. He had to make sure God's will was fulfilled.

Today that man is not only divorced, but also remarried. Apparently, God changed his will for him. He is still working in Christian television, mostly in Georgia and Texas. I heard from a good source that his income for helping several ministries spread the gospel is over one hundred thousand dollars per year. For a while he helped Jimmy Swaggart, the high priest of honky-tonk heaven, wage his holy war against Jews. On his television show, Swaggart showed some gruesome pictures of Nazi death camps and implied that the Holocaust was a consequence of Jewish nonbelief in Christ. Other enemies of the holy war waged by Swaggart and the former CBN executive were Catholics, liberals, feminists, homosexuals, and secular humanists. God's will may change, but some opinions never will—because they are held hostage by an inflexibility that cannot concede that another valid point of view can exist.

Do As I Say

The other member of my jury to bite the divorce bullet was never consumed with catching me break any laws. He just constantly preached to me about the sanctity of marriage. For a leader, he seemed a very insecure person, threatened by the creativity of those who worked for him. He liked tagging his name to his subordinates' ideas, and, indeed, the basis for his position as a division head was his spiritual maturity, not his professional and creative ability. Rather than acknowledge my contributions to the programming, he chose instead to focus on my apparent failure at marriage.

His seemingly picture-perfect marriage and his persistent preaching on the Christian perspective on matrimony served to make him feel superior to his subjects. He saw himself as a wise and holy leader. The pitiful part was that he was divorced prior to being "saved" and joining CBN, and while working there he married a very nice, bright young woman from one of the fundamentalist churches where he was an ordained deacon. It was easy for him to preach about the indissolvability of marriage. He had already made his mistake and now had a second chance with a wonderful woman who shared his faith conviction and let him be king of his castle. However, even after having two children, they were divorced. Once again, God must have changed his mind. While he no longer works at CBN, the man still toils in the land of Christian television that preaches a message he could not follow.

I wonder how these two men reconcile their former attitudes with their current situations? I wonder if they see the folly of their former judgmental beliefs? I wonder how they can still work in Christian television? I wonder if they will ever come to see that the "demon" they were driving out of CBN the day they helped fire me was a projection of themselves.

God's Secret Plan

During the writing of this book, I moved from California to New York, and in the process of packing and unpacking, I found an audio cassette. Taped onto the cassette case was a white label displaying the letters *G.S.P.* in my handwriting. I sat for a few minutes searching my mind for the meaning of those letters, but I could not recall either what they meant or what was recorded on the tape. With the tape player already packed, I stuffed the mystery tape in a box along with my curiosity.

A few weeks later amid the clutter of empty boxes and crumpled newspapers used for packing, I sat in my new apartment and played the tape. I heard my voice say the following words: "Today is February 21st, Wednesday, 1979, and today has been an absolutely amazing day. Now what this tape and others that will follow will do is attempt to record the events of a project that will be known as G.S.P.—God's Special Project. It's very unique, important, and for now top secret."

I then continue to say how I was sitting at my desk consumed with the writing of the soap opera when my boss, the gentleman whose "picture-perfect marriage" I just described, came into my office and began to tell me in a very hesitant fashion that he wanted to share something with me that was so big and so scary that he couldn't talk about it to anyone, not even his wife, but now he had to tell me. He said that he had been carrying something inside of him for a while and that it was a message that he believed was from the Lord. He appeared very nervous, as if he were afraid to tell me this secret. The secret was: "I believe that the Lord was telling me to get ready to televise—to capture—the Second Coming."

Now there was a project! We spoke for over an hour about his life and how things had led up to this order from God to get the cameras ready, but the project was so overwhelming that he just kept putting the idea out of his head. Nonetheless, God wouldn't let him forget. Finally he had to share his burden with someone. He needed to know if I agreed that this was truly a directive from God or if I would laugh at him, believing him a crazy lunatic.

As I listened to the tape I had two reactions. First, I couldn't believe I had forgotten this bizarre incident; second, I was frightened to hear myself speak in such a fundamentalist style—actually going along with this balderdash. The tape jarred my sleeping memory. At the time while I was listening to this man confess his secret thoughts, I had no idea what to make of it. I instinctively doubted that God would tell anyone to televise the Second Coming of Jesus, but I was touched by his sincerity.

Rather than affirm or laugh at his belief, I suggested that we both sit down with one other person and discuss the idea. The man I suggested was the guy with the rotten marriage who became my shadow in the "spy operation." At the time this audiotape was recorded, I still had great respect for this soon-to-be spy, and I knew that he and the man with the secret plan did not really like each other. Furthermore, he would not mince words or mask his feelings about the secret plan, and I thought he had the spiritual maturity and insight to deal with this matter. Much to my bewilderment, the tough-minded executive bought the plan hook, line, and sinker.

We prayed together and agreed that this would remain top secret—not even Pat would be told until we prepared a detailed document of our proposal for Pat's approval. We spoke of how massive a technological operation it would be to broadcast to every nation and in all different languages at the same time. The plans and contingencies would fill volumes, but we had to be ready so that when the Lord said, "Go," then it was go. We had to know just what to do and how to do it.

The greatest show on earth was in our hands. I wondered where we would put the cameras. Jerusalem was the obvious place. We even discussed how Jesus' radiance might be too bright for the cameras and how we would have to make adjustments for that problem. Can you imagine telling Jesus, "Hey, Lord, please tone down your luminosity; we're having a problem with contrast. You're causing the picture to flare." For me, how a plane gets off the ground is a mystery, so the concept of pulling together a project in which every person could witness the Second Coming of Jesus on his or her television—and in his or her own language—boggled my mind. Does everyone in El Salvador or Ethiopia even own a television? The tape indicated that I had some doubts about this Second Coming and Rapture stuff, but my love and concern for these men made the plan seem not odd. We believed God had chosen us—an improbable triumvirate—and we experienced a sense of calmness about this overwhelming revelation.

My spy believed even that during the millennium—a thousand-year period when believers will reign with Christ on a restored earth—he was going to produce a movie on the life of Moses. Clinically, this would be called paranoid-schizophrenia with delusions of grandeur. This is not unlike people who are so split in their identities that they believe they are Hitler, Napoleon, or even Jesus. But at CBN it was normal. In the world outside the walls of CBN such delusional states are treated with hospitalization and therapy. Inside CBN, budget allocations are made for their development.

CBN prepares all the externals—like setting a table for Jesus' Second Coming—when in all likelihood his second coming will be an internal event that each of us will eventually experience.

Life Out of Balance

There is no doubt in my mind that these two men loved God and were genuinely sincere in their efforts to serve him. I admired their dedication. The difficulties and problems in their personal lives caused both men to seek refuge and comfort in God. Religion for them had become a pain-killing drug. They were basically good men who really tried to be authentic Christians. Their respective conversions did not change their personalities or alter in any significant way who they were. Both remained strong, assertive individuals, and that trait got them to the top at CBN. However, the God of fundamentalist Christianity did not transform them into loving beings but rather into men who sought only exterior perfection in themselves and others. They lost all sense of spontaneity and joy. They became so saturated with the supernatural that they lost all sense of mystery and wonder. They failed to see the creative genius of their Maker. They became religious bigots who were so blinded to truth and reality that they could persecute the imperfect and, at the same time, actually believe that they were ordained to televise the Second Coming of Christ. Even though Scripture states that no one will know either the hour or the day when Jesus will return, these men will know in advance because they've got to turn on the cameras. They lived a life out of balance.

God Told Me

Sprinkled through these first three chapters are incidents in which people have heard the voice of God and responded to the message. I could allow myself to believe that God inspired and helped me write this book—in fact, wanted me to write it. Yet the message the book contains is in direct conflict with the message God is supposedly giving Pat Robertson to broadcast. I cannot claim that God wants this book written; although some of the circumstances that made the writing of the book possible seem almost miraculous.

In simple truth, there were no miracles performed in the writing of this book; I just attracted to myself what I sought and what I needed in order to write it. "Seek and you shall find," is a biblical statement that reflects a reality. I seriously sought answers to my many questions and sincerely wanted to write about my experiences. The energy of those twin desires attracted what I needed to fulfill them: books, events, people, and even a publisher came my way in such a seemingly extraordinary fashion that I could easily consider the remarkable series of circumstances that allowed this book to be completed to be supernatural. However, God is not behind every coincidence, nor is every serendipitous event a sign of God's support.

Life is filled with examples of ordinary people—both those who believe in God and those who don't—who have accomplished extraordinary feats by virtue of their own faith in what they were doing, despite the doubts of family and friends, and by inexhaustible persistence in being faithful to their dreams. What makes these people exceptional is that they sought something with every fiber of their existence—heart, mind, and soul—and they got it. The same is true for the religious people I met at CBN; except that they sought to spread the gospel of Jesus, and all the events on the road to any accomplishments they had were seen as help from the hand of God and a sign of God's blessing.

If God does exist, then it seems probable that he can speak to us; however, the communication would be more mystical than verbal. Without using words, we might hear God's voice as intuition—but only when we are on the same wavelength. The difficulty is learning to discern his voice from the clamor of voices within us. Was the voice we heard our own voice of reason, a projection of our own dreams and desires, an intuitive or psychic voice of understanding, a creative burst of insight, or the still voice of God?

The pentecostal movement neglects the essential *quality* of spiritual discernment and sobriety that was so important to the early fathers of the church. The emphasis on direct personal inspiration as well as the quest for extraordinary manifestations of the Holy Spirit can easily lead to spiritual delusion as a person seeks to excel in spiritual growth without proper humility and guidance. Whenever an inner voice demands or compels a person to do something, in all probability its origin is psychic or egoistic, but not spiritual.

The spirit or inner guidance that is most in harmony with authentic "spiritual" hearing is a message in the form of a suggestion or an offer of help. Spiritual experiences need to be examined in the light of the tradition of the church. Many fundamentalist Christians today ignore early church history. They believe they have received special blessings and confuse their own ideas with the will of God. This results in spiritual exhibitionism rooted in pride.

Looking Back

After I had been in Hollywood two weeks, I landed a job on the ABC soap "General Hospital." Soon I was consumed with feeding the nation a sea of emotional turmoil that the tormented characters drowned in each day. No longer was I spreading a message of salvation. But I never stopped searching for an understanding of what happened during those first two and a half years at CBN, and I painstakingly reviewed the events of my life that had put me on the one-way street to that capital of video Christianity.

My entrance onto the one-way street of fundamental Christianity was triggered by a failing marriage. I was forced off that Bible-paved highway-to-heaven because of the final collapse of that marriage. My marriage was an intrinsic part of the rebirth of my "relationship" with God and also of my exit from CBN. I cannot honestly tell my story of CBN without telling the story of that marriage. Unfortunately, they go together like movies and popcorn. Even today, that dead-and-buried marriage has a way of reaching out of its grave and touching my spiritual being.

Catch-22

After my ouster from CBN, my wife and I were divorced. The divorce was peaceful and amicable. We presently enjoy a kind, caring relationship and share the responsibility of raising our daughter. We speak frequently. On August 12, 1983, I visited her in Virginia Beach, where she still resides. During the visit, I went back to CBN for the first time since the day of my dismissal. As I toured the building, I was requested by the executive producer of "The 700 Club," who was also a vice-president of the corporation, to stop by his office because he had something important to tell me. Even though this man had been part of the jury on my last day, I still liked him, and I eagerly entered his office. As I sat in front of his massive desk, he told me in great detail of an ambitious project CBN was about to undertake.

It was producing a dramatic, prime-time series that would feature well-known actors. They had allocated sufficient money to guarantee a first-class production, and he wanted it to be produced in Hollywood. He waved before me a thick binder containing outlines and scripts and told me that all he needed was someone to head up the production. He offered me the producer's job, because he claimed that I was perfectly suited and qualified for the task. Almost. I had the writing skills and, most importantly, the network and Hollywood production experience. While he never disclosed an exact salary, I got the feeling it was in the one-hundred-thousand-dollars-a-year neighborhood, which isn't a bad neighborhood. I had no intention of going back into religious television, but the lure of the dollars and a massive Hollywood production was jumping up and down in my mind when he leaned forward, looked right into my eyes, and said, "There is, of course, one condition."

He paused, and I thought this was too good to be true. With utmost sincerity and clarity of speech and thought, he continued, "You will have to reconcile with and remarry your ex-wife."

I was too stunned to make a sound. The image of Pat Robertson asking, "Brother, did you sleep with her?" flashed in my mind. As I sat motionless in front of this Christian executive, I wanted to scream out, "How dare you play God?"

Playing God vs. God at Play

George Burns isn't the only person who gets to play God, a part he plays for fun in the movies. Fundamentalist Christian leaders also get to play God; but they don't play it for fun. They are deadly serious. I thought this executive knew me and was at least sensitive about the role that my marriage had played in my life. After all, he was very familiar with the details of the marriage, and that familiarity should have clearly illustrated the utter stupidity of that absurd condition for employment. His role as God did not require sensitivity and understanding because, for him, playing God only required an ability to be unbending, authoritarian, and judgmental—like his God. He knew the secret of my spiritual survival and success, and he just didn't want to share it with me, he wanted to clobber me with the truth: the highway to Heaven runs through your marriage. Without saying so, he, in effect, said—turn around and get back on the road, Buddy, because you are on a dead end street, a one-way street to Hell. The Christian executive didn't call me into his office to offer me a job but to grab my attention, cloak me in guilt, and "save" my soul. That's how he plays God.

But God does not hit us on the head to get our attention. I like to think that God sprinkles little crumbs—metaphorically speaking of course—along the path we have chosen to walk, and that those crumbs, if spotted and followed, will bring us together. He does not make us look for them or follow them. I don't think God is looking for people who only want the way pointed out for them; he desires and requires effort on the part of the traveler. He seeks seekers. He wants us to want to find him, and he stands ready to help us in our search; however, we must do the searching—mainly by learning to go against all our wrong conditioning.

God is the treasure, and we are the treasure hunters. He gives us each a piece of the treasure map, and if we all can put our pieces together we might find out that the "X" that marks the spot is deep within each of us. The spot is everywhere and nowhere. The treasure is so immense there's enough for everyone. It's so big it cannot be buried in any one place, so it was mystically broken up and buried within each of us. And each piece of the treasure is as valuable as the whole. We are each earthen vessels containing heavenly treasures. Seek and you shall find.

The crumbs and clues that I am following may be different from the clues you are following. In fact, there are no crumbs and clues—only understanding and truth. My treasure hunt—my search for the truth—may take me down a road that may seem ridiculous to you. The path we each take is called conversion. We are converted into something new as we travel—always growing, always changing. We each have our own conversion chronicle. We need to share them with each other. Here comes mine: it will reveal how I landed a part in the fundamentalist picture of God, a picture definitely not featuring George Burns.

4

A Conversion Chronicle

The electronic church feeds its television audience a little truth, a lot of emotion, and a literal interpretation of the Bible, and that mixture forms a recipe for guaranteed "salvation." The power behind the electronic church is the collective born-again faith of its staff and supporters.

A born-again encounter does not drop out of the clear blue sky. Events in a person's life must lead him or her to a place and a time when a total surrender to God is a viable option—and certainly not necessarily harmful. A person comes to that point ready and willing to take a leap in faith. Once that leap has been taken, there are few spiritual guides qualified to lead a person through the new land of faith, least of all the televangelist who may have helped him or her jump.

Tune in to almost any edition of "The 700 Club" and you will see how CBN has masterfully perfected the video technique of quickly, dramatically, and vividly reenacting the sinful events of a person's life that have led them to a born-again experience. The staged story is captured on video tape, then edited, narrated, and aired as a feature of "The 700 Club." We called these newslike reports "salvation testimony features."

If a man watching Pat Robertson calls CBN after accepting Pat's invitation to turn his life over to Jesus, and he tells the phone counselor that he has experienced salvation or some dramatic physical or emotional healing, the information is recorded by the counselor and passed on to a staff researcher. If the viewer's healing or salvation testimony is considered dramatic enough, the researcher will call the viewer to discuss the possibility of videotaping his story. If the conversation is fruitful, then a camera crew, producer, and an on-camera correspondent will soon arrive at the viewer's home, and the "miracle" will become a televised event aimed at inducing more miracles.

The December 3, 1985 edition of "The 700 Club" had a typical feature. It showed a divorced woman in her mid-thirties who, out of loneliness, frequented many singles' bars. The bars offered her no relief; instead, they gave her the opportunity to dabble in drugs. The picture tells the story as it shows the dejected woman sitting alone in a smoke-filled bar and seeking comfort in the bottom of a bottle. The convert has turned into an actress who portrays how she innocently fell victim to the snares of Satan. The camera paints a sad picture of the woman's pain.

Having set the stage, the feature cuts back to her home where she tells the reporter, with great emotion, how her two marriages both ended in bitter divorces and, worse, how her only child was tragically killed in an accident. Using all the video skills of any network documentary team, the taped living-room interview is sprinkled with dramatic cutaway pictures of her former husbands and dead child, as well as a staged scene that shows the dispondent and dispirited woman lying on her bed, curled up in a fetal position, and sobbing hysterically as the camera zooms into a touching and effective closeup of her tears. The simple interview is suddenly as compelling as any soap opera. It is visually stimulating and fast-paced: two essential elements of effective video storytelling. The feature can hook and hold an audience, which, of course, is its purpose.

After the feature embellishes how desperate the woman was, the audience gets to see how God can quickly and powerfully change any situation. In a dramatically staged reenactment, the camera follows the woman as she slowly lifts herself off the bed and morosely walks to her closet. The suspense mounts as she opens the door and gets out a shotgun. The only choice, she is convinced, is to end her futile and miserable life. However, this destructive moment contained an ironic twist: her arms were too short to hold the gun out in front of her and still be able to reach the trigger.

With tragic resourcefulness, we see her place the butt of the gun on the floor. With the barrel of the shotgun now pointing toward the ceiling, it is just a little taller than her waist; in this position she is able to bend over the gun so that it jabs her in the chest. In this awkward position her arms still can't reach the trigger, but her big toe can. Over a closeup of the toe on the trigger, she says, in an off-camera narration, that at this exact moment of deep despair prior to her soon-to-be self-inflicted death, her television set turned itself on—something, she added, that frequently happened—and she heard a voice break through the deadly silence saying that somebody was about kill him or herself and that he or she shouldn't because God loves that person.

The somber report turns joyful. We see the woman happily working at a new job in a child-care center, where her love for her deceased child has found a positive outlet. She enthusiastically proclaims the wonderous saving power of God and her mission to bring salvation to others. It is a very convincing story that is very well-produced. In fewer than four minutes, the home viewer gets to see a woman move from the brink of death to the fullness of life, and the sudden change certainly looks like a miracle and clearly illustrates that God plays an active and loving role in our lives—all we need to do is reach out and touch his saving power.

I don't know how much of the woman's real story was exaggerated by her enthusiasm for spreading the gospel, but as a television producer, I do know that her story was creatively enhanced in the reenactment and that the videotaped version of her conversion chronicle had far more dramatic impact than the lived reality. That is the nature of the medium: things look bigger and more vivid under the closeup eye of the camera. Moreover, some of the seemingly miraculous coincidences can be explained in very natural terms. A team of skeptics could have a field day dissecting the feature; however, more than likely, the woman was actually helped in her moment of crisis—a crisis that was psychological, not sinful—by the happy chatter of "The 700 Club." I have no doubt that droves of despondent viewers responded to that feature and also called CBN.

It is at this moment of doubt, despair, depression, and utter frustration at the futility of life that the fundamentalist stands ready, willing, and able to help. When a person has tried everything else—from drugs to drinks, from money to marriage, from psychiatry to self-help books—in order to fill or at least explain the void they feel within, then they are ready to respond to the fundamentalist Christian and grab the simple solutions waved before them. Why not, what do they have to lose? In many cases the simple solutions offered may be of temporary help.

The growth of the television evangelists, who mix into their blend of proselytizing and politicizing a caring attitude for the troubled masses, is virtually unlimited. Pat Robertson constantly reminds his audience that he and all the people at CBN love them and that CBN only wants to serve the viewers' needs. A message of "we care" is carefully woven into each show. If the role and mission of a ministry like

CBN were to sincerely reach out to the lonely and hurting members of society, I would laud their efforts. However, the caring, loving attitude they project is plastic and only a cover for their real purpose of preparing the planet for the return of Jesus. Moreover, their love is an effective tool for building bigger audiences, establishing broader voting blocks, and raising more money. Their growth will not stop until other concerned people—both religious and nonreligious—are ready to reach out in genuine love and compassion to the suffering who live among us. The religious right cannot and does not possess a monopoly of love.

There were many major events in my life that were stepping stones to a rendezvous with a born-again encounter and a job at CBN. The two biggest were leaving the seminary and entering matrimony. The best way for me to expose CBN is to expose myself, because, like so many other people who reached a point of no return, my conversion chronicle demonstrates the powerful effect of unexamined religious impressions and illustrates the appeal of a simplified and literal Christianity that easily cuts through the tensions and mysteries of life.

But First a Commercial Message

As a television producer, I used to get bags of mail from viewers. The fans of "The Doctors" let me know exactly what they thought about a character's impending death or a story's change in direction. Their imput frequently altered the course of the show.

Writing a book doesn't permit any audience feedback during its creation. I know that this chapter dealing with some personal material will generate one question, which I want to address before I start my own "salvation testimony."

Q. Why put a re-creation of my rather awkward sexual awakening in a book about the electronic church?

A. Because the "sins" of my youth contained the seeds of my sudden sainthood.

Shortly after my conversion, and without the aid of any theological training, I was turned from a sinner into a religious leader with pastoral duties. Granted, the religious community I led was small—a little over a hundred people—yet I held a position of spiritual authority and was expected to give spiritual guidance to many people who had a wide range of emotional and psychological problems. The power of the Holy Spirit supposedly made this possible and imbued me with the wisdom and discernment that I needed to teach and guide my flock.

Is a man, namely I, who was on the verge of divorce and brink of depression, who was so naive and timid that he entered a marriage simply because he lacked the conviction and courage to cancel poorly conceived and hastily made wedding plans, who didn't have the personal integrity and honesty to terminate a long-running adulterous affair that began two days after his wedding, and whose concept of sex was so devoid of any creative beauty and purity that he was attracted to the seamy, sordid sex of pornography, qualified to function as a spiritual guide to others simply because he was born-again, sorry for his "sins," could speak in tongues, and had personal charisma?

Absolutely not!

All across America, in churches and on television, men—and in some rare cases, women—who at one time in their lives were less likely candidates for heaven than I was in 1974 are the shepherds of souls and the undisputed experts on the will and ways of God. Dramatic conversion stories that make mine look boring abound in fundamental circles. I've meet convicted thieves, murderers, and men who have fathered a half a dozen illegitimate children and who now earn their daily bread by preaching. No matter how bad you were or how far you had strayed from God, it was possible for you to be instantaneously saved and to start a career of saving others. God's spiritual lottery turned a lot of losers into instant winners. But their conversion, salvation, and transformation has nothing to do with authentic spiritual growth and an honest search for the truth. That always takes hard work and continuous effort and is never a prize that can be easily won.

Soon after I was transformed from a sinner to saint, I was put, supposedly by God, in a position to create and produce television shows that would help spread his word and thereby save the world from its march toward eternal death. A March 27, 1980, memo to company officials from Pat Robertson stated that the Arbitron ratings for "The 700 Club" had jumped 35 percent from November of 1979 to February of 1980, thanks to the changes I made as producer of the show. I had the righteous stuff!

But did I?

The "holy" men who stand in front of a camera angrily proclaiming the good news of salvation are backed up by a huge, salaried staff of people whose backgrounds and beliefs are similar to what mine were when I worked at CBN. Despite being burdened with all the same secular worries as the rest of humanity—financial security, job advancement, health, children—somehow the staff members of a televangelist can still know beyond a shadow of doubt the will of God for each and every person on earth. The kind of faith that must take is impossible for other "mere mortals" to comprehend.

It has been more than five years since my ouster from CBN, and hardly a day has passed that some amount of time was not spent reflecting on my life as a minor-league religious leader and a major-league religious-television producer. What was I saying to my community and my viewers, and why was I saying it? At the time, I thought I was saying what God wanted said and because God wanted me to say it. After these years of arduous reflection, I now know that I was wrong on both counts. I did not know what God wanted said, and God did not choose me to speak for him.

However, all these experiences as a pastor and producer—no matter how confusing—have been beneficial to me. They have helped me to change and grow. The pain I suffered at the hands of my fundamentalist Christian faith actually helped me break through a thick, dull cloud of noncomprehension. Pain can be both positive and redemptive. For the first time in my life, I believe what comes from within me and not what is yelled into my ears, forced down my throat, or drummed into my mind.

I bought the message others, who claimed to speak for God, sold; the doubt came free of charge. But doubt cannot find truth until its wounds are healed. The dark and "sinful" side of my life before I bit into the fruit of fundamentalism needed to be examined and understood in order to be healed. Before that long, lonely look inside, my reasoning and my passion were at war. Sex was fun yet dirty; God was loving yet vengeful. The internal war frequently caused me to act without thinking and, worse, to think without acting: the perfect condition for surrender to the fundamentalist army.

Today, my reason and my passion have signed a truce and, for the most part, coexist in peace: I try to sit with my reason and let my passion move me. Reason tells me that my "salvation testimony"—that is, my "salvation" from the snares of fundamentalism—needs to feature a close look at the "sins" that fundamentalism tried to save me from. Sharing my story is sharing my healing.

My Early Life

Religion was a part of my life before I even breathed my first breath. My mother's religious life was as traditional as a Fourth of July parade.

Novenas to saints, stations of the Cross, statues of the Blessed Virgin Mary, Mass, and meatless Fridays were the floats of her religious parade. The living out of her conservative, pre-Vatican II Catholic faith was fully shared by my father. In the eyes of all who knew them, they were the perfect Catholic couple. Even as a Wall Street executive, my father attended daily Mass and engaged in rigorous fasting and abstinence during the holy season of Lent. A religious vocation for one of their offspring would have been a dream come true for my parents.

In the winter of 1946, Frances Straub was having a difficult pregnancy. She felt too old at thirty-eight to be carrying her third child. Weak and ill, she worried about the unborn child's condition. Complications in the final months were a cause of great distress for her. Frances, ever gentle in spirit, turned to her faith to help her through this time of crisis and did something my future Protestant friends would find ludicrous. She prayed to St. Gerard, who is the patron saint of hopeless or difficult cases involving pregnant women. My mother believed the Catholic teaching that claimed the saints are mediators between the living faithful on earth and God in heaven.

No one questioned the rather far-fetched notion that a holy, yet still mortal, person could die, be declared a saint by other men, and suddenly become an advocate for humanity and carry their prayers of intercession to the throne of God, who, of course, could hardly say "no" to one of his saintly creations. It seems silly and childish to think that a finite yet dead human being could carry the wishes of the living to God. If God is omniscient and omnipresent, then why the need for saints? There doesn't appear to be any reason, yet we had saints dedicated to every occupation and adversity under the sun. Teachers prayed to St. Gregory the Great, fishermen to St. Andrew, nurses to St. Catherine, and policemen to St. Michael. And there were saints who specialized in healing every known disease man could contact—St. James cured arthritis, St. Blaise sore throats, St. Lucy eye infections, and St. Giles concentrated on sterility. We even had saints that handled specific yet common problems: St. Anthony helped find lost articles, St. Joseph assisted women in finding husbands, and St. Barbara would be of help if you got caught in a lightning storm.

The fundamentalists I worked with at CBN vehemently attacked the satanic Catholic church's belief that the saints could help in a person's healing. The basis for their attack had nothing to do with the silliness of the concept but rather was based on a principle even more ludicrous than the healing power of the saints. The fundamentalist Christian believes that Satan causes illness by means of demon oppression, and he can take away an illness without opposing himself. They think that if a Catholic prayed to a saint for healing, Satan would heal the person because it would be to his advantage to deceive the sick person into thinking that the healing was the result of their prayers to the saint. The Bible never mentions anything about praying to saints. The fundamentalists believe that Satan uses the church teaching about saints to trick people into not finding God and into following unbiblical teachings.

Catholic children were encouraged to read the lives of the saints and to follow their holy examples. The false piety of many Catholic adults actually converted their veneration of the saints into something close to the worship of false gods. The saints became a Catholic version of ancient belief in various gods devoted to specific occupations and human needs. The statues of the saints became our modern-day idols. Theologians could state that the statues and pictures of the saints only served to remind us of the saint—the way that your child's photo in your wallet does—and that we should not worship the statue. But that is what many Catholics did.

It is odd to think that we were taught to trust in a dead human being rather than to go directly to God. Why did we bow down before the images of the saints, and why did we worship them rather than imitate them? Because spirituality had degenerated into superstition, and God had become not a spirit within us but a far-off, distant person who was so inaccessible that religion created a saintly messenger system to whisper our prayer into his ear.

I learned as a child to see the saints as perfect and myself as imperfect. Thus the seeds of guilt were sown, along with a belief that I needed some outside help in reaching God. Pat Robertson would become a living saint who could help me—and millions of others—reach God.

My mother believed her prayers were answered on March 31, 1947. During the height of a tremendous winter snowstorm, which jeopardized her safe arrival at the hospital, she delivered a healthy, robust baby boy. I was that baby boy, her hopeless case. My mother's belief that St. Gerard had successfully interceded on her behalf before the Almighty Throne of God resulted in her naming me after this little-known saint. I never cared much for the name, yet I guess it could have been worse. My pious mother could have prayed to St. Polycarp or St. Pancreas.

During my last year of Catholic grammar school, much to my parents' delight, I began to entertain thoughts of becoming a priest. It seemed like a natural choice. I was a very sensitive kid who was attracted to the message of Jesus. However, the choice was made difficult because I was bothered by the fact that the transforming power of Christ's words had little impact on the lives of the people I saw each day.

I grew up in the Borough of Queens, New York City, in a neighborhood called Richmond Hill. Even though the neighborhood is part of the largest city in the world, this little bite of the Big Apple maintained an almost small-town ambiance until the early sixties. Shopping malls and McDonalds were far in the future when I was growing up, but racial prejudice had arrived.

Richmond Hill remained white for as long as I lived there, yet within the hearts of many residents bigotry beat out its message of fear and hate. "The niggers have crossed Liberty Avenue," sounded like a progress report about an invading army, but what it really meant was that a black family had moved into a house in what had been an all-white section. The subtext of the comment left unsaid was that they were getting closer and what were we going to do?

As an eighth-grader, I had a difficult time reconciling Jesus' gospel of love with the daily reality of hate and fear that existed among the people who faithfully sat in church each Sunday and listened to the Word of God—yet walked out unaffected. I guess twelve-year-olds don't understand property values. Blessed are the children.

The rituals of worship seemed empty. People came to church late and left early. In between they squirmed as they sat on hard wooden pews or swayed from knee to knee during the times they had to kneel on the cushioned kneelers. To add to the boredom, nobody spoke Latin except God and the priest. If this really was God's house, and it was possible to tap into the creative source of power that formed the universe through this act of communal prayer, then it seemed that the level of interest should be higher. The enthusiasm I encountered many years later at Catholic charismatic prayer meetings and in fundamentalist churches seemed fitting. As a child I wondered how churchgoers could pray for an hour and then get in their cars and curse the parking-lot traffic caused by a slow Christian.

Unlike most kids that I grew up with, my going to church wasn't some kind of unpleasant obligation that required an unrealistic feeling of awe and silence. I liked things religious. I liked the mysticism of the Mass. For me, the priests and nuns seemed to be in another world. I thought they floated above the normal concerns of the people who were almost reluctantly kneeling in the pews or lurking at the back door in anticipation of the moment when the priest began to distribute communion, which was their cue to bolt out of the church. Through my idealistic young eyes, the priest's concerns were more noble and heavenly. I pictured them as people who healed the hurts of life.

In contrast, those of us who didn't live in rectories, monasteries, or convents seemed to hurl harms at each other through all sorts of acts of hate, bigotry, and prejudice. The lives of the saints had more appeal to me than any fairytale.

I wanted never to do anything wrong. I didn't want sin to be a part of my life. As a youth the priesthood seemed like a way of achieving a sinless experience. Now I know from first-hand experience that sin is very much a part of a priest's life. It's an important part of a saint's life. Even in today's permissive society many people would be shocked at the diverse sexuality displayed by some men of the cloth. Their sexual hunger demands a smorgasbord of fleshy treats—everything from altar boys to prostitutes. Fortunately the innocence of childhood is blinded to the realities of adulthood.

Despite the lack of any evidence supporting the effectiveness of Christianity on those I observed, I still wanted to follow Jesus as a priest. I began my trip down the priestly road as the world entered a decade of social upheaval, violence, rebellion, exploration, and exploitation. In the 1960s the world and I changed physically, emotionally, and spiritually. I'm not sure if it was the best decade to grow up in or the worst. What a mixture of influences! Consider the combination of the Cuban missile crisis, a presidential assassination, the Vietnam War, the birth of the Beatles, the launching of a man into outer space, the emergence of television, inner-city race riots, and the murders of Martin Luther King, Jr., and Senator Robert F. Kennedy.

In periods of radical social change and upheaval, the beliefs within a society undergo marked changes. Beliefs that once were the bedrock of the social order give way to new constellations of belief. The new beliefs then usher in new ways to find new meaning within the culture at large.

The individual, in periods of change, growth, and transformation, undergoes a process similar to that which takes place in the society. Beliefs once held dear and filled with meaning topple in the wake of ever more complex understandings of the life process. New, more viable beliefs are born.

In a sense, it is impossible to extract the man, the lone personality, from the constellation of physical, mental, emotional, social, cultural, and religious beliefs that color and make meaning of his personal reality. However, it is possible to identify which beliefs operate within an individual's psyche at various times in his development. My unique identity and personality were becoming manifest during an explosive historical period—but the explosion would blow to bits all my beliefs.

During these turbulent times, and at the tender age of thirteen, I entered the tranquility of St. Joseph's Minor Seminary in Princeton, New Jersey, in pursuit of a heavenly dream. The school was run by the Vincentian Fathers, whose formal name is the Congregation of the Mission, as a preparatory school toward the priesthood in that order. After four years of high school, the seminarian moved on to a college-level seminary for four additional years of study, then a two-year novitiate, followed by two years of study toward a master's degree in Theology. Finally, after twelve years of preparation and prayer, one reached the goal of ordination and received the sacrament of Holy Orders.

The sacrament of Holy Orders takes its name from the fact that the bishops, priests, and deacons give order to the church. They guarantee the continuity and unity of the church from age to age and from place to place. They've done so since the time of the Apostles, and—according to the church—they'll continue to do so until the establishment of God's kingdom in eternity. From the seminary to eternity is a long trip. I only made it through nine months. I never got to bring order to the church, but the church did manage to create a mess of my life when they made my adolescent indecisiveness and curiosity a crime and thrust me back into the real world.

The Seminary

Life inside the seminary was certainly far removed from the real world. It was a dark, dreary, and repressive society where everyone wore black clothing and constantly fought against their sinful natures. We had to go to confession every week. How many sins could a teenager commit inside a religious institution with a schedule that required that he spend more than ten hours a day in classrooms, the study hall, and chapel? Not many, but nonetheless we were urged to make daily examinations of our conscience in order to prevent sin from sneaking into our lives. In order not to have my entire weekly confession consist only of the sin of entertaining impure thoughts, I struggled to make up extra little sins—like being unkind to a classmate or saying *shit* during the heat of a basketball game.

Masturbation was the dreaded mortal sin that brought a stiff penance. We were told that masturbation was a sin despite the fact that Scripture does not make any direct reference to the "dirty deed." The seminary based its condemnation of the activity on an obscure passage, Genesis 38:6-10, which proclaims:

> Judah took a wife for his first-born Er, and her name was Tamar. But Er, Judah's first-born, offended Yahweh greatly, so Yahweh brought about his death. Then Judah said to Onan, "Take your brother's wife, and do your duty as her brother-in-law, to produce a child for your brother." But Onan, knowing the child would not be his, spilt his seed on the ground every time he slept with his brother's wife, to avoid providing a child for his brother. What he did was offensive to Yahweh, so he brought about his death also.

Ugh! What should a teenager—or adult for that matter—make of that biblical story? I doubt the "sin" referred to in the passage is masturbation but rather is Onan's failure to father children for his brother's wife according to the existing Hebrew marriage laws.

The seminary was an authoritarian state that treasured rigidity and buried spontaneity. Obedience was not simply required, it was a vow. Disobedience meant punishment—anything from a hard slap across the knuckles to being assigned an unpleasant work detail during scheduled recreation periods. The school stressed academic excellence and strict discipline, and those twin objectives ran counter to my nature. I was a daydreamer who didn't appreciate rules and regulations. One rule had us keep small sticks in our mouths in order to remind us not to speak during the silence periods.

We were even taught how to wash without touching ourselves. Well, maybe it wasn't that strict, but there was no way to express or understand adolescent thoughts or desires that dealt with the flesh. Normal thoughts and questions about human sexuality were considered "evil" and therefore couldn't be a part of a seminarian's life. We quickly learned that we were sinners. The dead language of Latin was far more important than the living thoughts of a confused teenager.

Initially, I adapted quite nicely to life in this priestly boot camp. On a practical level, I conquered the staleness of the cake that was served for dessert by soaking it in milk, thereby turning it into pudding.

But my problem was not practical. Doubts began to creep into my innermost thoughts as I questioned what I was doing in this place. I was searching for some deep religious explanation and motivation for my wanting to dedicate my life to serving God as a priest. I mean, after all, I didn't exactly hear a voice from Heaven asking me to follow him as a priest. I wasn't struck down like the Apostle Paul to be dramatically converted. I never really chose to be a Christian, much less a Catholic. My faith was inbred and a natural part of my childhood experience.

I still wondered what good it would do to bring Christianity to China; after all, the people living in Richmond Hill had been exposed to the message of Jesus since childhood, and it didn't seem to make them any better. At least on the surface most of my classmates didn't seem to be troubled by these kinds of thoughts. Later, I realized that most were afraid to raise probing questions or speak about emerging sexual feelings.

Wet dreams, or nocturnal emissions, as they were dispassionately called, were thought to be a dreaded curse that had to be covered up but never discussed. Ways of concealing stained pajama bottoms became a creative pastime. The evidence could be hidden but not the feelings. The all-male society fostered an artificial homosexual tendency that was both misunderstood and ignored, although it was not uncommon for two bright students to be dismissed at the same time for undisclosed reasons.

Many of us were terrified of our own nakedness in the locker-room showers, while others loved the soap-covered naked romps. No matter what was said or not said, thought or not thought, done or not done, the fact was that sex was alive within the bodies of the boys and priests, despite the fact that they rose each morning at 5:30 A.M. and scurried half asleep to a damp, dark chapel for morning Matins and Mass. Guilt over sexual fantasies made me feel I wasn't worthy to serve God as a priest. I vainly tried to ignore the thoughts and questions.

Denial and suppression didn't make the problem go away; it only increased the tension. The flesh was the enemy. The heroes of our faith overcame the enemy. That gentle giant of a saint who almost single-handedly renewed his church, Francis of Assisi, who managed to tame wild animals and live a life in harmony with nature, battled his own natural nature and devilish lust. Tradition has it that St. Francis was at times so tempted by the sight and thought of a woman that he literally stripped off his habit and threw his naked body into the snow and rolled around until he cooled off his hot flashes. The belief that the body's sexual urges could and should be overcome was alive in the seminary.

Writer Paul Hendrickson has eloquently captured the life I led in his book *Seminary,* in which he candidly examines his seven years as a seminarian and the years of guilt that followed his leaving. Reading his book, I felt as though I were in his class. The minor seminary he attended was in Alabama, but otherwise everything about the school sounded just like St. Joseph's. The following brief but shocking excerpt from his book describes his weekly meetings with his spiritual director:

> I would go in, sit in a chair beside his desk, talk for a short while, await his nod, unzipper my trousers, take out my penis, rub it while I allowed impure thoughts to flow through my brain, and, at a point where I felt myself fully large and close to emission, say, "Father, I'm ready now." He would then reach over and hand me a black wooden crucifix. I would then begin reciting the various reasons why I wished to conquer this temptation: because God had given me good health, a fine family, a sound mind. I always held the cross beside my penis, one hand on the crucifix, the other on my erect organ. Having thus systematically provoked myself to the ledge of mortal sin, and letting myself teeter there, I was now just as systematically talking the temptation down. Literally. The power of the crucified savior in my left hand was overpowering the evil of impurity and the world in my right.

This insanity passed for pastoral therapy to help a young teenager fight his impure thoughts; however, I think it was more like theological perversion. I didn't last long enough in the seminary to have had a personal experience like that of Hendrickson, but, after talking to many priests and former seminarians, I have no doubt that this type of sick activity was not an isolated incident.

Many involved in religious life make repression and guilt the cornerstone of their faith. The mere fact that they repress their humanity and bathe themselves in guilt is a sign that they do not fully believe in God's love and do not see themselves as being accepted by him. Their spiritual identity crisis denies the scriptural claim that "love consists in this: not that we have loved God but He has loved us." If that is true, then faith should lead a person to the realization that God loves them just the way they are. That wasn't the message preached at the seminary. Fear-forced repentance was the order of the day, just as it would be twenty years later at CBN. Counting our sins will add up to nothing; Christians would be better off forgetting their obsession with sin and stopping their worry about breaking rules. An examination of conscience should be on a much deeper level—concerned only with discovering what lack of love there may be in the heart. François Mauriac said, "The day I no longer burn with love, many others will die of the cold." It was very cold in the seminary—and even colder at CBN.

The concept of starting a person on the road to priestly ordination at the tender age of thirteen was begun in the sixteenth century in order to nurture a vocation early, before the temptations of the flesh ensnared the youth. The Council of Trent in 1563 assumed that if a young man could be protected from the harsh realities of the world by sealing him off from the influence of a decadent society, then the young man, planted behind the walls of a seminary, would bloom into a priest. Today, fundamentalist Christians are opening their own Bible-based schools for the same reason: shielding their children from the disastrous effects of an education that is so secular that "God is squeezed out of the classroom."

The greatest worry the seminary superiors had was the Christmas and summer vacations when their young men went home and were exposed to temptations. There was always a chance that some sweet schoolgirl would stir his sleeping passion and sin would surely follow. Girls were vocation killers.

With words unspoken, I was made aware as a child that celibacy and the priesthood were special, that sex was sinful, and that marriage was for mere mortals who did not possess the superhuman qualities required to be a priest or nun. When I attended Catholic grammar school, the boys were constantly urged by their mothers, the nuns, and the missionary priests who visited our school looking for recruits, to pay attention to the fact that God may have chosen one of us to be a priest. Many of us who as altar boys dressed up like junior priests wondered if we had gotten "the calling." Many impressionable young boys enrolled in minor seminaries. It's easy now to see how the specialness of "the calling" led to an elitist concept of the priest and painted a picture that was hard to live up to, and how the uncompromising demands of such a superhuman life led many a priest into alcoholism. I met my first alcoholic in the seminary. Somehow priests were supposed to be better; they were lifted up and placed on a puritanical pedestal— the scriptural principle that all Christians share in the priesthood of Jesus was lost.

Once planted in a minor seminary it became apparent to me that the concept of an idle mind being the Devil's workshop ruled my daily life, even though Scripture implored mankind to "be still and know that I am God," which sounds as if God is found in stillness and not frantic action. I craved inward stillness. Our daily schedule was hectic, demanding, and not conducive to soul-searching; yet, I found plenty of time to go deep within myself and even became preoccupied with my inner reflections. Actually I didn't find the time; I stole the time.

Between our rising at 5:30 A.M. and our retiring at 9:30 P.M., every minute was planned, and each new activity was heralded by the loud clang of a bell. The bell woke us. The bell signaled the end of the morning wash-up time. The bell urged us on to chapel. The bell cued the start and finish of meals, classes, recreation time, and study periods. My day-dreaming could only be stolen from study periods.

This was a time of silence when we sat at our individual desks, located in a large library-type hall. The desks were wooden, and each had individual desktop lamps. For everyone but me this was a time for feverish activity. Each seminarian sat at his book-cluttered desk as he attacked his assignments for the next day's classes. I saw this as the only unrestricted space during the day. This time was self-guided.

While my friends went back in time to translate a Latin text of Casear's Gallic wars, or spent time working some algebra formula or reviewing their compositions for dangling participles, I transported myself to distant and exotic shores on the wings of fantasy. I met interesting, intriguing people with whom I shared my Christian faith. Sometimes my flights into fantasy didn't take me to the far corners of the world but just across the field to our beautiful chapel. I saw myself fully arrayed in priestly vestments as I slowly lifted heavenward a large circular wafer after I had reverently whispered the words, "This is My Body."

At this stage of my life, I had not yet dealt with the theology behind those words and the concept of transubstantiation. I doubt that few Catholics understand this central tenet of their faith, which claims that the bread used during holy communion is actually changed in substance, but not appearance, into the body of Jesus. According to Catholic teaching, the sacrifice of the Mass is not just a symbolic re-creation of Jesus' death on the cross, but is a literal, actual offering of the flesh and blood of Christ to make a daily atonement for all our sins.

The Mass is identical to Calvary, a sacrifice for sin, and Jesus' suffering must be continually perpetuated to appease God. The Catholic church believes Jesus is still dying for the sins of the world. This teaching shows why fundamentalism is so violently opposed to Catholicism; they see the sacrifice of the Mass as unbiblical—and it is. The concept of eating the flesh and blood of Jesus—even under another form—is seen as barbaric. Television evangelist Jimmy Swaggart does not consider the Catholic church to be a true expression of the Christian faith because it is not totally based on the Bible. Both fundamentalism and Catholicism view the other as a cult. Both of them are right, but the latter happens to be very old, rich, and powerful.

As a thirteen-year-old I didn't need to understand all the theological implications because my childlike faith believed that Jesus was really present during the Eucharist. I did wonder why, however, if people really believed with all their hearts that they were actually receiving the body of Jesus and not just blessed bread, then why didn't they claw their way to the altar every day? For me, accepting the fact that the thin, stiff wafer was bread required more faith than believing the wafer contained the real presence of Jesus. Religion can be funny, but it usually isn't.

There was no doubt that I wanted to be a priest, but I did have my doubts on a much more subtle and troublesome level: Was this what God wanted me to do, or was it just something I wanted to do? Did I just like all the pomp and circumstance of the ritual? Did I really just want to wear a Roman collar? Was the priesthood a way for a shy, chubby kid to gain respect? Was I worthy of "the calling?" These were tough questions for a thirteen-year-old to deal with, let alone figure out the answers to during a short study period. I wanted to know how God talks to us and how I could hear his voice.

I was attempting to unfold the mystery of God in order to figure out why he selected me for the priesthood. I pictured myself so unworthy for this priestly life I had chosen that I actually began to believe that lie. The truth was that I was a good kid who was very innocent and filled with a desire to please others.

I spent four months in a spiritual and scholastic winter of hibernation snuggled up to my own thoughts. Almost in synchrony with nature, my doubts began to thaw along with the winter ice, and for some unknown reason I intuitively felt that God did love me, despite my own poor estimation of myself. We all crave acceptance for who we are. Yet the seminary constantly forced us to examine our own sinfulness. The priest, sitting alone in a darkened confessional box, became a stern judge who attempted to force good kids to be better out of fear. Most of the kids were afraid of the priests—at least when they were sitting in the confessional—because, according to Catholic teaching, the priest had the power to forgive your sins. He did not have to ask God to forgive you because he was a living representative of Jesus, and as you nervously knelt in the confessional telling the priest your sins it was the same as kneeling before Christ himself. Talk about power: if the priest forgave your sins, then God had no choice but do to the same. The concept of telling your sins to a human being in order to gain divine forgiveness is not only outrageously silly but also unbiblical.

In fact, it wasn't until 1215 under Pope Innocent III that private auricular confession became compulsory, and Catholics were required to confess and to seek absolution from a priest at least once a year. As a young teenager in a seminary, I feared a grilling from the priest in the confessional more than a drilling from a dentist.

A holy man should help people feel good about themselves, and his spirituality shouldn't include pressure or cause great uneasiness. Pressure denotes an absence of respect, a lack of love. Pressure is not God's way. The church and priests did not seem happy with who we were: yet, we needed acceptance in order to develop a feeling of self-respect. This is the key to the effectiveness of any cult—especially the cult of the electronic church. They convince you to look at your external "sinfulness" instead of your internal goodness.

Knowing that we're worthwhile unveils our potential. Only when we're loved can we become ourselves, but it takes great courage to believe in God's love and his complete acceptance of your existence when you have been convinced you are sinful. Even living in a world filled with hate, it is still possible for me to believe in God's love in a cosmic sense, but it is very tough to believe in God's love for me personally. Why me? Somehow during those early seminary days I managed to temporarily develop a faith in God's love for me despite my defects and doubts. My winter of doubt thawed into a spring of hope—but not soon enough.

While I was stuck in my circle of uncertainty about God and my "calling," the required academic standard of excellence marched ever forward, and my stolen study time made me miss the parade. The powers that be in seminary life didn't look favorably on a student who flunks religion and Latin. I managed to fake my way through the other subjects, but those two required reading and study.

After the midterm results came out, I was issued a stern warning. With my new-found confidence I attacked my studies with enthusiasm, and my grades improved noticeably. Despite my dramatic academic turnaround and support from my teachers, a new, strict headmaster pointed out that, while my third-quarter grades may have been excellent, the fact remained that, averaged in with the first two quarters, the combined result fell below the accepted minimum. It was bag-packing time. I was stung for the first time by the rigidity of unbending religious rules.

I pleaded my case against dismissal by telling the headmaster of my period of questioning and doubt and explained how I really wanted to stay at St. Joe's, pleading that my latest marks were a true reflection of my abilities. He almost bought it. He gently but firmly let me know that it was not possible to make an exception to the rule. He must have seen the disappointment painted on my face or realized the sincerity of my pleas, because he told me that once a seminarian is dismissed from the school, regardless of the reason, it is impossible to gain readmission, but in my case he would waive that restriction. He said he would help me gain admission to St John's Preparatory School, an all-boys high school run by the Vincentian Fathers in Brooklyn, New York, and if I successfully completed my high-school education in that institution and upon graduation still firmly believed God was calling me into the priesthood, then he would allow me back into the order. With tears in my eyes and determination in my heart, I left.

These details from my teenage years in the seminary reveal a picture and pattern that is amazingly similar to my life at CBN. Both the seminary and CBN frowned on individuality and tried to force people into conformity. The seminary had authoritative, ordained priests to enforce the rules, and CBN had God-appointed and anointed executives with their own secret police to catch rule-breakers and backsliders. Both the seminary and CBN preferred pressure to respect. Neither the seminary nor CBN could tolerate doubt or failure; and both had a love for unbending rules. Both organizations, claiming to represent God, lacked compassion—and, if nothing else, God must be compassionate. Both claimed they lived only for Jesus while preaching a message of damnation; however, Christ lived only to bring the world a message that we are loved by God—take it or leave it.

The fine points of these two faiths may have been different, but their methods of operation were the same. By carefully examining my life behind the walls of the seminary in light of my experience at CBN, I realized that I never learned the lessons of religious intolerance or understood that the creation of a spiritual fantasy should not be attributed to God—so the story was repeated in adulthood. Maybe history does repeat itself until the chain of error is broken.

At a young age I stumbled upon the problem of evil and the accompanying difficulty in reconciling the existence of a loving and powerful God with a world he created in which so much hate and suffering exist. Could the feeling of shame stop sin? If God does exist and if he is all-knowing, could he be thrilled with a person's piety and holiness if they were based on fear? Could fear-induced holiness merit the eternal rewards of "Heaven?" To all three questions, my answer would be, not very likely.

My priestly dream was buried a long, long time ago, yet until only recently it always managed to reach out of its grave and influence my life. For a long time I could not shake the feeling that I had missed "the call," and memories of the seminary clung to me like a frightened child to a parent. During my life no matter what choice I made that ran counter to the fulfillment of my childhood priestly fantasy—like becoming a television producer—no matter how much dirt I piled on the shattered and buried dream, it still haunted and influenced me. Shortly after leaving CBN, I stayed at the home of a priest friend of mine, and while he was out I put on his black shirt and white Roman collar and stood looking at myself in the mirror, and cried. The fantasy had not yet died. I even entertained thoughts of becoming a monk.

It is very hard to drop something that you believe with all your heart. I thought as I left the seminary that the church was my life, and without the church my life would be doomed. My personal salvation came twenty-five years later when I let go of all the lies that were programmed into me in the seminary and at CBN—lies that could not give meaning to my life—and gave birth to new beliefs. Giving birth is painful, but my heart no longer cries for what it has lost, because my spirit rejoices in what it has found.

CBN and the seminary had stripped me of my ability to look within myself during times of difficulty or doubt; they fostered dependence on senseless dogmas and a distant God. They had become my security blanket, and I couldn't let go—worse, I was afraid to let go. Now I know that my shame and guilt—just like my priestly fantasy—were nothing more than my own idle thoughts—*my* thoughts, not God's wishes. My emotions and conditioning had made God a monster and no amount of "old" religious piety and practices could make him less monstrous. Letting go of old beliefs—letting go of my religious security blanket—and searching first for myself and then for God was the only way to bring the dawn of a new awakening. But the search must begin in the frightening darkness of night where the path is not clear.

During the fourteenth century an anonymous monk wrote a treatise on spirituality entitled *The Cloud of the Unknowing,* and it became a classic in Christian writing. In a translation by William Johnson, S.J., the monk suggests that people should "not shrink from the sweat and toil involved in gaining real self-knowledge, for I am sure that when you have acquired it you will very soon come to an experiential knowledge of God's goodness and love."

Life After the Seminary

I did graduate from St. John's Prep, but I did not take advantage of the strict headmaster's moment of leniency and return to the seminary. The "I'll be back" determination that I took with me when I left the seminary drowned in a sea of freedom and guilt. Maybe the fears of seminary headmasters down through the ages about the ill-effects of a vacation on a vocation were well-founded. I might have survived a vacation, but three years on the outside proved more than I could handle.

Life outside the seminary walls offered options and choices that I never faced before. The seminary, like fundamentalism, controls its members through strong-armed tactics of bondage, and the individual's ability to make a thought-out, reasoned choice for himself is not developed; follow-the-leader is the modus operandi. Fundamentalists of any stripe fear freedom and don't think people should be free to be who and what they think they are—all must conform to the group's understanding of the laws of God. A CBN friend of mine was told that his long hair was ungodly.

Free from the dictatorial rule of the seminary, I could control many events of my day. Freedom was one of the subtle differences I had to adjust to during my first few days out of the seminary.

The early morning quiet walk to the chapel was replaced by a fifteen-minute walk through the noisy factory district that adjoined my neighborhood as I made my way to the subway. Clanging steel supplanted chirping birds. The train ride to Brooklyn took about fifty minutes and was an awesome adventure for a sensitive kid. I got to observe all types of people as the train wormed its way under a variety of ethnic neighborhoods. The morning rush-hour crowd wasn't exactly conducive to brotherhood as tempers flared almost daily to a level bordering on violence. The subway system itself was the winter home of the homeless who normally lived on the streets until the first frost of winter forced them to seek warm refuge underground.

Daily encounters with rowdy kids who attended the various rough-and-tumble, inner-city public vocational high schools were frequently a frightening experience. To them vandalism was a part of subway riding, and the station walls and train windows became a canvas for artistic expression of their inner hate. Often their hateful feelings were saved for the pristine pupils of parochial schools who traveled through their turf; this resulted in an innocent kid losing his books or teeth. Having survived the subway trip, you were ready for the really dangerous part of the journey: the walk from the station to the school.

One of my classmates was knifed to death on the train platform. The Myrtle-Willoughby Station reeks with the sour stench of urine. Red-wigged prostitutes wearing tight miniskirts stand guard at the exits. Diseased debris rots under a cloud of mosquitoes and bugs in a vacant lot. Liquor stores and pawnshops outnumber food stores. I walked past pimps, pushers, bars, and burned-out tenaments that still showed signs of people living behind the boarded-up windows. I cringed at roaches so big and bold that they didn't even run from light or man as they feasted on the slim pickings in the garbage cans. No one you pass ever smiles. Their solemn, taut faces reflect the hate and misery.

In July of 1964 the area exploded in violent riots. As a young high-school student, just out of the seminary, I walked through this valley of anger and despair, oblivious as a sleepwalker to the hatred and hopelessness housed within the decaying walls. I had no concept of a level of poverty that forced large families to live together in one small rat-infested room without any hope of escape. During my three years at St. John's I would learn about the plague of poverty, hunger, joblessness, discrimination, low wages, substandard housing and overcrowding. The church I loved seemed more concerned about banning the birth-control pill. I often thought that these malignancies I saw as I walked to school were problems Jesus would face and attempt to cure, not ignore. Within a very short period of time, I lost my interest in going to China as a missionary.

But of more importance at the time than those social concerns was my curiosity-impelled slide into pornography. The alluring pictures in the magazines I used to hide in my closet were soon augmented by the even more informative and erotic images of X-rated movies. The dingy, darkened theaters became my haven, even though I held the adult men sitting around me in contempt. I could rationalize and excuse my presence but not theirs.

The subway made it easy for me to get to the Times Square district of Manhattan that exposed me to an ever-greater world of lust and decadence. I loved the foreign nudist movies of the early sixties, whose repetitious plots always resulted in pretty girls undressing in forests or playing volleyball naked at the beach. The films portrayed a fun-filled erotic illusion of a self-gratifying, sex-centered life, but the theater projecting this image stood in dark contrast to its message. Most of the Times Square theaters that showed skin flicks were decayed corpses of their former selves. Seats were stiff, with torn upholstery and shaky arm rests. The paint-chipped walls looked as if they were about to collapse. The ornate sparkle of an old New York theater had given way to a litter-strewn death.

Once while sitting up front in the corner in an attempt to distance myself from the rest of the clientele, I was engrossed in the movie when I felt something at my foot. I wasn't sure if it was a touch or just a presence that I sensed. Tearing my wide eyes from the screen, I glanced down to the floor and was stunned to see a rat the size of a cat. With panic in my heart, I stomped my foot and the rodent scampered off and disappeared into a stack of trash.

I thought my attraction to these sleazy theaters made me some kind of pervert, yet in reality my presence was actually a natural response to repression. During my time in the seminary, sex was seen as an evil to be avoided. My parents' close-minded and close-mouthed attitude toward sex said very loudly that they thought it was dirty. My teenage sexual energy was normal and natural, yet I was led to believe it was abnormal and unnatural. The energy had no place to go but underground—hidden magazines. When they were discovered, I felt terrible guilt and, worse, thought my parents didn't like me. I resented them, first, for finding the stuff, and, second, for not helping me understand what was going on inside my body. Suppressed sexual energy must find a release somewhere, and usually it is in some unnatural or "perverted" way. Seedy movie theaters were a logical choice for me. There was nothing wrong with me. I was just deceived into thinking there was.

My teenage porn passion was hidden from all who knew me. The seen and the unseen me were as diverse as could be. But the lure of my hidden sexual expression and my perceived perversion made me believe that I was the most unworthy candidate for the priesthood. Maybe God didn't love me after all. The unrealistic picture of priestly piety and holiness became an obstacle to my achieving my childhood aspiration. I lived in a state of inner conflict, but my external righteous image was shattered by my parents' discovery of my magazines. I began to hate that part of me that was so easily aroused sexually, and I began to fear that neither God nor my parents accepted me because of that inner, mysterious urge. I didn't like myself and because of that negative feeling I began to crave acceptance from anyone.

Self-rejection is a vital step on the road to accepting and conforming to the beliefs of a cult. I was on the road. In a Christian's life most solutions to personal conflicts are tied to repentance. Life is ladened with poor decisions and unexpected curves. It is all but impossible to walk a straight and narrow path. Mistakes are a natural and unavoidable part of life's walk; the road to perfection travels through error. God would be less than God if he demanded absolute and constant perfection and did not accept us just as we are and where we are—and not as we could be or where we might be. The road is lonely, and we all need someone with whom we can share our innermost thoughts, someone who knows everything about us and still accepts us with unconditional love. I think that's the role God wants to play, but as a teenager I cast Him as a merciless tyrant looking for my slightest slip in order to slap me with retribution. The idea that I was worthwhile in God's eyes was as distant as the planet Mars. More than porno magazines and movies, I craved acceptance. I would marry simply because I thought my wife-to-be was the only person who would have me. Pornography provided some easily found but superficial joy and was little more than an escape from the dismal reality of repression and loneliness. There was so much lacking in me that I got whatever I could out of life in the easiest way.

All of us need acceptance, but acceptance doesn't mitigate the need for repentance. I could have been drawn to repentance by love but not driven by fear. In a theological sense, repentance is not a guilt-ridden trip where you feel bad about what you have done; rather, it is a change of direction away from those things that block unity with God. Sex is not a roadblock to reaching God, but excessive, self-centered sexuality is. I was never shown the difference; I thought that all sex was equally repulsive before God. I tried to repent, but the results were lousy and only produced more guilt and a greater sense of failure as I continually broke my promise to God that I would change my sinful ways. So my suffering intensified. I had no way of knowing that repentance is nothing more than waking up to the fact that something is wrong and needs change. Guilt, on the other hand, seeks punishment and usually gets its wish.

How does a kid—or even an adult—develop a change of mind and heart regarding a harmful habit? Years later at CBN I would learn a clever method: Bible brainwashing and force-fed guilt as the cornerstones of change. But for change to be honest and lasting much more is needed.

How sinful was my teenage sexual curiosity? The church's "Thou shalt not," authoritarian model of religion that was ingrained in my parents did not work for me as a teenager. As an adult, freed from the grip of a cult, I've come to believe that the major incentive for avoiding the "sins of the flesh" should be love. Jesus moved his followers by speaking words of love. He never mentioned mortal sin. Instead, Jesus gave humanity a glimpse of God's love and spoke of the importance of responding to that love. That revolutionary notion was the core of his teaching and the reason for his living.

Jesus was not interested in starting a church but only in changing some hearts. Jesus knew that the possible eradication of "sin" from a person's life would be the result of love, not force. Being taught that fornication is a mortal sin has seldom stopped a normal response to excited hormones. Nor does the threat of eternal damnation. On the other hand, the image of a tender and loving God gives birth to respect for our fellow humans and can convert sex into an act of giving and sharing. The persuasiveness of love can alter "sinful" behavior, but force and authority will have minimal impact on sexual promiscuity. I think that my pornographic passion was a symptom, not a sin— a symptom of feeling that I didn't count. I wonder what my high school days would have been like if I had thought of God as passionately loving or even had not been taught anything about God?

My sexual appetite may have been partially satisfied by girlie magazines and movies, but during this postseminary muddle and remorse, I developed a hunger that could be easily and openly indulged— and was.

Food in general and cookies in particular were consumed in quantities sufficient to sustain a small family. My high-school-long binge turned me into a 250-pound dumpling. On top of feeling terrible on the inside because of my alleged sexual sins, I now looked terrible on the outside as well. It's as if my innermost feelings of inferiority had manifested themselves physically. Add one hundred pounds of flab to my natural shyness and the flickering hope of a priestly life and you get the picture of how I graduated from high school without having ever kissed a girl even during that age of shifting moral values. Playboy pin-ups weren't so much a sin as an easy escape for a thoroughly rejected and naturally curious teenage blob. Cookies were relief, but the medicine became the disease.

As the summer of 1964 rolled in, I was rolled out of high school with no prospect of going to college on a full-time basis. The horizon held no appealing alternative to the priesthood. Three months into my seventeenth year I was about to face the real world—ready or not. My father hounded me about the importance of going to college, but I had no desire to pursue higher education. Perhaps my inner resentment of my parents led me to go against his wishes. In an effort at compromise, I agreed to attend night classes at Queensborough Community College as a nonmatriculating student while spending my days looking for a fulltime job. My cousin was an official at a major chemical corporation and, thanks to a gentle nudge from my mother, agreed to set up a job interview for me. Thanks to my lofty connection, a clerical job in the transportation department was mine. Almost. All I had to do was fill out some forms and take the company physical. I flunked the physical because of hypertension caused by my excess tonnage.

Things didn't look too good—in fact, they looked dismal. I'd go to the city each day pretending to look for a job, when in reality I'd hide in a darkened theater watching a dirty movie. I had no vision of the future. I started to hate myself, and by doing so I unknowingly took my first step toward the cult of fundamentalism.

Scripture claims that without a vision people perish. Within a short time televison would give me a vision and a future.

In the midst of my depression over losing out for a job because of rolls of fat, a roll of dice thrown by another cousin would transform me from a loser to a winner. Every year he got a summer job at CBS-TV because his neighbor was an executive at the network. That summer his job was in a department called Audience Services. He was hired to respond to requests for tickets from all over America to the "Ed Sullivan Show." The announcement of a guest appearance by a very special group from England brought an avalanche of mail. My cousin volunteered me to help handle the overflow. I was desperate, and even a temporary job was better than nothing.

Columbia Broadcasting System

As I prepared for my first trip to the CBS Broadcast Center on West 57th Street in New York City, America braced itself for a British invasion that would change the music world. Television not only was there but made instant heroes of John, Paul, George, and Ringo, as their uplifting sounds of love captivated the nation.

On my first day I was led to a room crammed with countless file boxes. Each box was filled with ticket requests for the Beatles performance. I was told that it shouldn't take longer than four weeks to open each letter and make the proper response. When I was done with the mail, CBS would be done with me. A four-week job gave birth to a twenty-two-year broadcasting career.

I diligently read each letter. Young girls offered everything and anything for a ticket. If I could only get my hands on a ticket, I could turn it into a ticket out of my virgin state. Some of the letters were very hot. Many of the young girls must have thought the Beatles actually gave out the tickets themselves. After reading a letter I sent out one of three types of standard negative responses based on their request. I enjoyed reading the letters so much that I finished my mountain of mail in only two weeks, which was half the allotted time. The supervisor congratulated me on my quick work and then wondered why, if I knew the job ended with the last letter, I would work so quickly. I had no clever response. He said that he would pay me for two more weeks, but it wasn't necessary to come in anymore. Not come in? Where else would I rather be?

The studios were the most interesting place I had ever been. I was bitten by the show-biz bug. I came to the studios each day and wandered up and down the halls. My bulging eyes looked everywhere. I may not have been ready to face the real world, but who said television had anything to do with the real world? The real world for me would become the world of make-believe.

A young man who scheduled lighting directors spotted me aimlessly walking the corridor in front of his office. He asked if I was lost. "Not exactly," I responded. I told him I was being paid but had nothing to do and no place to be. After laughing, he said that he could help me find a fulltime job, and he did. It was only a clerk's position, but I was on the inside. CBS became my home and my only interest.

Thanks to that inauspicious start in television, I had the opportunity to learn broadcasting from inside the premiere television network. I was selected for an executive-training program and became an executive before my twenty-first birthday. Altogether, during my time at CBS I had nine different jobs, the last being Senior Broadcast Control Supervisor.

My obesity and shyness forced me into a celibate state, and my smutty view of sex fostered a guilt-ridden inferiority complex, but CBS helped me break loose from those chains.

I was proud to work at CBS, and it helped make me feel good about myself. Television touches everyone. It's in everyone's living room, and we all have a natural interest in the behind-the-scenes activity of a studio. If someone asked me, "Where do you work?" My response of "CBS-TV" would always elicit a positive reaction. It didn't matter what I actually did at CBS; just the fact that I was around the glitter and excitement of show biz made most people envious—and made me special.

I began to look at the world through the CBS eye. Behind the eye of the camera I observed how people functioned in the cutthroat world of a creative business. At first I was appalled by the company politics, gossip, and back-stabbing, but the need to survive slowly taught me how to play the corporate game, though not how to enjoy it. The reality of the daily workday stood in stark contrast to the idealistic Christian principles that attracted but eluded me. The picture in front of the eye of the camera reflected a rapidly changing society as interpreted by the ratings-happy entertainment division. Television was creating a new reality for me as it exposed me to a world vastly different from Richmond Hill. I didn't stop to ponder who was shaping that reality or if it was a truthful reflection of life.

Network television feeds its audience a diet of junk-food shows, cooked to the taste of a twelve-year-old. The shows must have a broad sense of appeal in order to succeed, thereby making it necessary to aim the material at the lowest common denominator. For example, summer teenage viewers pushed "General Hospital" to the top of the ratings. The shows pretend to be reflecting life and current trends in America; yet, in reality, prime-time shows mirror the producer's view of life and the network's opinion of what the viewer wants to see. The camera does in fact blink and does not capture a complete picture of life. The CBS eye showed me a fragmented and distorted view of the world. Nonetheless, I became a television junkie, addicted not only to watching the tube but also to the production of the electronic images that shaped others. I was to become a video artist who created and lived in a world of fantasy—and one day would show America a fragmented and distorted view of religion.

I entered televison and early adulthood during an age of unrest and protest. When I rebelled against my religion, I no longer saw the need for going to church. I saw Christianity as a powerless set of misunderstood myths and man-made rules that trapped people in a maze of false beliefs instead of helping them transform themselves into a more true reflection of Jesus. I was in agreement with Gandhi's statement, "I like Christ, but I dislike Christians because they are so very unlike Christ." The Mahatma should have seen CBS, where church-going Christians cheated on their expense reports and made love in darkened viewing rooms and studios.

Even though I had no external use for the church, inside me I still felt a strong connection. In a very real way the church was my mother (a concept that was hammered into us at the seminary); and, while I was capable of rebellion, it was impossible to completely sever my relationship with the church. The occasional "Hi, this is your son" call—often in the form of a brief visit to an empty church—always managed to rekindle my dormant love for the church, a love that could not be explained or expressed. Even though the empty rituals and silly teachings of the church (like banning birth control) could not hold my interest, nonetheless I feared being damned by Holy Mother Church.

My early childhood training had led me to believe that the Church was God, and that without the Church there was no salvation. As a sexually frustrated young adult entering the work force, I didn't really believe that, but I was afraid to actually deny it. I would live in a spiritual limbo for twenty years before I had the courage and conviction to sever the tie and deny the lie I was told as an impressionable child. We save ourselves. Salvation is within each person, not inside any church.

For the sake of my mother, I pretended to go to church, but I only entered a church for such family events as a baptism, wedding, or funeral. Hatch 'em, match 'em, and dispatch 'em became my view of the ritualistic church. My secret disdain for the institution that my parents loved made it increasingly difficult for me to live at home. I wanted to be out of the house, but the economic reality of a clerk's salary forced me to live at home. My parents maintained a strong hold over me and continued to impose their will on my life. I teemed with resentfulness but lacked the money and conviction to leave. I was torn between outright rebellion and being respectful to them. I really did love them and was concerned to not hurt them. I suppose there was also a fear of rejection, that the people who gave me life might disdain their own creation. During the next four years the tension stretched until it snapped on April 12, 1969. On that day I would let my resentment rule my emotions, and I did something that I knew they would hate. Until that fateful and regrettable day, I lived a dual existence.

I was lonely and no longer content to just look at women in porno magazines, movies, or topless bars. I wanted to hold a real woman in my arms. But how—and more importantly, who? I read that frequently a guy's first full sexual encounter takes place in the arms of a whore. Having never even held hands with a girl, I figured that a street prostitute was going to be the only means of my sampling the forbidden fruit of womanhood. I was so timid that I couldn't even get up the nerve to approach one of the ladies of the night who lined 8th Avenue. Once, one walked up to me and asked if I wanted to go out. I was so scared and shy that I quickly responded with an emphatic, "No!" Still, I would look at the hookers and imagine which one I would confidently walk up to and ask out. The second time a hooker propositioned me, I mustered the guts to ask how much it would cost. She told me the tab would be twenty bucks. Then I wanted to know what we would do for that much money. She got the feeling that I was a cop—so she split. Jeez! Why was it so easy in the movies?

One evening after work, I was cruising the streets around Times

Square just looking and fantasizing when a neatly dressed Hispanic man in his mid-twenties asked me if I would be interested in a girl. What a question. Disregarding his alligator shoes and gold necklace, I calmly told him I might be, if the situation was right. I thought the part about the situation was pretty cool. He claimed he represented a couple of classy girls that he didn't let walk the streets. They just sit in his apartment and wait for the guys he brings up. It was his way of protecting his property from the cops or creeps who wanted more than just sex.

The whole thing sounded great to me, even though I wondered about what would happen if the girls were ugly. I wanted the first time to be with an angel. I shared my concern with the walking sex agent, and he said, "No problem. If you don't like my girls after you meet 'em, I'll give you your deposit back and you can take off." God, Monty Hall couldn't make a better deal. I gave him twenty bucks to escort me to the apartment, and once I finished with the girl I had to give her twenty dollars also.

After calculating the risks and the economics of the proposal, I agreed and anxiously followed him to a run-down brownstone located in the Hell's Kitchen district of the west side of Manhattan. I hoped the name of the neighborhood didn't have any religious significance to the deed I was about to do. As we climbed the exterior steps to the rubble of a once proud building, I intuitively knew this was not a smart thing to be doing. My lust overcame my flash of insight. Where were Ricardo Montalban and "Fantasy Island" when I needed them?

After passing through the outer doorway, we entered a small vestibule. On my left were a series of about eight doorbells. All the name plates were blank or missing. It was as if no one wanted to admit to living there. The wall on my right contained in-wall mailboxes for each apartment. The locks on many of the boxes were forced open. The paint-chipped ceiling revealed numerous old coats of paint now faded and soiled almost beyond recognition. My guide pushed open the unlocked inside door. A single naked light bulb overhead illuminated a dingy, dismal hall that was dominated by a worn-out stairway. The place looked like hell and smelled like death. I was beginning to get nervous, but still I followed him up the squeaky flight of stairs. My heart pounded in a mixture of anticipation and fear. Strange images flashed in my mind. I momentarily imagined that I was an undercover cop about to bust in on some junkie-killer. But this was no television show. I suddenly realized that this guy I was following could turn and beat the daylights out of me. I hoped he didn't have a knife. I wished I had a gun.

We reached the landing halfway to the second floor, at which point the stairs ascended in the opposite direction. The overhead light bulb had been smashed. The pimp turned in the shadows and looked me in the eyes and said, "Hey, man, you wait here for a minute." "Why?" I asked. "Listen Jack, I got to check to make sure the girls are ready—you know, not with a John. I'll be right back." Sounded reasonable, and besides who was I to argue. I stood there motionless. The minutes flew by without any indications that the coast was clear. As I listened to the sounds of a crying baby and an arguing couple from the floor above, I wondered if I could get laid without taking all my clothes off. Then it hit me. This guy isn't coming back. Why should he? I've been had. Kicking myself for being such a jerk, I turned and ran down the steps and out into the street. I was mad as hell. I didn't get the action I was craving, and I got taken for twenty dollars. I felt like a real fool. What a loser—I couldn't even buy sex in the middle of a revolution that flew the flag of free sex.

I took refuge in an Eighth Avenue pizza joint. As I sat in a corner stuffing my face I wondered if I was destined for a life without sex. The priestly vow of celibacy would have been a snap for me. I was determined, despite this depressing setback, to learn about sex—even if I had to climb the highest mountain.

Women, Women

A few days later, a couple of friends and I were gathered around my desk at CBS looking over a collection of brochures on upstate New York ski resorts. The young woman who was the boss's secretary and worked down the hall from us happened to walk by and overheard our conversation. Sarah loved skiing but had never skiied in the East, so she asked if she could come along. Her request wasn't enthusiastically received.

Sarah didn't have many friends at CBS or even in New York for that matter. She was originally from California but wasn't the kind of girl the Beach Boys sang about. She had only recently arrived in New York City. Later she told me that when she stepped off the plane she carried two worn-out suitcases stuffed with odds and ends left over from a rotten life in California. The move to the East Coast was more an escape than an adventure. She hit New York determined to start life over on her own terms. She said what was on her mind without much regard for other people's feelings, and it had a way of grating on people's nerves. Sarah had a zest for life and wanted to fit in at work, yet she was perceived by some as pushy and abrasive. Sarah had no sense of fashion and no use for make-up. She lacked softness and saw femininity as a sign of weakness. To make matters worse, she didn't trust people's motives and was a born skeptic. Yet, hidden beneath her coarse exterior, there lived a warm-hearted, wonderful person that no one ever got to meet. I had absolutely no interest in Sarah; however, I couldn't say no to her request to join us on the slopes.

My two friends and I sat crammed together in the front seat, and Sarah sat alone in the back as I drove north to the snow country. This was going to be my first time on skis, and I was brimming with excitement and expectation. As we approached the mountain, I was more overwhelmed by its size than its snow-covered majesty. My anticipation turned to apprehension, and I expressed some concern about the sanity of sliding down a snow- and ice-covered mountain on two long pieces of wood fastened to a pair of boots. My friends assured me that it was a snap, so, tossing caution to the cold, winter wind, I managed to stumble and tumble my way onto the chairlift.

I thrilled to the ride up the mountain and then spilled my way down the slope. After numerous falls, I managed to maintain my balance long enough to head downhill. I started to pick up speed, lots of speed. The exhilaration of zooming straight down the hill was shattered by the sudden realization that I had absolutely no idea of how to stop. Fear and panic took over when I found myself on a crash course with a group of people standing together in a line listening to a ski instructor. I screamed a frantic warning, and those who heard me scurried out of my way. My pudgy body, traveling faster than it thought possible without the aid of wings or wheels, collided with the ski instructor, and the impact sent him into a flying fall, while I somehow managed to continue sailing downhill. Leaving a wake of terror behind me, I was quickly approaching a cluster of trees, one of which I hit. With nothing but my pride hurt, I foolishly tried again, except with more caution. Nonetheless, I still took one tumble which sent me rolling down the hill minus my skis. I came close to turning into a gigantic human snowball. Is this any way to meet a girl?

After three unsuccessful runs at the hill, which was becoming bigger and bigger by the minute, my buddies abandoned me, and I decided that the warmth of the fireplace was what I needed. Once inside the lounge I realized that I was out of place there also. Everyone had on color-coordinated ski outfits that highlighted their trim, athletic bodies. I had on wet dungarees and a sweater that was stretched to its limits by my fat body. I was surrounded by great-looking girls, but the

odds were overwhelmingly against any of these almost-too-good-to-
be-true mountain maidens ever talking to me. I sat staring into the
crackling flames filled with a wish to experience the warmth of a girl.
I hated myself.

"Hey, what are you doing sitting here alone?" a female voice asked.
Is she talking to me? I turned to see Sarah. "Oh, hi," was my enthusiastic
response.

"What's the matter?" she inquired.

"Nothing. I just decided to give the ski instructors and the forest
a break. Besides, the lounge looks like more fun than a hospital, which
is where I'd wind up if I didn't stop skiing."

She smiled and said, "Hey, it's no fun skiing alone. Why don't
you join me, and I'll teach you the basics."

There we sat. Alone together amid a mountain of fun and friendship. "Sure, why not?" I replied rather than face that fire all day. It
wasn't bad. In fact, it was nice having someone to talk with and to
share the chair-lift rides. Almost as if by magic, the natural beauty
of the panoramic vista was magnified by sharing the experience with
Sarah. Being able to say, "Look, isn't that beautiful," and having her
agree managed to enhance the scene. Sarah's patience converted my
slipping into skiing. By the day's end I was able to make it down
the mountain without endangering innocent bystanders or trees.

As we stood together on the summit of Hunter Mountain, we were
both perched on the edge of transition.

I had no way of knowing that this pleasant day would change
my life. Every event of our lives, no matter how seemingly unimportant,
has the potential to have a profound impact on all subsequent events.
Two lonely, hurting, rejected people would sit together on a chair
lift sharing a ride up a mountain and never be the same again.

The change was almost unnoticed in the beginning. I still had no
special interest in Sarah, but I no longer avoided her. In fact, conversations became commonplace, and the coming Christmas season would
turn those incidental office chats into an official date. Nobody is immune to the festivities of the Christian celebration of the birth of their
Savior. For Sarah, the season made her usual loneliness even more
painful. For me, Christmas created disillusionment. Beneath the com-
mercially induced glitter and merriment is buried the message brought
by the baby whose birth is remembered but whose teachings are forgotten. It seemed like a strange time to stop and thank God for his
presence when so many were lifeless, hurting, hungry, and dying in a

strange war. The circumstances were not occasions for celebration. They were really reasons for anger. Even during this holy season when hearts seem more loving, there was no yearning for the helpless and hurting—those here among us and in places we know only through tragic headlines. The darkness of conflict and the frailty of humanity obliterated my awe of God's gift born in a manger. For me Christmas was a time of sadness stuffed under the joyful lights of a tree.

This Christmas was a little different for Sarah and me. We went to the movies and marveled at the decorations that adorned the streets.

As everyone was preparing to greet 1968 in style, it became apparent to Sarah and me that we had no plans or prospects for fun. "Say, how about we do something together on New Year's Eve?" I asked.

"Sure," she said without any hesitation. For her a night with a chubby Catholic, who was two years younger than she, was better than nothing. For me, anything was better than watching my parents twist a noisemaker in an effort to welcome a new year that would probably be a carbon copy of the old year. They seemed to need the past in order to hold them together in the future. I wanted a future that ignored the past.

As the big night approached, we were both still very inept at being with a member of the opposite sex. Sarah thought Greenwich Village would be a good place to ring in the New Year. Even though the area is sprinkled with jazz clubs and pubs featuring folk music, we wound up in a nightclub that specialized in vulgar, blue humor, although we didn't realize that until after we had been seated and ordered drinks. So we sat, like invaders from outer space on a voyage to another world. We spent the night gaping at the weirdos.

Around 10:45 P.M. I realized that at midnight tradition would have everyone kissing. My stomach became nauseated, and the drink I was nursing made it worse. I couldn't tell her I had to go home. Our first kiss was going to be ushered in by the tick of a clock during a freak show. Would she even expect or want a kiss? Do I make the first move? Woody Allen hadn't yet made his first movie, so I didn't know it was okay to struggle with stupid stuff like this. I wished I could have kissed her then—only to avoid the next hour's worth of nerves.

"Three, two, one." The place exploded into a frenzy of celebration. I stood still. Sarah cautiously leaned toward me. Oh, God, here it comes! I made a slight move in the direction of her mouth. Zap! It happened so fast, almost between heartbeats, that I nearly missed it. Our lips had barely touched when we both beat hasty retreats to our seats.

Our mutual love of the mountains and skiing opened the door for us to spend a great deal of time together during the winter months. We took a number of day trips to Hunter Mountain. Weekday nights became increasingly booked with movies and plays. The world of exotic restaurants became a part of my lifestyle. Sarah loved to dine at French restaurants. My gastronomical tastes had never been exposed to anything fancier than my mom's burnt pork chops. I'm not sure Mom knew what seasoning was, and her repertoire of meals was limited. The specialty of the house was leftovers. Now I came home burning with excitement about some new kind of food I had eaten, and my parents became increasingly more curious about this woman with whom I spent so much time in restaurants.

Despite the time we spent together, we still never held hands, and our kisses never expanded past isolated pecks. There were few physical displays of affection, and sex played virtually no part in our friendship. We talked. We took in the sights and sounds of the city. We frequented art museums and the Broadway theaters. Despite the compatibility we could muster for these social outings, we had absolutely nothing in common except our loneliness. We were hardly ever in agreement about anything, especially religion.

Sarah was a Jew who thought she was an atheist but probably was an agnostic. The Jewish part was enough to make my parents sick. They didn't like her, and they had never even met her. My parents' inquisitiveness became obsessive. What did I do during all the time I spent with this girl? Who is she? Where are her parents? An endless stream of questions. I wasn't hiding anything. I just didn't think the topic of Sarah was their concern. After all, we only hung out together. I certainly wasn't in love. They couldn't accept the fact that Sarah was simply a good friend. They should have known how I spent my time before Sarah.

I knew bringing Sarah home would ignite flames of hate. Bowing to pressure, I finally brought my friend home to dinner. The initial visit was an instant disaster. My brother thought she was a Communist. My father thought she was a Christ-killer. My mother thought she was a loose woman. My sister thought she was obnoxious. The visit didn't clear up anything and only intensified their worst fears and stimulated even more probing questions. Why did she leave home? Who was she running from? Why did she move here alone? Doesn't she miss her family?

My answers were unacceptable, so they invented their own. They speculated that she must have been married before. Our friendship was turning into a soap opera. What dark, dirty secret was she covering up? What did we do in her apartment? They didn't think that nice girls lived alone. My family found Sarah opinionated and abrasive. Blinded by bigotry and fear, they could not see that Sarah was a fragile yet fine person.

Sarah wanted to be liked and to feel a part of a family, but, thanks to her loveless childhood, she had no inkling of how to gain acceptance. She never knew the warmth and security of a close-knit family, and I felt sorry for all the hard times she endured growing up with parents who didn't want her or her younger brother. They once tried to put her away in some cruel institution. She grew up isolated and with no self-respect. I admired the way she overcame all the adversities life had dealt her and was able to make a new life for herself. Beneath her hardened exterior there beat the heart of a very warm, wonderful, caring person.

Our friendship and concern for each other didn't mean we were destined to spend our lives together, but events and our own immaturities joined us together in a futile attempt to make that happen. Sarah shifted my interests away from the porno theaters of Manhattan and exposed me to the world of art, culture, and the theater. Sarah gave a lot to me. I gave a lot to Sarah. We were both changing and learning how to care about a person. I deeply resented my parents' negative attitude toward her.

Despite our mutual caring, a mountain of differences soon became too much to overcome. We always went and did whatever she wanted. I thought I was being the perfect gentleman. She enjoyed the attention and respect, but deep inside she wanted me to provide more direction. She projected an image of complete independence, yet she longed for someone to lead the way, at least on dates. I just wanted to make her happy—what we actually did was unimportant.

Late one March night, a discussion about all that took place that culminated in her calling me "a mouse, not a man." I lost my temper and stormed out of her apartment. For dramatic effect I screeched the tires as I pulled away from the curb and sped down the block. We went back to ignoring each other at work.

I was alone again, and more than anything else in the world I wanted a romantic relationship with a girl—not friendship or sex but romance.

The only obstacle to the fulfillment of that desire was fat. Lots of fat. I had tried more times than I cared to remember to lose weight, and the results were always failure. But my past efforts lacked two significant ingredients: motivation and determination. No fancy diets this time. No counting calories either. Forget drugs, doctors, and science also. Willpower did it all.

I started with a seven-day fast, after which I ate only one small meal a day for almost three months. The result was a net loss of 91 pounds. I went from 250 pounds to 159 pounds. I was physically born again.

My physical change was so overwhelming that relatives who had not seen me for a while failed to even recognize me. I was skinny, and it felt great. With the loss of weight came a gain in self-confidence.

In May of 1968, I was filled with a new hope and outlook for myself. One evening after work, another seemingly unimportant event took on monumental significance. I was taking the Long Island Railroad home, but instead I was transported to the land of romance.

I boarded the train, turned left, and headed down the narrow aisle looking for a seat. Suddenly, I thought I saw a vision. There before me sat a girl who stole my heart. She gave me new meaning to the word *beautiful*. I slowed my pace to a crawl in order to get a longer look at her face as I passed her. Her long golden hair had a whisper of a wave and partially covered one side of her delicate face. The hair provided a touch of mystery as it partially hid her soft, gentle features and sky-blue eyes. She was alone. She didn't have a book or paper, yet she seemed very preoccupied. As she stared blankly into space, her head was tilted ever so slightly upward and leaned a touch to her right side. She was lost in thought and really didn't notice anyone around her. God, how beautiful and enchanting! What was she thinking about? I took one step beyond her seat and came to a dead halt; but my mind was moving at the speed of light. The seat next to her is empty—so what—she wouldn't talk to you—yeah, that's right—no, wait—I look great—new sport jacket and all—she wouldn't have talked to the old fat me—go back and sit—no—yes. That sequence of progressive reasoning took but a few seconds, but the turn to return to her seat seemed to take an hour.

Trying to conceal my excitement, I calmly slipped into the seat next to the dream. Now what? Did she notice me pass her and come back? Doesn't matter, I'll just sit here and be cool. My eyes darted sideways in an attempt to steal quick unnoticed glimpses. She was hundreds of miles away in deep thought; I was beginning to get lost in my own fantasy about her. I had never had that kind of instantaneous infatuation with any female.

Ever so softly came her first words, "Excuse me, do you know the time?"

She spoke. The dream talks. She spoke to me! Thank God, I can tell time. "Nine-forty," I said after nonchalantly glancing at my watch.

"Has this train ever left on time?" she chuckled as she shook her head in an annoyed, negative fashion. I got lost in the movement her shaking head created in her long, silky hair. God, I just can't stare. Say something quick.

"I think that's against railroad policy," I responded in a futile attempt at humor. Oh damn, she smiled but isn't going to say anything else. It's up to me or it's over. "Do you take the same train every night?" Not that clever, but the answer could be helpful, and besides I got it out without dribbling or stuttering.

"Yeah, it's always late, so I always make it." Pretty funny, but it would have been nice if she asked if I took this train every night.

"You work in the city?" Oh nuts, that was a dumb question; of course she works in the city. "Yes, at Gimbels. It's just a short walk, but by the time we close it's still a rush to make this train."

Gimbels. Great. I'll open a charge-account tomorrow. Suddenly a silence invaded our space as I ran out of things to say and questions to ask. "That's a neat RFK button you're wearing. Where did you get it?" There is a God, and he made her talk when I couldn't. I'll go to Mass in the morning and thank him.

"I work for the senator," I said, knowing that might draw a response out of her.

"Oh, how exciting. What do you do?"

Ugh! Now I'm cornered and in trouble. I wanted to say that I wrote his speeches rather than admit I only hand out the campaign buttons to anyone who asks. Inspiration. "Well, actually I work at CBS-TV, but I'm a campaign volunteer for Bobby."

"Have you ever met him?"

"Sure, just last night he was in the office." Okay, so I stretched the truth a bit. I did see Kennedy at his campaign headquarters. That's almost meeting him, and he did toss a smile in my direction.

"What do you do at CBS?" That's the magic question. Now I'm on a roll. I can talk about CBS for days, and most people want to listen.

We never stopped talking, and I did not get off at my station. As the train pulled into the Long Beach Station, the last stop, Emily said, "Gee, you live in Long Beach too?"

"Not exactly," I said with a wry smile, "I live in Valley Stream." She twisted her pretty head in a quizzical fashion and said, "But Valley Stream is six stops back. You missed it."

"I would have missed you more." God, what a great line, and it came out so naturally.

She smiled, looked at me for a few seconds, and asked, "Would you like to walk me home?"

This must be a dream—if it is I don't want to ever wake up. "I would be honored," I replied with utmost sincerity. We walked along the beach and talked for more than two hours. I asked her if she would see me again, and she said that she would love to.

The next night we had our first date. The start was magic. The end was tragic.

Emily. Emily. Emily. The name stands as a monument to an unparalleled bomb-bursting first love. My memory of that love and of Emily set a standard for my feelings of love that I believed could never be matched again. The picture of her that hangs in my memory is better than any photograph because it has erased all her imperfections and left only a pure image. I was totally captivated by her beauty, charm, exuberance, and style. I loved the way she spoke and the words she chose. I loved the texture of her voice and never got bored listening to her animated utterances. She was feminine, soft, and gentle. Oh, and her body. She looked equally great in a dress or jeans and a tee-shirt. With a bow in her hair, she was beyond compare.

Emily embodied my every boyhood desire. From that serendipitious train ride until the end of the summer, every moment that I could squeeze out of a day was spent in Long Beach. It didn't take my parents long to realize that this girl was very special to me. I was always staring off into space with a smile on my face. I didn't mind their endless stream of questions or even find them an intrusion on my privacy. I loved talking about Emily, and I knew they would love to hear what I had to say about her.

"Yes, she is a Catholic; her uncle is even a bishop." "Yes, she lives at home, but she and two of her girlfriends rented a beachhouse for the summer." "Her father is a respected businessman in Brooklyn and is also involved in local politics and is going to run for public office." The answers proudly rolled off my tongue.

Her first visit to my home gave birth to a collective sigh of relief from my family. "What a sweet, charming girl," was my mother's instant analysis of Emily. Emily said all the right things. She knew how to ingratiate herself with my parents and pulled out all the stops in an effort to win their approval. Little did Emily know that just not being an opinionated Jew would do the trick. Little did my parents know that their worst fears about Sarah were unfounded, and that beneath Emily's sweetness and polished sophistication was a sensuous core they would have considered sinful.

Emily was twenty-two years old and had just graduated from a prestigious Catholic college. Her parents were conservative in their religion, politics, and morality. Emily was trying to escape that image. Dressed in jeans and a sweatshirt, Emily could have been a poster pin-up girl for the flower children of the decade. At a time when virginity was beginning to be perceived as a plague rather than a virtue, she had made it so far without "losing it." This was a problem for her. She wanted to discover the joys of sex, and the rented beach-house would be her *Santa Maria*.

As I picked Emily up for our first official date, I had no way of knowing her plans for a summer of surfside sex. Just talking to her was a thrill beyond my wildest expectations. As we walked to a fancy French restaurant, one Sarah had discovered, Emily took hold of my hand. That simple touch could have sustained me for years. After a wonderfully romantic dinner and drive to Long Beach, we took a quiet moonlight walk along the oceanfront. We stopped and faced the water. We were holding hands. I was in heaven. I turned my head to watch the evening breeze playfully blow through her long hair. She looked at me, smiled, and kissed me. Our first kiss stands in stark contrast to the first time my lips touched Sarah's. I got so excited by Emily's affectionate kiss that I was totally flabbergasted. No one had ever touched me the way that she did that day. We stood silently staring at each other's smiling faces. The emotion of that moment would affect the rest of my life. As we walked back to the beachhouse, we made plans to meet the next day.

I spent the next day watching the clock. I was at Gimbels' side door an hour early. When Emily walked out of the store, she was wearing a white sundress and had a yellow ribbon in her hair. The bounce in her step made me feel that she was glad to see me. I couldn't believe I was seeing her three days in a row; I felt so very proud. I hardly got out "Hi" when she gave me a hello kiss. Following a candlelight dinner, she suggested we head for the beachhouse where we could talk.

But talking was the farthest thing from her amorous mind. If she had sat any closer to me during the drive to the beach, she would have been on my lap. With her arm around my shoulder, I sped down the Southern State Parkway. We had the radio blasting, and she energetically sang along with each song. I was beside myself with excitement. I knew in my heart that I was in love.

I had this chivalrous notion that sex wouldn't be right—after all, it is sinful and dirty. Mixed-up thoughts about honor and respect contradicted the message my aroused body was sending. We got to the beachhouse, and "mysteriously" her two girlfriends had vacated the place. We sat on the couch in the dimly-lit living room. It was so hot that even the ocean breezes didn't help. We sat and chattered. She kept creeping closer. Before I knew what had happened, we abandoned the cramped couch and were on the rug-covered floor—in each other's arms. We were both filled with passion but empty on experience. I didn't know what to do next, but Emily knew what she wanted done, so she led the way. She placed my hand on her still-clothed breast. When I did not get her message, she reached behind herself to unzip her sundress. Sensual passion was a stranger in my life, and its sudden, unexpected arrival was far too much for me to handle. I lost all control and had an untimely eruption in my pants. My entire body went limp. My ecstasy instantly turned to nervousness as I worried what Emily would think. Much to my relief, she giggled, and we held each other tenderly for a long time. We may not have made love, but nonetheless it was a night of sheer delight.

The next night I once again picked her up at Gimbels. She got into the car carrying a Gimbels' shopping bag, which she tossed into the back seat. We drove to the beach. As we pulled up to the bungalow, she let out an annoyed, "Oh shit!"

"What's the matter?" I asked, fearing the worst.

"My friends are home," she responded as if the girls had committed a crime.

"So what. They do live there," I said innocently.

"I know. It's just that I bought something special for you today," she said with a mischievous smile on her face.

"What?"

"Well, I wanted to surprise you by wearing it first."

With my curiosity aroused, I asked, "Let me see it now."

She started to say she couldn't when an enlightened look spread across her face. She impulsively jumped into the backseat and excitedly removed a see-through, sexy negligee from the bag. With little-girl innocence, she said, "Don't look yet," and she began to take off all her clothes. My disbelieving eyes were glued to the back seat. Once into the negligee, she looked at me, smiled, and said, "Well, what do you think?"

"I think I better move the car," I said in a near-panic. I drove the car as fast as I could to a more remote section of the block. Once parked in a more darkened spot, I leaped into the back seat, and we kissed in a violently passionate manner. Oops! Premature ejaculation number two. I got frustrated. She got dressed. Still, she seemed unperturbed and danced her way toward the house. Before entering, she turned and blew me a kiss.

The next five weeks were filled with heavy petting and touching without ever having intercourse. We were very close to "going all the way" one night when her friends burst through the front door. Emily was frustrated. I was content. I think that she genuinely loved me; however, I wasn't fulfilling her summer goal. She wanted sex and had not planned on falling in love.

One day she was alone on the beach when a guy a few years younger than she managed to strike up a conversation. He wasted no time getting Emily into bed. Emily wasted no time getting what she wanted. She didn't plan on seeing this teenager again, but for some reason his being the first took on mystical importance. So, she saw both of us for most of the summer. I treated her like a queen. Bill gave her what she also wanted. He was Jewish, and despite her sexual revolution her Catholic faith still meant something to her. He was a beach bum with no education or job. Still, Bill eventually won her undivided attention because of the physical hold he had on her.

Emily tried gently to explain all this to me, but no words could ever ease the pain. I loved her and would always love her. One question hounded me for a very long time: Why didn't I make love to Emily? For a long time I thought it was just because I was a gentleman. Remember, this was 1968, long before young adult sex was an accepted fact of life. However, that explanation only scratches the surface, and I now realize that there is a much deeper and more accurate explication.

The church had created an image of woman that was modeled on the Blessed Virgin Mary. Sex was dirty. So dirty, in fact, that the ever-pure Mary had to conceive the Baby Jesus without having to be stained by the squalor of sex. Sex was something you did with a hooker if you couldn't control your perverted and unholy urges. I wanted to make love to Emily, but I thought those "lustful desires" had to be suppressed. I thought that the sex of pornography was ugly and something to hide and that sex outside of marriage was pornographic.

I had accepted a stupid premise: that if you don't love someone then you might as well go all the way, but that if you did, you must wait for marriage. The church fostered a dumb belief that a man had in his power the ability either to use and abuse a woman or to treat her as a love object, which meant making her a living Blessed Virgin until he married her; and, further, that a man had to choose between the two extremes of sexual exploitation and sexual repression. It is no wonder that women played a subservient role in the church; they might be good enough to be a nun, but never a priest. And a priest had to be so good that he could never have sex. The priest in me could not make love to the girl I loved because I chose to turn her into a Blessed Virgin. Emily had other ideas, and I was left to struggle with my obsessive, compulsive behavior.

My obsession with the church, despite my mild rebellion, made me deny my natural sex urge and thereby forced it into the gutter. The church's antisex message had been so hammered into me during my twelve years of Catholic schooling that it had become an indistinguishable part of me. Without knowing it, the church's neurosis had become my neurosis. When I was alone with Emily, the little "voice" that said "don't" was not mine, it was the voice of Holy Mother Church—and it was wrong. I wanted to give Emily all of me, totally, exclusively, and forever—that doesn't sound unchristian to me.

The church's problems about women's sexuality are still evident today. The Pope stands firm in banning birth control, denying women the option of becoming priests, and demanding celibacy for priests. The church seems more concerned with sex than sanctity. Cardinal O'Connor of New York continues to fight against homosexual rights. The official Catholic church, just like many fundamentalists, does not have a high regard for women or sex.

As the summer ended, I was alone again. More than alone, I was despondent. With Emily, I knew happiness beyond compare; without her, I knew only despair. I went from feeling great to thinking I was second-rate. Life after love had no satisfaction and was filled with confusion and one big "What now?" My self-confidence level was at an all-time low, even though I was thin. I thought of myself as a dismal failure without much of a future. Even if I could fall in love again, it wouldn't do any good—it would never feel the way it should. Even life at CBS lost its luster; the trip to the top seemed so long that I speculated I would spend another forty years on the periphery of television as some kind of clerk.

Sarah Again

One fall afternoon I was walking up West 57th Street, headed for the subway. It was three long city blocks from CBS to the train. The walk was uphill, and the street formed a wind tunnel into the Hudson River. It wasn't an easy walk. As I huffed and puffed my way along, I heard the distinctive sound of an old Volkswagen Beetle horn break through the cacophony of city sounds. Beep, beep. I kept walking, ignoring the sound. Beep, beep. My head turned curbside and there, creeping her way up the road, was Sarah behind the wheel of her little German car. Waving enthusiastically, she blurted out a big "Hi!"

I responded with my normal lethargic response to her presence, "Oh—hi."

"Want a ride?" she beckoned.

Tired of fighting the hill and the wind I said, "Why not?"

As I settled into her tiny car, she asked, "What's new?"

"Nothing much," was my weak response.

As we hesitatingly communicated for the first time in six months about such things as my weight loss, her new car, and CBS politics, I distinctly remember thinking, "This is my lot in life." I meant, of course, Sarah. In that negative thought the seeds of a twelve-year disastrous marriage were planted. It ended at the Christian Broadcasting Network.

Back then, the Bible for Sarah was a collection of silly, outdated, and barbaric stories, and for me the Scriptures were important yet misunderstood. In the end the Book would take on major significance for us both and drive us apart.

Sarah and I picked up where we left off, just in time for another ski season. The one difference this time around was that we had a little more physical activity. The return of Sarah to my life mortified my family. More questions and gossip.

I didn't want to lose the only girl who spoke to me, and by December Sarah and I speculated about a possible August marriage. After breaking the news to my parents, things became increasingly impossible at home. I began to think it would be a good idea if I moved out of the house and lived on my own before the wedding. I disliked Long Island and thought a move to the city would be perfect.

In January of 1969, I informed my folks that I wanted to move out of the house and get my own apartment in the city. From their reaction, you would have thought I shot my sister.

"No way," was their categorical response.

"What do you mean 'no way?' I'll be twenty-two in three months." I was reminded that my father was the youngest of twelve and that most of his brothers and sisters had at least six children, and no one ever left home before marriage. "Okay, fine. I'll get married as soon as I can."

In an open act of rebellion, I moved the wedding up to April. Of course, my parents thought I wanted to move out in order to move in with Sarah. That was not my intention; yet they figured we spent all our time in bed. Just like the church they so loved, my parents saw evil where none existed—in my closet and in Sarah's heart.

Sarah and I talked about divorce before we were married. Even though I was no longer active in church life, the ingrained Catholic position against divorce lived within me. "Marriage is forever," I argued with Sarah. Her position was simple and pragmatic: Sure, we'll get married, and if it doesn't work out we'll get a divorce with no harm done. We were both wrong—marriage is not always forever; divorce always hurts.

Our marriage was built on immaturity, ignorance, and desperation. Despite numerous conflicts between Sarah and me, as well as mounting protests from my parents, an April date was set for our marriage in the local Catholic church. Sarah and I attended a few meaningless pre-nuptial conferences with a priest. There were a host of pledges made, many of which we both soon forgot. Sarah agreed to allow any children to be raised Catholic but argued with the priest that she didn't want them to attend a Catholic school. It was a ridiculous debate that clouded the potential problems of our partnership.

I had no idea of the importance and impact of my choice to get married. I didn't know what marriage was all about. The experience was a far cry from a sacred calling from God. According to the priest, by virtue of our marriage we would signify and share in the mystery of that unity and fruitful love that existed between Christ and his church. We did not see marriage as a vehicle to holiness or as an irrevocable sacred covenant. That was the church's pipe dream.

The priest told us we should nourish and develop our marriage by undivided affection, which would well up from a fountain of divine love, while, in a merging of human and divine love, we would remain faithful in body and in mind, in good times as well as bad. Yea, right.

Four days before the wedding I received a phone call from Emily. No, this isn't a plot from "General Hospital." She had to see me. I eagerly agreed without informing her of my plans for the weekend. We met the next night. She cried her heart out as she told me how dumb she was for staying with "that beach bum." I told her how she hurt me and that I was getting married on Saturday. We were both in a state of shock as we sat parked in an isolated section of Staten Island. I told her that I loved her very much and that I would cancel the wedding. We held each other tightly.

I wanted to cancel the wedding but didn't know how to do it. I was frightened and confused. I didn't want to hurt Sarah. I didn't know if I could trust Emily. What about all the catering arrangements and the guests? How would I tell Sarah? I couldn't sort it all out, so I remained silent.

Two days before the wedding, Sarah found a cigarette lighter in my car with the inscription "Emily." She looked upset as she asked, "Whose is this?" It was the moment of truth. I choked. Maybe I was a mouse after all, because I didn't have the guts to tell the truth. In order to avoid any confrontation or inflict any harm, I lied. "Oh, gee, I bet it's Joe's. He's seeing some nurse and he must have dropped it after the bachelor party." She bought that. And I bought the fruits of that lie. I lived the lie for twelve years.

The wedding day came and I was sick. I dragged my way to the church praying for some kind of disaster—like a plane crashing into the church—to thwart the dreaded ceremony. I stood in front of the priest, motionless. I was in a deep fog. I never heard any of his words. Even the waiters at the reception had more fun than I did.

I called Emily two days after the wedding. We met. We cried. We made love. It was the most incredible experience. It was six months too late.

Three days earlier I was a virgin. Now on my second shot at intercourse I was committing adultery. Emily was still emotionally bound to Bill. I was legally bound to Sarah. And we were in love. For the next three years we made love on a weekly basis. After our flights of ecstasy, we often joked how Bill and Sarah would be perfect for each other. We had the greatest of times during our secret rendezvous.

One night we fell asleep and I awoke in a panic at 3:00 A.M. How was I going to explain getting home at this hour? Emily was sound asleep. I dressed quickly and scribbled this note:

Emily,

We fell asleep. I had to leave but didn't want to wake you.

Love,
Gerry

The next morning Bill paid an unexpected visit to Emily, who by now had her own apartment not far from where I lived. He let himself in with his key and discovered next to his sleeping girlfriend my note. They had a big fight. Afterward she told me we couldn't go on like this. And so it ended. I've never seen or spoken to her again.

Love and Marriage

Life with Sarah was a charade. Much of the time I worked nights or weekends and she days, so we didn't have to spend a lot of time together. My family eventually accepted Sarah but never with much enthusiasm. With Emily gone there was no way Sarah could keep me satisfied on any level. Yet I wanted to be faithful and even had a half-baked notion of trying to make something out of our marriage. I didn't feel guilty about my three-year affair with Emily; I rationalized that my marriage was a blunder and that I loved Emily. Now that Emily was no longer a part of my life, I wanted to try harder with Sarah. Initially, I didn't look for some other girl to take Emily's place; I didn't think anybody could. Once again I was ready to accept "my lot."

But before long, I began to take refuge in the pages of porno magazines and the flickering images of skin flicks. I was looking for love in all the wrong places. With a photographer friend, who also worked at CBS, I even started to take X-rated pictures. I was drowning in a sea of decadence that included a torrid six-week affair with a topless go-go dancer who had modeled for us. I hardly seemed like a candidate for sainthood or a person who would, within months, be leading prayer meetings.

The engrained Catholic belief about the indissolubility of marriage left me an emotional cripple. Instead of working at reviving my dead marriage, I chose to bury myself in a world of fantasy—dreaming about finding real love. I might have lost Emily, but I had bought the myth of romantic love: a myth that claims there is one someone "out there" who is going to be my perfect mate and that together we will be able to meet each other's needs and that we can live in perfect harmony. It is a lie. I've wasted untold hours daydreaming about such a perfect love or desperately trying to find it; yet, no one could measure up to such a love. Especially Sarah. I was always ready to fall in love and that was the problem. Love is not something you "fall" into; love is something that takes hard work to achieve. In his book, *The Road Less Traveled*, which has had a long life on both hardcover and paperback best seller lists, M. Scott Peck writes:

> Of all the misconceptions about love the most powerful and pervasive is the belief that "falling in love" is love or at least one of the manifestations of love. It is a potent misconception, because falling in love is subjectively experienced in a very powerful fashion as an experience of love. When a person falls in love what he or she certainly feels is "I love him" or "I love her." But two problems are immediately apparent. The

first is that the experience of falling in love is specifically a sex-linked erotic experience. We do not fall in love with our children though we may love them very deeply. We do not fall in love with our friends of the same sex—unless we are homosexually oriented—even though we may care for them greatly. We fall in love only when we are consciously or unconsciously sexually motivated. The second problem is that the experience of falling in love is invariably temporary. No matter whom we fall in love with, we sooner or later fall out of love if the relationship continues long enough. This does not say that we invariably cease loving the person with whom we fall in love. But it is to say that the feeling of ecstatic lovingness that characterizes the experience of falling in love always passes. The honeymoon always ends. The bloom of romance always fades.

I wanted to be one with another person—one in a mystical, not just sexual, sense. As infants we see ourselves as one with the universe. A baby cannot distinguish itself from its surroundings. All is one, and there are no boundaries. In time the infant develops a sense that he or she is a separate entity . . . there is a "me." The infant learns it can move when it wants to move and that its surroundings will stay still—it is starting to learn who she or he is and who she or he is not. Gradually the child begins to understand that it is not its crib and has its own arms, legs, voice, and will. The child is learning about its limits and boundaries and has dropped its belief that it is one with the universe. According to Dr. Peck the knowledge of these limits is known as ego boundaries, and the development of ego boundaries is something that continues through childhood into adolescence and even into adulthood, but the boundaries established later in life are more psychic than physical. With the expansion of these ego boundaries comes loneliness. Dr. Peck writes:

> Most of us feel our loneliness to be painful and yearn to escape from behind the walls of our individual identities to a condition in which we can be more unified with the world outside ourselves. The experience of falling in love allows us this escape—temporarily. The essence of the phenomenon of falling in love is a sudden collapse of a section of an individual's ego boundaries, permitting one to merge his or her identity with that of another person. The sudden release of oneself from oneself, and the dramatic surcease of loneliness accompanying this collapse of ego boundaries is experienced by most of us as ecstatic. We and our beloved are one! Loneliness is no more!

With the exhilarating sensation of falling in love comes the belief that love can conquer anything and that together—united in love—the lovers can solve all their problems. The future seems forever bright, but the fantasy soon fades and is buried beneath the problems of daily life and the reality of individual goals, likes, and dislikes which may not be in harmony with those of the person we love. The ego boundaries that had expanded to include another person begin to shrink back to their former limits. We are no longer one, but two very distinct people who begin to fall out of love. Dr. Peck writes in his highly acclaimed book that:

> At this point they begin either to dissolve the ties of their relationship or initiate the work of real loving. By my use of the word "real" I am implying that the perception that we are loving when we fall in love is a false perception—that our subjective sense of lovingness is an illusion. However, by stating that it is when a couple falls out of love they may begin to really love I am also implying that real love does not have its roots in a feeling of love. To the contrary, real love often occurs in a context in which the feeling of love is lacking, when we act lovingly despite the fact that we don't feel loving. Falling in love is not an extension of one's limits or boundaries: it is a partial and temporary collapse of them. The extension of one's limits requires effort; falling in love is effortless. Once the precarious moment of falling in love has passed and the boundaries have snapped back into place, the individual may be disillusioned, but is usually none the larger for the experience. When limits are extended or stretched, however, they tend to stay stretched. Real love is a permanently self-enlarging experience. Falling in love is not.

I believe that a great deal of the rampant infidelity that exists in marriage today grows out of a search for romantic love; however, real love cannot be found in a fantasy but grows out of the true acceptance of each other's individuality and separateness—and that takes effort.

I wanted Sarah to be Emily—and she could never be. Because I never had the feeling of "falling in love" with Sarah, I believed that I could never love her; and the Church's edict that marriage is forever only increased the pain. When I fell in love with a woman at CBN, I thought I could have it all: leave Sarah, keep my job, and live forever in a garden of romance. What a fool! I had made it to my mid-thirties without learning about love. Love was only a romantic notion without any meaning. The Church, the wife of my childhood, spoke about love yet in reality did not teach me anything about authentic self-enlarging love—it was concerned about enforcing bedroom morals and completely ignored the issue of helping people overcome loneliness by becoming truly one. Instead I learned about "love" from the movies, which taught me love was magical and instantaneous. I was not able to grow until I divorced the wife of my childhood and the wife of my adulthood and could take a fresh look at life and decide for myself which beliefs and myths are real and which are false. What I had been taught to believe, both by the church—the peddlers of mythology and morality—and the movies—the peddlers of fantasy and ecstasy—was not helpful to my growth; in fact, those beliefs drugged me into a state of despondency and complacency. I pretended to stay married to Sarah and the Church—in reality I despised them both but feared leaving either one of them. I needed to forge for myself more viable beliefs in order to give meaning to my life. However, the double divorce—Sarah and the Church—was postponed for ten years because I was about to embark on a course that would not challenge my childhood beliefs but intensify them and increase my pain. I was about to step into the twilight zone of a cult.

Two years after Emily and I parted company, Sarah became pregnant. The prospect of fatherhood shocked me into attempting to correct my sordid behavior. Sarah and I attended Lamaze birthing classes. We both stopped smoking for the sake of the baby's health. We decided to buy a house because our Queens apartment was located in an area that was riddled with crime and not a safe place for a mother and child to be walking around. Extending ourselves to our financial limit we purchased a big, but rundown, house in New Jersey. The upcoming birth was bringing us closer together, yet our constant arguments made our life together a joke.

After our daughter was born, the real problems came home. Sarah had a difficult time adjusting to motherhood. The crying baby scared her to death, and she seemed totally ill at ease caring for an infant. To complicate matters, the house was in need of a tremendous amount of work. We went through 55 gallons of paint in a futile attempt at making it at least look good. We were financially strapped and desperately trying to cope with a bouncing bundle of energy.

I loved the baby and wanted us to be a family. Sarah would have positive feelings for the infant in time, but for now she had to return to work in order to retain her sanity. I cared for the four-month-old child from sunrise until about three-thirty in the afternoon, at which point the baby went to sleep. The babysitter arrived, and I departed for work. Sarah got home as the baby's nap ended. She fed her, and it was soon time to put the baby to bed for the night. I got out of work at midnight, came home, and collapsed. That cycle continued for months.

I had two full-time jobs, and the changing, cleaning, feeding, and walking of my daughter was the harder of the two. As my love for the child grew, so did my hatred for Sarah. Enough of this stupdity. I located a good divorce lawyer. I knew Sarah wouldn't want custody. It would be easy.

Before the first meeting with the lawyer and before I informed Sarah of my plans, I got a little case of the nerves. I needed to talk to someone. Because of my deep love for my sister and her husband, they became ideal candidates for my soul-searching chat. What I didn't know was that they recently had had a born-again encounter with God. A God I had long ago forgotten. They lived in Albany, New York, which is about a three-hour drive upstate, and as I drove north I began to enter the one-way street of spiritual fundamentalism that would take me, Sarah, and our daughter to the capital of evangelical television and would terminate with an unbelievable dual twist of fate and faith.

I was on the brink of conversion—conversion from an imperfect person coping with the normal tensions of life to a religious zealot who had all the answers to life. My life was about to start over—I was going to be born again.

5

A Word from the Lord

Driven by despair, I headed north on the New York State Thruway toward Albany. After leaving the congested, noisy New York City metropolitan area, the road gently winds its way through lush valleys and majestic mountains providing the traveler with a breathtaking panorama of beauty and freshness. The peaceful rolling landscape was a welcome relief from the pounding beat of the crowded city streets. The year-round wonder of the road pales to insignificance when contrasted with the colorful spectacle created by autumn. 1974 was no different; the vast expanses were ablaze with color as the trees put on their amazing technicolor dreamcoats.

Despite the season and the vista, my drive was not filled with exhilaration. I was despondent and scared. I felt cornered and trapped. Everything had gone wrong in my life. I hated working nights at CBS; the responsibility for coordinating the prime-time shows was awesome. Worse than the pressure and the late hours was the fact that I was stuck deep inside the technical bowels of broadcasting life.

I detested the house we had purchased and dreaded all the work it generated. I had gone from being an apartment dweller to being a house painter. When I wasn't painting, I was repairing. The garage had a massive hole in the roof. The roots of the trees in front of the house had pushed up and cracked the sidewalk. The wooden steps to the porch had rotted away. The fence around the front yard was collapsing. The doorbell didn't work. The plumbing leaked and converted the basement into an indoor swimming pool.

The furniture that fit snugly into our Queens apartment was all but lost in the space of the five-bedroom house we called home. We needed rugs, storm windows, baby furniture, and a host of household items; yet, all the money went into mortgage payments. I would have gladly given the deed to the dump to the termites, who obviously enjoyed the house much more than I did. They just ate the place up!

But the tortures of the job and house were nothing compared to the utter futility of the marriage. I hated Sarah more than I thought it was possible to hate anyone. But that hate hurt. The opening verse of the Prayer of St. Francis, "Lord, make me an instrument of your peace. Where there is hatred let me sow love," still haunted me from my childhood. I was sick from my inability to even care about Sarah. As a child I had had aspirations of being a priestly instrument of peace; yet, as an adult in my own home there was a state of open warfare. I saw myself as a failure.

It seemed as if the war was without end. Love was only a dream. For years I couldn't face the possibility of a divorce. Ingrained religious concepts and a fear of hurting Sarah stood in the way. Divorce was not even in harmony with the kind of marital love that I dreamt about. Giving without possessing were the clouds my dream rested upon. I wanted to give myself to someone in an act of love that was pure, permanent until death, and exclusive. I was not capable of my idealized form of love with Sarah, so my vivid imagination transported me to a fantasyland where I envisioned what life would be like with almost any female I met. Maybe I was looking for a new "Emily."

Sex wasn't important to my world of make-believe. What was important was creating an atmosphere of sharing and caring. Sex was always exploitative for me and therefore lacked beauty. I wanted sex to be an expression of giving, not taking. I imagined sex as being pure and beautiful, but lived with the reality that it was evil and dirty. Even with Sarah. Such is the result of a repressive sexual upbringing in which the body from the waist down is considered evil. The failure of my marriage to live up to my fairy-tale expectations pushed me farther from Sarah. Despite my unhappiness and loneliness, I always had difficulty arranging a funeral service in order to bury the dead marriage of living partners. This time it would be different.

Having a chat with my sister and brother-in-law about my plans for ending the marriage didn't seem to have the potential to change my life. I never anticipated a pow-wow with God that would postpone my marital split for seven years. All I wanted to do was tell somebody what was on my mind and know they would care enough to listen. I wasn't seeking a solution, just understanding and support.

As I drove north, I replayed the events of the last six years over and over in my mind. The drive took me past Hunter Mountain, and I cursed that first day. I desperately wanted my family to know that the marriage was not born in love and was a tragic mistake from the moment of its conception and that I could no longer prolong the agony of living in the state of undivorce—legally married but emotionally single. I had to put an end to the life I was living. No matter what they said in Albany, I could no longer live as a hypocrite. I would explain that I had to end the marriage for my survival and sanity.

I spilled my guts to my sister and her husband as I told them the unhappy details of my marriage. They were generous in their sensitivity and caring. While they supported my solution to the problem, they still hoped for an alternative.

I didn't know at the time that their marriage, which had all the outward appearances of perfection, had recently traveled down a shaky stretch of track and almost derailed. They spoke freely not of their troubles but of their solution.

Without knowing it, I was listening to my first salvation testimony—and it worked. Their revelation piqued my interest, and I listened intently as they described how a new personal relationship with God had helped restore and renew their marriage. As they spoke, I realized that my past preoccupation with my own troubles had blinded me to the subtle changes in their lives that I had seen without seeing. On recent visits I had noticed Bibles lying around and recalled how God did creep into conversations. They even said prayers before meals. Yet I never attached any significance to these glimpses of change. Now their words brought life to those overlooked actions.

I had a difficult time understanding how important God was to them. They radiated a godly glow. They had taken guitar lessons in order to accompany themselves while singing Christian songs at night in their living room. Because of my love and respect for them, I suppressed my skepticism and accepted the plausibility of their conversion experience. However, I did argue that a spiritual conversion would not save my marriage. There was no marriage, never was. It was all a sham and couldn't be redeemed. Jokingly, I told them that I thought God got out of the miracle business a long time ago. Besides, Sarah would never go along with all this God stuff. I didn't realize that the gentle smile they gave in response to my arguments was the result of a faith that now believed all things were possible with God—even to Sarah becoming a Christian. They assured me that they wanted to share their new-found faith with me, not to miraculously save my marriage but because it would be good for me under any circumstances.

It was not their words that I trusted but their lives, and so when they invited me to attend a charismatic prayer meeting I said, "Yes."

The desperation I felt in my life made me a prime candidate for becoming "born again." The concept of spiritually wiping the slate clean and starting all over is very appealing. Having made a total mess of my life by following my own senses and reason, why not turn to God and let him straighten everything out?

Born again is an expression that is normative to Protestantism and identifies the experience of rebirth in Jesus Christ. For Catholics rebirth is the result of an infusion of the Holy Spirit and is described by the term *baptism in the Spirit*. If you wanted to seek out such an experience, you would go to a charismatic prayer meeting. Catholics who attended charismatic prayer meetings and were baptized in the spirit are known as Pentecostals or Charismatics.

Pentecostal is a term used to describe people who believe that the power given to and manifested by the apostles on Pentecost was not some ancient event that took place during New Testament times in order to get the church rolling but is something that is available to all people for all time. According to the New Testament, the Holy Spirit of God came down from Heaven and filled the first followers of Christ with a power that changed their lives. They spoke in tongues, preached with boldness, and radiated the joy of Jesus. Pentecostals seek out this infusion of the Holy Spirit. The external signs of this inner manifestation are speaking in tongues, a thirst for reading Scripture, and a passion for saving souls.

Charismatic simply refers to the gifts of the spirit that are called *charisms*. For example, a person could have a charism or gift of healing. The religious usage of the word has nothing to do with the popular usage, which describes a person who has a personal magic or magnetic charm. In Christian terminology, a charismatic is someone who has received and demonstrated the gifts of the Holy Spirit, such as the ability to speak with wisdom, the ability to speak with knowledge, the ability to speak in tongues, the ability to interpret tongues, or the acquisition of such miraculous powers as healing. It is interesting to note that Pat Robertson has received all those gifts of the Holy Spirit—or at least that is what his followers think.

When I walked into my first charismatic prayer meeting I had no idea that within a short time I would be leading a prayer group of my own. Nor could I realize that I would speak in tongues, preach, conduct seminars on how a person becomes filled with the Holy Spirit, and lead healing services. Soon my only passion would be that of saving souls. The pornographer was about to be transformed into a pulpiteer. The soon to be sinner-turned-saint would declare war not only on his own sins but the sins of others. I walked in as an unworthy sinner, and in a short time I became hypnotized into believing I was saved, which led me to project my former unworthiness onto unsuspecting "sinners" whom I must save in order to remain "good."

The first prayer meeting I attended was held on a Sunday night in a high-school gymnasium. As I entered, clutching my skepticism tightly, I momentarily thought I had walked in on a high-school pep rally. This didn't look like a gathering of Christians. Everyone was beaming with enthusiasm and oozing with love. At first, it was so overwhelming that it appeared fake and threatening. I couldn't imagine why all these people were so happy and excited. People greeted each other with whole-hearted hugs instead of spiritless handshakes, with "Praise the Lord" instead of "Hello." I felt as though I were drowning in a sea of smiles.

If my frown or occasional forced smile didn't betray the fact that I didn't belong there, then my empty hands surely did. Everyone was holding Bibles, which came in all different sizes and versions. I rarely had seen a Bible outside of church or off the top shelf of a bookcase in someone's home.

As I wondered if this open display of love could be real, the Scripture verses came to mind in which Jesus said something to the effect that you would be able to recognize his followers by their love for each other. If that were true, then perhaps these were real Christians.

The large rectangular sports arena was filled with hundreds of chairs that were set up to form rows in gigantic concentric circles. In the center of the circle sat a group of well-groomed young musicians. The pervasive happiness soon manifested itself in a joyful noise as the musicians literally burst into a festive song. It was like a triumphant battle cry that led all to their seats. The upbeat songs seemed to have the power to arouse the gathered crowd into a spirit of open worship. No sitting or kneeling with hands folded and heads bowed in this athletic house of worship. The people stood and clapped and sang with a vitality that I had never before seen or heard in any church. Some of the worshipers actually jumped and danced with joy. Being in a gym made me feel more as though I were watching the last minutes of a championship basketball game than the opening of a church service. Jubilation abounded as this unusual adoration society shouted out their praises to the Lord.

In total disbelief, my eyes kept panning the room. Everywhere I looked people stood with their arms and hands held heavenward as they praised God. A chorus of "Hallelujah," "Praise the Lord," and "Jesus is King" filled the rafters with a clamorous praise. I recalled how the Bible frequently, especially in the Psalms, urged us to give praise to God in all things, but I never imagined that a group could so openly and with such intensity do just that. I had no understanding of what was happening, but I did have a flickering notion that it was rather glorious.

There was no pussy-footing around; these people really liked God, and they let him and everybody know it. The enthusiasm was contagious. I felt like joining in, even though I had all but forgotten the God they so freely exulted. Just as I was being drawn into this unorthodox form of worship, some weird events made me want to beat a hasty retreat to the door.

I began to hear strange sounds. It sounded like repetitious babbling or some unusual foreign dialect. People were speaking in tongues. If that wasn't odd enough, they soon began to sing in tongues. This mysterious, supernatural type of prayer was eerie. Some of the people looked as though they were in a trance. Not only did I not understand what was happening, I was also frightened by it. I felt as though I were surrounded by religious nitwits. Everything inside me wanted to head for the exit; but, out of respect for my sister, I stayed. I listened carefully, and somehow the many strange-sounding syllables and words being sung blended together into a beautiful harmony. Later I was informed that the Holy Spirit had orchestrated the plethora of sounds into a single, united hymn of praise to God. I considered that explanation to be ludicrous.

After about a half hour of singing, praising, and intense prayer, a man, standing in the center of the circle holding a microphone, officially greeted and welcomed everybody. He asked us to be seated. That was good news for me. He spoke energetically about the good things the Lord had done during the past week. I had never heard anyone who wasn't a priest speak so naturally about God; yet his belief that God was so actively involved with the affairs of the community seemed unnatural. He read something from the Bible and then made some comments on the passage. His remarks were brief and supported the biblical promise that God seeks our worship and, in fact, dwells in our praise.

I wondered why God was so egotistical that he needed our praise —especially this kind of wild cheering praise. The speaker then asked those assembled to share as the Lord led. I did not understand exactly how the Lord led someone to speak; yet amid a quiet murmuring of prayer, individuals would stand and read a passage from Scripture or disclose something personal about themselves and how Jesus had helped them. Some people fought back tears as they proudly proclaimed that God had healed them of various ailments or how a "lost" family member had accepted Jesus. Each testimonial to the power of God was followed by a rousing round of applause and numerous exclamations of "Praise the Lord."

Then a loud voice boomed out an unintelligible message that sounded frantic and important. I later learned that he was delivering a prophecy to the community, but the message from God was delivered in an unknown tongue. (Leave it to God; he's such a kidder.) The speaker stopped his string of strange words, and a silence fell upon the place. People gently and repeatedly whispered the name of Jesus. Every eye but mine was respectfully closed. Most faces had a strained and solemn look as if they were struggling to hear God's voice. I would have been overwhelmed to have just heard God clear his throat; yet these people expected God to speak to them and give them an explanation of the prophecy. A minute of hushed silence, which felt like an hour, had passed when a forceful loud voice broke through the strained stillness. This time the words were in English; however, for me, the message was foreign. The speaker was giving an interpretation or translation of the message spoken in tongues. Of course, God was telling him what to say. This interpretation was what everyone was so prayerfully waiting to hear. The shocking thing to me was that the man spoke as if he were God.

"My people, yes, you are my people and I am your God," was how he began. With all the heads around me bowed in awe, I secretly squinted to spot the speaker. He stood tall, swaying back and forth as if under some mystical power or trance. Around his neck he wore a chain with a large wooden cross. His eyes were closed so tightly that a frown formed on his forehead. It was spooky. I had never heard about this kind of stuff in the seminary. I couldn't believe these were all Catholics. This messenger of God ended his urgent words with "Thus saith the Lord your God."

As he sat down the place burst out in spontaneous praise and worship. I broke out in a sweat. The musicians added to the fervor of the moment by playing a song that started "God has spoken to his people," with a tempo that sounded very Israeli in style and flavor. Everyone rose from their seats and ardently sang the song as they rhythmically clapped their hands and stomped their feet to the beat of the folksy music. They had no doubt that God had spoken, but I had plenty.

A quick peek at my watch revealed that an hour had elapsed, and I speculated on how much longer this could last. Nobody looked as though they were in a hurry to leave. My sister shot concerned glances my way as she periodically checked to see if I had skipped town. My hopes for a quick ending faded as a tall, middle-aged priest holding a black leatherbound Bible stood up in the center of the circle. With impeccable enunciation and the flair of a Shakespearean actor, the priest read a long passage from Scripture. Then he began to preach. But this was no ordinary preacher. This guy was funny, dramatic, dynamic, and had the timing and delivery of a professional entertainer. He had the audience in the palm of his hand as he pranced up and down the aisles waving his arms and the Bible in exaggerated gestures. This was pure show biz.

I couldn't decide if I liked the showiness or not, but he got and kept my attention. My first impulse was that the man was a phony or at best a priest who should have been a stand-up comic. However, his homily was inspirational. After twenty minutes I was mesmerized, not by his delivery, but by the power of his words. The priest said things about God and love that rang true. Some of what he said gave me a slight case of the "guilts" yet the tone of his talk was not "hell, fire, and brimstone." He brilliantly mixed thoughtful theology, sound biblical exegesis, and a personal love for God into a presentation that was spellbinding and left me hungry for more. I knew that if this priest were a part of this group, then I might come back again, despite the fact that I was uncomfortable with most of the ninety-minute meeting. I was now curious to find out about what I didn't understand.

The drive back to my sister's following the meeting was sprinkled with questions and observations. They were thrilled that I might consider going to another meeting. I tried to contain their optimism by stressing that I was just mildly curious and not on the verge of conversion. (I should have thought about what curiosity did to the cat.)

Once back in New Jersey, the daily routine of playing mother by day and breadwinner by night left little time for reflections about God. Yet I had this gentle underlying feeling that the people I had witnessed did have a sincere love and concern for each other. I was fascinated by that, and it enabled me to ignore all their spiritual abnormalities like speaking in tongues and prophesying. During this time, when I felt so alone and nervous about my future, the warmth of the friendship I had felt in Albany beckoned me to return. I figured that I could drive up to Albany on a Sunday afternoon and head home immediately following the meeting.

During the next few months I made the trip as frequently as I could, and each time I attended I learned a little more. I bought books that dealt with the spiritual gifts. I thought my pursuit was more on an intellectual level than a response to a personal need for holiness or salvation. I liked the people, and I wanted to learn about the religious experience that accounted for their inner and outer joy. In retrospect, I now realize that I wanted their acceptance and that that was going to require conformity to their beliefs. The practices I first thought to be odd gradually became less so.

During this time, the initial meeting with the divorce lawyer took place. His legal mumble-jumble was more confusing than helpful. Somehow my preoccupation with the prayer community took on a greater priority than following the lawyer's advice. My lawyer's cutthroat approach to my problems had little appeal, but my growing circle of friends in Albany seemed to hold the secret for happiness, and that held great appeal.

Sarah was perplexed by my numerous visits to Albany, but seeing as I tended to be a bit warmer following one of my religious pilgrimages, she didn't press me for many details. Besides, I barely understood what I did myself, so I could hardly explain it to her.

Divorce still weighed heavily on my mind, so I sought spiritual help for my problem. I had a few counseling sessions with some of the best teachers and spiritual directors in the community. One was a Franciscan priest, who was one of the founders of the community. He was a charismatic leader in both senses of the word. We had some in-depth talks about my marriage. While he believed that the healing power of God could turn my miserable excuse for a relationship into a loving marriage, he seemed to have a practical streak also. He told me I had an open-and-shut case for an annulment.

The Catholic church does not grant divorces and steadfastly upholds the indissolubility of marriage. The church dogmatically proclaims that marriage is forever—period—except for one legal loophole. Under certain restricted circumstances, the church, after a thorough investigation, can declare that a marriage was invalid because it failed to meet minimum ecclesiastical requirements and therefore could be terminated with the church's blessing. In effect, the church law said that due to certain psychological and spiritual problems that were not known prior to the wedding, the marriage was not valid in the eyes of the church and God. They were not actually ending the marriage; they just declared that there never was a marriage. You couldn't end something that had never begun. If extenuating conditions were brought to light and carefully examined and confirmed, then there would be no godly reason to prolong the mistake. It wasn't meant to be a spiritual short-cut to divorce. Annulments have always been rare and take a long time to obtain. Only those who were genuinely concerned about their spiritual life even bothered with the arduous process, which was conducted by a marriage tribunal consisting of priests—experts on marriage.

As divorce became more prevalent in our society, the Catholic clergy had no effective way with which to deal with a failed marriage. To ease their growing frustrations and to avoid losing church members because of the unpopular antidivorce position of the official church, the grounds for an annulment were gradually broadened and the process shortened. More and more annulments were sought and granted. Fundamentalists, who also firmly believe in the indissolubility of marriage, saw this Catholic version of divorce as an insult to God and the people involved, especially when one partner did not want the divorce or there were children involved.

In my case, my frame of mind on my wedding day made a mockery of the sacrament. According to the priest, my mental and spiritual attitude invalidated the effects of the ceremony. The marriage was legal and binding in the eyes of the state but not the church. His advice was simply to end it and go in peace. He suggested I repent and rebuild my life on godly principles and not carry unnecessary guilt. The bottom line, claimed the priest, was that God hadn't joined us together and wasn't trying to keep us together. The priest's advice ran counter to the unwritten rule in charismatic and fundamentalist circles that considered divorce to be the one unpardonable sin. I ignored the best piece of spiritual advice I would receive during the next ten years and chose instead to follow the voice of the majority which believed a vow is a vow. It may be of interest to note that the enlightened and compassionate priest is no longer a priest.

Others in the community recognized the annulment option as being an authentic choice in my situation, but urged me to first work to make the marriage real. Learn to love your wife and marry her again before God. That was a far-fetched plan; however, trying harder at making the marriage work seemed reasonable, and if my efforts failed I could still apply for an annulment.

While frequent trips to Albany had awakened my childhood interest in God and were spiritually stimulating, they also offered some problems. The more spiritual books I read, the less certain I became about the divorce or annulment. The uncertainty only increased the domestic tension as I vacillated between learning to care and moments of deep despair. I got caught up in a mental tug-of-war. I could eloquently debate myself on the merits of leaving Sarah and also of staying. I was told that my mind was a spiritual battlefield because the Holy Spirit was attempting to lead me to righteousness but Satan was fighting to thwart those efforts. Not wanting to side with Satan, I started to listen more to the advice of this fanatic fringe of Christianity than to my own instincts.

The dichotomy I faced was simple. On the spiritual level, I was beginning to think that the marriage could and should work. On the physical and emotional plane, I wasn't interested in saving the marriage. From the fundamentalist point of view, that contradiction translated into the obvious fact that the spirit is willing but the flesh is weak; therefore, I must conquer the flesh. Little by little, the spiritual influence began to dominate my life, but its fruit was not peace and joy.

My thirst for spiritual insight and understanding could not be adequately quenched by sporadic visits to Albany. I needed a steady source of spiritual drink, so I began to search for a local community of charismatic Catholic believers. Much to my delight, I discovered a small prayer group that met in the basement of a Catholic church on Friday nights and that was only ten minutes from my home.

I walked into my first New Jersey prayer meeting far less skeptical than I had been for my initial encounter with the Albany assembly of believers, but I still had many unresolved doubts and still was tottering on the brink of divorce. Within a very short period of time those doubts would dissolve, and I would stand firm in my resolve to heal my moribund marriage. A spiritual illusion, masked as the Truth, was about to bait its hook. As I descended the stairs to the small Franciscan church, which had been a mission outpost at the turn of the century, I was alone, a little frightened, and a little depressed. I was drowning and reaching out for help; I was about to be reeled into the ship of salvation.

I was greeted with the warmth and open arms that are characteristic of charismatic gatherings. The smiling reception is not accidental or even spontaneous. Even though all the participants are supposedly filled with the joy of Jesus, they don't take chances when it comes to effective evangelization and growth in numbers for the community. A special "greeters team" is formed for the distinct purpose of caring for new people until they become joined to the life of the community. I didn't know it then, but I've come to realize that our ascent toward God begins with a descent into ourselves, because our greatness lies not so much in our ability to remake others or the world as in our ability to remake ourselves. But trained "greeters" stood ready to transform me.

Team members were selected for their spiritual maturity, friendly personality, and ability to communicate. The Holy Spirit could have taken the night off. Making a stranger feel welcome became their holy duty. I was introduced to key members of the group. I was given coffee. I heard a brief history of the community and glowing praises of its leader. The schedule of events for the evening was explained. I was shown a book table and given the option to buy or borrow a book. I was encouraged to attend regularly.

I was also steered away from members who were not playing with a full deck. Because the warmth of the group makes everyone feel special and wanted, it draws a lot of people who have serious psychological and emotional problems. If your only encounter on the first night was with some unstable zealot, you might never come back, and the team made sure that didn't happen. The greeters team subtly tries to determine where a new person stands in his or her relationship to Jesus and the church and if he or she has been involved with drugs, the occult, secular humanism, or Eastern religions. (The internalized nature of Eastern religions poses a serious threat to the group dynamics of fundamental Christianity.) These probings are an attempt to discern if the new person is open to receive the spiritual gifts, especially the gift of tongues. The ultimate objective of the greeters team is to guide a new person into a seven-week "Life in the Spirit" seminar which culminates in the baptism of the Holy Spirit. Having achieved this goal, they have won another soul for Christ. I know all this because for a long time I would be in charge of the "greeters team" and would win many souls for Christ. Or so I thought.

Not knowing that much of the enthusiasm was orchestrated, I was impressed and touched by the warmth of my greeting that first night. The meeting was very similar to the one in Albany; however, the size of the group was much smaller, numbering only about forty people. I was more comfortable with this smaller, more intimate gathering. The folding chairs were placed in about six rows of circles, with the musicians and leaders sitting in the innermost circle. As in Albany, the prayer meeting consisted of enthusiastic singing, speaking and singing in tongues, Scripture readings, personal testimony, loud vocal praise and worship, and a teaching by the leader of the group. As spontaneous as it appeared, the meeting was—I would learn later—very structured and, by virtue of repetition over a period of time, very ritualistic. You could even turn tongues on and off.

Just as in Albany, one person made a difference in my coming back again. Rob Ochman was about to become my guru, my spiritual master and teacher. He was a short, slender man in his early forties who had prematurely gray hair. Seven years earlier, the then playboy-financier had a dramatic encounter with God, after which he abandoned a lucrative Wall Street career in order to devote his full time and energy to spreading the Gospel, despite the fact that he had a wife and three kids to support. Following instructions from God, he began conducting prayer meetings in the basement of the church, even though nobody showed up for the first two weeks. One by one, people joined his solitary effort to praise God in a new, enthusiastic fashion. Although the group made only insignificant gains in its membership the first few years and many of the church regulars considered the prayer meetings weird or strange, Rob remained faithful to the Lord's command to gather in his name.

When Rob began meeting alone in the church basement, the charismatic renewal movement in the Catholic church was still relatively young. It started at Duquesne University in 1967 when four people prayed for the gifts of the Holy Spirit, and then the movement spread to Notre Dame. Within ten years the national coordinating board would be able to fill regional stadiums with fifty thousand Catholic Charismatics, all of whom would profess the belief that Jesus Christ was in the stadium and that the Holy Spirit was there, too, moving in them and speaking through them. I attended one such huge rally on the campus of Notre Dame in 1977. It seems incongruous that a movement previously associated with lower-class Protestantism and fundamentalism would take root in two prestigious Catholic universities. That, of course, demonstrated that the Charismatic or Pentecostal movement could only be of God.

While the Pentecostal experience has its roots in the New Testament, the manifestation of the gifts of the Holy Spirit, especially that of tongues, was rarely reported in Christendom from A.D. 100 to the year 1800. The modern Pentecostal movement is about 85 years old; the seeds for this unorthodox religious practice were planted in the Wesleyan revival of the 18th century. The Protestant Reformation emphasized the importance of a believer establishing a personal relationship with the Lord. This personal acceptance and subsequent knowledge of Jesus was the result of God's unmerited grace, which insured salvation for the believer. However, John Wesley taught that there was more to Christianity than just salvation. He believed that the Christian could attain absolute sanctification and be assured of reaching heaven by losing all inclination to evil and gaining perfection in this life. Wesley's method for holiness spread like wildfire and gave birth to the

Methodist church, whose moral standards at one time outlawed the use of alcohol and tobacco, and banned dancing, card playing, gambling, and attendance at the theater. John Wesley taught that saved, committed Christians could expect to receive a second burst of grace from God in the form of baptism of the Holy Spirit, which would enable them to reach complete holiness.

A split began to develop among the many followers of Wesley over the two distinct moments of grace from God. The itinerant evangelists who roamed the American frontier in search of souls stressed the importance of the first outpouring of God's grace, which resulted in a personal conversion and a new relationship with Jesus. These God-fearing, Bible-believing men would storm a town, set up their tents, and begin to preach the gospel to anyone who would listen. At the end of their fiery message they would invite sinners to come forward and accept Jesus as their personal lord and savior. The meetings were filled with hymn singing, loud praying, shouting, and hand clapping. They also had their share of alleged miracles, healings, and casting out of demons. A carnival atmosphere abounded along with emotional excess. Because of the educational level of both ministers and people, the revivals were often characterized by overly simplistic catechisis, biblical interpretations, and theology. For example, some sects insisted that all church singing be done *a capella* since they found no mention of organs in the Bible.

Other followers of Wesley not only stressed the two different moments of grace but actually placed more emphasis on the attainment of holiness from the second encounter with the Almighty. They started the Holiness movement, and they referred to this second step on the road to perfection as the Holy Ghost baptism. A Methodist minister in the Holiness movement opened a small Bible school in Topeka, Kansas, in 1900. The school's forty students used only one textbook: the Bible. Their only assignment was to search the Scriptures to see if they could uncover any biblical evidence for this second baptism. They came to the conclusion that speaking in tongues was the only consistent and conclusive sign that a person had received the baptism of the Holy Ghost. The minister and his dedicated students began to pray diligently not only for the baptism of the Holy Ghost but also for the physical evidence of its reception—speaking in tongues. On January 1, 1901, Miss Agnes Ozman started the new year off right by speaking in tongues during a school prayer meeting and thus became the first white person to demonstrate glossolalia in the Pentecostal revival.

Out of that humble and unsophisticated beginning in Topeka grew a strain of Christianity that has flourished beyond imagination. Worldwide Pentecostal membership is estimated at over ten million, including over three million in the United States. The largest single Pentecostal church is the Assembly of God, which has more than 1,500,000 members in this country. The best known Pentecostal television preacher is Oral Roberts, who was ordained by the Pentecostal Holiness Church.

The amazing Pentecostal growth isn't confined to rural southern towns. You can visit over 350 Pentecostal churches in New York City, although most of the churches are the store-front variety. Pentecostal believers were long considered a fanatic group of "Holy Rollers" until the early 1960s when the practice of speaking in tongues infiltrated such mainline Protestant denominations as Episcopalians, Lutherans, and Presbyterians. For the most part these mainline Pentecostals prefer to remain in their own denominations and exercise their gift of tongues in private prayer meetings. By the 1970s, Pentecostalism had spread to the Catholic church, and an estimated five hundred thousand Catholics, including priests and nuns, participated in Charismatic prayer groups. Many people saw this alleged outpouring of the Holy Spirit as evidence that Jesus was attempting to reunite his severely splintered church, but in reality the movement resulted in even deeper theological splits and biblical disputes.

Pentecostals believe in a literal interpretation of the Bible and condemn the teaching of evolution as unbiblical. This helps reinforce the popular belief that the movement consists of half-crazed, uneducated religious zealots. On the contrary, most members are very stable individuals who have just bought into a very captivating belief-system that promises a quick cure to all of life's problems. They regard the incredible growth of the Pentecostal experience as a sure sign of God's presence in the movement. I tend to think that the rapid blooming could better be attributed to an effective recruitment system, a simple master plan from the Bible, that gives the members a high degree of confidence, a flexible organization, and an experience (speaking in tongues) that produces a fervent commitment to the cause of evangelization. Growth in a religious movement is not an indication of God's presence in or support of the movement. The Unification church has flourished wildly, but Roberts and Robertson would not acknowledge that that indicates that God really did call the Reverend Sun Myung Moon to America to prepare this nation for the second coming of the Messiah by leading us into national repentance, as Moon claims. Nor would I.

I joined the church-basement prayer group just as the existence of the Charismatic renewal was beginning to sink into the consciousness of many Catholics. Most "Sunday only" Catholics considered the "tonguers" to be a bunch of lunatics for whom Sunday Mass was not enough. Conversely most Charismatic Catholics believed unspirit-filled Catholics to be spiritually immature and almost un-Christian. Quickly the Charismatics developed an elitist attitude that allowed them to judge the quality of another person's relationship with God. However, more and more people were starting to at least check out a prayer meeting, maybe out of curiosity or because the members did seem to be the happiest people around. Rob Ochman was determined to attract and keep more people.

Rob detected in me more than just a passing interest in the Charismatic movement. He perceived in me a deeper hunger for God and the ability to absorb all the things he had learned. As the community grew, he needed help in sharing the leadership, and I was unknowingly being groomed for that responsibility. First, he had to get me filled with the Holy Spirit; events in my life were going to make his task easy.

I carried my personal problems into the prayer meeting in hopes that I would be shown a way to wash them away. That's the first element of conversion. Every person who has a born-again experience has a need, and he or she is persuaded that Jesus has the only solution. The evangelical Christian must first present a plausible case for the unbeliever to believe that Jesus can cure his or her ailment. Here is how they accomplish that seemingly Herculean task.

The warmth of the smiles and apparent affection has its attraction, but even more alluring is the perception that they have something of great value and are willing to share it with you. They don't play "I've Got a Secret." Members are eager to proclaim their testimony, their personal story of how a new personal relationship with Jesus had dramatically transformed some prior hopeless situation. I must have appeared ill at ease because some of the men were quick to tell me how uncomfortable they were during their first prayer meeting.

"My wife had to drag me here in the beginning, but now I wouldn't miss it for anything" was the type of exuberant claim that subtly told me to hold on for a while and I'd also fall in love with the community. I met a chemical engineer, a printer, a psychologist, and a coffee distributor. And while this divergent group of men were united in their open love of Jesus, they seemed very real; yet, except for the crosses they so proudly wore, they didn't come across as especially pious— these trained "greeters" knew better. In an almost unconscious fashion I formed the premise that a few hours of my time couldn't hurt and that I should give them a chance to prove themselves.

Once I made that informal decision to come back for a few more weeks, I asked how this baptism of the Holy Spirit actually happens. I was told that all questions would be answered along with the actual reception of the baptism during special "Life in the Spirit" seminars. This short course in spirituality ran for seven weeks, and it was imperative that I attend each class. The seminars started in two weeks, so, with the gentle nudging from members of the "greeters team," I elected to take the seminars.

The seminars are well-planned and very effective. The dropout rate for those who begin the course is very low. To the participant they appear to be a series of informal talks given by your average next-door-neighbor type who was uncomfortable standing up in front of a bunch of people and giving a lecture. This less-than-slick presentation seems harmless and gives no sign of being a carefully calculated plan to lead the participant into a new dimension of faith. Each talk is followed by a discussion group. It seemed so simple that I couldn't imagine that this collection of poor communicators made up of middle-aged housewives and common laborers would be able to deliver a life-changing message or be capable of manipulating their audience.

But behind the informality and almost amateurish presentation there was a well-conceived and finely-tuned master plan. While a team of familiar people gave the talks and led the discussion groups, everything they said and did was based on a manual that was developed and produced by a large prayer community in Ann Arbor, Michigan, that was the national headquarters for the Pentecostal movement within the Catholic church. The group had no official ties with the church and acted solely as a collection of individual Catholics who were faithful members of the church carrying out their own private enterprise of salvation. The manual is a 183-page book which leaves absolutely nothing to chance. It was designed for use by the team members, and the participants have no knowledge of what lies ahead except for a vague outline of the topics.

Today, when I read the manual, I conclude that the talks consist of a series of psychological manipulations. Some critiques of this training manual liken the process to practices used by communists, Boy Scout leaders, Dale Carnegie lecturers, and even public school teachers, noting a similar technique, methodology, organization, and even language. The manual gives minute details concerning the conducting of the seminars and the roles of the tutors and the participants. No room is left for the inspiration of the Holy Spirit.

It was as if the people who put the manual together and those who conduct the seminars consider the souls of the participants to be wandering in some murky middle ground between the armies of God and Satan; therefore, the soul must be persuaded to fall under God's banner. They believe that the devil spared no effort in tempting us, so these modern-day crusaders could spare no effort in saving us. The manual is a major weapon in their arsenal, and they are constantly seeking ways to improve it based on its use in the field. What looked like a simple seminar aimed at providing me with some helpful information was in fact a deadly serious business bent on selling God and salvation.

Prior to the start of the seminar, the team leader trains the teams by feeding them Scripture passages to support the position that they must become spiritual craftsmen and that the Lord is entrusting to their care the priceless soul of a person whom they must serve with utmost skill. With the aid of a leader's manual, he guides the team members in the proper way to lead the discussion period following the talk and suggests the questions that would best stimulate dialogue with the participants. He also teaches them how to avoid or duck troublesome issues.

During the first night of the seminar, the team members' goal is to get the audience excited and motivated to attend all the sessions. I was told of God's love, mankind's sinfulness, the power of prayer, and how widespread the Pentecostal renewal was. A year after I was a participant in these seminars, I was leading them. What follows is a portion of an introductory talk that I gave and recorded on an audio cassette:

> The purpose of these seminars is to help you establish a personal relationship with Christ. We want to help you make Jesus the center of your lives and experience the freedom and change that will take place. Everyone can expect that God will do something for you during the coming weeks. No matter what route you took to get here tonight, behind your desires and the circumstances that led you here is God himself. He really brought you here, and He is not someone you can't have contact with because He loves you and wants you to have an abundant life. Too many of us have settled for far too little of what Christianity has to offer, too little of what God really has for us.

I then spoke of the reality of Jesus in my life and how I overcame the separation between myself and God that resulted from my sinfulness. I conducted six of these seminars within a two-year period, before graduating to CBN and using television to manipulate my audience.

I got very good at leading the seminars, but did I really know what I was doing? I was a performer who followed the manual blindly. After all, the writers of the manual were superstars in the Charismatic renewal, and they knew what was best. What I have come to see, especially during my time at CBN, is that the naive religious conscience of the fundamental Christian has no need of intellectual proof in matters of faith, and no argument, regardless of how well-researched or articulated, can sway them from their belief. The aim of the seminars, as well as of evangelistic television, is to lead people into a new belief system based on biblical promises.

A woman who was a math major and possessed a highly analytical mind was probing the merits the impact of a born-again experience had on her two best friends. Like so many people, she was glad that this simplistic religious experience seemed to be helping her friends cope with their problems, but she seriously doubted that all this Bible stuff was for her. Nonetheless, her friends convinced her to attend a meeting, and during her first hesitant visits to our prayer community she was touched by the apparent sincerity of the love she saw flowing between the people. She became more curious and attempted to use her logical mind to analyze the source of the happiness and love. She asked many probing questions that couldn't be answered to her satisfaction. One day, out of frustration, one of her friends said, "Why don't you stop analyzing everything? Your problem is that you are looking at this through your mind's eye and must look at it through your heart's eye." Seeking understandable answers to sincere questions concerning matters of faith is looked upon as a roadblock to conversion that is cleverly placed by Satan. Blind faith is what is required.

In order to make sure that knowledge, especially scientific knowledge, didn't make inroads into the Christian thought process, the apostle Paul ordered his followers to bury their intellect. He warned them in his first letter to the Corinthians, "If any man among you seems to be wise in the world, let him become a fool." If a non-Christian asks serious intellectual questions of a soul-seeking Christian evangelist, he or she will simply be told to forget the wisdom of the mind and turn to Jesus in faith. A fundamentalist Christian's inflexible attitudes concerning such important issues as public morality, school prayer, homosexuality, evolution, divorce, women's rights, and abortion appear foolish to a nonbeliever because the fundamentalist is encouraged to be foolish, and therefore no truth-seeking dialogue can exist. When knowledge is the enemy, there is bound to be big trouble. Eastern religious teachings say the mind is a tool for finding God and that we should use our intellect, because faith comes after tenacious inquiry, not before.

Modern historical knowledge has shed new light on the Bible, but the fundamentalists prefer to read in the dark and ignore the new archaeological discoveries that have been made that provide a clearer view of the history of biblical times.

Written over many centuries, the Bible contains an amazing variety of religious beliefs and practices as it reflects the changing conditions of the times in which the various books were written. The fundamentalists' absolute reliance on a literal interpretation of the entire Bible automatically exalts it above scholastic criticism. Placing the Bible on a pedestal makes confusion the nature of religion, causes psychological trauma in a person struggling to decide what to believe, and leads to unbridgeable divisions between churches and people as well as ill-will among friends and family. I was encouraged to read the Bible but not with an open mind.

When the introductory seminar is completed, the course gets serious in the second week as it nudges the participants into turning to the Lord by stirring a groundswell of faith. The night centers on the concept of God's love, which is biblically backed by the Gospel of John in which the evangelist wrote, "For God so loved the world that He gave His only Son that whoever believes in Him should not perish but have eternal life."

The manual provides a comprehensive plan of attack for the team members by providing them with a goal, the dynamics of the session, a detailed outline of the presentation, and a question to be used during the discussion period. We are told that Christianity isn't a restrictive morality and is much more than loving our neighbors. Authentic Christianity is a deep personal relationship with Jesus that results in his being the center of our lives and filling us with happiness, peace, and joy. The following is an excerpt from a talk I gave on May 20, 1977:

Some of you may ask why more people have not yet experienced this new kind of life? The answer is simple, but at the same time most of us don't like hearing the answer, because the answer is sin. I personally didn't want to hear that I was a sinner, because the world had conditioned me to its "situational ethics" by saying, in effect, that if something feels good, do it. This type of evil ethical standard teaches us that we should respond to whatever the situation is, because there is no sin or evil. Our only concern should be what feels good to us. This kind of thinking motivated man to respond out of selfishness and not out of self-giving love. Well, as I began to grow in the Lord, I realized sin did play an important part in my life. I started to learn that the truth is that man is sinful and separated from God by sin, and therefore we cannot know God's love and share in God's life with others. I have learned and believe in the depth of my heart that sin is never merely a private affair. Every sin disrupts the community of the people in God.

When one Christian fails to become what he can be, others, too, fail to become what they can be. In Paul's letter to the Romans we read, "All have sinned and come short of the glory of God," and because of that, today men have become indifferent to God. Paul also writes, "Because men refused to ackowledge God, they are full of all kinds of wickedness, greed, and hate." I believe that this age's growing indifference toward God hinders us from even recognizing our wickedness. We try kidding ourselves into thinking we can reach God by our own efforts, using ethics, philosophy, drugs, and even religion instead of putting Christ at the center of our lives.

Only in some kind of hypnotic state could I have spoken those words. I certainly didn't understand the implications of the thoughts expressed. But the validity of the statement is not important. It is the power of a religious experience that could have me deliver such a message that is vital to understanding the spread of fundamental Christianity and its ability to drastically change the way people think and look at life. More than Christianity, this is a cult of results: it produces emotions and experiences, and while these experiences and emotions have little to do with reality, they seem real to the convert. It is a religion of extremes—either you hear God directly or you are hopelessly fallen. Televised Christianity is a form of mass hypnotism which can forge a powerful coalition capable of legislating a biblical morality. There was an element of truth in my talk, but it is buried beneath a false notion that the world is an evil enemy. I went on about how we have to turn to Jesus and he will help us overcome our sinful nature. I gave my attentive audience a brief version of how I began to turn back to God during my visits to Albany. I witnessed to God's power by describing my marital problems and how God changed all that:

> Through the prayerful counsel of Rob Ochman, I began to develop a more healthy attitude about my marriage and realized it was worth the effort to make it work. He taught me what it means to love, the commitment that it involves, and the spirit of dying to oneself that is needed. My wife and I are beginning to come together as never before, and some deep problems are starting to fade away. My marriage today is at the healthiest stage of its eight-year life, and the outlook for the future is even more promising.

Well, it didn't turn out to be as promising as I had proclaimed.

The third week of the seminars took on the awesome topic of salvation. The talk dealt head-on with sin and our need to be saved from its deadly effects. I always expected a mass exodus following this presentation. The audience was told that God intended the world to be peaceful, one in which justice and happiness reigned supreme. Instead, we have riots, poverty, racial conflict, and war. Technological and social changes appear to be beyond man's control. Society and government are not working. Everybody has problems. Loneliness, anxiety, depression, and failed relationships are all around us. After painting that gloomy picture, it was claimed that behind all of society's problems and each individual's problems was Satan and that we can't beat him or lick the problems without the help of God, even though we try to do it ourselves.

The speaker, with the manual's help, points out the obvious failures of secular humanism, of educators who know everything but can't stay married, of business executives who can make a bundle of money but are losers at home. It's funny—yet sad—how the fundamentalists make the demise of a marriage symbolic of all that is wrong in the world. It is effective because the majority of the participants have some type of marital problem, but ironically the cure-all baptism will frequently intensify those problems. The speaker also puts down Buddhism, yoga, meditation, and traditional Christianity. After hearing about Satan's role in temptation, the audience learns that Jesus came to defeat Satan and that he died for our sins and gives us new life.

The first time I heard this straightforward proclamation of the gospel without compromise, I found my mind lingering on all the problems confronting the world. I nodded in agreement to the premise that the world is pretty screwed up and doesn't look like it's going to get straightened out; however, I doubted the Devil's part in the problems. During the discussion period I was surprised that a number of people had suspected that the Devil's handiwork was behind our troubles. I found that hard to swallow, but I did think that no matter what the cause was of the manifested evils and wrongs that are clearly visible, God certainly could fix them. The thought that God works through people to bring about improvements in the human condition was plausible and in fact made Christianity a big deal, since Christians united in love could be a leaven for change in a troubled world. The talk of sin didn't scare me away because, after all, this was a group of nice people speculating about a not-so-nice subject. It was interesting and harmless. By not denying their Devil theory, I was taking my first timid steps toward conformity to the belief.

The next seminar turned away from the bad news and focused on the good news. The good news offered was that each person could have a new life by being baptized in the spirit. Most of the participants responded to the personal testimony of the speaker who described his or her baptism and the difference it made in his or her life. While the salvation talk was mostly theoretical, this personal presentation usually made a powerful change in the participants' attitudes. Few people dropped out after this talk. As I listened, a new faith and a new desire to change my life were quietly forming in my heart.

To ensure that the participants' enthusiasm did not waver and in fact was nourished, the various team members made sure they got together privately during the week with each participant. The follow-up informal meeting allowed team members to answer any nagging questions or lingering doubts about the baptism. The meeting also fostered a feeling of community and made the potential convert feel important. Team members didn't want to take a chance that Satan would turn the participant's heart into stone during the week, so they provided ample opportunity for reassurance. The team members' reaching out was more a response to a method than to love. As a team leader, I was never fond of these one-on-one visits and thought of myself as a pushy salesman trying to close a big deal. Yet, the group dynamics of the team approach turned me into a spiritual salesman. If the participants had any doubts about trusting God, he or she was told that those fears and concerns were natural and most likely came from Satan.

After the fourth session a great sense of anticipation builds for the people attending the seminars. They had been told that during the next seminar they would learn about speaking in tongues and the following week would actually be baptized in the Spirit, and their lives would start over. Just as a child awaits the gifts Santa brings, these spiritual children eagerly await the Spirit's gifts. They are now willing to believe the unbelievable. The seminars are working to perfection as they lead the participants into the belief that the Holy Spirit will enable them to experience God's love, will help them hear God speaking to them, teaching them, and guiding them, will endow them with a new way to pray, will enable them to read Scripture in a way that the Word will come alive, and will enable them to heal and be healed. The participants have been told that Christians are not powerless and that they will soon get the power they've misplaced.

Within two weeks this seemingly simple series of talks will have masterfully transformed a person from a casual Christian into a committed Christian. The manual is packed with information on how to skirt any doctrinal issues a participant may raise, such as one moment of grace versus two moments of grace.

The fifth week is dedicated to final preparations and a dress rehearsal for the big night as the speaker helps his audience turn away from everything that is incompatible with a Christian life. Encouragement is the key, but repentance and faith are also pushed. The presentation reiterates that God is going to make us an offer we can't refuse. After all, he is the Godfather. He wants to give us a new life. He wants to change us and heal us. He wants us to be part of a supportive Christian community. All we have to do is turn to him. According to the talk we are involved in wrongdoing and must start doing what's right. Repentance is a change of direction away from the things that led us away from God to the things that draw us to him. One-third of the talk stresses that we must be obedient to God. A list of the wide range of things we must avoid includes non-Christian religions and sexual intercourse outside of marriage.

Then the talk shifts to the need for faith. Faith becomes important because we need it in order to believe God's promises. The seminars help manufacture faith as they provide people with a trust that allows them to step into the unknown regions of spirituality. Here's a segment from the talk that deals with faith as I explained it to one of my classes:

> What is faith? Faith means relying on what God said. We realize that before us in scripture we have the written revealed word of God, so we must turn to scripture and put our faith in it and know that if something were in scripture then it's true. We know that everything God says is true because He does not lie. Our Christian lives are based on facts, the facts contained in the scripture. We put our faith in facts and our feelings follow. First we put our faith in what Jesus has said, then our feelings will follow naturally. I'd like to share with you a passage from scripture to help illustrate faith and also a lack of faith. It's the story from Matthew's gospel about Jesus walking on the water. "Directly after this He made the disciples get into the boat and go ahead to the other side while He would send the crowds away. After sending the crowds away He went up into the hills by himself to pray. When evening came, He was there alone, while the boat, by now far out on the lake, was battling with a heavy sea, for there was a head wind. In the fourth watch of the night He went toward them, walking on the lake, and when the disciples saw him walking on the lake they were terrified. 'It's a ghost,' they said, and cried out in fear. But at once Jesus called out to them saying, 'Courage! It is I! Do not be afraid!' It was Peter who answered. 'Lord,' he said, 'If it is you, tell me to come across the water.' 'Come,' said Jesus. Then Peter got out of the boat and started walking toward Jesus across the water, but as soon as he felt the face of the wind, he took fright and began to sink. 'Lord, save me!' he cried. Jesus put out his hand at once and held him. 'Man of little faith,' he said, 'why did you doubt!' "

When Peter stepped out of the boat he was looking at the fact that Jesus said "come." He put his faith in that word and that faith held him up—not the water. But as Peter began to lose sight of the faith he put in Jesus' word, he began to sink. As he began to sink he yelled out, "Lord, save me," and Jesus put out His hand at once and held him up. This parable has great significance for all of us today. There is much insight we can gain. Besides learning what faith should be, we can also learn what our lack of faith can cause. When we begin to doubt and let our feelings take over, we lose faith, and we also begin to sink. Jesus saves us from the sea of temptations, because we put our trust in Him. We put our faith in the fact that He can and will help us through anything. The story has real meaning for us, because only Jesus can save us from drowning in eternity. When we see the fact that God promises us something, we can expect that it will happen to us. All we need to do is claim the promise of God.

If only it were that easy. That kind of silly biblical commentary and reasoning is common in Charismatic and fundamentalist circles. My talk helped those participants who didn't feel excited about the baptism to do it anyway. I tried to give scriptural support to the kind of blind faith that is required, yet my entire argument was based on the fact that the Bible is the revealed word of God and is completely true. When I attended these seminars for the first time I held no such belief; yet I was brainwashed into accepting that viewpoint and soon found it easy to convince others.

Despite the supposed unimportance of feelings in the conversion process, the rest of the talk helps prepare the class for the reception of the gift of tongues, which makes people not only feel as though they have gotten something tangible from the baptism but also boosts their emerging faith. During this portion of the talk the soon-to-be spirit-filled Christians are told what to expect the next week, along with more scriptural support for the baptism. Here's how I explained tongues:

What can we expect during the baptism? Well, we can expect to experience the same things that happened at the first pentecost. We read in Acts 2:4, "And they were all filled with the Holy Spirit and began to speak in tongues as the Spirit gave them utterance." Something happened to them. They were filled with the Spirit, not just some, but all. They did something also. They began to speak in other tongues as the Spirit gave them utterance. Some of you may be concerned about tongues and may not fully understand what takes place or see what importance it could have. That's a normal reaction. However, it's important for you to realize that tongues is a beautiful gift from God, and while scripture does say that tongues is the least of the gifts of the Spirit, it is still desirable by all of us. I look at it this way: If God wants to give us a gift that He thinks we need, then I want it and you should also. Trust that the Lord will reveal the beauty and the importance of the gift to you personally. How then do you yield to this gift of tongues? Well, it's just a matter of beginning to speak. Think of a syllable, speak it out, and trust God to give you the words. What happens is that we begin to pray in a new way as the Spirit prays for us from within our souls and it goes directly from our souls and out our mouths, bypassing our minds with its built-in filters of prejudicial and human ideas that we would normally incorporate into our prayers. The Spirit prays to the Father for us in a new way that releases us, frees us and brings us to a new level of prayer. The Spirit is not taking over us, He is simply allowing us to pray in a freer way. It's important that you begin to speak. If God were to inspire you to write a letter, you would have to pick up the pen and write and He would supply the words. So it is with tongues. God is inspiring you to pray and you must speak. He'll supply the sounds and the words.

Nonsense. These were not my own thoughts, but the reality of tongues in my life prompted me to believe and preach them. Much of Christianity is split over tongues. The Reverend Jerry Falwell doesn't advocate the practice, but Pat Robertson believes it's a normal part of a Christian's prayer life. Left unsaid, in Pat's view, is the fact that if you don't pray in tongues, you are not a normal Christian, and your faith experience is lacking.

For the person who has a desire to change his or her life and is predisposed to believe and want the biblical promises of Jesus, the oddity of tongues seems to fade away. In fact, the most skeptical of the participants in the seminars became the most ardent practitioners of tongues. I personally didn't speak in tongues when I was baptized in the Spirit, and I couldn't help but feel cheated. I was reassured that I would eventually pray in tongues. I wanted to pray in tongues and in fact felt pressured to do so. When I listened to people praying in tongues it sounded very easy to do, yet I had difficulty letting go of my apprehensions and actually just speaking a syllable and allowing it to flow from there. Then one night during a period of fervent prayer, I let a few meaningless syllables slip past my lips. "Ah sa wen tiz hay moyoh hobnit." Suddenly a burst of unintelligible words came pouring out of my mouth. I was in a state of spiritual ecstacy. It was a high, and I loved it.

The next week I stood up during the prayer meeting and proudly proclaimed what a release it was to give in, step out in faith, and pray in tongues. With great enthusiasm, I told the smiling faces that were looking at me how the last week had been terrific thanks to my new prayer language. "I used to get so aggravated with the traffic in the Lincoln Tunnel on my way to work," I told the community, "but last week, instead of getting annoyed, I prayed in tongues. It was wonderful and funny. I mean, can you imagine: tongues in the tunnel!" People laughed and applauded my reception of the gift. I was now one of them and there was no turning back.

In no time at all the strange words that I formed became a natural and normal expression of prayer. But was God forming the words, or was it my desire? Was it some distant or ancient language I was speaking or a bunch of babble? Linguists have difficulty identifying these tongues when they have been recorded and studied. The Pentecostals strongly object to an academic analysis of their God-given language of prayer by asserting that there are almost three thousand languages spoken around the world and that no linguist could possibly recognize more than a few dozen of them. I never stressed the idea that the tongues spoken in our meetings were actually a foreign language but instead considered the sounds a type of ecstatic speech used to praise God when ordinary or known words failed to articulate the adoration felt in the soul.

With time the practice of speaking in tongues became second nature, and the alleged divine gift became commonplace and predictable. During a prayer meeting I could sense when an outburst of praising God together in tongues would occur. Trends began to form, and a new ritual was born. When the normal English verbalization of prayer began to diminish in volume and intensity following a sustained period of communal worship, one person would begin to speak out in tongues—supposedly at the urging of the Holy Spirit. The unknown words would gently rise above the hushed English words of praise and mystically hover there until one by one members added—almost on divine cue—their voices, now also praying in tongues.

The worship gradually grew louder and more fervent. It was as if our worship had been running out of gas, and so the Holy Spirit refueled us with high-octane tongues in order for us to go further in our worship. The dying worship had become electrified, and people lost all sense of restraint and literally shouted out praises to God in an unknown tongue. The community had become lost in a worship that reached such a feverish pitch of emotion that you believed that God was in the room and actually inhibiting the praises of His people. We were one in the Spirit. You could feel the power of God—or at least what we thought was the power and presence of God.

To an outsider, this wild, unabashed, strange-sounding form of worship seemed bizarre at best; yet, to the worshiper, it gave a sense of being united in spirit with God, as if he or she had joined some heavenly host of angels gathered around the throne of the Almighty. During these periods of prayer, I felt as though I had left the planet and all my problems behind me. In reality, it was little more than spiritual scream therapy. The psychological effect of a group praying in tongues tended to bind the people together, as well as increase individual faith. I had no doubt that I had found "it." This is what tongues is really all about: to lead people to believe they have found the truth. I was now one of them.

During my time in the prayer community and at CBN, I had one nagging concern about tongues that stemmed from my observation that people developed a pattern or individual style in the exercising of this gift. Rob Ochman's speech pattern always sounded the same. Pat Robertson never varied the way he spoke in tongues. The words they spoke became familiar to them and to those who heard them. Just as various accents are prevalent in the country, different people developed various inflections and a cadence in their unknown language. The same "words" would keep coming up, only in a different order. That seemed too human to me. I thought that God might have provided an infinite variety of unknown languages and not always reduce this special gift to a string of words and pattern of delivery that could always be identified with a particular person. During a prayer meeting, I began to associate various expressions of tongues with specific people, not by the sound of the voice but by their developed method of speaking in an unknown language that had become familiar to them. I had this passing notion that if God really were the giver of this gift, he would have done better.

Recently, I thought it might be helpful to attend a Charismatic prayer meeting and do some updated field research. I had not attended a prayer meeting in years. Nonetheless, I prayed in tongues. I was very surprised. I didn't plan it or think that I would. It had nothing to do with the Holy Spirit. It was purely a behavioral reaction. I believe that tongues is something you learn; and, like bicycle-riding, once you have learned it you never forget how to do it. The gift of tongues is a present you give yourself. The seminars build a person up to the point where he or she can part for a time with intellect and unleash emotions. I do not believe it is a gift from God.

There is nothing inherently wrong with praying in tongues as long as it is used as an aid to prayer or as a meditative device to help free the mind from the concerns of the day and focus on the true inner self. But when speaking in tongues is elevated from a tool for entering a deeper, more spontaneous level of prayer to a divine manifestation of God's presence, then the practice becomes dangerous. A person who doesn't speak in tongues is considered inferior by many Charismatic Christians. Tongues cannot be a litmus test for authentic Christianity—but it is at CBN.

"Heblab romkar edmont mekob dondey" could mean "God is great and the giver of all things " to some people and be simple gobbledygook to others, but in either case it should not be a barrier to love and understanding. No matter what the "gift" of tongues is, the fact that it helps turn a person into a religious zealot and creates a spiritual superiority complex negates whatever cathartic good it may contain. Speaking in tongues follows a stress-filled situation that leads a person to seek an emotional release from his or her problems. It is nothing more than a cathartic, learned behavior. Speaking in tongues cannot be a sign of holiness, and I am convinced that for many the "gift" is little more than an act. I believe the result—if not the aim—of tongues is to create a closed community, a cult.

The talk portion of the fifth seminar concluded by pointing out the obstacles that stand in the way of God's big offer. The roadblocks placed by Satan are: a person's feeling as though he or she doesn't deserve God's gift, a fear that the personality will die during the spiritual rebirth, a feeling that he or she doesn't need God's gift, and the fear that friends and family will think he or she has gone crazy. Following Paul's advice to encourage the faint-hearted, the team members once again visited each participant during this last week prior to the big night. After all these talks about God's love and Satan's power, it would be difficult for the Christians-in-training not to show up on the coming Friday graduation night and have someone lay hands on them while praying that they receive the baptism which will change their life. In fact, the seminars were so effective that most people could hardly wait.

The Gospel compelled us to be fishers of men, and the night we prayed for the baptism of the Holy Spirit became the time we reeled them into the boat. It took our little community more than five weeks to hook new people; with the power of television, Pat Robertson can accomplish the same thing in a matter of minutes.

The act of praying for baptism of the Holy Spirit is extremely simple and consists of one short prayer that can be said in less than thirty seconds. The hours of preparation and work were an attempt to make this brief piece of time last for an eternity. All born-again, spirit-filled

Christians can recall one brief moment when they turned to the Lord
in total honesty and sought his help. The moment is usually preceded
by a period of personal frustration and problems. They have tried
everything else, so now it's time to give God a shot. The seminars are a
highly orchestrated, thoroughly researched attempt to bring people to
this moment of surrender.

On the night of the baptism we left the basement and assembled
all the participants around the altar of the church. As the community
members sat silently praying in the pews, the team leader spoke to his
class. He started with a reading from the Gospel of Luke that concluded, "If you then, who are evil, know how to give your children
what is good, how much more will the heavenly Father give the Holy
Spirit to those who ask Him!" Jesus said these words, so the participants
know they are true and now are going to act on them and claim the
Holy Spirit.

But first the team leader again talks about tongues, by encouraging
the people not to limit what God can do in their lives by not seeking
something God thinks is worth having. He tells them that the Spirit
doesn't use them like a puppet and that more is needed than just
providing the Spirit with a loose jaw. You have to give the Spirit some
raw material to work with by uttering a sound even if it seems to be
meaningless, because the Spirit can give us the gift of tongues more
easily if our mouths are moving and we are making sounds. The class
is instructed not to analyze the sounds or worry that it is only baby
talk. I told one of my classes, "If you ask God for the gift of tongues,
he's not going to give you baby talk. Yeah, I know it sounds like your
vocal chords and your tongue are doing the work, yet those sounds are
like clay which the Holy Spirit molds into a new language of praise."

After being conditioned and primed for tongues, it is time for
exorcism. Team members command any evil spirits that might be af-
fecting the participants' lives or trying to block this work of the Lord to
leave. Nothing dramatic ever happened during this rite of exorcism, except for one incident when a young lady began screaming and ran
from the church. With the Devil-chasing over, the team members then
lay hands on each participant, and they pray together a prayer that
renounces Satan, affirms a belief that Jesus died for their sins, promises
obedience to the Lord, and asks for a manifestation of the Holy Spirit.
This is a moving experience, since the community seated in the pews
are filling the sanctuary with praise and beautiful songs. Those being
prayed for are filled with a sense of peace and joy. The place is
flooded with tears and a wonderfully warm feeling of a family reunion.

Hugs abound.

As each person is prayed with, he or she is urged to yield to tongues. A team member might even whisper something spoken in tongues into a participant's ear, interjecting an occassional "You can do it!" Amid an atmosphere of Christian love that rules out the fear of feeling foolish the novice speaks out, "Da da dat." The team member excitedly says, "You got it," the person believes it, and suddenly the flood gates of gibberish are flung open.

It's an unforgettable high. Some people think they see angels or hear trumpets and harps. Others claim they have had an out-of-body sensation and felt their souls hovering above the altar. Afterward, the leader reminds the newly spirit-filled Christians that Satan can tempt them into confusion about the night. He couldn't keep you from receiving God's gift, but he can rob you of it by convincing you that you didn't get it. "When doubt comes, tell the Devil to get lost because you belong to Jesus," was my standard advice. They are also warned not to expect all the problems to go away but to look for the new way the Lord is working in their lives.

Quite simply, the night is a turning point for everyone who goes through it. They now have a fire for God. They are consumed by things spiritual. They hunger for Scripture readings. They are driven to spread the Gospel. They declare war on Satan. Most people turn into strangers in their own homes and into oddities to their friends because they now see sin everywhere and want to shove the Bible down everyone's throat. It takes a long time for enthusiastic converts to realize that they can't force-feed the Bible to friends and family. They become impatient with friends and family who get nervous or don't believe them when they claim that God speaks to them. The estrangement from their personal circle of friends and family tends to bind converts to their new spiritual family of friends. Pat Robertson even has commercials that dramatize this feeling of alienation and then offers a book and cassette on how to deal with the problem—offers to sell, that is.

The last week of the seminar stressed living a life in the spirit through growth and becoming more like Christ. The importance of community is hammered away as being essential to that growth and to living a life in harmony with God, because living apart from the community will cause spiritual death, and we can only grow together. Rob Ochman's favorite way of illustrating that principle was to point out that the best way to put out a fire in a fireplace was to pull the logs apart, and a good method of starting a fire was to put the logs together in the right order. The message was clear: We needed each other to keep the fire of Jesus' love burning within us and to set the world on fire for Jesus. The Devil loves to isolate Christians. The fact was that we couldn't stay together twenty-four hours a day, but many people wished we could.

I could never have envisioned the change that the direction my life would take when I committed myself to attend those seminars. Not only did I now go to Mass on Sunday, I went every day, just like in the seminary. Pornography no longer held me in its grip. In fact, I had a bunch of magazines tucked away in a dark corner of my attic, and it was not enough for me simply to throw them out. I burned them in my fireplace as if it were some kind of sacrificial ritual. It felt good; however, the glossy pages of my smut collection didn't burn easily and created a heap of identifiable ashes that were tough to clean up—but not as tough to clean up as my ash heap of a marriage.

Those old problems that led me to this new life in the Lord wouldn't go up in smoke like my magazines. Conversely, my new-found faith and Christian zeal stirred up sleeping memories of my days in the seminary. Guilt set in as I believed I had made a dreadful mistake by not becoming a priest. I really wanted to be a missionary for Jesus, but I was living with a woman who found the message of Jesus to be absurd and his death barbaric. If there were a God, she used to claim, then he could save mankind in any manner that he chose and not just the way that the Charismatics believe he does. Further-more, it didn't seem very smart or God-like of him to concoct a compli-cated and humiliating plan for salvation that demanded the torturous execution of his son. If that weren't bad enough, this all-wise and all-powerful God then buried the truth of his primitive plan in a sexist Bible that most of the world would never have the opportunity to read, and they therefore would be damned to Hell for not knowing that Jesus is the only way to Heaven. Sarah's insightful and logical argu-ments annoyed me, and my anger prevented me from responding with any kind of coherent answer. In an ironic twist of faith that seems almost fictional, Sarah would wind up a cameraperson on "The 700 Club," and I would wind up writing a book that exposes the dangers of fundamentalism and Christian television. As a television producer I would reject such a change in plot.

During the early days of my spiritual renewal, as Sarah and I battled about God and an assortment of more human concerns, I knew that Sarah probably had more genuine concern for people than most members of my community. And she tolerated my involvement with the prayer group. Still, it seemed that the emotional gulf that existed between us could never be bridged. Rob Ochman tried to help me solve my marital dilemma through counseling. Even though we quickly hit a deadend, Rob didn't consider divorce or annulment as an option.

Ochman believed my shattered priestly vocation was part of my marital problem, so he suggested a way for me to partially fulfill that childhood dream. He told me about a new program in the Catholic church called the permanent diaconate in which married men were ordained to serve as ministers in the church and said that I could be a deacon. Rob thought I could be a missionary to my own parish, as well as to my family, friends, neighbors, and the people at CBS.

Thanks to the shortage of priests, the church felt it was important to reinstitute the ancient office of deacon, which had become merely a symbolic final step on the way to the priesthood. Married men would be allowed to perform any of the duties of a priest except for presiding over a liturgy and hearing a confession. They could preach, bring communion to the sick, perform weddings, serve as chaplains in hospitals and prisons, and they could administer a parish. Rob was one of the first ordained married deacons in the area, and with his sponsorship I was accepted into the program and began three years of night school in order to prepare for this ministry.

I studied theology, Scripture, and church history. It was all fascinating and stimulating. There was one Charismatic in my class who quit because a Scripture scholar taught us that a literal interpretation of the Bible was dangerous. The teacher claimed there really were no such people as Adam and Eve. They were just symbolic. He taught us about redaction criticism, which looked at the Bible through the theological motivation of the author as it is revealed in his arrrangement, editing, and modification of traditional material. We learned literary criticism, which looked at the New Testament as unselfconscious popular literature and attempted to understand its aesthetic structure and force. The most intriguing study was form criticism, which presupposed that the written Gospels were developed out of an oral form and that it was important to determine which of the words or deeds attributed to Jesus go back to Jesus himself and which are likely to have been a product of the early church.

Most of what I studied regarding the Bible would be condemned by my friends at CBN. For most fundamentalists open-mindedness implies timidity or weakness. To my Charismatic classmates, their Bible-based faith was challenged by the probing biblical scholar who was viewed as in need of salvation. While I shared the same Charismatic

expression of my Christian faith, I nonetheless found the classes interesting, and I absorbed what was helpful and ignored the rest.

As part of our education we had to choose an area of service we
would specialize in after ordination and begin to get practical experience through on-the-job training. I wanted to either preach or work
with troubled youth. I studied homiletics, which teaches how to give a
sermon, and actually delivered a homily from the pulpit of a large
church during a Sunday liturgy. It was a thrilling experience; and,
more importantly, two members of the congregation were so touched
by my talk that they got in touch with me afterward and joined the
prayer community. I also worked as a counselor at a home for retarded
teenagers for six months and as a counselor in a New York City shelter
for teenage prostitutes and runaways for an additional six months.
Those jobs were very demanding but even more rewarding.

During this time Sarah had lost her job and was now more than
content to stay home and care for our daughter. Her fear of motherhood had faded, and by the time our daughter began to walk Sarah
had become a wonderful mother. This allowed me to have more
normal hours at CBS and devote most of my free time to the prayer
community and the diaconate program. My life was full despite the
emptiness of the marital relationship. I became a member of the
pastoral team that governed the prayer community. I even led the
prayer meetings and conducted various community workshops. Between my full-time job at CBS, the on-the-job training as a counselor,
preaching, teaching, and leading the prayer meetings, I was a perpetual
motion machine for three years.

Television had always been my life, but now I wanted a life of
service to others. Watching the shows on CBS through my new Christian eyes only magnified that desire, but it was impossible to sacrifice a
well-paying job when I had a house and a child to support. I had no
idea I could make a bundle of money in religious television.

Despite all these religious activities and spiritual "growth," the
marital situation was a sore which refused to be healed. Playing deacon
was not going to help; something more was needed. Rob Ochman
prayed with me for a healing of memories. He believed that the
memories of two particular days, the day I left the seminary and the
day I got married, were not only painful for me but were also binding
me to the past and not letting me grow into a loving husband. He
wanted to help me go back over those memories and turn them over to
the Holy Spirit's healing touch so that those two past hurts could no
longer control me. He realized from our many marriage-counseling

sessions that I never really wanted to get married and that I deeply regretted that day. Rob thought those feelings blocked my ability to love Sarah and give myself completely to her in order for our marriage to prosper. Deacon Rob was about to attempt to alter my remembrance of that fatal day by making me see that God did have a hand in our wedding.

During a meditative state and under the guidance of my spiritual guru, I envisioned the seminary. I saw the priests and my classmates. A picture of the recreation hall popped into my mind. I could see clearly the black-and-white square floor tiles that seemed to have a pale yellow glaze on them from years of waxing. Rob told me to picture Jesus in the room. Under Rob's suggestive power, I saw Jesus talking and listening to the people with me. Jesus stood by my side. I felt good about being there with Jesus. Ochman told me to see the headmaster's office on that last day. The priest is giving me the bad news, and Jesus is there with me, his hand on my shoulder. As I dejectedly walked out of the office, Jesus put his arm around me and whispered into my ear, "It's okay. Don't worry." My guilt about doubting and flunking was lifted. Rob said that this wasn't an exercise for my imagination but rather a sharing of the situation with Jesus, letting him uproot the hurt, anger, and resentment and replace those negative feelings with God's forgiving and healing love. Sounded good to me—although I probably would have felt better if Jesus had given the headmaster the "high sign."

Rob then made me switch scenes to the wedding day. As Sarah walked down the aisle, I saw Jesus standing next to me in the front of the church. He wasn't wearing a tuxedo. He knew I wanted to run, yet he comforted me and helped me to stay. Jesus heard me say, "I do," and he didn't try to stop me. The exercise tried to help me accept the fact that I was married, because in my mind I really wasn't. Believing that my mind was now mystically changed, Ochman urged me to become physically closer to Sarah. I was told to start by holding her hand and touching her in a tender way.

I had wanted to do that, but it had always felt like an obligation. The healing of memories made me feel great that day and filled me with confidence that I could and would fall in love with Sarah, and that would make our marriage real. The effects of the inner healing session lasted two weeks. The hopes only raised my expectations, and the reality increased my disappointment and guilt. In fact, my interest in pornography was soon rekindled and only finally died out years later when I experienced a love so pure and genuine that it finally made pornography ugly to me. Life and maturity, not religion and fear, helped me break the bad habit I learned as a teenager.

There are no quick fixes, and God does not whisper in our ears easy solutions to our problems. Earlier I mentioned that the Lord supposedly directed a woman to send Pat Robertson a book. That seems to be a common practice among fundamentalists.

One day Rob Ochman handed me a book, and on the inside cover he inscribed the following message:

> Gerry,
>
> Enclosed herein is a word from the Lord.
>
> May it bring Joy, Peace, and Love.
>
> Rob

It had a soapy title like *Marriage Forever*. It was written by a Christian woman and was intended to help married men better understand women so through that understanding they could build a better marriage. She explained in the book the why and the wherefore of the female mind and that the man needs to supply the emotional needs of his wife so that she will eagerly satisfy him in every way. She claimed women are illogical and should submit to their husband's leadership. She had biblical proof for that, as well as loads of other stupid ideas concerning women and marriage. The book jacket gave no indication of the woman's qualifications for writing such a book, and it simply stated that she was an actress who had written a play.

Sarah was nothing like the woman the writer described in her book. In fact, if Sarah had read the book she would have thrown up. Yet this garbage was given to me as coming from the Lord. God had nothing to do with the book, let alone placing it in my hands. Rob's well-intentioned gesture aimed at healing my marriage became mixed up with his own personal vision of how life should be.

I felt that I ought to find romantic love where none existed. It was not enough that I no longer hated Sarah. It didn't matter that we were becoming friends. I talked more with her. I provided for her well-being. We even went on a weekend marriage encounter, which was touted as being able to turn a marriage around. We left half-way through the weekend. It wasn't enough that we were kind to and tolerant of each other. None of this was Sarah's fault. She never knew the depths of my negative feelings and cared very much for me. I was not able to respond. For me the situation was no longer miserable, but I felt my marriage was empty. I only found contentment in my ministry.

Within three years of my spiritual rebirth, the worst part of my existence shifted from the home to the job. I was unhappy at CBS and wanted to work full-time for the Lord. One, day while sitting in my office at CBS, I had the television tuned to a local station when "The 700 Club" came on the air. I had never seen the show before, but the Christian message coming from the tube caught my attention. My first impression was that the show was a poorly produced program, yet it said some good things. As I sat there watching I thought, "Gee, wouldn't it be neat to work at a Christian television station? Yeah, but that's not possible because they are all Protestants and would never hire a Catholic—even a fundamentalist Catholic."

Just then I felt the words "Nothing is impossible with Me. Write them" penetrate my being. In the prayer community—as well as at CBN—I was recognized as having received the gift of prophecy, and so I was familiar with the physical sensations that accompanied a word from the Lord. I believed at that moment, while I was sitting at my desk at CBS, that God was telling me I could and should be working at CBN. God said write, so I wrote a letter that minute. I told them my background, both professional and spiritual, and mailed the letter that day. Within two months I was working full-time for the Lord—just as I wanted.

But it was still a tough decision. Sarah wasn't thrilled with the move but agreed to go. It was hard to shut the door on fourteen-and-a-half years at CBS; even though I was unhappy, it had been my life for a very long time. I had only a few months to go to complete my studies for the diaconate; and it was difficult to walk away from being ordained a deacon. I loved my community and my pastoral post. Yet, I felt God was calling me into this new ministry where I could reach the world. This was my new vocation. I couldn't say no to God; I had to go.

As further "proof" of divine intervention, the letter I sent to CBN was forwarded by the personnel office to someone whose area of responsibility would have had no need for my services and who would have chucked the resume. The interoffice envelope containing my mis-directed letter "accidentally" wound up on the desk of the one person in the organization who could recognize my potential. I didn't hear anything for two weeks after writing, so I decided to call and make sure they had received it. I had no idea whom to ask for; and, despite the fact that I asked the operator to connect me with personnel, I was "accidentally" connected to the head of network operations. This man never answers his own phone, as all his calls are carefully screened by his secretary or his assistant, but my call "accidentally" came in on his private line—a number which few people knew—and "coincidentally" no one was there to pick it up. The busy executive had just finished reading my resume and was about to call me, when he answered his private line and discovered me. What a "coincidence!" Those accidents and coincidences were considered to be a sign that God wanted me to work at CBN.

An extreme saturation in a religious atmosphere leads to all thought tending toward a religious interpretation of daily natural events. Coincidence and luck appear to play no part in a fundamentalist Christian's life. Before we ended our "coincidental" conversation, I had a reservation on a flight to Virginia for an interview.

I thought that setting sail for the foreign shores of fundamentalism would make my life complete. It made it completely different.

6

The Foreign Shores of Fundamentalist TV

My early days at CBN were like a dream come true. Even though my job had none of the outward appearances of my teenage fantasy of carrying the gospel to such foreign shores as China or Africa, nonetheless, inwardly the dream became a reality when I stepped onto the foreign shores of fundamentalist television. I was a space-age missionary who could reach out to the world without leaving my own backyard.

The modern-day television missionary is able to remain safely inside his studio cocoon surrounded by people who think just like he does and support him completely; he does not have to venture out on his own into potentially hostile environments as did the missionary heroes of earlier ages.

The missionaries of yesterday were solitary men with deep convictions and courage to match. They left their native lands and sailed to unknown regions in order to live among wild and uneducated people for the simple reason of saving them from final damnation. They were the noblest of dreamers and adventurers. They truly believed that there was no salvation outside of Christ for anyone. Out of love, they risked death in order to bring eternal life to those who did not have the chance to hear about God's plan for salvation. Christianity for these missionaries—just as for their space-age counterparts on television—meant the total renunciation of all other religions and, as a result, became a form of religious imperialism.

Christianity is essentially a missionary religion, and true Christian faith not only requires but demands zealous missionary activity even at the expense of interreligious dialogue. It is not reasonable to expect

missionary outreach, whether door-to-door or via television, to diminish, because ardent recruitment is not an option of the faith but is a
requirement—even if the fulfillment of that requirement violates the
rights of others. Evangelization, as practiced by both the missionaries
of yesterday and the television preachers of today, is an act of spiritual
violence; dialogue, on the other hand, is an act of sharing.

I came to CBN with the intention of sharing my faith through my
broadcasting skills and proclaiming over the airwaves the message that
Jesus is Lord. I honestly thought that I was going to use the medium I
loved to send out a message of love. Instead, I became part of a team
of people who exploited the medium by making it a modern means of
mass manipulation by cleverly packaging indirect messages and
making outrageous claims in the name of God.

In July of 1980 I received a letter from a vice-president of a local
television station in Toledo, Ohio. Actually, it was a carbon copy of a
letter he had sent to one of his viewers who had written the station
protesting a show I had produced. The viewer's letter to the station
was also included, and it said:

> I just finished watching Channel 13 from 6:00 A.M. to 7:00 A.M. It was a
> terrible reactionary religious program which did nothing but slander
> the gay population of the viewing audience. Why do you broadcast
> such one-sided garbage? What sort of rebuttal time do you have to
> offset this?

The vice president replied in part:

> Their reference to homosexuality was a religious interpretation, which
> is usually negative on the subject. Both sides of the issue of homo-
> sexuality have been discussed many times on various programs in the
> past. In fact, just yesterday, a positive side of the issue was the subject
> of the Phil Donahue Show.

I'm sure the theme of the show that I had produced was more like
"homosexuals are sinners" than "Jesus is Lord." My message had
changed—and so was I changing.

Air Pollution

During my first year out of CBN, I was contacted by reporters from
the *Washington Post* and the *Los Angeles Times*. Both papers were

running stories on the growth and goals of CBN. The Christian soap opera was highlighted in the articles. As the creator and original executive producer of the show, I was tracked down at ABC in Hollywood in order to get my comments. I imagine that they had hoped I was a disgruntled former employee with an ax to grind and something nasty to say. I only stated that I believed Pat Robertson was a man of integrity, and I made no comments on either the show or my departure from the ministry. I said so little that I was never mentioned in either article. In fact, during most of my post-CBN days, I defended their right to exist and to produce television shows from any point of view they wanted.

But now, after several years of study, I seriously wonder what these religious programs are doing polluting the public airwaves. However, they have become so big and so institutionalized that they are beyond attack—or at least an attack that could seriously damage them. Nobody in public life wants to appear to be anti-God, and any criticism of these righteous video vicars is easily converted into an attack against God; nor is it wise to be seen as tolerant of any of the list of evils that the fundamentalists are trying to uproot from the American soil, because then you can be classified as pro-sin. "Go Sin" is not a campaign slogan that is likely to win any elections.

Not only are the superstar servants of God almost untouchable, their company is frequently sought by the powerful and influential. Jerry Falwell is no stranger to the White House. Politically it is not smart to appear to be against God. Whenever elections draw near, politicians are drawn not only to the front pews in their churches but also to the electronic church. Legislators like Senators Robert Dole, Richard Lugar, Strom Thurman, Orin Hatch, and Paul Laxalt have no hesitation about sitting down with Pat Robertson and discussing politics on a religious television show. The fundamentalist ministers have become—thanks to television—mainline, powerful, and beyond criticism. They know God; and, more importantly, they can deliver votes. They are now an accepted part of the American scene. However, they have not accepted the American scene—they want to repaint it with the blood of Jesus. And I helped them.

Play Ball

The death of my goal to simply share my faith by producing wholesome shows reflecting the ideals of Jesus and providing an alternative to the shallow offerings from the networks died quickly; so quickly, in fact, that I hardly noticed or mourned its passing. I was surrounded by people whose faith experiences seemed superior to mine. I knew television; they knew God. I felt that I lacked their spiritual insights, their commitment, their dedication, their determination. The people at CBN played religious hardball, and they took the game very seriously. You played the game their way, or you were off the team. For acceptance, either personal or professional, you needed to conform and display unquestioned belief in their dogma of salvation. God was spoken of openly, freely, and frequently. It was as if anything that didn't have to do with spiritual things was not worth talking about, especially if you traveled in the circles of upper management. Yet, I loved talking about movies and the New York Yankees. There were a few renegades on the staff who occasionally liked to engage in a conversation that centered on the theater and not the tribulation.

Before long the political, social, and spiritual gospel of Pat Robertson began to sink into my consciousness. I was being absorbed into a new belief system and pattern of behavior. Slowly, a new "me" began to emerge. I enjoyed the challenge of my new job as well as the attention I received as the new kid on the block. At CBS, I was just one of the troops; at CBN, I was a troop leader. I relished all the perks of being a boss. I was an instant celebrity, and it was fun. My quick acceptance was due to a memo that was issued in order to introduce me to the staff. Before giving any details about my professional background, the division head let it be known that I stood on holy ground by writing, "First, Gerry is a brother." That meant I was one of them— spiritually speaking. My Catholic Charismatic involvement gave me the same language, but not the same attitude. At times I feared that they would discover that my faith wasn't as firm as theirs. I loved my job and wanted to fit in, and before long I did. There were times when I was uncomfortable with my new-found fundamentalist faith, but my need for acceptance in order to survive and earn a living outweighed doubts, and I managed to ignore my discomfort with some of the stagnating spirituality. Besides, I had mistakenly thought that the message being broadcast was harmless. It would have taken a great deal of courage to question some of the beliefs and practices, and the last thing I wanted to do was to make waves when I was attempting to become part of the team.

Masquerade Party

I did manage to maintain a degree of individuality; however, my changed faith had so brainwashed me that I was incapable of making a reasoned and independent choice on a wide range of nonreligious issues; that became Pat Robertson's role. Most of the staff had a difficult time interacting with people—even family and friends—who did not share their faith. Together, under Pat's anointed leadership, we controlled a major communication tool that could touch society on an emotional level—and viewers responded to our twisted message. Television was an easy way to get converts to our brand of Christianity, converts who would eagerly use the political process to turn their private beliefs into public policy. I had become a space-age missionary who carried, with the help of space-age technology, a stone-age message of intolerance. Hardly noticing, I had changed.

And I thought when I set sail for the shores of Virginia Beach that I was going to produce programs that radiated with a spirit of love and hope. Was I wrong! When I landed in my new missionary country, I believed that I had crossed the border between genuine spirituality and a cult imitation. I cut myself off from my family, my friends, my past, and moved into a new society of people chained together by a common experience that made them special and separated them from the unsaved. They were bound together by chains of fear and pride. They feared living without each other, and were too proud to live with the rest of the world. Having been mysteriously transformed, they were filled with a less-than-holy desire to transform the world. My new cult society hid safely behind a masquerade of Christianity and television, and many observers lack the insight and courage to unmask them and expose their religious halloween party. It's easy to get angry at them, hard to understand them, and impossible to defeat them. I can only hope to show them as they really are.

During my time at CBN, I faithfully maintained a practice of saving every memo I wrote and every memo I received. This is a common practice among freelance producers. My memo saving at CBN was done independently of my secretary, who had her own official file of my correspondence that would eventually wind up in the company archives or, maybe in my case, the county dump. When I cleaned out my office on the day I got fired, I took along with me twelve thick binders overflowing with memos and production notes on all the shows I had produced. They sat unread on the top shelf of my closet for years. One day I decided to reread every memo. It took two full days to complete the task, since the words frequently transported me back in time on the wings of wistful daydreams. Some of the memories the memos triggered were warm, some sad, some bitter, and some funny. After reading all the material, I was overwhelmed with the overall theme and tone of the writings: Satan is attempting to thwart the will of God. The collective impact of all the memos revealed tension and paranoia. In order to unmask the Christianity of the staff, I would like to share a few samples from my memo collection.

His Solution

The following excerpt comes from a memo dated June 4, 1980, and was written by a woman field producer. She was young, bright, talented, and endowed with beauty and charisma. Her smile could light up a room. Her job was to put together salvation testimonies and required her to travel around the country with a camera crew. The memo detailed numerous technical equipment problems that she had encountered on a recent trip she'd made to New York City in order to tape the testimony of a young girl who had been afraid to go outside for five years until Christ changed her life.

> When we got back to the hotel, however, we found the audio during 98% of the major interview [with the girl] was badly garbled and unusable. According to standard procedures, we should have just dropped the story and filled out the appropriate forms when we returned home. But I just couldn't do it. There's something about being there and talking with the real people like Linda whose lives have been so dramatically transformed and see the tears in her father's eyes as he told us what God had done. . . . I just *knew* that the Lord would be honored in the airing of that story, and that we just couldn't buckle under to the devil and let all that good shooting be wasted. So, after much thought and prayer, I rescheduled my shooting days in New York, and went back the next morning to reshoot the interview with Linda. Unfortunately, it was raining, so we had to shoot it indoors instead of the lovely outdoor setting we had used the day before, and Linda was tired out and not as sparkling.

The crew also taped an interview with William Simon, former U.S. Treasury secretary. After detailing the technical troubles that plagued the Simon interview, she continued:

This particular New York trip cost over $1,000 excluding salaries. A new videocassette recorder costs only $2,500, and this is only one of dozens of shoots that have been crippled or lost over the past few months. One of the biggest side effects of the equipment problem I see is the spirit of the crews. Every cameraman that I've worked with in the past six months is fired up, creative and enthusiastic when we start a shoot. But after the first day with equipment problems, there's usually a noticeable difference in attitude. And I know personally how hard it is to shake the discouragement and disappointment over troublesome gear. I'm sure this is one key area Satan knows he can weaken not only our enthusiasm and creativity, but our on-the-road testimony for Jesus Christ. I'm not coming to you to gripe, but merely ask for your concerned prayers in this area. Something has to be done. One Christian leader I heard recently made this comment: "God loves to put us in situations where we can't see a solution—then He can expand our frame of reference so that we can see His perspective and His solution." Whatever God is trying to show us or teach us in this situation, I would ask for you to pray with me that we clearly see His solution in the very near future.

(signed) His servant

The memo indicates how anxious they were to get the healing testimony on tape. They did not function as investigative reporters but as producers of a commercial that would honor and help sell their God while pretending it was a journalistic coverage of a miracle. They were easily moved by the emotions of the "healed" girl and the tearful father. The crews' emotions turned to frustration when they failed to capture the girl's story. Assuming for a moment that God did heal the girl, is it necessary to magnify the works of the Lord? Does God, who they believe is the creator of the universe, need their feeble help at polishing his tarnished image? Their distress at losing the testimony indicates that they would answer yes to both questions.

They were quick to blame Satan for the troubles, but I wonder if it ever crossed their minds that perhaps their boss—God—didn't want this story told. After all, the next day it did rain, the girl was cranky, and the piece, even though it did air, lost its original luster. It should work both ways—if the Devil can stop something, so might the Almighty. For the CBN staffers, however, bad news always came from Hell, and good news came from Heaven. And what should be made of the spirituality of a Christian crew that can become so easily dispirited and distressed when confronted with problems? The memo clearly states that following these aggravating difficulties they were no longer able to be good witnesses for the Lord, which means they were grumpy and irritable instead of happy, redeemed children of God. The

Bible they love suggests rejoicing in all things—both good and bad.

Note the part prayer played in the story and the memo. The producer justified going against company policy by reshooting the girl's testimony because she had prayed about it, and God didn't say no. In writing the memo, she doesn't demand—as a professional—any specific or practical action; instead, she seeks—as a Christian—only joint prayer in finding a spiritual solution. For CBN staffers, prayer somehow motivates and sanctifies any activity. Almost anything you do is okay as long as you prayed about it first.

"I was praying and I had this idea . . ." was far more effective than, "I had this idea. . . ." Finally, the Christian leader's quoted comment in the memo clearly distorts and spiritualizes a simple fact that all problems become opportunities for growth as people strive to overcome obstacles. Human beings are problem-solving agents. The most successful people are good problem solvers. God isn't sitting around all day trying to cook up trials and troubles from which we can learn. Can you imagine God getting up in the morning, stretching, and instantaneously calling to his mind every person on the planet, and for each one of them think something like this: "Let's see, for Gerry Straub I think today I'll have his typewriter break in order to teach him patience and resourcefulness." Sounds silly, yet that is the comic reality of the Christian leaders' understanding of human problems.

The most basic question that the memo raises is: Was the Devil causing the technical failures in order to make the crew crazy? Of course not. The problem was simple: CBN sent the crew out with old, poorly maintained equipment and expected them to work miracles. You don't need prayer or the wisdom of Solomon to realize that the solution had nothing to do with a lesson from God but was simply better equipment. Yet somehow this rather natural management problem of carefully determining when the time is right for the most cost-effective replacement of existing equipment and also establishing a preventative maintenance schedule was turned into a satanic struggle. Bad management was the only "devil" I saw at CBN.

God Didn't Tell Us

While developing "Another Life," I received a number of letters from a woman who claimed that God was telling her to go to work at CBN as the head writer of the soap opera. That is a very difficult and demanding job that requires very specialized writing talents, and the woman had virtually no writing experience of any kind. Even the Devil wouldn't have advised her to apply for the job of head writer. No matter how ludicrous the woman's suggestion was, I felt that as a Christian organization we should at least respond to her out of kindness—especially after her third letter. The following is a response written by one of my assistants:

> I am responding to your letter of October 13th, hoping the Lord is your portion and joy today. I was glad to hear of your eager interest in helping CBN in its mission, yet, too, as a brother in Christ I was a bit concerned too. I was concerned because of your insistence that the Lord had been telling you for some months to go to work for CBN. He may or He may not be doing so. I feel an obligation as a brother in Christ to share with you along these lines. You see, often times our desires are so strong that we miss the true leading of the Lord. When I received Christ as my Savior, I was pursuing a professional writing career in Hollywood, California. I had had a degree of success and was being represented by a literary agent. But, yet, when God called me He led me into some very menial jobs for several years to break me down that He might build me up spiritually. I washed cars for a living, mowed grass, drove a cab and so forth. Yet all the time, He was schooling me in His word, fitting me into a local body of believers and preparing me for the work He had for me. At first, I had to become a broken and yielding vessel. You have talent. You have a desire to serve the Lord. This is good, but I want to caution you to make sure that any leading from the Lord is confirmed by His word and the counsel of others who may be spiritually older in the Lord than you are, like a pastor or elder in a church. The Bible clearly teaches us that there is wisdom in a multitude of counselors. When you say that the Lord has been telling you to go to work for CBN, don't you think our heavenly Father would be kind enough to tell us here at CBN, too? But, you see, He hasn't. We already have a head writer for the new soap opera. The realistic possibilities of your working with us at this time are quite remote. That's why I caution you to be careful when you feel God has spoken to you to go someplace or to do something. Pray about it. Ask God to confirm it specifically. If He doesn't, forget about it and go on walking by faith. I praise God for your thinking about us, and I pray that the Lord will use your talents one day, soon. May God bless you and increase you.

I guess it is easy for some poor soul who sits home day after day watching people on religious television to claim that God spoke to or led her in this or that direction, to want for herself that same kind of communication and direction from God. Thanks to shows like "The 700 Club" many people are finding it easy to proudly announce that God has spoken to them. CBN gives them both the example and the courage to expect godly intervention in their lives. The notion that

God has favored you with his words, wisdom, and advice is really rather egotistical.

When I reread the letter written by my assistant, I could not help but stop and think about his response in light of what has happened to the both of us since I asked him to write to the woman. This is the same man who pushed pamphlets on the toll-keeper and the former network executive. He wrote the woman as a wiser and spiritually older brother in the Lord. That gave him the authority to counsel her. Yet his counsel grew out of his experience as a new Christian when God supposedly broke him down by making him work at menial jobs.

As he tells it, before God saved him and then afflicted him with a string of slavish jobs, he was a writer on the verge of making it big. In truth his credits and experience were slim, and I tend to think that he did not continue to work as a writer after his salvation because his writing wasn't working and therefore not selling. I did a great deal of agonizing over his talent or lack of the same. I had his writing evaluated by a number of impartial professionals, and the general consensus was that he didn't have much potential as a writer. In fact, I did not originally even hire him as a writer. Following his conversion, his outlook on life became so narrow and judgmental that his writing suffered even more as it became more moralistic and less marketable. He wouldn't even consider working on something that he considered to be less than Christian. That left mowing lawns until he heard about the Christian soap opera and contacted me.

He, too, wanted to be the head writer. I hired him as a member of the production staff because I believed he had the fundamentalist strain of spirituality that had to be woven into the stories in order for the partners to support the project. I never met anyone who could quote Scripture better, and that was my weakness—among others. He had a Bible passage for every occasion. For example, it is common practice when applying for a job to send the prospective employer some letters of recommendation. Well, this man had to attach a scriptural basis for his doing so:

> Having just finished our phone conversation of this day, I thought it might be of some interest to you to have these letters of recommendation. They are a few years old, but speak of my qualifications, abilities and character. "Let another man praise thee, and not thine own mouth . . ." (Prov. 27:2).

Under his signature in parentheses he wrote Phil. 2:13, which sent me scurrying off after a Bible in order to find out what the second chapter and thirteenth verse of the apostle Paul's letter to the Phillipians said. "For it is God which worketh you both to will and to do His good pleasure."

It may have pleased God to have him work at CBN, but not me. I always felt that hiring him was a mistake; and, after I got the heavenly boot, his influence on the soap grew. He turned the show into a religious drama when it had originally been a drama that included some religion. Miracles and the Bible abounded. One of the show's characters was on the verge of death and lay unconscious on his hospital bed. Following prayer by visiting friends, he woke up, sat up, pulled out the tubes and the life-support systems that entrapped him, and got out of bed, miraculously healed. The room was suddenly filled with songs and shouts of praise as the healed and the healers thanked God for his demonstration of power. This spiritual fantasy and heavy-handed way of selling salvation cost about $14,000 per show and played to virtually nonexistent audiences.

The writer's stories were didactic, preachy, moralistic, and boring. He was always in conflict with anyone who did not seem to be a mature Christian in *his* eyes. He believed God had called him to CBN. I think his job on "Another Life" was more a fluke than a favor from the Lord. He no longer works at CBN—having lost his job when "Another Life" was cancelled due to lack of viewer interest—but he still tries to write for God. The sad part was that he really was a very kind and nice man whose pain for all the unsaved people who were doomed to hell was genuine. I grew to like him despite his intolerance. For a long time, I worried that his understanding of the way God operates might be correct—he seemed so sure.

The biblical principle he wrote about in his letter that ensures wisdom in a multitude of counselors is not true if all the counselors think the same way; however, a multitude consists of many people who would think differently, and to listen to and evaluate all the various pieces of advice offered by a diversified multitude would lead to a decision that might be founded in wisdom. But a fundamentalist Christian would never seek or accept advice from someone who does not think like a fundamentalist Christian. Many times I sat with ministry officials gathered together around the long, highly polished table in the private conference room adjacent to Pat's office and heard Robertson share his latest visions and plans for CBN. We thought there was safety and wisdom in the numerous counselors assembled. But disagreement and differences of opinion seemed to be reserved only for the actual methods of implementing the presented plan. The vision always went unchallenged because we all thought alike—like Pat.

The Grand Alternative

God seemed to give everyone an idea for new and improved ways of selling the old gospel of salvation. Part of my time at CBN was spent as the assistant director of network programming, and that position included the responsibility of reading and evaluating all the heavenly ideas for television shows that people believed God wanted CBN to produce. One such idea came in a letter from an Oral Roberts University graduate who had majored in European history and minored in telecommunications. After some introductory comments he wrote:

> While at school I participated in every available aspect of television and radio production, but dedicated myself to writing. I found myself being drawn towards humor and science fiction, though all forms of dialogue interest me. After graduation I decided to remain in Tulsa and try my hand at freelance writing. A brief stint as a political satire and humor columnist for a California publication and several scripts proved educational, but I felt like God had something special in mind and that is why I wrote CBN. I feel that the potential for CBN is great. Throughout the world, the Devil has saturated every form of communication with ungodly garbage. Of course you are aware of the lack of quality programming the three networks have to offer. (By "quality" I mean content and emphasis, not money—they have plenty of that.) To me, CBN looms as the Grand Alternative. Instead of serving to erode our society, the family unit, and moral values, CBN can counter with positive programming that affirms that which is right—that which heals. It may sound corny to some, but it's the way I feel. Just *who* CBN reaches is important. There are so many Christians with radio and television ministries, but they all seem to be focusing their ministries within, to their own followers. Their audiences are very limited. I think God wants to reach *out* today . . . to touch the many people out there who aren't fortunate enough to be within the fold. That's why the expansion of CBN is so very important to me. Preaching and teaching the Word is important, but if that is the *only* programming much, if not most, of the potential audience is lost. If the Devil can take an attractive program and use it to destroy subconsciously, why can't God take an attractive program and heal? Maybe not with angels singing and John 3:16 emblazoned across the screen, but with something good, something upbeat. I say all this, not to be preachy, but just so that you'll know how I feel. I see science fiction as a potentially powerful media device. Everywhere I look these days there is science fiction and fantasy. *Star Wars* set box office records, and why? It really didn't say anything terribly new. The essential theme was good vs. evil and that's a theme that's been around for a long time. Since Genesis! No, I think what *attracts* people to sci fi is external—the setting, the fantastic gadgetry— but what *holds* them successfully is very basic drama . . . human characters

working out human conflicts and supplying human needs. While the setting may be far-out, the actual message can be simple . . . and godly. Science fiction is an attractive means of communicating and not necessarily expensive. A weekly series would contain the same dramatic elements of a western or soap, but the setting would be in another time and another place. So what it boils down to is this. I have some ideas, I love to write, and I want to serve the Lord. I would be glad to send you any samples and clippings, if you desire. Thank you, Mr. Straub, for your time. I am grateful for any consideration that you give me.

People really thought that CBN was capable of anything, that we were going to save the world through television, and that God was sending them to help us. But what about this young man? The writing he had done proved educational, which means not profitable (when you learn a lot, you don't earn a lot); nonetheless he was confident he could help us help God. Obviously, he was more sophisticated than the woman who insisted that God wanted her to work at CBN; however, despite his sophistication, he still firmly believed that the Devil had infiltrated mass communications, especially television.

The programs on the networks may be garbage, but they are not Devil-made. They only reflect the economic reality that dictates that the quickest way to make a buck in television is to program to the lowest common denominator. The producers making the shows and the network executives making the choices as to which shows air are not secret agents for Satan; they are ordinary people—many are even religious—who struggle in a very creative and highly competitive field to earn a living. It takes years to learn the creative crafts they love and even longer to gain a working understanding of a fickle business that changes with the seasons. Most of the people working in television want to do something special or meaningful but are content to be able to do anything. Very few people make it big in television. You can earn seven thousand dollars one week and the next week be on the unemployment line.

The young letter writer wanted to reach out to those people who were turned off by Bible-thumping preachers. He wanted to soften the message so that it was more palpable for the "lost" viewer. I tried that, and it doesn't work—viewers are too smart and not easily tricked. In his youthful naivete and idealism, he ignored the financial requirements of producing effective television and thought that on a low budget he could compete with the networks for viewers' attention. Furthermore, the television preachers must pitch most of their material at the already "saved" because they are the ones sending in the money. I learned from CBN's soap opera that you must keep the donors happy. If you get too secular, they get mad, and the ministry doesn't get their money—and you get your walking papers. The January 1986 CBN Telethon, a week-long event that was the major fundraiser for the year, fell short of the amount they needed in pledges to cover the operating budget by one million dollars per month. After the exhausting beg-a-thon, everyone knew that jobs would be lost—whose and when were the only unknowns.

It was unfortunate that this bright young man had been deceived into thinking that his love for writing and his love for God are incompatible unless he functions as a writer within the restrictive confines of Christianity. I'm sure that whatever talent the young man has will be wasted if he continues to think that God has something special for him. He must make something special for himself. CBN is not a grand alternative, as he suggests: it is a grand delusion.

In His Service

I could easily fill a couple of volumes with commentary on my memo collection. They demonstrate how pervasive and perverted the spirituality was at CBN. It invaded and affected every area of our lives as it twisted and distorted reality into an unseen spiritual warfare. The simplest events in life took on complicated religious significance. For example, one woman believed that every time her hands sweated it meant that God was speaking to her. Once when a real-estate agent was showing her a house, her hands began to perspire, and she took that as an indication that God wanted her to buy the house. It was a clear (although wet) sign from God. Later in the day, the real-estate agent showed her another house and again the woman's hands became moist. Her conclusion: God must want her to buy both houses for some reason he would make clear later even though she could barely afford to buy one house. The purchase of a house can be a nerve-wracking experience, and a normal response for many people when they become nervous is to have their hands turn clammy and moist. Seeing the hand of God in a damp hand that is the result of a natural and human reaction to tension is a rather schizoid response.

Without realizing it, we were spiritually oppressed and psychologically battered people who blindly followed the crowd as we marched triumphantly toward God—trampling on the ungodly as we prayerfully goose-stepped our way down the salvation highway that led to glory land. It has taken me five years to deprogram myself from the detrimental effects of my time at CBN. After spending the winters of 1984 and 1985 in virtual frozen isolation and solitude watching the snowflakes joyfully dance in silence as I scribbled down my thoughts on CBN spirituality, I've come to see how CBN nearly stole my life, my friends, my very soul—and how lucky I was to escape.

The memos remind me that while I worked at CBN, I marched right along with my fellow soldiers in Christ's army. In the summer of 1979, I was asked to conduct a comprehensive study of a very vital department within the programming division. The ministry was growing faster than its ability to manage it. Due to ineffective leadership, morale at the time was down and communication between management and staff was poor. The workers lived each day going from crisis to crisis. The staff saw money being wasted due to poor planning, yet they were underpaid and overworked. Some people felt used and abused—and worse, they didn't think anyone cared. The frustration grew so intense that steps had to be taken to turn things around and improve the decaying morale.

My job was to analyze the problems and complaints and to offer concrete recommendations for improving the operation. I spent two draining weeks conducting intensive interviews with all the staff members in an attempt to develop an accurate picture of the problem. I compiled thirty pages of typed notes, and from that material I composed a nine-page memo that included sixteen specific proposals that I felt needed to be implemented as soon as possible to rectify the departments' difficulties. Like a good spiritual leader, I began and ended my report on a spiritual note with Scripture quotes: I opened with, "My goal is God Himself, not joy nor peace, nor even blessing, But Himself, my God," and closed with, "Where there is no vision the people perish."

Perhaps the opening quotation reflected a subconscious fear that my tough analysis, which included one firing, two demotions, and a major internal restructuring of responsibilities, would be considered arrogant or self-serving. On a conscious level, however, I believed that I was God's agent for change. Either way, biblical quotations never hurt and often helped set the tone. The language used and beliefs expressed in my report indicated my conformity to the CBN doctrine. In fact, I sounded like a hard-liner. My report contained these comments:

> The world is treating us with a shrug while we're putting out a program we hoped would revolutionize the world. Where is the dedication and commitment to excellence?

We give someone a key job and pray they can perform. We need to hire fully competent people who don't need on-the-job training, but have on-the-job experience. Is a national program the proper place to train a person with absolutely no experience in what you are giving them charge to do?

We are blessed with excellently motivated people willing to give totally of themselves, but how long can we expect them to give 100% when we provide them with such a poor working environment? We depend on a person being spiritually mature and willing to totally sacrifice themselves in order to keep them on the job.

It is my overriding belief that what besets "The 700 Club" more than anything else, is a lack of an identifiable vision and purpose which unites the staff and commits us to a revolutionary work in presenting Christ to an unsaved world. There seems to be no real understanding of to what degree we are an evangelistic organization dedicated to aggressively bringing men and women into the Kingdom, and to what degree we are charged with ministering to the spiritual needs of the partners, the men and women who pay the bills and make future telecasts possible.

The mixture of my spiritual sensitivity and business reality impressed Pat Robertson greatly; and, as a result, my personal "stock" rose swiftly. Nearly all of my recommendations were acted upon, and the situation did improve noticeably. However, Satan was not behind the problems nor was God behind the solution. It was just that common sense defeated inexperience and poor judgment. I had been working at CBN about fifteen months when this memo was written, and by that time I had bought the belief that the world needed to be saved, and I was quoting Scripture. Conformity and unquestioned belief are vital to being accepted, and I really wanted to be accepted by my new society of friends.

Memos were the life blood of the ministry. We loved writing memos. I once suggested that we buy our own forest in order to cheaply meet our ferocious appetite for paper. If a memo was a document that merely conveyed some simple information, like a schedule or an announcement, and was therefore not overtly religious in tone or substance, then the writer would at least use a religious closing like "In His Service," or "His Servant," or "Your brother in the Lord," or "Yours in Christ." There was no doubt who the boss was. We were bound together by the belief that we had found the truth.

Planning a Club

Much planning went into each edition of "The 700 Club." Mounting a live ninety-minute program five days a week takes an incredible amount of coordination. The work is demanding, and the pressure is great. The key to a successful program is preplanning. Themes for each show had to be established, guests selected, features and testimonies planned, and show formats written. On any given day while one show is airing live, at least three weeks' worth of future shows are in various stages of development. It is a massive juggling act. Each week a group of people would gather together for a formating conference, and we would share ideas for shows still far off in the future. At this meeting, each show begins to take some kind of form. Things like scenic requirements and guest travel arrangements and accommodations will be set in motion. Possible salvation testimonies will be discussed, selected, and assigned to crews.

What follows is a brief description of the themes of some of the shows we decided to produce and some of the profiles of guests we invited to be on the show. This information was taken from my notes written during the conceptual formating meeting which, as the producer, I chaired. This is not fiction; this really happened. I was there!

Themes

Will The Russians Stop at Afganistan? A look at Soviet aggresion and its threat to Western Europe and an examination of the reasons for current unrest in Muslim and Hindu countries.

The Working Woman: How to triumph in times of family crisis, and how to plan for business success without compromising family values.

Our Genetic Futures: Who should play God? A discussion of the national conflict over test-tube baby clinics and just how far science and government should go to decide our future.

Marriage in the 80s: Will it work? A look at the institution of marriage and its problems along with a teaching on the importance of the family structure.

When Cancer Strikes: Looks at a woman's struggle with cancer and an unfaithful husband.

Age of Materialism: A review of materialism and its effects on young people.

Israel on Center Stage: Probes the current political and social climate in Israel.

Be Not Deceived: Exposes how Hinduism is not a path to God.

Don't Worry: Teaching and ministry on why Christians can live free from anxiety, and how to differentiate between worldly worry Christian "rest."

How the Mighty Have Fallen: Examines reasons why so many Christians are backsliding and illustrates principles from God's Word on righteous living.

Thy Neighbor's Wife: A look at the sexual proclivities of America's adult population and a review of the appropriate scripture on the subject. Show will feature a prostitute who became a missionary.

Mood Management: A look at the great American love affair with maintaining an artifically induced high.

America's Religious Heritage: Leaders in education, government, and business were frequently Christians. We challenge Christians to take back the territory we've surrendered to the world.

The Road to Armageddon: A look at the facts leading us to believe the world is coming to an end, followed by a call for viewers to receive Christ.

Not Married: Looks at why more and more young people are determined to remain unmarried and what can be done to effectively evangelize this hidden group of single adults. Show stresses the role of family in giving stability to society.

It's a Miracle: Presents real-life testimonies of people who insist miracles do happen despite the intellectuals who claim they do not.

Beyond and Back: Will probe the stories of men and women who have died, seen heaven or hell, and have returned to tell about it.

What's Wrong With American Business: An analysis of the severe problems undermining the productivity of the American worker and the resulting decline in the standard of living. Program's ultimate emphasis will be what the Bible says about the relation between the worker and his employer.

Soul Winning: Examines the right to evangelize the world, the techniques used, and a measurement of how the worldwide crusade is going.

Training Up a Child in The Way He Should Go: A look at methods directed at bringing Bible foundations and faith principles to young people.

Banned: Tells what Christians can do to prevent the federal government from wiping out all obscenity laws from the books.

One Nation Under God: Looks at the moral drift in America.

Psychiatry and Religion: The history and validity of psychiatry and its relationship to spiritual counseling.

Guests

An Endurance Horse Rider tells how he was saved after living a full life of wine, women, song, and dope. He went from jailbird to real-estate agent with God's help.

Evangelist tells how God raised his failing grades to the honor roll level, delivered him from bad habits, met his financial needs, and healed him of severe injuries suffered when a plane propeller hit him and nearly took off his nose.

Veterinarian/Farmer tells how he was transformed from a fearful, weak, worried Christian into a spirit-filled faith healer living an abundant life. He shares how the Lord is working in veterinary science.

Singer who was into the occult, reincarnation, and Eastern philosophies before being saved. He is now an evangelist with an international CB ministry to truckers as he talks about Jesus via CB radio.

Reporter for a Trotskyite publication was heavily into alcohol, drugs, and Marxism. While dating a Christian lady, the presence of Jesus came into the room, and he was saved. He married the woman, and now he is the religion editor of a local paper, and he uses his column to expose astrology as a tool of Satan and managed to get the paper to drop its daily horoscope feature. The Spirit has given him a revelation similar to Pat's regarding the return of the Lord in the near future.

Housewife whose father was an alcoholic and wife beater who exposed her to pornography when she was in the fifth grade. She became an unwed mother when she was 17 and later married an ex-convict. She got involved in an adulterous affair and fortune telling before she was thrown into jail for stealing. Once out of jail, she divorced her first husband and married a race-car driver who had a violent temper and a lust for other women. She had a miscarriage and divorced him. Depressed, she cried out to God, and He heard her plea. She gave up dating married men and remained single for three years until God answered her prayers and sent her the perfect husband. They both backslid briefly when they got interested in reincarnation. After rededicating their lives to the Lord, she took fertility drugs, got pregnant, and was diagnosed as having cancer. Following the advice of God, she refused to follow the doctor's request that she have an abortion. The baby was miraculously born healthy. She still has cancer.

Those themes and guests hardly sound as though they would combine to make a healthy, balanced, and inspirational religious television show. It is difficult for me to believe that I actually produced "The 700 Club" and that the host of the show wants to be president of the United States.

You're Next

When I reread the profiles of the guests, I could not help but get the feeling that I was reading a comical parody of fundamentalist Christianity. But it wasn't funny back then—salvation was a very serious business. The staff were sincere in their beliefs and totally dedicated to their mission of slaying Satan and saving souls—and no sacrifice was too great for such a vital task. For the most part, low wages and hard work didn't deaden the enthusiasm with which they served their God. Mismanagement and insensitivity were the only morale breakers; however, even those could be overcome by faith and fear of the Devil.

The late 1970s were a time of great expansion for the ministry. God was blessing us with tremendous growth in both size and scope, and massive amounts of money were being poured into the construction of the new headquarters center and university buildings. It was an exciting time that filled the staff with a sense of pride. Yet at the same time, some financial belt-tightening was needed in order to hold down the costs of the day-to-day operation. The ambitious construction projects pushed the ministry to its financial limits, and every penny was important. In fact, by the spring of 1978, the dollar crunch was so bad that, in an effort to economize and to cut operating costs, we had to cut twenty-four people. I personally had to choose and inform a number of those fired. It was a very dark day in the Kingdom of Light. The firing of twenty-four staff members sent shock waves of worry through the ministry, as everyone quietly wondered, "Am I next?"

I'm sure that an impartial review of the various functions performed by the dismissed employees would have revealed some waste and that justification for the elimination of a number of positions could have been established. However, that is business talk and does not address the spiritual implication of the sudden firings. Those twenty-four dedicated people who had faithfully served the ministry believed that God had called them to CBN, and their sudden termination seemed cruel and ungodly. The unasked question on everyone's mind was: How could a monumental building be going up and staff members be cut down?

The firings caused such a commotion that on Sunday, June 11, an all-staff prayer meeting was held to seek God's guidance and to restore our sense of purpose. At the meeting Ben Kinchlow, the tall Texan cohost of "The 700 Club," gave an impassioned speech that implored the staff to defeat the satanic fear that was spreading through the ministry like a deadly cancer. The head of personnel thought that Ben's message was an inspired word from God and was so important that he had the text of the plea released as a memo to the entire staff. There is no single memo or document in my possession that more clearly illustrates the ministry-wide paranoid schizophrenia that exists at CBN. Here is the complete text of the "inspired" message:

I want to tell you I travel all over America, and I see people everywhere and people of all kinds: people who take an afternoon off and fly me around in an airplane because they have nothing else to do; people who live off of $20 a week—that's all this lady makes—$20 a week. These are the kinds of people I see all over America. I want to tell you something—the one common unifying bond that they all have is that they love CBN, and believe that God Almighty is speaking to them and they believe that the people here at CBN are something special and those people out there are sacrificing. I mean they are literally going without things in order to make sure that this ministry goes forward. I want to tell you something—I believe in a lot of cases that they have more confidence in what God is doing at CBN out there than some of us do here at CBN. The devil can't destroy you from the outside so what do you do if he gets inside. Let me tell you I really feel strongly that fear has grabbed around a bunch of people's hearts here at CBN. It is just like he is just whipping our hearts like this with fear and people are afraid. Can you imagine that born-again, spirit-filled, redeemed Christians working in the midst of one of the most powerful ministries today are walking around with fear gripping their hearts? Let me tell you something—the devil tried that on me. I heard the news that 24 people had bit the dust and the devil said, "You're next!" If you're not very careful, you start listening to him and the next thing you know you start agreeing with him and the next thing you start looking around for your next job. I said, "Wait a minute." I said, "Devil, you didn't give me this job, and you can't take it away." I said something else, "Pat didn't give me this job and he can't take it away. God brought me to CBN. It didn't have anything to do with talents and abilities I didn't have. He brought me here because He wanted me here. He had something He wanted me to do and when He gets tired of me being here at CBN—I'll be on my way out, but not one instant before." How many in here believe God brought you to CBN? If you don't believe that God brought you to CBN, then you ought to be looking for a place to leave. But if you believe that God brought you to this ministry—I believe that God has people in this thing that He brought specifically for a specific purpose—and He's got you here and He's not going to turn you loose until He gets ready to turn you loose and you ain't going to be able to stay one second beyond that moment. Let's stop walking around fearful, intimidated and afraid. Man, turn the job over to Jesus and you don't have nothing to worry about. Turn your finances over to Jesus and then you don't have nothing to worry about. Turn your family over to Him. I can go anywhere in the world and the devil comes and gets on my case. He says, "Now that you landed in Detroit, I'm going to jump on your family like that." That don't bother me. He says, "Ain't you worried about that?" I say, "No, I don't have no family. I gave my family to the Lord." Now if the Lord can't take care of my family, then I'm going to find somebody who can. That's the way I feel about my job. If the Lord can't support me then I'll go back out there and get a degree and find someone who can. God brought us here. Let's let the joy and the peace and the power of God come in here. God's going to supply our needs because He promised to, and let this spirit of fear that has bound us up and keep us worried about it—get rid of that stuff. Man, God's working and God's got everything under control. Praise the Lord!

Ben vividly reflected the spirituality at CBN: It is childishly dependent on an all-powerful Father-God for an external, parental, and consoling influence on one's life. The people cheered Ben's message and shouted out praises to God. The hyped enthusiasm helped still the fears; we had nothing to worry about—"God's working and He's got everything under control."

Before being born again, Ben Kinchlow was a Black Muslim follower of Malcolm X. One day Ben was driving a sports car around a race track; he was traveling 80 miles per hour, smoking a cigarette, and listening to rock and roll. Suddenly, he asked if God was really out there, and he was instantly filled with the knowledge that he was. Ben was also filled with sorrow for his past sinfulness. He was saved. He quit his job and started to minister to street kids and soon became a spiritual superstar. No one found it odd that this second-most visible member of CBN had rather lengthy conversations with the Devil. Or that the Devil speaks in English slang. Of course not. Such schizoid behavior as hearing Satan speak is commonplace.

I heard a Charismatic pastor of a church that many CBNers attend claim that the Devil had told him that God had lifted his hand from his life and that he would never feel the Spirit of God on his life again. He then told his spellbound congregation the agony that it caused him until he realized the Devil was just lying in order to trick him into cursing God. The pastor then said, "I'd rather have God lay His hand on me and whip the daylights out of me than to lift His hand and never deal with me again." The Devil spoke to people, and they spoke back. No one found it odd that normal concern about the possibility of losing your job was turned into a trick of the Devil's and that people now felt guilty that their faith was so weak that they bought the lie of Satan and wallowed in worry.

But what about the twenty-four martyrs who lost their jobs? Did God just get tired of them being at CBN? If not, then who was responsible for the trauma they suffered from being fired from a job they believed God gave them? Was it the Devil or mismanagement and shoddy stewardship of the funds donated by the poor people who "are literally doing without things in order to make this ministry go forward"? Those were Devil-asked questions and therefore did not require an answer.

The communal, cultic ecstasy of the prayer meeting worked its magic. Those not fired buried their fears, forgot their friends, and got back to the business of selling salvation. In time, the building was completed, the university opened its doors to closed-minded education, the ratings went up, the donations increased, and the staff grew. Maybe the twenty-four were lucky—I know that I was the day I got fired. I also know that I would be terrified to have the president of the United States be a person who has daily conversations with both God and the Devil.

Back in 1978, I didn't ask many probing questions. Who had time? My job kept me so busy that I once was ordered to take a vacation because they feared I might work myself to death. The challenge of working one-on-one with Pat as the producer of "The 700 Club" left little time for debates with my doubts. I was too busy being zany!

Zany Does as Zany Sees

One executive at CBN attributed my surviving and even thriving as a producer to my zaniness. Pat was extremely tough on a producer. His demands often were unreasonable and, worse, unpredictable. He had no interest in hearing why a sudden idea he had just before he was about to go on the air couldn't work; he only wanted it to happen. He had no patience with technical limitations or human imperfections. I came to believe that his own shyness and preshow nerves contributed to his daily explosions and rantings. He literally feasted on producers for breakfast, and I became his corn flakes.

Pat really knew what he wanted, and he had a great sense of what would work, but the production team could rarely meet his high expectations. The producer felt the full force of his frustrations as a performer. No one wanted the job of being alone with Pat in his dressing room before the show in order to explain the day's program. He was never happy with the material presented to him, and at the last minute tried to change things around, leaving the producer with the headache and burden of trying to reconstruct the show to suit his mood that day. Producing "The 700 Club" was considered a thankless and almost impossible job—but I loved it!

The exhilaration of live televison and the excitement of the daily boxing bouts with Pat were a combo to which I quickly became addicted. Life on the edge was a thrill and a natural high. But more importantly, Pat and I had a creative chemistry between us that really bubbled. He challenged me. I excited him and never said no to any of his last-minute inspirations. We clicked together, and the shows sparkled; they had an energy people could feel. Pat seemed to go for my sense of the absurd. A couple of short stories illustrate that and at the same time reveal a little something about Pat's character.

Once during a conceptual formating meeting, a Christian psychiatrist was recommended as a guest. I argued against his appearance on the show because I felt that he would make Pat uncomfortable—a condition that guaranteed trouble for me. Pat found much in the field of psychology to be nonsensical and felt that all the guidance and help a person needed to straighten out his or her life was found in the Bible—not on an analyst's couch. However, everyone in the meeting felt very strongly about booking this noted author and teacher. I agreed to allow him to appear on the show; however, I requested that one of the team members be in Pat's dressing room with me on the day of the show in order to hear first-hand what I predicted would be Pat's strong negative reaction.

When the day arrived, we stood together in the dressing room waiting for Pat's grand entrance. Robertson rushed through the dressing room doorway, forced a smile of greeting, and headed for the make-up chair that sat in front of a huge mirror. As the make-up man applied Pat's make-up, I handed the host the format sheet for the show that was to begin in about five minutes. The format sheet detailed the sequence of events and the amount of time allotted to each item, including an interview, a teaching, praying, videotaped reports, salvation testimonies, and commercials pushing Pat's book or the university. The format sheet is the show's road map, and if Pat throws it out, we get lost. He read it over in stern silence. Then I handed him a set of fact sheets on the day's four studio guests. The fact sheet capsulized everything Pat needed to know about the person he would be interviewing, including short biographies, quotes from their books, and possible questions.

Pat immediately pulled out the fact sheet on the psychiatrist. Standing next to Pat, I glanced into the mirror to take a quick look at the formating team member who fought to have the psychiatrist as a guest. He stood quietly in the corner. Pat suddenly broke the calm and blurted out, "I'm sick of so-called Christian psychiatrists." Pat looked me squarely in the eyes and angrily stormed on. "What makes you think this glorified English teacher is qualified to offer psychological counseling to the saints?" In his usual blunt, insensitive manner, Pat had zeroed right into that portion of the fact sheet which noted that this scholarly man held three separate master's degrees, one of them in English, a subject he briefly taught. Pat chose to ignore the long list of professional accomplishments the doctor had achieved and picked out his love of English as a reason to invalidate his work in psychology. Without ever blinking or losing eye contact with the unreasonable host, I snapped back, "Because he has a great beard! Let's get going, we have less than two minutes to air—if you hadn't been so late we could have talked about it." We remained in a stare-down for what seemed like an hour, and then he finally exploded into a hearty laugh. He got up, and we rushed off to the set, where he was greeted by a thunderous round of applause from the studio audience.

I had been right and, as it turned out, so were the people who lobbied for the psychiatrist's inclusion on the show. He was articulate, interesting, and very informative. It was a terrific interview. After the show, as Pat and I were walking together toward his dressing room for our normal postshow rap session, Pat put his arm around me and said, "You were right; he did have a great beard. Hey, how do you think I'd look in a beard? I think I might look more authoritative and distinguished." I told him that nothing could help him, and we both laughed. I won the battle—this time.

The story was told during the next formating meeting, and the dressing-room observer said, "Gerry's genius is that he combats Pat's absurdity with even far greater absurdity. Instead of getting hooked up in a useless debate based on reason, he just shot back a stupid response and then confronted Pat with his tardiness. Pat had no recourse but to laugh—he knew he was wrong and was just blowing off steam, and Gerry would have no part of it."

God's Super Bowl

Moving into the new building was one of the biggest moments in CBN history. And one of the most sacred. To mark the occasion, a grand opening dedication program was planned to cap off a week of festivities and celebrations. I was given the job of writing and producing a live ninety-minute, spectacular show. Shot at night outside the building, with many dignitaries in the large audience, the show included Dr. Billy Graham, the Virginia Philharmonic Orchestra, a prestigious all-black choir, a metropolitan opera star, and a Christian rock star. It was hosted by Efrem Zimbalist, Jr. The show concluded with a massive fireworks display over the building as the choir and orchestra performed the Hallelujah Chorus. It was truly an extraordinary production that more than surpassed Pat's expectations.

Rarely does any television production use more than five or six cameras. Well, I requested ten cameras to cover the extravaganza that I planned. In all honesty, that was a bit excessive, but when I get excited about a show I have a tendency to get carried away. For example, for this grand-opening special I envisioned an electrifying shot of the massive crowds, the three stages, the orchestra, the building highlighted by powerful headlights, and the spectacular fireworks display crowning the entire picture with a rousing rendition of the famed Hallelujah Chorus underscoring it all. Pure show biz.

Naturally, I asked to have a camera placed in a helicopter to capture the scene I had in mind. No dice, said the powers that be in the operations division. It was considered too dangerous and too expensive. Besides, I was being a bit too theatrical. But I was determined to give the viewing audience goose bumps of pride in the building they had built with their contributions. So, instead of a helicopter, I had a camera platform built that would tower over the crowds as it reached skyward some nine stories. It worked: The closing of the show brought a flood of tears, and to this day it is still talked about as one of the all-time emotional highs of the ministry.

Despite the eventual success of the program, during the planning stages I had many obstacles to overcome in order to execute my concept for an emotionally charged night that would give glory to God. My methods were not understood, and many of my requests seemed extreme—and, in fact, were. At a network, there are people and policies to hold in check those creative tendencies that border on the outrageous, but at CBN I had almost free rein. The operations division at CBN, who were responsible for the equipment and the operators, couldn't understand why I demanded so many cameras, and they felt I had to be stopped. The division manager, whose opinion Pat held in very high regard, went to Pat to register his concern about my immoderate requests, which he felt were too costly and supercilious. He did a great job convincing Pat that my request for ten cameras was excessive and unreasonable. During his appeal to Pat, he happened to mention, as a basis for his argument, that the network coverage of the Super Bowl only uses ten cameras on the actual game, and that is the single biggest sporting event on television. So, surely a simple grand-opening special couldn't possibly need ten cameras. Pat agreed with the executive's logic and told him that he personally would inform me that I could have only nine cameras.

When Pat told me of the executive's problem with my exorbitant camera request, he saw my disappointment and annoyance. He said, "Brother, be reasonable. They only use ten cameras on the Super Bowl. Come on—you don't need that many."

I responded, "I happen to think this show is far more important than some stupid football game. I'm only trying to give the very best to God, who gave us the very best television center in the world. In fact, I wanted to ask for an eleventh camera that would be looking out the third-floor window of your office. It would make a great reverse angle shot of you on the stage addressing the crowd. Such a high, wide shot would be very dramatic, and just the thought of it gets me excited—but—if you say nine cameras is the limit, then I'll live with nine cameras."

Pat caught my fever and fervor, smiled, and declared, "You're right, Brother, this *is* more important than the worldly Super Bowl. I'll order operations to give you those eleven cameras. Don't worry—I don't care how much trouble it is for them or how much it costs." I made up the eleventh-camera request while I was talking, and it did turn out to be a great shot. What I was able to do was press Pat's pride button. Out of this building we were dedicating to God, the gospel was going to be proclaimed to the entire world, and Pat was not going to shortchange this special occasion one bit.

After such an exhilarating production, a producer frequently feels a big let-down. The all-consuming energy needed to pull a show of that magnitude together suddenly has no outlet, and, perhaps even worse, the producer is no longer the center of attraction. The day after the show, I stood alone in the massive lobby blankly staring out the window at the site of my triumph. The tension and fast-paced craziness were gone. Workers were busy dismantling the three stages and the towering camera platform. I felt sad and empty. The dream was over, and the remains were being removed. Unnoticed, Pat walked up behind me. He must have sensed my emptiness; maybe he felt the same way. He tenderly put his arm around me and softly said, "You done good." Pat was not big on tossing compliments, so while that comment sounded understated, it meant a lot to me. I turned to him. We both had the start of a tear in our eyes. We spontaneously exchanged a big hug of mutual affection. I had become, in that moment, his star; he had become my master.

My Tour Guide

Earlier I recounted an incident in Jerusalem in which Pat and I didn't see eye-to-eye regarding the use of wine during a Holy Thursday communion service that we broadcast live from the alleged Upper Room. After that broadcast, which went very smoothly despite the rough goings before air time, Pat and I headed back to our hotel in Tel Aviv. Alone in the back seat of the chauffeur-driven Mercedes limo, Pat, feeling good about the telecast from the historic location, said, "Well, what did you think about the show?"

The thrust of my heated response clearly indicated that I was angry at his preshow behavior, and I wasn't referring to the wine incident. I let him know how I felt about the caustic manner in which he issued orders to people that were in conflict with my instructions to the crew and, worse than that, dealt with production details that should not have been his concern. He was nervous and not aware of the total picture, so he had barked out commands that were counterproductive to my efforts at coordinating the event.

The building had been crowded with tourists, and the monks who ran the place seemed ill at ease with all the equipment being lugged in. They appeared unable to cope with annoyed tourists whose visit to the sacred shrine was being delayed by our short televised service. I thought that one monk was on the verge of kicking us out. In the midst of all this frantic activity, I had to take time out to undo the confusion caused by Pat's commands. Then, Pat sent me on a wild goose chase for a hair brush because he had suddenly become unnerved at the thought that his hair was sloppy.

After venting my displeasure in very forceful and explicit terms, I said something rather dumb, I guess out of my total frustration with the man: "Furthermore, we've been in Egypt and Israel for a week, and

I haven't gotten to see a thing but the back seat of this car. We just zoom past all sorts of historic and interesting places without even pausing to take a quick picture. When are you going to give me a chance to see some of the sights?" He looked at me in utter amazement. He stuttered out a mild apology for his actions before the show and seemingly ignored the silly sightseeing plea. He changed the subject to our upcoming trip to Lebanon, and still feeling my oats I told him that I didn't want to go unless I functioned as the producer and he as the interviewer. He agreed, and during the rest of the drive back to the hotel he explained in great detail the biblical significance of Jerusalem. I listened, but the lesson sailed over my head as the passing scenery captured most of my attention.

The next morning, as was my daily custom, I hit the streets early and secured for Pat a couple of international newspapers so that he could stay abreast of events in the world, as well as the stock market and the price of gold. I hated it when he gave me lessons in economics. With his papers in hand, I waited his arrival in the lobby. The schedule was light that day, consisting of a few meetings in Jerusalem with government officials. Pat emerged from the elevator of our luxury hotel looking calm and content with only a trace of tiredness in his eyes. We got into the limo. As we were driving he ordered the chauffeur to stop at a large church. He turned to me, and with a wry smile on his face, he said to me, "You wanted to sightsee, go ahead. This church marks the spot where Peter had the vision."

The expression on my face must have formed a question mark— what vision? After a slight, silent pause, he said, "You know, the story in the tenth chapter of the Acts of the Apostles where Peter went to the roof of a house to pray and saw Heaven thrown open, and a large sheet was being lowered to earth by angels holding the four corners, and on the sheet were all sorts of animals, birds, and insects."

I hadn't the foggiest idea what he was talking about, but said, "Oh yeah, right."

He sat back and unfolded his newspapers and said, "Well, get going—we don't have all day." I jumped out of the limo and walked around the church while he read the papers.

I returned to the car some ten minutes later, and as I climbed into the back seat and closed the door I said, "Thanks."

Without ever lifting his eyes from the newspaper, he said with a gentle touch of humor, "Don't ever say I didn't let you see the sights." I think he enjoyed the little gesture that was his way of saying he was sorry for being so rough on me at times.

However, the next day we were in Lebanon, and we clashed again. After driving in jeeps with armed military escorts past bombed-out buildings that litter the villages of this beautiful but war-torn country, I was setting up for an interview with Major Haddad, who was then the powerful head of the Southern Lebanese Christian militia, when Pat once more tried to play producer.

I wanted to shoot the interview in the "60 Minutes" style. I carefully set a table in the corner of a dining room in the run-down hotel where the interview was going to be conducted. For visual effect, I placed water bottles and other interesting items on the table that I'd covered with a brightly colored tablecloth that stood in contrast to the dingy room. I placed the table itself in a spot where the background behind the Major would capture the starkness of the room and where the light from a nearby window would highlight the interview area.

I informed the cameraman that during the interview we would keep the camera exclusively on the Major, and when Pat was asking questions we would pull back and shift from close-up to wide shots and then gently zoom in to a tight shot as the Major responded to the question. During the interview, we would use an audio-cassette machine to record Pat's questions, and after the interview we would reposition the camera and have Pat re-ask the same questions, only this time the camera would be either looking over the Major's shoulder at Pat or Pat would be on a close-up. When we return to Virginia, I explained, we would edit all the material together, and it would be visually stimulating and fast-paced due to the many camera cuts and camera movement.

The crew loved the idea but claimed Pat wouldn't go for all the razzmatazz and wouldn't put up with asking the questions twice. While we were talking, Pat burst into the room, looked around, grabbed two chairs, started walking toward a blank wall, and began to tell the crew that this was where he would do the interview. Great, I thought, two chairs up against a dull wall, both facing the camera for twenty minutes—boring, boring, boring.

Pat seemed to have no need to consult me, so I just started walking out of the room. As I got to the door, Pat shouted from across the room, "Brother, where are you going?"

Much to the crew's surprise, I said, "For a walk. You don't need me. I should have stayed in Jerusalem and gone sightseeing. You want to produce and conduct the interview—go ahead." I turned to leave, and he called me back. We huddled alone in a corner, and I told him my plan for the shoot. He listened, was intrigued, and said he would do it my way. I don't recall what the interview was actually about, but it was newsworthy enough that one of the networks used a portion of it on their nightly news. Pat looked as good as Morley Safer or Mike Wallace, and he loved it.

Caveat Emptor

What the stories about the psychiatrist, the grand-opening show, and the Middle East trip illustrate is that Pat Robertson is very human, not the God people believe he is. He can be tough, yet tender. He can get angry, yet be understanding. He can be serious, yet laugh. He can be demanding, yet caring. He can be cold, yet sensitive. He is in the public eye, yet very shy. He is both a ruthless politician and a driven businessman. Pat is a complex man whose dedication, determination, ambition, creativity, and endurance seem to be without limits. This dominating father-figure is held in awe by the staff. They ignore his faults and flaws because they believe that God has chosen him to lead them. I admired him greatly; in fact, I grew to love the man. I hung on his every word. I never tired of watching him or listening to him. The way that he handled difficult people and tough situations never ceased to fascinate me. He challenged me to reach far greater levels of creativity than I ever had before.

As the years passed after my ouster, I still respected Pat, even though I was beginning to see that his views and beliefs were not the gospel truth. Even during the writing of this book, I never lost my fondness for the man; however, I resent what he does in the name of God and regret that I helped him do it. Pat has made many mistakes over the years and has damaged a number of people. He is not simply a bright, intelligent, and articulate star of fundamentalist television and a possible candidate for the presidency; he is a threat to all free-thinking, freedom-loving Americans who respect the dignity of humanity and who desire to live in peace and harmony with each other and the world.

To his growing audience, Pat offers salvation for sale, and if you buy it you'll pay a high price for nothing. You'll mortgage your mind, your emotions, your family, your friends, and your very soul. He'll be the richer; you'll be the poorer. *Caveat emptor,* let the buyer beware.

For me, what began as a dream come true turned into a true-life nightmare—a nightmare from which it took me more than five years to recover. I still cannot believe that, after I escaped this religious loony bin, my ex-wife bought Pat's message and actually works for CBN. Seeing her name on the show's closing credits still sends shivers of disbelief up and down my spine. Sarah was converted from an open-minded, inquisitive explorer of life to a closed-minded, unquestioning deplorer of much of life. It can happen to anybody. Caveat emptor!

7

The Deadly Mixture

During my post-CBN search for understanding, I initially was not very concerned with the political power the fundamentalist could wield; nor was I aware that the emerging coalition they formed was potentially very dangerous. My main interest was theological, not political.

I was buried under a mound of so many questions about God that concern about the political ramifications of the religious political right in America was impossible to consider. In digging my way out from under all my questions concerning the existence and nature of God, and man's relationship to a supreme spirit, my main tool was books. I read histories of and commentaries on all faiths, as well as scholarly studies in the fields of philosophy, psychology, and sociology that specialized in the religious side of humanity. A secondary tool was talking to spiritual leaders and concerned laymen about their experiences: I attended university seminars and conferences held by gurus, visited monasteries, and talked privately with dozens of ministers from many different denominational backgrounds. I was like a giant magnet that attracted any written material or conversation that dealt with God. I became extremely sensitive to people's inner feelings about God, how they arrive at their understanding of the Almighty, and how that understanding affects their daily behavior. My awakened awareness of the many roles God plays in people's lives gradually opened my eyes to the politics of God.

Each day as I read the newspapers—usually two—scissors sat next to my cup of coffee. I clipped out any article that had to do with God or what people thought God wanted done. I placed these "religion" articles in a folder that I marked "Holy Terror." I had read *Holy Terror: The Fundamentalist War on America's Freedoms in Religion, Politics and Our Private Lives,* by Flo Conway and Jim Siegelman (Dell, 1984), and was terrified by the things that people did in the name of holiness. A few examples follow.

A man from Glen Haven, Colorado, was charged with child abuse in the death of his five-week-old daughter because he failed to provide her with medical attention when she was suffering from pneumonia; the father claimed he was a fundamentalist Christian who treated his child with prayer because he believed "God is my doctor." At his trial he stated, "The Lord is my defense."

In Ensburg, Pennsylvania, a fundamentalist Christian couple who denied medical treatment to their two-year-old son who was dying of a five-pound abdominal tumor, because they said that the Bible precludes medical treatment, were found guilty of involuntary manslaughter and endangering the welfare of a child. The couple believed that seeking medical help would have been a sign of a loss of faith in God, whom they believed healed through prayer alone.

In Elyria, Ohio, a thirty-two-year-old man was found guilty of involuntary manslaughter in the death of his three-year-old daughter. The child, along with her two sisters, aged two and five, was not sick; however, the child died of starvation because the father believed that "spiritual food" was more important than a balanced temporal diet. During his trial he refused to answer any questions, and, claiming that Jesus was his lawyer, he spent much of his three-day trial reading the Bible.

In Albion, Indiana, a faith-healer and his wife were charged with reckless homicide and child neglect in the death of their nine-month-old daughter and were sentenced to ten years in prison after they refused to renounce the practice of praying to cure illness. The judge asked the father if he would seek medical help for his other children if they became ill, and the father replied, "I still can't sin against the Lord." The judge asked the same question of the wife, and her response was, "I have to stand by my husband; Jesus bore it all on the cross."

In Onalaska, Wisconsin, a man who identified himself as "Elijah" and believed he was a biblical prophet whose mission was to crush the worship of idol Gods, stormed into a Catholic Church and opened fire with a shotgun, killing a priest and two male parishioners during a Mass for children. The "prophet" of God had spoken to the priest prior to the service and expressed his concern over the priest's allowing young girls to read from the Bible during the liturgy.

Not all of my clippings were that terrifying. Some were funny, like the report on Mr. T, the star of television's "The A Team," who said, during an interview on "The 700 Club" that he wore "a lot of jewelry because I serve a rich God." Some of the articles I clipped confirmed the suspicion that some television ministers are saving more money than souls. For example, in the fall of 1984 it was reported that Jim Bakker, who once worked for Pat Robertson, and who was the original host of "The 700 Club" and who now heads his own Christian television network and hosts the popular "PTL Club," bought a $449,000 vacation and retirement home in Palm Springs, a 1984 Mercedes-Benz costing $45,000, and a 1953 Rolls Royce costing $55,000. Several weeks before his big spending spree, Bakker told his loyal viewers that he had given virtually everything he had to his religious broadcasting efforts, that the ministry was facing its biggest financial crisis, and that he needed immediate help to pay the bills in order to continue to do the Lord's work and spread his word.

Before long, my "holy terror" folder gave way to a small box, and in the space of six months I had a large file box stuffed with clippings. As my collection grew thicker and thicker, I could not help but notice that the vast majority of the articles were extremely political. During the 1984 elections it seemed that God had become a political football. With a gentle push from their pastors, people were taking their religious beliefs to the ballot box as a way of oppressing other people— in the name of God.

The Republican Party even pleaded with the pastors to help get out the "God" vote. Prior to the 1984 presidential elections, Senator Paul Laxalt, who was the national general chairman of the Republican Party and President Reagan's reelection committee, sent a letter to eighty thousand fundamentalist Christian ministers asking them, in overtly religious language, to help register their congregants and endorse Reagan:

> Dear Christian Leader,
>
> As chairman of Reagan-Bush '84, the President's authorized campaign committee, I am writing you to ask you to play a significant role in what may very well be the most pivotal election of this century. President Reagan, as you know, has made an unwavering commitment to traditional values, which I know you share. In addition, he has, on several occasions, articulated his own spiritual convictions. As leaders under God's authority, we cannot afford to resign to idle neutrality in an election that will confirm or silence the President who has worked so diligently on your behalf.

The letter ended with a call for the preachers receiving the letter to "organize a voter-registration in your church and join us to help assure that those in your ministry will have a voice in the upcoming elections—a voice that will help secure the reelection of President Reagan and Vice President Bush."

I read the letter, and an alarm rang out a warning in my head. I was used to preachers talking for God but not for a nationally known politician. Who appointed the Republican Party and the fundamentalist ministers as "leaders under God's authority?" The letter even enraged conservative columnist William Safire, who wrote, "that political proselytizing is surely so unethical as to be un-American."

The letter was an arrogant attempt at equating party politics with Christianity by suggesting that God was a Republican and that the Christian thing to do was to vote for God's anointed favorite—Ronald Reagan. The letter was a vile attempt at twisting theology into a political platform, as is done in Iran by the Ayatollah Khomeini. Claiming that God has endorsed a candidate is repugnant politics and rotten religion.

The letter helped me realize that religion and politics is a volatile and deadly mixture whose significance I was no longer able to ignore or avoid and that the scope of this book must include the political aims and clout of the televangelists, who have turned your television set into a twentieth-century bully pulpit that preaches a selective morality packaged to look like Christianity and which pronounces, in the name of Jesus, a blessing on certain political candidates.

Political Soldiers for Christ

"The Lord spoke to me and said He is seeking militant believers." That sentence was spoken in October of 1985 on "The 700 Club" by a female singer during an interview with Pat Robertson. God had "told" the perky, pretty entertainer what type of follower he was seeking while she was alone in her hotel room in Nashville. Pat has long felt that most Christians were wimps who feared standing up for God in the political arena, so he quite naturally smiled in agreement with the singer's statement. I could not help but think that the singer's speaking for God and Pat's believing her divine revelation proved that the twin defects of arrogance and ignorance, which often go together, were well met in this interview.

The chat ended with host and guest joining hands in a prayer imploring God to bring a revival to America and to give Christians the insight and courage to join their voices together and to stand up and fight for what is right for America. What America needs, they believe, is the total eradication of immorality and evil. The militant seeker they think God seeks is armed with righteousness, and his or her voice is a voice of hatred that screams out a rhetoric of condemnation of what the fundamentalists consider evil. The militant believer that the "God" of the New Right is seeking is filled with a passion for a holy war that will seek out and destroy evil—and whomever he believes to be God's enemies. At CBN, the militant believer's unbending rigidity and intolerance made him or her unable to live harmoniously within a pluralistic society. The evil enemy is anyone who disagrees with their prophetic vision and understanding of God. Dissenters are devils who need to be exorcised from society. The soldiers of CBN hate the un-American, immoral, and ungodly enemy—but, of course, in a "Christian" way.

The Politics of Unforgiveness

The God Squad of television preaches a gospel of guilt that is based on the principle that we are all basically evil—sinners bound for eternal damnation in Hell. It's that simple and it needs to be, because the television preachers must tailor their trivial gospel so that it conforms to the video reality of providing easy answers for hard questions. The complexities of television production and the nature of the medium do not permit an in-depth analysis of any problem, and the television preachers understand the importance of the thirty-second solution.

CBN produced a series of slick, short film spots (produced by a born-again Jew) that were commercials for the notion that the secrets for finding happiness, health, and wealth can be found in the Bible.

Maybe President Reagan saw that commercial, because in proclaiming 1983 as the Year of the Bible he said, "Can we resolve to read, learn, and try to heed the greatest message ever written—God's words and the Holy Bible? Inside its pages lie all the answers to all the problems that man has ever known." That last presidential sentence contains the key to being a hit on Christian TV: the ability to both oversimplify and exaggerate. Pat Robertson could walk up to a blank blackboard, which he frequently does on his show, and within minutes chalk out a quick plan for salvation. Keep it simple, keep it moving, and keep it entertaining was the threefold key to success that I used while producing "The 700 Club."

The television preachers offer the bare fundamentals of faith and ignore the complex theological issues that will either bore the audience or provide them with opportunities for disagreement. Pat Robertson is successful because of his tremendous ability to communicate the impression of absolute certainty. Pat is a refuge of certainty in an uncertain world that is overwhelmed by the complexity of choices it faces. According to Pat, God has a message and a plan that leaves no room for ambiguity in spiritual, ethical, and moral matters. The gospel of Pat Robertson and the power of television is a marriage made in "heaven," and it effectively procreates a message that the world is going to Hell unless it turns from its evil ways. I believe that Pat's mission is to legislatively remove evil from our government and society by seeking political control. He wants to be God's policymaker in America.

What is this "evil" that the militant believers in God's army under the command of Pat Robertson are determined to defeat? I believe that, for the most part, this evil exists primarily in the minds of those who wish to eliminate it. Psychologists call this "projection." Fundamentalists like Pat are engaged in a never-ending effort to maintain the appearance of goodness and moral purity by denying their own badness and shortcomings and projecting their own "evil" onto others. Evil is seen everywhere but within themselves. When Jesus said, "Do not judge, and you will not be judged," he wasn't suggesting that we never judge others but, rather, as the next few verses make perfectly clear, that we should judge ourselves before we judge others.

"Why do you observe the splinter in your brother's eye and never notice the plank in your own? How dare you say to your brother, 'Let me take the splinter out of your eye,' when all the time there is a plank in your own? Hypocrite! Take the plank out of your own eye first, and then you will see clearly enough to take the splinter out of your brother's eye" (Matt. 7:3-5). Purification through self-criticism is required before making a moral judgment. The militant believers I met at CBN were trigger-happy when it came to judging others but feared facing their own failures—and for one good reason: self-criticism is painful because it eventually requires a person to change by eradicating imperfections that are found. Pointing a finger at the evil in others is infinitely easier; however, scapegoat spirituality does not work. I could not help but think that many of the militant believers at CBN were in reality the Pharisees of today—the sinless self-righteous who never suffer the pain of looking within and changing themselves.

A man who has been directing "The 700 Club" for years—a most critical and influential job—had no trouble capturing on videotape Pat's rhetoric about the "sins of the flesh," and then, after taping of the show, cruising the building making passes at the women or uttering sly and nasty sexist comments disguised as humor. Being able to admit our own "sinfulness"—without worrying about our brother's—helps us to resist our own inclinations toward wrongful or unhealthy behavior.

Henry David Thoreau wrote, "When we are shocked at vice we express a lingering sympathy with it. Dry rot, rust and mildew shock no man, for none is subject to them." Those words by the great American thinker and writer at first appeared a bit strange to me; however, after giving them some thought, I realized that the sentiment expressed applied perfectly to my life.

During my postconversion days and time at CBN, I devoted a great deal of energy to venting my anger at the perils of pornography—even to the point of condemning cable-television systems that allow "R-rated" movies into a home. No good Christian would allow a cable hook-up in their home or subscribe to HBO. I now see more clearly that pornography still held me in its grip, and I was not free from its lure. Plagued by guilt because I was still attracted to that kind of un-Christian material, I waged a "holy" war against the evil enemy I had not been able to defeat. That was much easier than trying to understand and change whatever it was inside of me that sparked my interest in smut. As Thoreau understood, I was shocked and angered at the vice mainly because I still had a lingering sympathy and communion with the trash.

I wonder if the same thing is not true of the television preachers who are obsessed with the desire to eliminate all forms of what they consider indecent behavior. Today, while I cannot condone the widespread production and distribution of pornographic material and consider it detrimental to minors, I no longer rile against it, because it no longer appeals to me. I no longer label those who make it or enjoy it as evil. At worst, they are people who don't know any better. I've changed, and I'm not going to try to change others—they must do that themselves. Searching for sins in others helps no one. Evil cannot be destroyed by hate; it can only be healed by love.

God does not use force, and neither can Christians. In fact, God does not even punish us; he can create, but he cannot destroy. By creating us in his image, God elected to give us free will—if he hadn't, then we would be mere puppets. This gift of free will prevents God from using force against us—a shotgun marriage isn't based on love—and limits him to simply standing by and letting us be. God voluntarily put his unlimited power in check—permanently. God can only help us and will never hurt us. If we don't want God's help, he'll let us go our own way—which, in a way, is our punishment. God never forces us to choose him, nor does he use force to prevent us from committing unspeakable atrocities against each other.

The Bible says that in his mercy and love, God not only forgives us our failures—when we see them and make a sincere effort to eradicate them—but he also forgets them. The sad thing is that we don't love ourselves enough to forget our own failures; we hang on to them and let the guilt ruin our lives. Nor do we love enough to forget the failures of others. God always forgets; Christians rarely do. The militant believers who control fundamentalist Christian television want God to unleash his power in an act of retaliation against the evil-doers around the world, and they'll even help.

The Politics of Sin

According to CBN theology, Hell is a place where sinners get to feel the flame of God's wrath. Roasting together for eternity will be murderers and unbelievers. Pat Robertson wants the government to act as God's law-enforcement agent on earth, and there is no reason to wait for Hell to start punishing sinners; we can throw them into the slammer now. The televangelists believe that through sin this country has turned its back on God, and eventually we all will be punished for it. Their mission is to save the nation by removing the sin, even through the force of "holy" legislation.

Who defines what sin is? *Sin* really is not a moral or legal term. It is a religious term that refers to man's offenses against God, and it has no meaning without an awareness of God and his holiness. Sins are expressions of man's separation from God through disobedience and are manifested in such acts as murder and such attitudes as lust and hate. However, it is extremely important to realize that religious wrong—sin—is not the same as legal wrong—crime.

Our civil laws deal with offenses against each other and society, not our failure to follow God. Simply stated, civil law is concerned with overt acts, not inner attitudes. As Jimmy Carter pointed out, lustful thoughts are offensive to God, but they are not punishable as a crime before mankind. Some sins are also crimes—like murder and stealing; but some sins are not crimes—like idolatry and slothfulness. Moral knowledge and responsibility are possible apart from religious belief and the sense of sin.

The radical religious right has no right to dictate their morality to the nation or punish what they think is sinful and evil. Holiness is much more than perfect observance of moral law. A truly religious person considers himself a sinner because he or she is most keenly aware of how far he or she is from perfect holiness. Holiness is not reached by the simple eradication of sin; it is reached through an awareness of personal imperfection and perserverance in striving for personal perfection and unity with God. Christ is not found by simply responding to a television preacher's invitation to accept him; Christ is only found in seeing how you help nail him to the cross. Holiness cannot be mandated or converted into the law of the land. Pat Robertson is wasting his time praying for a national revival. What is needed is personal enlightenment. Pat Robertson is wasting his time and his followers' money trying to scare the world out of Hell.

It is essential to realize that at CBN, alcoholism is considered not an illness but a sin. That is a critical distinction, because sympathy and understanding are not required for sin. The so-called sins of homosexuality, adultery, and abortion do not require understanding or tolerance; what is required is elimination by means of political and legislative force. No wonder the God of CBN is looking for militant believers; there is a political "holy war" to be fought and won. The irony is that the CBN staff really believes it is saving people from burning in Hell. Another irony is that there is no such place as Hell!

In his 1947 book, *The Pain of Christ and the Sorrow of God*, Gerald Vann wrote:

> Hell is essentially a state of being which we fashion for ourselves; a state of final separateness from God which is the result not of God's repudiation of man, but man's repudiation of God and a repudiation which is eternal because it has become, in itself, immovable. Pride can be hardened into hell, hatred can be hardened into hell, any of the seven root forms of wrongdoing can be hardened into hell.

Sin basically isolates us from God and each other—and that is Hell. Hell is not a place where God sends us; Hell is a reality we create.

God forgives and forgets; Christians can do no different. God is not seeking militant believers; that is not God-like and is purely a projection of Pat Robertson's infantile understanding of the Almighty. We were not created evil, nor can some unseen Devil force us to be evil. However, as Erich Fromm suggests, we can become evil slowly over time through a long series of personal choices. God gave us free will, and Pat Robertson and the religious right cannot take it away from us. What better way to conceal one's sinfulness from oneself, and others, than by hiding behind the disguise of piety. The pious, plastic Christians at CBN were certainly not free of sin, yet they never ceased in their efforts at removing the moral wrongs they saw in society. They truly believe our nation is dying from immorality and that the only hope for America is for Pat Robertson to be living in the White House. But that will be a black day.

The Politics of Absolutism

On September 16, 1981, Senator Barry Goldwater entered a speech into the record of the U.S. Senate that stands in stark contrast to the sentiments expressed by the Christian singer during her chat with Pat. In the months prior to the speech, the conservative senator from Arizona had proudly pushed for the nomination of Sandra Day O'Connor, also from Arizona, as the first woman Supreme Court justice. No sooner had President Reagan announced that she was his first choice for the post, then Jerry Falwell and the rest of the religious right severely criticized the president's selection because O'Connor had supported legalized abortions when she was a member of the Arizona legislature.

During a press conference, Goldwater was asked what he thought of Falwell's suggestion that all good Christians should be against O'Connor's nomination. "I think every good Christian ought to kick Falwell's ass," was the senator's blunt response. After O'Connor's nomination was confirmed, Goldwater spoke out in more eloquent style. The first section of the speech traced his own conservative career and pointed out how in politics, as in life, there can be no absolutes; every person and his or her opinions must be at least considered. The senator then said:

> However, on religious issues there can be little or no compromise. There is no position on which people are so immovable as their religious beliefs. There is no more powerful ally one can claim in a debate than Jesus Christ, or God, or Allah, or whatever one calls this supreme being. But like any powerful weapon, the use of God's name on one's behalf should be used sparingly. The religious factions that are growing throughout our land are not using their religious clout with wisdom. They are trying to force government leaders into following their position 100 percent. If you disagree with these religious groups on a particular moral issue, they complain, they threaten you with a loss of money or votes or both. I'm frankly sick and tired of the political preachers across this country telling me as a citizen that if I want to be a moral person, I must believe in "A," "B," "C," and "D." Just who do they think they are? And from where do they presume to claim the right to dictate their moral beliefs to me? And I am even more angry as a legislator who must endure the threats of every religious group who thinks it has some God-granted right to control my vote on every roll

call in the Senate. I am warning them today: I will fight them every step of the way if they try to dictate their moral convictions to all Americans in the name of "conservatism."

Jerry Falwell speaks for God. Jimmy Swaggart speaks for God. Peter Popoff speaks for God. Jimmy Bakker speaks for God. Pat Robertson speaks for God. And God seems to be saying to these ministers that Barry Goldwater is wrong about there being no absolutes in politics and that he does want followers to be militant, to force their moral convictions on the nation, and to fight for goodness and the American way under his almighty banner.

One commercial message that runs repeatedly on the CBN Cable Network proclaims that in a troubled, confused, and violent world there *are* absolutes: namely, God still governs the affairs of men. The slick spot asks, "Where are the voices of reason?" and then answers its own question with, "They are being trained at the CBN University School of Public Policy." Watch out, Barry; watch out, America.

And how do these "prophets" of God and their loyal followers respond to criticism—whether from government officials, the press, or individual citizens: with "holy" arrogance, of course. Two examples, first from a follower and then from a prophet. In response to a *Newsweek* article that was critical of Jimmy Swaggart, a minister from Wise, Virginia, wrote the following letter to the editors, which *Newsweek* published in the June 13, 1983, edition of the magazine:

> I am very disturbed by your vicious attack on evangelist Jimmy Swaggart and his organization. I'm a born-again, Bible-believing, Holy Ghost-filled, tongue-talking Pentecostal preacher and I want the world to know that I stand behind Brother Swaggart's kind of preaching. The Bible plainly warns, "Touch not mine anointed, and do my prophets no harm," so I'm afraid your writers have sealed their doom.

How can a piece of Scripture from another time, place, and culture be applied to Swaggart and a journalist? Who says that Swaggart is a prophet of God? If a reporter investigates a public figure like Swaggart and then, in print or on the air, raises some legitimate questions about Swaggart's beliefs, practices, and goals, how can that be construed as harming a "prophet" of God and, according to the Bible, dooming the reporter? The answer to all three questions is arrogance and ignorance.

Pat Robertson has publicly rebuffed critics of his theo-politics by suggesting, "You are trying to silence a prophet of God. The Bible says this, 'He [God] removed kings for their sake saying, touch not my anointed and do my prophets no harm . . . God himself will fight for me against you—and He will win,'" Turning dissent into ungodliness is un-American and has no place in a public debate in a free society.

The Politics of Intolerance

The United States is truly a remarkable country, and one of its most admirable traits is that it manages to maintain a sense of stability and unity while there exists within the hearts of its people deep differences that force fellow citizens further and further apart. Tolerance is a virtue any American can be proud to proclaim; however, we must be careful not to allow it to die from atrophy.

Hop on any crosstown bus in any city and you will encounter people with totally diverse views of life: a virtual busload of varying beliefs, goals, creeds, and gods. Sitting side-by-side, sharing the same ride are people who believe that our society is held together by the glue of Christian morals and ethics, and people who believe that supernatural beliefs stifle natural behavior and cause all kinds of hang-ups, guilt complexes, and deep neuroses. Some see Christianity as the only means to salvation, others see Christianity as highly repressive. Some believe in reincarnation, others await Armageddon. Some live a life of chastity, others find fidelity in marriage an impossibility. Some want their kids to pray in school; others want the schools to teach sex education. Some believe in a woman's right to have an abortion, others want to bomb abortion clinics. Some drink or do drugs, some are teetotalers.

Despite the diversity, they all can ride—for now—side-by-side on a bus. However, the gap between believers and nonbelievers is widening, and the struggle between secular and religious people is growing more intense. The conflict between the faithful and the skeptical is irreconcilable. The Christian appears irrational to the secular man; the secular man appears sinful to the Christian. Also caught between the two opposing factions are some people who suffer a good deal: those who are unable to accept or reject faith and are at war with themselves, doing as they please without finding inner peace. The religious person lives for God, attempts to keep a tight rein on his or her carnal nature, and tries to be cheerful and charitable—despite occasionally slipping into an impulsive, natural, instinctive, and less-than-godly act of humanness. The secular person is the center of his or her own universe and lives without external restraints and guilt. The secularist may or may not think God is dead; it really doesn't matter because life provides more than enough interest and relevancy—there are business deals to close, golf games to win, museums to visit, movies to attend, trips to foreign countries to plan, and all kinds of sex to enjoy. Both types of people know exactly where they stand, and the gulf between them is probably unbridgeable. Between these extreme types lie the mass of Americans: a mixed breed of the spiritual and secular. This uncommitted group is the target of the televangelists. Some of these people in the middle might go to church, but for some their attendance is irregular and ritualistic. For some their faith is lacking, and their lives are restless. Natural impulses and temptations do battle with a poorly trained spiritual conscience; however, being a little bit secular and a little bit spiritual leaves a person very weary and fatigued. The televangelists stand ready to offer them a fresh new start and the restful waters of salvation.

The time is nearing when the fence-sitters in the middle must make a choice. It is becoming increasingly more difficult to be a spiritually secular chameleon. The secular camp is pushing for the removal of all social restraints and is fighting for the rights of homosexuals, complete freedom of artistic and literary expression, and preservation of a woman's right to abortion on demand. The religious army is battling for school prayer, strict blue laws, tax breaks for religious schools, and a ban on abortion. The battle lines are clear: both the secularist and the fundamentalist know exactly where they stand; it is tougher for the casual Christian or the slightly secular to stay neutral. Most people seem to be leaning toward a secular outlook on life, which is why Pat Robertson is urgently trying to get the people in the middle to take a giant step into the security of salvation—move to the right and fight.

Pat Robertson and Jimmy Swaggart constantly preach that the secular humanist is a vile enemy—a serpent in sheepskin out to devour weak Christians. By gaining control of the middle, Robertson and his fellow prophets believe they can legislate their brand of Christianity into the law of the land. Voting is no longer just a constitutional right for the religious right—it is a new commandment from God. And God's prophets tell his people how to vote. "The 700 Club" is not just a religious television show—it is a political base of power.

While I was at CBN, I never took seriously the political clout the ministry carried and thought that Pat's political banter was harmless daydreaming. I grew tired of hearing what an idiot Jimmy Carter was, nor could I understand Pat's devotion to Ronald Reagan. I thought that the evangelical legislative goal was impossible to achieve; however, closer examination of American history clearly shows that Christian-sponsored legislation was once rampant and that history could repeat itself.

During the nineteenth and early twentieth centuries, the church's moral and religious authority was pushed to the brink of extinction by the mighty growth of science and the insights of Charles Darwin, and in a frantic attempt at keeping their private moral codes alive Christians managed to incorporate them into public law. The will of God was enforced by the state, as laws governing sexual conduct—requiring marriage licenses and prohibiting adultery, sodomy, fornication, lewd behavior, pornography, and prostitution—were passed. Blue laws grew out of the Christian observance of the Sabbath and handcuffed Jews and atheists alike. The virtue of sobriety became the law of Prohibition. The sin of gambling was restricted by state law, and some communities even banned dancing because the Baptists believed it was evil. Laws dealing with morals became impossible to enforce, and during the past thirty years most have been repealed or ignored. The church's effort to enlist the state as an agent of moral authority failed, because in a democracy the growing secular segment of society can repeal the laws and because, more basically, it is not the state's function to enforce the Bible.

The militant Christians of today want to legislate their divinely inspired morality into the law of the land. The modern secular world has become unbearable to the fundamentalist because of its blatant disregard of the Bible and the laws of God. It is impossible for fundamentalists to accept liberal abortion laws when they firmly believe abortion is murder; they cannot idly stand by as the state becomes a partner in a deplorable crime against the creative powers of God—even though they do support such "justifiable" homicide as the death penalty and war. The religious right believes that the secular humanist has created a demythologized religion that breeds moral decay. The militant Christian is not content to be a Christian within a secular nation; he wants this to be a Christian nation. While they have every right in a democracy to fight for laws against abortion, what has become clear to me is that militant Christians cannot compromise without feeling that they have lost the faith, and without faith they would face only death. Moreover, a free exchange of ideas with a person who believes he or she has a monopoly on the truth is impossible.

Pat Robertson wants to change our society by bringing it back to biblical principles. Not only has he expounded that goal on "The 700 Club," but he has also established a fully accredited university for that purpose. The school has more than five hundred students from nine countries and offers master's degrees in communications, law, and public policy. On the February 25, 1985, edition of "The 700 Club," the president of the university said that the purpose of the graduate school was to "change the way America thinks." On the same broadcast, he also claimed that "the Lord wants us to establish a law school." The graduates will take—according to Pat's plan—their degrees and their militant Christianity into the marketplace in order to change the system from within—all for Jesus, of course.

Jesus, however, never established himself as a political reformer or sought to overthrow the secular government or the Jewish leaders. His only concern was for establishing a spiritual kingdom that could live within the secular kingdom. Jesus didn't play power politics. Jesus neither planned any coups nor plotted any treasons. He never started any schools to train followers in the art of spiritual warfare. Jesus never rejected public law or public authority. What drove his detractors mad was that the kingdom of Jesus was immune to the politics of the Jewish Pharisees and the Roman procurators. Today, the militant followers of Jesus fail to follow their leader's lead as they press on for religious solutions to secular problems through political reform. Jesus would be ashamed.

The radical Christian right are entitled to their views (some of which I even support with varying degrees of conviction) on all the issues of the day, and they have every right to strive to influence public action. However, they violate the bounds of reasonable democratic discourse when they say that those who oppose them are not simply misguided or wrong, but sinful, intolerant of religion, and unpatriotic. Policy debates should not be transformed into theological disputes, and political dissent from fundamentalist belief should not be twisted into an un-Christian act.

The first victim of a political battle fought with self-righteous arrogance that flagrantly disregards reasonable discourse is tolerance. If tolerance falls into disuse, the citizens of this nation may well have a difficult time riding on a bus with one another. Our mutual tolerance must not be simply passive; we need to make a positive and cordial effort at understanding each other's beliefs and practices without necessarily accepting or sharing them.

I had to make an effort at tireless tolerance, which, at times, was almost impossible. I may totally disagree with the rantings of the Christian right; nonetheless, I must refrain from hating them or denying that their thoughts and ideas may contain some truth. Yet, at the same time I know full well that my honest and long attempt at understanding Pat Robertson and the effect of religion on my life, will, according to Pat, seal my own doom. He makes tolerance very difficult.

The Politics of Deception

At 11:15 A.M. on Thursday, October 17, 1985, armed guerrillas from Lebanon's Communist Party blew up a radio station located in Southern Lebanon, just two and a half miles from the Israeli border. The blast destroyed the station that was operated by High Adventure, an American-run missionary broadcast service owned by George Otis, a wealthy businessman from Van Nuys, California. George Otis is a friend of Pat Robertson and a frequent guest on "The 700 Club." CBN provided some financial assistance in building the radio station's transmitter. The station was not destroyed because it preached the gospel but because it supported an Israeli-backed militia known as the South Lebanon Army.

During our 1979 Middle East tour, Pat and I visited, under militia escort and protection, the radio station which already bore the scars of mortar shells that had hit the building but had not knocked them off the air. George Otis conducted a live interview with Pat, and while they were on the air my crew videotaped their conversation for use as a feature on "The 700 Club." An Israeli soldier told me that there was a good chance that the station would be lobbed with mortar shells as they spoke. Just the thought of that made me nervous. The militia had named the desolate road that led to the transmitter, which was located in a remote corner of a beautiful valley, "Pat Robertson Blvd." At the time, I thought it was a little peculiar having a road that went nowhere in a remote section of a small war-torn country named after a powerful television preacher from America. Pat didn't seem to mind; in fact he had me tape the soldiers digging a hole and planting the pole that carried the sign with his name on it. It did look silly standing in the middle of the field, and I speculated that it would be removed as soon as we split.

I never gave the visit to the station and the transmitter or George Otis' mission to broadcast the Christian Gospel and right-wing politics in a Shiite Muslim dot on a map halfway around the world any more thought until 1985 when George Otis popped up in a book entitled *Reagan Inside Out,* an unofficial campaign biography aimed at luring evangelicals into the Reagan camp. The book was written by a CBN board member who now heads CBN University and is the former journalist who made a feeble attempt at inaugurating Pat's dream of his own news operation. The book reports that Reagan and his wife clasped hands in a prayer circle with a small group of lay evangelists, one of whom was George Otis.

George Otis began trembling, a sign that God was about to give a message he wanted spoken to those gathered—as he prayed aloud. Filled with "the Spirit of the Lord," Otis prophesied of Reagan: "If you walk uprightly before me, you will reside at 1600 Pennsylvania Avenue." Suddenly, I knew why Pat was such a devoted fan of Ronald Reagan and worked so hard to insure that his friend George's prediction come true. The businessman, the journalist, and the preacher had all deceived themselves by Pentecostal emotionalism to think that God had a hand and an interest in American politics.

God is not a member of any political party, nor are Ronald Reagan and George Bush "God's instruments for rebuilding America," as Jerry Falwell claimed during his deliverance of the benediction at the 1984 Republican convention. Many people think Ronald Reagan's public piety lacks conviction because he rarely even attends church—not that church attendance is a sign of spirituality. Why should the president go to church when he can stay at home and tune in Pat Robertson or Jerry Falwell and receive pastoral counsel and political advice in a single shot—or pray, for all I know? Pat and Jerry are happy to provide Reagan's militarism and social Darwinism with a theological base. Mixing politics and religion is the ordained mission of the televangelists, and as a group they are committed to bringing America back to the Bible—but even that smacks of deception.

I was never an American-history buff, so it was rather easy for Pat Robertson to convince me that our nation was founded on biblical principles. I took his word for it—after all, he seemed so sure of the facts that there was little reason for me to doublecheck them. Besides, even the dollar bill carries the message, "In God We Trust." I shouldn't have been so trusting. Now that I have checked the facts for myself, I've learned that fundamentalism has managed to distort American history—just as it distorts the Bible—by quoting selectively from the historical record and mixing in its own fantasies. In doing so, it had created the false myth that America was founded on biblical principles and that separation of church and state somehow did not exist as a founding principle from the very beginning.

There is no denying that the New World was settled, in part, by devout Christians; however, they did not share the same beliefs or even a common vision of faith. Pilgrims and Puritans settled in Massachusetts. Anglicans settled in Virginia. Quakers settled in Pennsylvania. Dutch Reformers settled in New York. Each group tried to convert their specific beliefs into the law that governed their colonies. It quickly became clear that for the nation to stand united, it could not be divided by religious differences and that a new method of government needed to be developed in order to avoid religious persecution. The ingenious plan that was conceived by the founding fathers actually kept God out of the governmental process. Despite the religiosity of many early settlers, the majority of the colonists did not belong to any church.

Jerry Falwell claims, "The foundation for our government, our laws, our civilization, the structures of our homes, our states and our churches have come from the word of God." If that is true, then it seems odd that *neither the Bible nor God are mentioned in the Constitution.* It is not my intent to digress into a discourse on American history. All that is needed to refute the fundamentalist fabricated version of American history and at the same time illustrate their facile ability at the art of deception is to list some statements that were written by some of the people who played a part in the formation of our nation. Their words speak for themselves.

> The United States is in no sense founded upon the Christian Doctrine.— George Washington

> It does me no injury for my neighbor to say there are twenty gods or no God. It neither picks my pocket nor breaks my leg.—Thomas Jefferson

> I do not believe in the creed professed by the Jewish Church, by the Roman Church, by the Greek Church, by the Turkish Church, by the Protestant Church, nor by any Church that I know of. My own mind is my own Church.—Thomas Paine

> God requireth not a uniformity of religion.—Roger Williams

> The day will come when the mystical generation of Jesus, by the Supreme Being as his Father, in the womb of a virgin will be classified with the fable of the generation of Minerva in the brain of Jupiter. But we may hope that the dawn of reason and freedom of thought in these United States will do away with this artificial scaffolding, and restore to us the primitive and genuine doctrines of this most venerated Reformer of human errors.—Thomas Jefferson

The evangelicals of his day tried to sink the presidential aspirations of Jefferson. They labeled him an infidel and claimed his election would ruin the country. Jefferson was a member of the Episcopal church, but his views horrified the evangelicals. Jefferson preferred reason to divine revelation and doubted the divinity of Jesus, who he thought was simply an extraordinarily good man. Jefferson led the fight for the disestablishment of Anglicanism as the state religion of Virginia, and that worried the Evangelical Congregationalists in New England because they considered it an assault against religion, since

their religion was still established by law in Connecticut and Massa-
chusettes. Jefferson did not appear to acknowledge and heed the will
of God, and the evangelicals resented the way he seemed to belittle
religion. With Jefferson as president, the evangelicals feared the
churches would become temples of reason. The fear of reason still
grips the evangelicals of today.

The following sentiment was expressed in a letter to the editor of
the *Albany Times-Union* and published in the paper on November 19,
1985: "When men compromise the Word of God and through the
process of rationalization make it say what they want it to say, they are
committing the same age-old sin of rebellion that Adam and Eve committed by listening to Satan, the father of lies."

How can using the mind that God gave you in order to rationally
and reasonably attempt to read and understand ancient writings of
fellow humans be a sin of rebellion? Evangelicals and fundamentalists
are proud of their respect for the Bible; however, by using the Bible for
purposes for which it was not written, they treat the book with appall-
ing disrespect and expose religion to contempt. This might sound
shocking, but according to Matthew 5:31–32, 33–34, and 38–39, Jesus
himself did not believe all the Bible. Look it up. Jesus specifically
disagrees with three passages in the Old Testament, namely, Deuteronomy 24:1-4, Leviticus 19:12, and Exodus 1:24. And, now look at
Matthew 5:17–19 (and 43–48) and read how Jesus stated that the Jewish
law is still valid, and then read Paul's Letter to the Galatians 3:24–26,
and you will find that Paul disagrees with Jesus and claims that the old
laws are no longer needed. Even Genesis presents two creation accounts.

Jefferson was not Christian enough to be president according to
the evangelicals, so they waged a campaign of fear and hate to keep
him out of the White House. They might have succeeded if they had
had television as a weapon. I'm sure that the evangelicals who opposed
Jefferson were sincere, just as the people at CBN are very sincere, and
I don't fault them for their desire to promote godliness in the public
square. Yet, the great religious outcry against Jefferson turned out to
be unjustified and ironic. Jefferson's public policy comported well
with Christian values and his Christian respect for life was exemplified
in his great reluctance to commit the nation to war. Jefferson turned
out to be among the most moral, honest, and upright of presidents.

Let us, then, fellow citizens, unite with one heart and one mind. Let us
restore to social intercourse that harmony and affection without which

liberty and even life itself are but dreary things. And let us reflect that having banished from our land that religious intolerance under which mankind so long bled, we have yet gained little if we countenance a political intolerance as despotic, as wicked, and capable of a bitter and bloody persecutions.—Thomas Jefferson

During almost fifteen centuries the legal establishment known as Christianity has been on trial, and what have been the fruits, more or less, in all places? These are the fruits: pride, indolence, ignorance and arrogance in the clergy. Ignorance, arrogance and servility in the laity, and in both clergy and laity, superstition, bigotry and persecution.—James Madison

I do not find in orthodox Christianity one redeeming feature.—Thomas Jefferson

The divinity of Jesus is made a convenient cover for absurdity. Nowhere in the Gospels do we find a precept for Creeds, Confessions, Oaths, Doctrines and whole carloads of other foolish trumpery that we find in Christianity.—John Adams

The Bible is not my Book and Christianity is not my religion. I could never give assent to the long complicated statements of Christian dogma.—Abraham Lincoln

As to Jesus of Nazareth . . . I think the system of Morals and his Religion, as he left them to us, the best the World ever saw or is likely to see; but I apprehend it has received various corrupting Changes, and I have, with most of the present Dissenters in England, some doubts as to his divinity.—Benjamin Franklin

Jerry Falwell ignores the sentiment from the pen of Benjamin Franklin and instead loves to use the following quotation from the author and publisher of *Poor Richard's Almanack*, "God surely was no idle spectator when this great nation was born in his name and with his grace." However, during the Constitutional Convention in Philadelphia, an aging Franklin moved for daily prayers, "imploring the assistance of Heaven, and its blessing on our deliberations," and the motion failed! Why would Falwell quote a man, who was, according to Fallwell's understanding, doomed to hell for his denial of the divinity of Jesus? Jefferson was wrong: religious intolerance has not been banished from our land, and today's zealots even try to rewrite our past in order to support their vision of the future.

For the fundamentalist of today, the enemy is the same as it was in Jefferson's time, only the names and faces have changed. Dissent is still linked with the Devil. Charles Stanley, former president of the Southern Baptist Convention and star of his own televised church service, claimed in 1984 that the Equal Rights Amendment was "a satanic attack upon the American family." Jerry Falwell has repeatedly proclaimed that his opponents are the servants of Satan.

During the 1984 presidential elections Reverend Falwell used the same tactics of fear against Walter Mondale that his fellow Christians used unsuccessfully against Jefferson, when he said, "We're fighting against humanism, we're fighting against liberalism . . . we are fighting against all the systems of Satan that are destroying our nation today . . . our battle is with Satan himself." On June 24, 1984, Falwell announced a list of 208 members of Congress who had "voted against freedom for our children." Jerry's list, which he wanted displayed "on the marquees of the world" turned out to be a roster of representatives who voted against the administration's policies toward Central America. Pat Robertson compares the freedom fighting Contras in Nicaragua with the defenders of the Alamo.

In 1978, a group called Christian Voice began issuing *Congressional Report Cards,* with the scores indicating how a member of Congress voted on fourteen key moral issues. A perfect score of 100 reflected the highest level of morality. Morality, of course, for this Christian group was tied to the Bible and ultra-right-wing beliefs. Oddly enough, a congressman who was convicted of accepting an ABSCAM bribe— Richard Kelly—and a congressman who confessed to having homosexual tendencies—Robert Bauman—both scored a perfect 100. In contrast, two ordained clergymen badly flunked the morality test. Robert Drinan, a Catholic priest, was given a zero; and Robert Edgar, a Presbyterian minister, received a score of 8. According to Christian Voice, it is antifamily for a member of Congress to support shelters for battered wives and immoral to vote for funds for the National Science Foundation. Of course, they believe that good Christians must support cuts in federal aid to education and increases in defense spending. In its *Presidential Biblical Scoreboard,* published in 1984, Christian Voice labeled Mondale a "Humanist/Presbyterian," rather than a sincere Christian.

Christians did play a vital role in the formation of this country, but they were not all of one mind, nor did they function in perfect harmony in establishing the will of God in America. President John Adams mocked the Christian reverence for Scripture and thought the idea of the incarnation was nonsense. Pat Robertson's annual commemoration of the pious pilgrims planting of the cross on the shores of Virginia Beach paints only part of the picture of the historic event. The fundamentalist of today wants to sanitize American history to suit his beliefs.

The very freedom fundamentalists enjoy that allows them to openly express their views on God comes not from God, as they suggest, but from less-then-religious men who had a natural belief in being fair and just. Preachers, said Jefferson, "dread the advance of science as witches do the approach of daylight and scowl on the fatal harbinger announcing the subversions of the duperies on which they live." The fundamentalist of today, just like those in Jefferson's day, have no choice but to hate and scowl at science. For example, the scientific work of Darwin made it impossible to ignore biological evolution even though it damages the historic credibility of a small part of the Bible. That terrifies the fundamentalist. After all, no Adam and Eve means no fall, and no fall means no sin, and without sin the fundamentalist would be out of business.

Today's video preachers cannot bring us back to a place we've never been. Their claim that America was founded on biblical principles is false and pure deception. They want us to believe that this is—or should be—entirely a Christian nation. According to a report in the August 8, 1985, edition o the *New York Times,* in early 1985 an Education Department official located in Denver gave a speech denouncing the "godlessness now controlling every aspect of our society." The speech asked how these developments could happen "in America, this land of freedom, this Christian nation?" Another departmental official had the speech widely distributed. After a California man sent a postcard to the Education Department's Denver office protesting the distribution of a speech asserting that the United States was a Christian nation, he received an angry response from an official in another government agency in Washington. The letter, written by a former fundraiser for Reagan, claimed that the California man's knowledge of "this country's history and structure of government was minimal at best." In a postscript, the offical told the protester: "When you die, you will give your account to Jesus Christ, your creator, who happens to be Christian. I hope you are prepared." How did a simple postcard of protest that asserted that under the Constitution, the United States had never been a Christian nation, reach Washington? The battlers of Satan seem to have an effective network of watchdogs. It is interesting to note that the official's mother was an assistant director of the White House office of public liaison with evangelical and fundamentalist Christians and conservative women.

While working at CBN, I was convinced that this had been a Christian nation from the very beginning and still was then in the seventies. The viewers of Pat Robertson and Jerry Falwell should not be duped by the convincing nature of their communication skills, and they should test what they hear being preached as the whole truth.

The Politics of Virtue

The shepherds of the electronic church may have abandoned thin rods and staffs for a satellite; however, they broadcast an image of themselves as being as virtuous as the shepherd who left his flock of ninety-nine sheep in order to go look for the one sheep that was lost. Even if you don't completely believe the message that is beamed into space and back down to your living room, you are, nonetheless, left with the impression that the messenger is a man of virtue.

Exactly how virtuous are these modern-day shepherds of souls? Can any one person, or any one faith, or any one political party be the epitome of virtue and the possessor of true moral excellance? Virtue is so rare and so ephemeral that it is difficult to know exactly what it is—let alone recognize it within a person, a system of belief, or a political party. Virtue is a conformity to a moral standard of right and is manifested in a positive and courageous power to act in a meritorious manner. Virtue seeks the high ground of human potential and strives for purity of intention while steadfastly refusing to travel the way of expediency and follow the lower instincts of human nature.

Tune in to any of the televangelists and you will quickly learn who they consider virtuous: themselves. They don't even consider each other virtuous; I frequently heard Pat Robertson knock Jerry Falwell. The televangelists proudly display their virtue like a trophy on a mantle; nor do they hide their sense of moral superiority on the top shelf of a closet. No matter what political position Pat Robertson takes on an issue, he is assured that he is ultimately correct both in his understanding of the issue and in his solutions to humanity's problem because he is, above all else, a good man; and, more often than not, those who oppose his views are basically viewed as not good people, thereby making their insights automatically invalid despite the logic of their thought or the purity of their intentions.

The gospel according to television claims that it is impossible for a bad—that is sinful—person to have a good idea; goodness cannot flow out of badness. Deviation from the God Squad's understanding of truth is an indication that a person cannot be good, and therefore his ideas are bad. The funny thing is, though, that during most of my last nine months at CBN, I was engaged in "sinful" activity and certainly veered from their understanding of truth, yet I still had many good ideas that helped push Pat's ratings up.

Pat Robertson's rhetoric is ablaze with his own goodness, which is either self-proclaimed or implied by a parade of guests who salute his goodness, fine character, and the courage of his moral convictions. Pat has virtue on his side and contempt for opinions that are not as virtuous as his.

Virtue is not the sole property of the new Christian right; both the left and the right, as well as the religious and the secular, lay claim to the prize of virtue. Liberal Democrats act as though they are the only people with hearts, and conservative Republicans believe they are the only people who know how to think clearly. They both play the politics of polemics that pit people against right and wrong. Liberals are against nuclear war as if conservatives were for war. Conservatives are "pro-life" as if liberals were "anti-life." In this troubled and complex world everyone wants to be on the side of goodness.

Pat Robertson and the rest of the video preachers want to divide everything into camps of good and bad. The viewers then need only endorse the opinions of the "good" preacher in order to feel good themselves. They feel good to be against the bad, that is abortion or any other action deemed sinful. Moreover, the viewer doesn't have to be a person of authentic virtue to at least feel virtuous, because he or she can acquire a virtuous feeling by simply associating with the "virtuous" preacher. But virtue is not a train you board—even if the engineer is a television preacher; virtue can only be acquired through experience and practice over a long period of time. Virtue cannot be bought or taught—it springs from deep within when watered by the fire of life. Pat Robertson tries to teach virtue to a viewer he only values for his or her vote—a vote for Robertson's version of the truth.

The virtuous from both the left and the right know who is good and who is bad, who is naughty and who is nice; but despite their similarity in claiming virtue and their tactic of attacking the virtueless, the preachers who represent the new Christian right have—besides God as an ally—a major weapon in their arsenal that the other side does not have: television. Viewers should heed the advice of George Orwell: "Saints should always be judged guilty until they are proven innocent." The same holds true for the virtuous: The preachers and politicians who claim or imply they possess virtue may not. Moral superiority is easy to claim but difficult to obtain. The danger of the politics of virtue is that we each fail to see the goodness in the other side and project onto others the deficiencies that are our own. It's politics that speaks without thinking, listens without hearing, and sees evil where none exists. The virtuous man who has God on his side is capable of untold atrocities. The horrific barbarities committed under Hitler were perpetrated by a populace overwhelmingly "Christian." Their hatred was clothed in righteousness and patriotism. Reason and religion, charity and "holiness" were not on speaking terms then, and they are not on speaking terms today in many churches and on most Christian television shows. "Don't reason, don't let doubt in," was a plea I heard over and over again at CBN. We were all members of the church of the open Bible and closed mind.

Let us Reason Together

As I reached the completion of this book, I was awash in a sense of relief. The struggle, the anguish, and the pain would end. I no longer would have to get up each day and focus my attention and efforts on dissecting and explaining my life as a fundamentalist. I could return to the land of the living—cured. I could look ahead and not back. Yet, I know that I cannot stop searching for understanding and truth.

The writing of this book helped me to see that I was in a state of confusion and depression prior to my rebirth in Christianity, because I was unable to make a reasoned choice regarding the direction of my own life. I could not let go of old beliefs about marriage even though they were unreasonable, especially when applied to my situation. As a child, I was fed dogma and not trained to use my own mind. I learned readin', writin', 'rithmatic, and religion—but not reasoning. Later in life, when I walked into my first prayer meeting, I checked what little ability I had in the art of reasoning at the front door and tried to make a religion out of a nice feeling. We cannot make a religious shrine out of our better moments, which is exactly what happens after one receives the not very reasonable "gift of the Holy Spirit."

Steven Allen wrote an essay that was included in a book entitled *The Courage of Conviction*, edited by Philip L. Berman, in which well-known people discuss their beliefs and how they put them into action:

As I argued in *Beloved Son*, a book about my son Brian and the subject of religious communes and cults, one result of proper early instruction in the methods of rational thought will be to make sudden mindless conversions—to anything—less likely. Brian now realizes this and has, after eleven years, left the sect he was associated with. The problem is that once the untrained mind has made a formal commitment to a religious philosophy—and it does not matter whether that philosophy is

generally reasonable and high-minded or utterly bizarre and irrational—
the powers of reason are surprisingly ineffective in changing the believer's mind.

I'll say "Amen" to that. I had a difficult time changing my mind
about all I had accepted as truth after my sudden conversion and
during my time at CBN. I had to learn not to fear reason and to trust
my mind. I wanted to be accepted by my community in the church
basement and by my coworkers at CBN, and I wanted it so badly that
I willingly suspended my own disbelief and embraced their unreasonable beliefs. It was called faith, but it was a peculiar brand of faith. I
know that this book will anger a lot of people and that I will be the
object of much hate, but it does not bother me. I don't need people's
love if the price is my mind. They do not—and cannot—have all the
answers. Steve Allen expresses exactly how I feel after my long journey
of exploration into the realm of religion when he wrote in the same
essay:

> It is possible to do what millions have done, with varying degrees of
> satisfaction: accept one prepackaged philosophy or another and try to
> live by its precepts. A few individuals, over the centuries, have led
> edifying and productive lives by such means. But all the saints who
> ever lived could convene in one meeting hall of modest dimensions.
> And no philosophy, sadly, has all the answers. No matter how assured
> we may be about certain aspects of our belief, there are always painful
> inconsistencies, exceptions, and contradictions. This is true in religion as
> it is in politics, and is self-evident to all except fanatics and the naive. As
> for the fanatics, whose number is legion in our own time, we might be
> advised to leave them to heaven. They will not, unfortunately, do us the
> same courtesy. They attack us and each other, and whatever their pro-
> testations to peaceful intent, the bloody record of history makes clear
> that they are easily disposed to resort to the sword. My own belief in
> God, then, is just that—a matter of belief, not of knowledge. My respect
> for Jesus Christ arises from the fact that He seems to have been the
> most virtuous inhabitant of Planet Earth. But even well-educated Chris-
> tians are frustrated in their thirst for certainty about the beloved figure
> of Jesus because of the undeniable ambiguity of the scriptural record.
> Such ambiguity is not apparent to children or fanatics, but every
> recognized Bible scholar is perfectly aware of it. Some Christians, alas,
> resort to formal lying to obscure such reality.

At the young age of thirteen, hidden behind the walls of a seminary, I became a doubter. My career as a doubter had a short life, and it
quickly ended in suppression. Now over a quarter of a century later, I
am once again a doubter; only this time I wear my doubt like a coat of

armor. As a doubter, I reject the external expressions of all religious faiths, yet I am cognizant of the importance of religion in internal or personal human experience. The noted scholar and secular humanist Sidney Hook wrote, in an essay also contained in the book *The Courage of Conviction:*

> It may be hard to separate the existence of organized religion from personal religious experience, but it is possible to distinguish them. It is only the first with which I have been polemically involved. In a statement made long ago, which still expresses my considered view, I wrote:
> "So long as religion is freed from authoritarian institutional forms, and conceived in personal terms, so long as overbeliefs are a source of innocent joy, a way of overcoming cosmic loneliness, a discipline of living with pain or evil, otherwise unendurable or irremediable, so long as what functions as a vital illusion, or poetic myth is not represented as a public truth to whose existence the once born are blind, so long as religion does not paralyze the desire and the will to struggle against unnecessary cruelties of experience, it seems to me to fall in an area of choice, in which rational criticism may be suspended. In this sense, a man's personal religion justifies itself to him in a way his love does. Why should he want to make a public cult out of it? And why should we demand that he prove that the object of his love is, as he believes, the most beautiful creature in the world? Nonetheless, it still remains true that as a set of cognitive beliefs about the existence of God in any recognizable sense continuous with the great systems of the past, religious doctrines constitute a speculative hypothesis of an extremely low order of probability."

All I can add to Professor Hook's statement is, as Pat Robertson says on "The 700 Club," "Amen and amen."

Epilogue

This book has depicted one man's spiritual journey played against the backdrop of Christian fundamentalism and television; mostly it was about religion and persuasion. My belief is this: The two do not belong together because the basis of all religion is love, and the nature of love does not include persuasion. Love is for giving and forgiving. My intention in writing this book was not to condemn the religious outlook of the fundamentalist Christianity that permeates religious television. My goal was to open, as fairly as possible, the doors of understanding regarding the way fundamentalists perceive God.

Dostoevski wrote, "Nothing is easier than to denounce the evildoer; nothing is more difficult than to understand him." If we substitute the words *different religions* for *evildoer* in that quotation, the new sentence would be equally true. We dislike and frequently fear what we do not understand. When the subject is as complex as the deeply rooted religious views of humanity, then a true understanding might be impossible. Ultimately we may never understand, but we must persist in our efforts to try.

Our future survival rests on our ability to listen to and to love one another, to know and respect one another. Dialogue and understanding must become a part of our existence. It is paradoxical that religion, which should unite us, is in practice frequently divisive and the cause of many unholy wars between individuals and nations. For interreligious dialogue to be effective, the participants must be willing to learn and ready to change, which is impossible if you are convinced that you hold all the truth and that the other person lurks in the darkness of ignorance or error—or evil. We must see some truth and goodness in each other. Dialogue is impossible for Christians who regard everything outside the Bible as evil and all nonbelievers as doomed.

316

A "holier than thou" attitude is a dead-end street that does not allow them to see any holiness in Hinduism or Buddhism.

Even more harmful is claiming to be specially chosen by God because that belief leads to triumphalism and chokes any exchange of ideas. Dialogue is a process of receiving and accepting, and there is no room in true dialogue for a feeling of superiority. How can a Buddhist respond to the Christian doctrine that there is no salvation outside of Christ? What of the vast majority of humankind that live outside of the Christian church—and always have? The search for God is a basic feature of the human spirit, and one can never quite penetrate the mystery of religions. All religions need, and have, men and women of God who live completely for God and show others a way to God. God, in His love, shares Himself with everyone out of the richness of His mercy and in a rich variety of cultural ways. Our differences should not be turned into walls that divide us; without the walls our differences have built, we can begin to share and perhaps stand together without being united. Our intellects tend to suffocate dialogue; only the heart can pump life into dialogue.

There are more than three billion people on the planet (fewer than a billion are Christians), and while we share lots of similarities, no two of us are identical. No two of us sees or understands things in exactly the same way. The human mind is extraordinarily complex; and, even with the insights gained from this generation's technological advances and scientific reseach, we are still only at the threshold of understanding how the mind works. There are indications that we only use about 10 percent of our brain power. No matter how much gray matter we use or don't use, the mind functions differently for each of us because the same idea or experience is never understood in exactly the same way by any two persons.

This is especially true of spiritual concepts. We each have our individual filtering processes that consist of all we've seen, heard, and done, and they influence our retention or rejection of any concept or experience. It never ceases to amaze me that, after going to a movie with a group of friends, we can pile into the car and embark on a discussion of the film as we head home and be left with the impression that we each saw a different film. Our individual uniqueness indicates that God isn't into mass production.

The mystery of creation is how God can put himself in each one of us without repeating himself. A sign of His infiniteness is that every creature is an original—we're not cookie-cutter copies. The oversimplified religious message broadcast by the born-againers does not respect the *individuality* of each human being. We cannot all hear and respond to their understanding of salvation in exactly the same way or even in the way they want us to respond. The fundamentalist intention is to unite us in Christ, but their tactics tend to separate us by dividing us into camps of good and evil. Our acceptability then is based on our response to their view of the truth, yet each of us has a deeply felt need to be accepted as he or she is and not by the conformity of his or her belief. Acceptance is liberating. Separation is devastating.

When I am loved in that deep sense of complete acceptance, then I am free to become my authentic self—warts and all. The gospel according to television does not liberate you as a viewer and allow you to be yourself; it only wants you to become one of them—by stripping you of your fundamental need for a sense of personal worth. Fear of Hell is their most effective sales pitch. They paint a picture of an eternal chamber of horrors that is fueled by creating unbearable guilt and then offer an attractive alternative that stems from the sacrifice of the cross. But do they offer the only holy alternative or a somewhat less-than-holy choice? A holy man or woman gives people the freedom to be themselves. He or she does not pressure. Pressure implies a lack of respect—and even a lack of love. This is not God's way; it's man's way. Pat Robertson is a man, not God's anointed prophet. A respect for God that is based on fear is not only despicable but also useless.

While each person searches for the meaning of life, it is vital to realize that man is a mystery in the midst of a mystery. That dual mystery of man and God does not have a simple solution, and the search for clues will not end until the author of the masterpiece reveals himself in the end to all the readers. Until the end of the book, which is a work in progress, we must be tolerant of doubt and permit each other to follow the clues they discover and believe to be important. Columbo and Kojak caught killers following distinctly different insticts and methods.

There is more faith in honest doubt and sincere searching than in half the rules and tenets of any religion. As a Christian, I am no longer embarrassed by the fact that I find the New Testament bewildering, difficult, obscure, confused, and confusing—because in its mysterious way it still causes me to think, it creates healthy uneasiness, and it sometimes leads me to authentic growth through positive change, as Jesus reveals God to me when I meditate on his life and words. Openness to faith, which is the power of goodness and truth to overcome sickness, suffering, misery, frustration, fear, oppression, and injustice—our self-created hell on earth—does not require persuasion or certainty but begins in compassion and awe of the mystery of life. But until the author—God—reveals the solution to the mystery, is it possible for us to live in a harmony that is free from the unharmonious effects of both religious indifference and intolerance? Perhaps a pearl of wisdom found in the words of Norman Cousins can answer that salient question about the future of mankind. In his wonderful book *Human Options,* Counsins wrote:

> We may not be able to persuade Hindus that Jesus and not Vishnu should govern their spiritual horizon, nor Moslems that Lord Buddha is at the center of their spiritual universe, nor Hebrews that Mohammed is a major prophet, nor Christians that Shinto best expresses their spiritual concerns, to say nothing of the fact that we may not be able to get Christians to agree among themselves about their relationship to God. But all will agree on a proposition that they possess profound spiritual resources. If, in addition, we can get them to accept the further proposition that whatever form the Deity may have in their own theology, the Deity is not only external, but internal and acts through them, and they themselves give proof or disproof of the Deity in what they do and think; if this further proposition can be accepted, then we come that much closer to a truly religious situation on earth.

And maybe closer to a peace that lasts—a peace that is based on mutual respect and love for one another and that grows out of a concerned and constant effort to try to understand through a dialogue that is honest and kind at the same time. It causes me great sadness that the electronic church I served cannot accept any of Norman Cousins' propositions and does not seem willing to understand or tolerate other spiritual points of view.

Perhaps our common prayer should be inspired by that gentle flower from Assisi, St. Francis—easily a saint for all faiths whose unselfishness, openness, defenselessness, and love for all creation make him a model for dialogue—who asked God to help him understand rather than be understood. He must have realized that there are no shortcuts to understanding and that he would need plenty of help. And so do we. *Francis traveled the road from sinner to sainthood by not giving up.* And so must we, because there are no short-cuts to sainthood and salvation.

Postscript

The publisher of this book asked me to write a personal postscript that would inform the readers where my spiritual odyssey has taken me. He thought that the answer to the question of where I now stand vis-à-vis my Christianity was not only important but a fitting conclusion to the book. I initially resisted the idea because I believed the book said everything I wanted it to say, and nothing more was needed. However, upon reflection I realized that the writing of this book brought my lifelong spiritual odyssey to a new land of understanding and faith—which should be shared.

It has been three months since I completed the writing—a long enough time to calmly inspect the impact this writing has had on my personal beliefs. The fact that I had dramatically changed was so self-evident that shortly after the manuscript was delivered to the publisher, I felt compelled to visit my older sister, remove my mask of socially acceptable conformity to standard Christian beliefs, and reveal my true inner identity, which could no longer be classified as "practicing Christian." I love my sister very much, and I feared that much of what I had written would upset her—even hurt her. That bothered me. Even while I was writing this book, the conflict between my desire to express the truth as I understood it, and my concern about upsetting members of my family with my frankness in detailing personal events in my life and in expressing opinions about Christianity that are diametrically opposed to theirs, caused me considerable anguish. I had to warn my sister about what she eventually would be reading—everything she wanted to know about her brother but was afraid to ask. I hoped she would love the "new" me as well as she had the person she always thought I was. We had a marvelous evening of sharing and understanding. By both of us expressing the almost unexpressible nature of our deep-seated faith and beliefs, we drew even closer despite the tremendous difference in our world views. Our love for each other was able to bridge the religious gap that could have separated us. Since that wonderful night, my sister no longer tells me that she is praying for me, but I know that she is—and I am glad because her prayers are flowering expressions of her love. The dialogue between us is now much more meaningful and deep. I appreciate and admire her faith; she understands and accepts my doubt.

I may not be a "practicing Christian," but Christianity is still a part of me—it's in my blood. I can soften its impact on my life and thoughts, but I cannot ignore its existence within me. However, that does not make me a Christian—at least not in the orthodox or traditional sense. I am not an active member of any Christian denomination, and I rarely attend any church service. In fact, I did not even go to church on Christmas Day or Easter Sunday (days that manage to draw even the most marginal of Christians to church). My Christianity is somewhat like a nationality—Catholicism, Anglicanism, and Orthodoxy are the major cities of my spiritual homeland, and, no matter how far I roam from them, they still manage to pull at my heartstrings during certain times of the liturgical year.

Well, if my Christianity is little more than an inherited part of my overall makeup, and I am not a card-carrying, churchgoing, Bible-believing Christian, then what am I? I dislike labels in general; however, if for the sake of clarification I need to label myself I would choose secular humanist. That does not imply that I am comfortable with all aspects of secular humanism or even all secular humanists.

Secular humanism attracts a broad spectrum of people—some are more tolerant than others, some are more militant than others, some are more open-minded than others; some believe in God, and some don't. Do I believe in God? No, I do not believe "in" God—I believe in the probable existence of God and the absolute importance of searching for my own personal truth. I am a secular humanist who is strongly influenced by the teachings of Jesus and somewhat influenced by the teachings of Buddha.

I believe life is a mystery to be lived and not a religious problem to be solved. I do not think it is possible to use our finite mind to find the infinite, because God resides beyond our comprehension. Yet wisdom can only be gained through a thorough investigation. Enlightenment, transformation, and growth are not found in the answers handed to you by others but grow naturally out of questioning. The ability to constantly question has two enemies: the desire for constancy and the holding of convictions. Questions give birth to change, and consistency demands stagnation. (Next year I hope that I'm not as ignorant as I was this year; consistency requires that I be just as ignorant.) Questioning requires an open mind. Convictions demand a closed mind, and, as Nietzsche writes, "are more dangerous enemies of the truth than lies."

I respect the tenets of all faiths without fully accepting the dogmas of any religion. The abbot of an orthodox Christian monastery in Cambridge, New York, once told me that "Christianity is not a religion, it is a way of living." If the truth of that sentiment were a reality in the lives of Christians, then those who offer salvation for sale on television would be out of business faster than a flick of the dial on a television set. Until that time, I will continue to seek, to doubt, to wonder, to ponder, and to question. I support secular humanism and consider it to be a breath of fresh air battling the pollution-filled smog that religion pumps into the atmosphere. The Christian zealots who dominate television are living examples of Winston Churchill's definition of a fanatic: "A fanatic is a person who can't change his mind and won't change the subject."

My spiritual odyssey and the writing of this book have taught me that truth and serenity lie sleeping in silence and solitude.

March 31, 1986
New York, New York

Update: "Playtime Is Over"

"If it wasn't for Pat Robertson, nobody would ever have heard of Gerard Straub," shouted an angry gray-haired woman in the television studio audience. At that moment, I would have gladly chosen anonymity rather than being assailed and slandered on television and radio by the army of fanatical supporters of a candidate for the presidency who artfully rewrites the facts of history. After grabbing the microphone from the hands of the show's host, the woman's countenance changed from that of a mild-mannered grandmother to that of a wild animal about to pounce on its prey. Her voice was loud, piercing, and filled with hatred.

The date was October 20, 1987; the place, the studios of WOR-TV in Secaucus, New Jersey—a city from which you can see the majestic skyline of Manhattan. I was the guest on "People Are Talking" and the audience was peppered with people from "Americans for Robertson." Armed with righteousness but devoid of common courtesy, they booed and hissed at me during the interview because I had played a videotape of the Reverend Robertson saying something he had vigorously denied ever saying. More on that later. The evidence that Robertson had lied to a reporter from *Time* magazine did not sway their opinion; it only roused their resentment.

The granny-turned-tiger shrieked: "You say he lied. Let's hear what Pat Robertson has to say. I am so tired of listening to newspapers and men like this [waving her finger at me] who come up to dirty Pat Robertson."

One overweight woman, who looked as though she had just come from the Tammy Faye Bakker school of make-up and was decked out in a bright red suit garishly accentuated by large gold earrings and topped off with a beehive hairdo, loudly and proudly proclaimed: "Pat Robertson is a man of God." She said that we hadn't heard what Pat really meant and asked the host if he had a vertical relationship with God. I knew I was in trouble before entering the studio, because as I walked across the parking lot I spotted a bumper sticker carrying the message "Come to Jesus, or go to Hell."

On October 6, 1987, during an hour-long interview on KPRC Radio, an NBC affiliate station in Houston, Texas, a listener called and asked me, on the air, "What do you think of Jesus Christ?" The trick question had come about forty-five minutes into what had been a very difficult show because the vast majority of the callers were fundamentalist Christians who strongly opposed my critical views of Pat Robertson and his mix of religion and politics. I could hear the hostility in the callers' voices and could sense their frustration at my being given the opportunity to challenge their belief-system on the radio. Yet, I felt I was holding my own, calmly responding to their attacks and giving reasonable answers to their questions.

One woman, however, did leave me speechless. A few minutes before her call, I had read a few of Robertson's sentiments about women, as expressed in one of his books. Robertson had written that a "woman has voluntarily surrendered a portion of her autonomy to her husband when she marries" and that a "wife should submit to his leadership." It was Stone Age thinking on Pat's part and I thought that his opinion on the role of women in marriage would trigger a tidal wave of outrage from the female members of the audience. My quoting from Robertson's writings was a new tack I had just started using during radio interviews. Rather than blab on about what I thought to be the potential dangers of a Pat Robertson presidency, I decided to let his own words on the devil and women give the audience insight into Pat the man, and his words on government give them insight into Pat the politician. I was simply holding him accountable for his own words.

The plan backfired with a resounding boom! The lady flatly fired back that Pat was right, that the key to her successful marriage was her submission to her husband. Moreover, she continued with conviction, if her husband does something that she does not agree with, she goes along with whatever it is and prays that God will give him a dose of wisdom and then he'll change his mind. Her marriage sounded like a game of follow the dummy. Fortunately, I didn't have to respond to the woman because the host of the show immediately jumped into the fray and asked her if she had a mind of her own. The two launched into a heated discussion, which the host, overcome by disbelief and getting nowhere, quickly concluded. Well, maybe the plan didn't backfire; it did manage to ignite a sense of outrage in at least one male—the host.

No matter what tactics I employed in an interview, no matter whether the show originated from the Bible belt or from a large northeastern city, no matter whether the host was prepared or not, or sympathetic to my position or not, I could always count on trick questions to get me to say that the Bible wasn't the divinely inspired, errorless word of God, or to get me to admit that Jesus Christ was not God. Hearing either statement from me was all that was needed to completely invalidate everything I had said in the minds of the Bible believers. For them, my mind had been deceived by Satan and therefore nothing I said was worthy of even the slightest consideration. My answer would label me an unbeliever, a heathen, or an atheist.

I felt as if I were pounding my head against a stone wall. This public battleground seemed like the worst possible place to conduct a fair examination of beliefs. It was not conducive to a meeting of minds; it only inflamed the differences between them. No matter how closed-minded or unreasonable a caller or audience member appeared to be, somehow I felt, perhaps naively, that if we had the chance to sit down at the kitchen table for an evening of chatting over a couple of cups of coffee, we could calmly share our thoughts about Jesus and the Bible and, at the very least, begin to understand each other and maybe even narrow the gap between us. Abraham Lincoln said, "I don't like that man; I must get to know him." You don't get to really know anyone through the media; you get to know certain images of them. Radio and television are artificial and are no substitutes for the face-to-face communication required for meaningful dialogue. Of course on these media I could inform reasonable people about the hidden dangers of the unreasonable beliefs and political goals of fundamentalist Christianity, but I also wanted to reach out to those people who had already bought the "salvation" Pat had been selling. Maybe I felt that my years at CBN had made me at least partly responsible for Robertson's being such a good salesman. But once they bought the eternal package, nothing could persuade them to return it, least of all my satanic thoughts transmitted over the polluted secular airwaves. One radio talk-show caller was so upset by my comments that he suggested, on the air, that I should be shot.

And so it goes, and has gone, since publication of the first edition of *Salvation for Sale*. Even after more than eighty radio interviews and a dozen television appearances, I still haven't gotten used to being probed and battered in public. Private matters of adultery, divorce, and faith were turned into grist for the media mill. And it was no fun constantly explaining the circumstances surrounding my ouster from Robertson's Christian Broadcasting Network or responding to the false charge that my book was little more than a case of "sour grapes." Even for someone with more than twenty years of experience behind the camera, being *on* camera, under the bright lights, and in the hot seat getting grilled by a host who is only looking for short, snappy, simple answers to tough, complex questions was extremely nerve-racking. Being somewhat oversensitive, and seeing myself as more contemplative than controversial, the sparks of fury that the book touched off caught me off-guard and caused me considerable emotional stress.

The upheaval of introspection that I experienced while writing the book were intensified after publication. To make things harder, my personal crisis became public. On the bright side, I was warmed by the numerous letters I received from readers who were touched and helped by the book. Many people wrote to thank me for convincing them that it was okay to doubt. One gentle and kind elderly Christian woman from Indiana has been corresponding regularly with me; we exchange views and frequently recommend books to each other. She, too, decried hatred in the name of Christ. Perhaps the most touching letter came from a lesbian in her mid-thirties whose live-in lover came from a strict fundamentalist background. Her nine-page letter detailed the agony of a loving relationship being constantly threatened by confused religious beliefs and bigotry. She read parts of the book aloud to her lover and it helped them deal more openly with the problem.

During the post-publication period, I slowly began to see that I still had a lot to learn about the dark side of Christianity. But, more important, despite the cathartic value of writing it all down, I realized that I had still not fully recovered from the deadly effects of the Robertson cult. I began to see from my own experience and hearing of those of others that it takes a long time to recuperate.

The Pearlygate scandals touched off by the "Give to Me or God Will Kill Me" fundraising campaign of Oral Roberts and the sexual indiscretions of Jimmy Bakker thrust fundamentalism into the spotlight, and as a result many former fundamentalists began to openly discuss their negative experiences.

It was during this time that I uncovered information about Pat Robertson that was more shocking and scandalous than I ever imagined. A new portrait of Pat was slowly emerging, one drastically different from my CBN-days image of him as a sincere, sensitive man honestly seeking to serve God. The respect I always had for Robertson, still intact long after my firing from CBN, began to dissolve while writing this book, but I still harbored a vestige of admiration for him, probably because he had such a tremendous impact on my life. He was bright, talented, articulate, clever, creative, forceful, and a man of towering strength. I came to think of him as a father for whom I would do almost anything. That feeling is hard to shake, and realizing that I had been so wrong about him was unsettling at best. The hard, cold facts slowly began to reshape my opinion. Now, almost two years since completing the book, the admiration is gone. It has been replaced by outrage at his deception of innocent people and his all-consuming desire to eliminate what he considers to be evil. When I first began to see the serious faults in his theological perspective, I simply considered him misguided but harmless. I was wrong. He is not harmless; he is dangerous. Robertson's secret agenda for transforming America into a "holy" nation, as well as his hope for a worldwide physical manifestation of a secret spiritual kingdom needs to be exposed.

Most people think politics and religion don't mix. However, for Pat Robertson it is essential that they mix. It is also a divine command that religion and politics merge to form a new, more powerful gospel of activism and aggression. While politics has always been an important part of Pat's life—his father was a United States senator—it has for most of his adult life taken a back seat to religion, which he considered a much higher calling. In the eyes of a fundamentlist Christian, it is infinitely more important to be a prophet who hears directly from God than to be president of the United States and hear only from people and polls. Why then did Robertson give up the role of prophet to make a bid for the presidency? The simple answer, according to Pat, is that God told him to do it. Putting skepticism aside, which is a dangerous thing to do when dealing with self-appointed prophets, let's assume that this is true. Why would God want His prophet to be president? Because, according to Pat's deep-seated belief, God has a secret plan for the salvation of humanity that He has kept hidden for centuries. But now, conveniently, He has revealed His plan to Pat, His chosen servant, and to a few of his friends. The sacred scheme is the Armageddon scenario, which consists of the following essential ingredients:

The Bible can and must be interpreted literally.

God's justice outweighs His mercy.

God has a chosen people whom He loves and prefers over all other humans; the Jews are God's chosen people.

God gave the Jews a Holy Land; the modern state of Israel is that ancient, biblical, and mystical Holy Land known as Zion.

Israel's enemies are God's enemies.

Both Christian and Muslim Palestinians are expendable; God has divided time into seven periods, known as dispensations. One of those dispensations will include a catastrophic nuclear holocaust resulting in a horrible bloodbath that will engulf the earth and kill not only nine million Jews but also all those who do not confess the Lordship of Jesus.

Jesus will triumphantly return to earth to lead his Christian forces to victory over Satan and the Antichrist.

Some Christians believe that in the height of battle the faithful will be plucked from the earth and zipped off to the safety and tranquility of Heaven—this event is known as "the Rapture." Others believe that Christians will be protected during the battle and will survive to reign with Christ for a thousand years on a restored earth.

God is not concerned about Hindus, Buddhists, or any other non-Christian religion.

The lucky ones who make it to Heaven will not be tormented with the memory of their friends and family burning in Hell because God in His mercy will erase this memory from their minds.

War with the Soviet Union is inevitable, and almost 85 percent of Soviet troops will be killed.

The Dome of the Rock, which is the most sacred of Muslim shrines, located in Jerusalem, must be destroyed and in its place must be built a Jewish temple.

More than forty million evangelical fundamentalists, including Pat Robertson, Jerry Falwell, Jimmy Swaggart, Hal Lindsey, and Kenneth Copeland, believe all or most of this thumbnail sketch of the Armageddon scenario.

Before looking at this bizarre plan for salvation in more detail and the ramifications of it for people who simply want to live in peace on this planet, I would like to digress briefly to what I think are Pat Robertson's real reasons for giving up the ministry for politics. It is important to realize that, despite Robertson's religiosity, he is basically a political animal. In fact, outside of the realm of religion, politics and economics are the consuming interests of this highbrow evangelist—with the exception of owning and breeding pedigreed horses.

One of the things that most surprised me when I first became the producer of the "700 Club" was Pat's vehement Carter-bashing during our prebroadcast chats. He seemed to loathe the born-again president, who was guilty of the sin of being soft on communism. Politics always weighed heavily on Pat's mind. As he and I traveled together throughout the Middle East, to such politically and religiously important countries as Egypt, Lebanon, Jordan, and Israel, getting our hands on the latest editions of the major international newspapers in order to keep abreast of political events was equally as important as daily prayer and Bible-reading.

Off camera, Pat was never more energized or emotionally charged than when he was talking about politics, which more often than not was the main topic of his conversation. I remember how I had to struggle to feign a comparable level of interest or risk losing his attention. To bore Robertson was professional suicide at CBN. His political discourses were sprinkled with facts and figures to support his position; it was as if he had instant access to a computer databank of statistics and political history, but with the occasional Reaganesque mixing of fact and fancy. He always managed to get in the last word. As with his religious convictions, Pat displayed a high degree of self-assurance regarding his political point of view, but he was frustrated by those who couldn't see the obvious truth of his position. He saw liberals as guilty of plotting a massive conspiracy to overthrow the truth that God wanted manifested in the political realm. Pat acknowledged no ambiguity of doubt when it came to either politics or religion. There was no separation between the two in Robertson's mind. He could not tolerate Christian wimps who were too fearful to stand up in the public square for righteousness and for stamping out the immorality and evil that pervades our society.

Robertson, along with most of the people I worked with at CBN, wanted very much to reform society. But, as Thomas Merton pointed out, correctly I think, "Nothing is more suspicious, in a man who seems holy, than an impatient desire to reform other men." The great American writer Ralph Waldo Emerson, who observed our nation during most of the nineteenth century, felt that the desire to reform others is a waste of time. Gay Wilson Allen writes in the introduction of his biography of Emerson: "He refused to join social reform movements because he believed individual action was better than collective enterprise. Unless the individual could be improved, there was no hope for society. His own reform began with himself."

Now fully reformed himself, Robertson wants to reform others and urges fellow believers to militantly express their religious views on the battlefield of politics. "Thou shalt vote" is for Robertson a commandment from God; voting is not simply a privilege or duty. Still, getting out of the religious boat and walking on political waters was not a natural or easy step for the preacher. Something happened that forced him into running for public office—namely, a failed prophecy that clearly indicated that he had not heard God's revelation correctly.

Pat was obsessed with the imminent return of Jesus. In 1980, he openly expressed his belief that the Day of Judgment was at hand and explained how both current events and the ancient writings of the Old and the New Testaments supported this conviction. He boldly predicted that by 1982 a major war would erupt in the Middle East and that this would trigger a seven-year period of tribulation that would culminate with Jesus establishing His kingdom on earth—and we'd better get ready. The evidence he cited was as follows: the increase in the number of earthquakes and divorce; the spread of secular humanism and communism; spiraling inflation and sin that threatened an economic and moral collapse; the increase in military threats confronting Israel; the acceptance of false religions and the denial of the existence of the devil; the projected global shortages of food, fuel, and water; the increase in terrorist activity; and the collapse of many political systems. For Pat, earthquakes were not geological shifts that released pressure, they were warning signs from God that released a passion for saving souls.

As I briefly mentioned in the Prologue, which, at the time it was written, was based solely on my memory and not the concrete evidence I now have, biblical writings helped Pat paint the following bleak international political picture that would develop prior to the return of Jesus: Tensions in the Middle East will explode into a major war when Russia invades Israel. The communist force will be wiped out; but as a result of the war, the oil supply to Europe and much of the world will be severed. The bottom will fall out of the European economy, causing total chaos. A charismatic dictator will seize the opportunity to take over the ten nations that comprise the European Common Market. Economic order is quickly restored, but the dictator turns out to be a wolf in sheep's clothing—in reality, the Antichrist, who despite his benevolent exterior is evil to the core. Jesus, the military Messiah, will return to earth, destroy the dictator, and establish his everlasting kingdom of justice and peace. Before all this happens, suffering will be the order of the day as a result of an increase in earthquakes, volcanic eruptions, hurricanes, and drought, and also because of the possible calamity of a nuclear war.

This picture of the world to come was not impressionism painted with speculation, it was realism depicted from conviction: During a post-Christmas 1979 private retreat at a wealthy friend's home in Florida, God told Pat Robertson that doomsday was coming.

This scenario was dramatically revealed in great detail on January 1, 1980. The occasion was the New Year's Day all-staff prayer meeting at CBN. Filled with the normal optimism that the first day of a new year brings, along with the yearly opportunity and resolve to wipe the slate clean and start over, we all enthusiastically gathered together for prayer and fellowship on the first day of not only a new year but also a new decade. That spirit of bright promise was quickly doused by Pat's promise of the coming fires of wrath. In Chapter 3, I wrote about how frightening it was for me to play back the audiotape I had found that detailed God's wish for CBN to start making plans for televising the Second Coming of Jesus. But when I recently came across an audiotape of that New Year's Day prayer meeting, I sat in stunned disbelief for three days. I played the tape over and over again. Talk about a smoking gun. The tape captured the Pat Robertson that neither the public nor the "700 Club" viewers ever got to see. Because there were no cameras and he was speaking to the most faithful of his followers, Robertson was able to rip off his mask of reasonableness and reveal his true identity: a mad, modern day version of an Old Testament prophet of doom, whose God merely mirrored his own human frailty.

The audiotape I found was buried in a box of odds and ends of my past. Ironically, it may provide the only authentic look at the insanity that passed for reality at CBN. Pat recorded all his formal talks. At the time, there would have been no reason for me to want a permanent record of such a despicable message of fantasy, horror, and hate, except for one small thing—my vanity. Before Pat spoke, there was a period of prayer and worship that included singing in tongues. As this praise began to wind down, I stood up and read the last six verses from the Book of Zephaniah from the Old Testament. Robertson considered the reading to have been inspired by the Holy Spirit as a confirmation of the message he was about to give.

After his talk, you could sense a ripple of fear moving through the staff, and I stood up and reread a portion of the Scripture I had delivered earlier and followed it with this comment: "Yahweh is saying here that He will exalt with joy over us, that He will renew us by His love, and that He is going to dance with shouts of joy for us! So, beyond not fearing, I mean that it is a pretty gloomy picture you paint, but we are not supposed to have fear—beyond not having fear, we should be shouting with joy because He's dancing with joy over us."

Pat chipped in with, "Amen."

I continued, "I think that's an important part, we should be more joyous through this and not just be resolute that we're not going to be fearful."

"Exactly," Pat replied, "that's beautiful. And He is going to restore our fortunes, and we're going to—actually we're getting ready to get the kingdom, when you see these things come to pass."

I was the bright bookends of his dark message. And my vanity wanted a record of it, so I asked the guys in the audio department to make me a copy of their recording of the meeting, which went unplayed until recently.

Now, almost eight years later, I wonder how I could have so completely turned off my mind that Robertson's words did not raise a question about his sanity when I first heard them. It was a long—more than an hour—rambling, paranoid, almost incoherent talk that mixed many Old Testament quotations about an avenging God with direct messages from God, which Pat had written down on lined, legal-sized yellow pads, and a lengthy lesson on the Middle East. Robertson sounded like a modern-day Ezekiel, whose ancient writings form the foundation for Pat's prophecy. It is incomprehensible to me that any person who had delivered such a deranged, absurd, cruel message could one day sit in the Oval Office. What follows is a lengthy selection of the highlights—or perhaps "lowlights" is more fitting—of Prophet Pat's message. I think these unedited passages adequately convey the maniacal tone of his talk.

Each year, at least for the last decade, I have said to the Lord, "What kind of year is it going to be?" Each year, the Lord has said to me, "It's going to be a good year for the world." And I came back the next year and think it's going to be terrible, and the Lord said, "It's going to be a good year for the world." And I do it again, and the Lord said, "It's going to be a good year for the world." And I've gotten this written down [on] these yellow tablets, and year after year that's what was said. I asked the Lord, "What about this year?" And I didn't get the same answer. I got a different answer. And He said, "It will be a year of sorrow and bloodshed that will have no end soon, for the world is being torn apart and my kingdom shall rise from the ruins of it." We're not going to have good years for the world anymore.

I've been struggling for the past few months in relation to the Christian's role in government. As you know, a number of Christian leaders in America have been meeting together—Jerry Falwell, Bil Bright, Billy Graham, Adrian Rogers, . . . head of the Southern Baptists, Bob Jones, Ben Armstrong of NRB. I've been in several meetings with these brethren, some to pray, some to express our concern about this nation, the course of the political life of it, and the course of the spiritual life of it. And there has been a great deal of pressure for us to get actively involved. And I've had calls from one multimillionaire who wanted me to get involved personally and said, "I'll put up the money or help you raise it." So, all these things are happening.

I said, "God what do you want?" And that was a few weeks ago, and the Lord led me to a Scripture where he said, "I did not come to judge the world but to save the world."

Later He said to somebody who came to Him with this request, the man said, "Lord, make my brother divide the inheritance with me." And Jesus replied, "Man, who made me a judge or divider over you?" And the Lord made quite clear that when He came on earth, that He did not come to take over the Roman Empire. The Church ultimately did it, but He didn't. He came for one purpose—to save sinners. He came to lead people to salvation. He came to point them to a new way, a new life and the experience which would get them out of this world and into a new kingdom. But yet, you read in the Bible, and it says that the kingdoms of this world have become the kingdoms of our Lord and His Christ. He said to His disciples, "You who have been with me will sit on twelve thrones, judging the twelve tribes of Israel." Paul said, "Don't you know that the saints shall judge the angels." And yet, you see Jesus said, "I'm not a judge." And yet He tells His disciples they are going to be judges. The Bible says, "I'm not a judge or divider, I'm not going to have anything to do with governing your temporal affairs whatsoever." And yet the Bible says, "The kingdoms of this world are going to be the kingdoms of our Lord and His Christ."

But you have to ask yourself this question: How would a Christian— let us assume that we took Spirit-filled Christians, that every member of the Cabinet was Spirit-filled, the President was Spirit-filled and the Senate and the House of Representatives were Spirit-filled. But you've got a country filled with homosexuals, people who are living together outside of wedlock, who are engaged in drunkenness, fornication, drug addiction, crime, and violence. Now what are we going to do with those people? Are we going to kill them all? Are we going to put them all in jail? How are you going to enforce righteousness on them? Well, you really aren't. You just aren't going to do it from any temporal type of legislation. And we wring our hands and say what a mess the government is in, but the government is giving the people what they ask for, essentially. I mean, there was an article in *U.S. News & World Report,* this last issue, that says they have now put in an executive ruling in the government that there cannot be any discrimination against homosexuals. The reason is that there is a move now by the administration to counter a charge by Governor Brown that there is discrimination against homosexuals. So there can be no discrimination in hiring against homosexuals. But if you were in charge of things, would you let that happen? You wouldn't!

He [Jesus] was witnessing to me—and I believe I'm hearing Him right—that He has taken about all He is going to take of the drunkenness, and the drug addiction, and of the ungodly behavior, and of the blasphemy, and the perversion in the name of God, and the things that are going on in the world. He's had it up to here. And the hour of His wrath has come. But before He establishes His kingdom, when He's going to rule and allow His people to get participating in that, which He will do, He's going to shake the world right to its foundations. And while it's getting shaken, beloved, you're going to get scared to death. And He told me, in one of the clearest things He said, "Don't be afraid of anything." He said, "I'm going to protect you. Do not be afraid. Fear not." But I'll tell you, you'll see Chrysler Corporation in a tailspin, you'll see hundreds of thousands of people out of work, you'll see all kinds of problems with the gold market, and the oil, the people in long lines, and you're not going to be able to do this and the other—and you're going to get scared.

A few years ago, 1973 I believe it was, I was in the Hilton Hotel in Dallas, Texas, and I had been on the "700 Club" from our studios in Dallas the night before and we did it at night, and it was late by the time I got to bed, and I didn't get up till it was nine o'lcock, I think, in the morning. And I turned on the radio in the room—or attached to the television—and it said President Nixon has ordered an emergency. The troops at Fort Hood are being called off their leaves and brought back in and he scrambled the Air Defense over Houston.

And I thought, that sounds serious. Why didn't I know anything about it. So I got on my knees and I said, "Lord, what is happening?" And I opened my Bible to the Book of Amos, and in the Book of Amos it said, "Does the Lord do anything without revealing it to His servants the Prophets?" And I said, "No He doesn't." And He said, "Did I reveal anything to you?" I said,"No You didn't." He said, "Did I reveal anything to any of your friends?" I said, "No." He said, "Well, there isn't anything happening."

And sure enough, nothing happened. It was a nice exercise, but didn't anything happen. Because He hadn't shown it to any of His people. There was no word. But the Lord has assured us in His word that when something begins to happen that He is going to tell us about it, that we will not be groping blindly in the darkness, but that we will know what's going on. Now if I'm hearing Him right, things are starting to happen. What is started over in the Middle East is not going to stop short of a war. I believe in the next two years, I would put it at '82, but dates are risky, there is going to be a major war in the Middle East. I don't see how it can stop.

Now they [the Russians] are going to make the move, and that's what God is saying—we've got a couple of years. It's going to start. They are not going to let up from now on. I mean, from now on it's going to be bloodshed, war, revolution, and trouble. Because the prize is too big. It's just too big. The United States is going to spend $90 billion this year on oil. Just the United States to these people [Saudis]. They've got so much money over there they don't know what to do with it all.

But the Bible says that's exactly what's going to happen—that Russia along with the nations of east Europe will join in a try to make a play for the whole world, and they are going to do it, and God said He is going to defeat them there. But what do we think is going to happen? Well, while this is going on, the United States is going to be putting more and more troops in here, and we'll get into some kind of war. Whether it's a big atomic war, I don't know. But we'll have a war, and while we do it somebody is going to blow up the oil fields. And there is going to be an ungodly bunch of burning. The Bible talks about Edom. Now Edom is more down here, but if Edom included Saudi Arabia, it says it will be a perpetual burning. Well, you can imagine what would happen if you set fire to all those oil fields. You couldn't get them back under control, and there would just be billowing black clouds over this whole area—for decades.

But what's going to happen if all of a sudden we have 50 percent less oil? Your power goes out in the big cities. You don't get to drive your automobiles. Factories are closed down; people are out of work. There is an awful lot of dislocation. They're going to be starving. There are going to be bread lines. There are going to be riots. People are going to go crazy. They just took the lights out in New York for twenty-four hours recently, or whatever it was, and they had 3,500 looting arrests. And they destroyed and looted billions of dollars in one city just overnight. What would it be like if all the major cities—? But it will hit Europe first, and then it will hit the U.S., and it will happen very quickly, and all of a sudden the oil flow is stopped and the world's currency is crazy and the people are out of work and there is great suffering and there is great hardship. Now you can get over it. The United States is relatively self-sufficient. But there is going to be a six-month period, eight-month period, twelve-month period, of a really hard way to go. And, when people begin to get in that situation, they may forget their kinky little sex deals, and they may forget their drugs and booze and so forth, and they may say, "Hey, maybe we better turn to God." And when that happens, they are going to start turning to people who know the Lord—hopefully us.

Now, God says He is going to destroy them [the Russians] at this point, so the Soviets, as far as I'm concerned, are going to go down, but how many people's lives are they going to take with them nobody knows.

God in His infinite wisdom permitted the Soviet Union to take over the countries of Poland, Hungary, Austria, East Germany—not Austria—Czechoslovakia, Rumania, Bulgaria.

In 1981, one year from now, Greece is going to join the European Community of Nations. [Note: They did not.] And it will make a ten-nation confederation, which is what was written about in Revelation, that there was going to be some kind of a ten-headed thing that's going to come out of something that died before . . . the death and the new life that was an offshoot of the old Roman Empire.

There will be ten nations who are going to be absolutely in desperate condition. They won't have any electricity. They won't have any factories. They won't have any industrial output. They won't have any employment. They won't have any raw materials that we have. They won't have food. They are going to be in critical condition. Now, what happens when ecomomies get in critical condition? Well, they look for a strong leader to get them out of it. And they'll give their power to anybody—be he devil, or be he God—anybody who can give the answers. In the Depression of 1932, when we elected a new president, far-out right-wing congressmen voted a New Deal Democrat everything he wanted. Any power he asked for, they gave him; any emergency legislation, they gave him; because you had to get people fed and you had to get them back to work. Didn't make any difference what you did—just let 'em eat. Well, that sounds to me like the perfect setting for a guy that may be called the Antichrist.
    Now the Bible talks about a seven-year tribulation period. . . . Seven years, three and a half of that's going to be relatively easy, and then three and a half years of persecution against Israel, and problems. And the guy's going to supposedly make a deal with Israel, because Israel is going to be strong. You see, they won't have been burned up in all this. This man is going to make an arrangement with the Israelis and then will begin some kind of a special type of persecution and difficullt days on the rest of the earth.

When Europe goes down, all the lesser developed countries are going to go back to tribal primitivism.

So, if this man in Satan's power can pull off a few miracles and rebuild quickly and put together the dictatorship—that could happen overnight almost—then indeed he might be in a position to challenge . . . Israel. There is one scenario we don't know about—the Bible doesn't tell us—that possibly the United States and Russia might just blow each other out of the way and then Europe will be all that will be left. It will be in chaos, but it might be all that's left. We don't know . . . for sure what's going to happen. All we know for sure is that the U.S. is going to stand against Russia and that Russia's going down. We don't know particularly beyond that. But you've got seven difficult years. That takes you through 1989.

It doesn't have to be Chinamen to fulfill Kings of the East. . . .

China can make it. China doesn't use any oil now, they've got their own and everybody rides bicycles.

What's going to happen to the Christians? I believe that we're going to see a fulfillment of the 91st Psalm. I think that we're going to see stuff crashing around us, and it won't come nigh us. God is going to protect us, I am convinced of it. I am convinced of it. That's why He's saying do not fear. I wrote down a few things—where did it go? Here—that I felt the Lord was saying to me. The Scriptures, you know, in Revelation 11, says now is the time to reward my servants the prophets and those that fear God, and—I'm paraphrasing now—to begin to make right the wrongs on the face of the world. And I believe our way . . . and he said to destroy the destroyers of the earth. The time has come to make things right.

These are some selected Scriptures in Zephaniah, I really believe this has applicability today, although it pertained to a time in Israel. Zephaniah the first chapter and the second verse through second chapter and the third verse—these are some selected Scriptures: I will utterly consume all things from off the land. I will consume man and beast. And I will cut off man from the earth. For the Day of the Lord is at hand. For the Lord hath prepared a sacrifice and hath bid His guests. That day is a day of wrath, a day of trouble and distress, a day of wasteness and desolation, a day of dark and gloominess. And I will bring distress upon men that they shall walk like blind men because they have sinned against the Lord, and their blood shall be poured out as dust.

You know gold hit 525 yesterday, and this Scripture says that neither their silver nor their gold shall be able to deliver them on the day of the Lord's wrath. Bunker Hunt was in my office a couple of weeks ago. After he was here, he said he had a little interest in silver. We learned that he bought 75 million ounces of gold. He made $630 million between Christmas Eve and New Year's Eve on that gold. It went from 20 to 29.75. I mean silver, I'm sorry, silver—on that silver. He made more money than most of us make in a whole year. All right, but the Bible says that neither their silver nor their gold shall be able to deliver them on the day of the Lord's wrath.

Now, the Lord [said]—take this prophetically or what ever: The end of all things is at hand. Behold I am coming quickly and my reward is with me. Use the time you have left to win souls to me. I will send the resources and the concepts of what are needed to win people to the Lord Jesus Christ.

Now Isaiah 22, verses 12 through 14, has this to say: In that day did the Lord God of Hosts call to weeping and to mourning and to baldness and to girding with sackcloth. And behold joy and gladness, slaying oxen, and killing sheep, eating flesh and drinking wine. That's the world that we see around us, you see. Now's the time when this whole world ought to be in a time of fasting and prayer. You see, we're starting this New Year with a time of fasting and humiliation and prayer and seeking God. But the world is—last night was out eating flesh and drinking wine and killing sheep, if you will, and slaying oxen, joy and gladness. The Bible says the prudent man—this is Proverbs 22:3—foreseeth the evil and hideth himself; but the simple pass on and are punished.

And another prophetic type word: I am the Lord God Almighty, the nations are in my hand, their rulers are like water. Nothing can hinder my plan, no man can block it. I have ordained it the foundation of the world, and my name will be glorious for I am God. My plan is to gather nations into the valley of vision, and I will contend with them there. Their horses, their riders, their tanks, their artillery will be as nothing before my power—I will render them helpless, useless. Their planes will not fly when I rain fire and brimstone upon them. My world will not be destroyed. Terrible things will happen but my world will stand.

Now we're coming to harvest, and Jesus said we're wheat; and he's going to gather the wheat into His garner. But the chaff is going to be burnt up with unquenchable fire We haven't seen Jesus do that yet; but he said, "My kingdom is going to arise out of the ashes of the old world." The old things that's here Jesus can't use in His kingdom, He doesn't want it. He doesn't want fornication. He doesn't want adultery. He doesn't want various types of promiscuity. He doesn't want homosexuality. He doesn't want drunkeneness. He doesn't want bloodshed and murder. He doesn't want the blasphemous lips, and the greed of mankind. He doesn't want their rejection of Him, and the world's system is so corrupt that He can't do anything with it, except to say: "I'm going to shake it and tear it down and start all over again with my kingdom, with my people. The wheat He's going to gather into His garner. And He says to us, "Let's get out and start bringing in some sheathes, some wheat into the garner," before the time when He says to the other angels, "Thrust in your sickle and reap, for the harvest of the world has come." Two harvests: one of wheat and one of the grapes of wrath. I think we're into it. I think this year we're going to see it.

He's prepared His dinner and He's invited His guests. He's called on the fowls of the air to come and eat the flesh of princes and captains and mighty men. The great supper of the Lord God Almighty is an awesome thing. The slain of the Lord will be many when you get a world that there is little or no redemption for—like it was in the days of Noah: the slain of the Lord were many. Because men had turned their hearts so far away from God, He said, "There's nothing more I can do with you."

When some of these things happen, there's going to be a tremendous spiritual revival. That's what God says. He's going to turn some of the residue into flaming evangelists. They're going to declare His glory.

Jesus Christ is going to be glorified and then He is going to come back again. And He's going to establish a kingdom and He's going to turn it over to us and say, "All right, run it. I taught you the principles, run it. I've cleared the decks for you, now it's your world. You run it."

There's one thing we ought to keep in mind: Playtime is over, you know, for everybody. Playtime is over. We're talking about anguish in the world. We're talking about Cambodia's being repeated. We're talking about refugees. We're talking about desperate poverty. We're talking about anguish of mothers seeing their children die of starvation. We're talking about the broken spirit of men out in bread lines on the street that haven't got any work and their whole attitude is being changed. We're rioting and looting, and the animal nature of man is coming out—unrestrained in places. We're talking about difficult times.

A hell of a way to spend New Year's Day. Robert G. Ingersoll's comment that "God so loved the world that he made up his mind to damn a large majority of the human race," accurately sums up Robertson's manifesto from heaven. None of the more than five hundred people who listened to that dreary message thought it was odd or off the wall. Pat was on speaking terms with God, and we simply followed where God led Pat. The insanity of the Jonestown mass suicides has become more understandable to me. Nobody thought Robertson was headed for the loony bin. Now Pat's got them believing that God is leading him down the road to the White House. On November 8, 1987, the day after I transcribed the audiotapes of that prayer meeting, I woke up to the following headline on page 26 of the *Los Angeles Times*: "Robertson Nips Bush in Maine Straw Poll." And just one week later

Pat garnered 37 percent of the vote and a second-place finish in a nonbinding Florida straw poll of delegates. Playtime is over!

Nineteen eighty-two came and went—and nothing happened. Jesus tarried and Pat squirmed. Did the prophet goof in his prophecy? You bet he did! Even an attempt to revise his original prophecy to read "1984" proved inaccurate. Of course the cunning commander can tell his faithful army of followers that only his timing was wrong, and not the details. After all, it's been two thousand years since Jesus' alleged ascension to heaven; what's a few more years—a mere blink in the eye of eternity! For Pat, the truth is simple: Jesus is coming soon, and so is big trouble. However, the Bible-believing followers of Pat Robertson must ignore the Bible teaching found in Deuteronomy 18:22, where Moses instructs the people to ignore a prophet whose prophecy doesn't come to pass. They seem to pick what they like from the Bible, as if it were a fruitstand, and disregard what doesn't feel ripe or seem appetizing.

Pat Robertson did not treat his prophecy lightly, and the delay must have caused him concern. I can vividly recall the anticipation that permeated CBN as Pat and the staff awaited the unfolding of the events Pat foresaw. This aura reflected Robertson's twofold approach to the coming Armegeddon plot: Don't worry, and get ready. Getting ready, for us "real Christians" at CBN, meant learning how to become less dependent on the rest of the world. When the global economic system crumbles, we would be prepared, and hence our suffering would be less and our overall chances of survival greater.

Robertson urged us to get ready for the day when money would be useless by implementing a barter system for exchanging goods and services between Christians. If you were skilled in auto mechanics, then you should fix your dentist's car and in return he would take care of your cavity. I remember wondering if a dentist would accept a story from me in exchange for a drilling from him. Land on CBN's property was turned over to the staff for growing vegetables. Pat frequently proclaimed that, when the world food supply was running short, we could survive on soy products. He was very high on soy beans for a while.

Another aspect of getting ready was launching an intense effort at spreading the Gospel and saving souls. There was a theory that Jesus wouldn't return until every person on earth had an opportunity to hear the Gospel and accept or reject its claims. Regardless of each individual's opinion of that theory, everybody felt it was important at least to try to save family and friends from the coming doom.

Pat's tremendous skill at communicating a sense of absolute certainty was crucial to holding down the level of worry. Pat knew the score because God had given it to him, and we trusted both Pat and God. The message was simple and clear: No matter how bleak the fate of the world, ultimately, after a period of terrible trial and tribulation, the future will be bright for those who give their hearts to Jesus. Pat's formula for attracting and holding people works like a charm: Exploit their fears, their frustrations, their anger, their alienation, and their anxieties, and then skillfully offer them hope, relief, community, and guaranteed salvation.

I believe that Pat's failed prophecy of Doomsday and the Second Coming played a vital role in his decision to test the political waters. I realize that for those who base their thoughts and actions on the terra firma of reason, the deluded world the Reverend Robertson inhabits is like something out of a religious freak show; but, in order to understand what makes a man like Robertson tick, it is essential to grasp the significance he places on correctly hearing God's voice and doing the job that God has assigned him.

Robertson believes that God chooses certain people to perform specific tasks. For example, Pat maintains that centuries ago King David was chosen by God to lead Israel and that in 1980 God chose Ronald Reagan to lead the United States. Now Pat believes that God has a very specific and very important job for him, and that particular belief is the basis for every move he makes, including his running for the presidency of the United States.

The December 14, 1987, issue of *U.S. News & World Report* quotes Robertson as saying in September 1987: "I have made this decision [to run] in response to the clear and distinct prompting of the Lord's spirit. . . . I know this is His will for my life." It also quotes a remark Robertson made in July 1987: "Do I know the will of God? Of course, I do." But the job Pat believes God has chosen for him is not just to be the leader of the greatest country on earth; it is also to help to usher in the return of Jesus to earth. It may sound far-fetched and utterly ridiculous, but the ramifications of this belief are too immense to ignore or simply to dismiss as silly.

Before anticipating how Robertson's beliefs would affect the United States—and the entire world—were he elected president, let's first turn the clock back twenty years to a fine spring day in 1968, when Pat first got the notion that God had something very special planned for him. It was a time of great expectations for the infant Christian Broadcasting Network. Supporters and workers festively gathered together to celebrate the dedication of the expanded and renovated CBN head-quarters building, which overlooked a sleepy little creek in Portsmouth, Virginia. The growth of this fledgling Christian television operation was unquestionably a miracle to the devotees of Pat Robertson, and clearly a sign that God's hand was guiding the ministry and its charismatic leader. Armed with only a mandate from God and with virtually no money, in less than a half-dozen years Pat had turned a small, rundown, poorly equipped television station, whose signal could travel only a few miles, into a flourishing religious broadcasting empire. It is indicative of Pat's vision and ambition that he named his infant organization the Christian Broadcasting *Network*. Imagine a network consisting of one little dilapi-dated UHF television station. CBN's growth is a testament to Pat's brains and ability as well as to the gullibility and longings of his followers. To credit God would be to degrade the very concept of God.

Still, as the faithful convened that day, it was God who got the glory. But Pat got a message. In Chapter 1, I tell of the following prophetic pronouncement that was delivered by a member of the CBN board of directors at the luncheon banquet: "The days of your beginning seem small in your eyes in light of where I have taken you, but, yea, this day shall seem small in light of where I am going to take you. . . . For I have chosen you to usher in the coming of my son."

To Pat Robertson and everyone who heard these words, it was clear that God had spoken. Logic and reason had been discarded, but at great peril. No one said, "God said *what*?" No one questioned the authenticity of the telepathic message from the Almighty. Assume for a minute, that an infallible Deity does send messages to his or her human creations. The message receiver is still a human being capable of error. The message received cannot be considered to be the *absolute* truth. However, in the mind of the fundamentalist Christian there is no need for logic or reason. Logic and reason were designed by Satan to trip us and have been replaced by blind faith.

I believe it was that dubious message from Heaven that planted the seeds of the Armaggedon scenario in Pat Robertson's subconscious. Imagine, the creative force behind the universe—again, assuming that there is such a being—using Old English words like *yea* and speaking through a person who has been recognized by his community as having received a gift from God that allows him to receive specific messages directly from Heaven, telling an almost-lawyer turned preacher that he will someday be the head usher at the biggest event—or, more accurately, the last event—in the history of the world. To those who have not traveled in Pentecostal circles, this may sound pretty silly; but, for those who believe, it is very real. It fuels their very existence. For those who adopt this bizarre belief system, usually out of a deepseated emotional or psychological need, life without God—a God who can and does communicate directly to selected individuals—is not only incomprehensible, but also not worth living. For them, God is the glue that holds everything together and without Him life would collapse under the burden of malignant immorality, uncontrolled decadence, and widespread lawlessness.

To me, it is perfectly understandable that fundamentalist Christians are threatened by a person who claims to be an atheist. They have absolutely no framework from which to even begin to understand how a person can reach the conclusion that God does not exist; and such a conclusion automatically makes the atheist an enemy of God—and God's enemies are their enemies.

The message Pat Robertson heard in the spring of 1968 so excited and energized him that by the mid-eighties he had turned CBN into a $230-million-a-year operation that beamed it's version of Christianity around the world. Pat's achievement is proof that he should be taken seriously.

During the dozen years that followed the prophecy, Pat was a perpetual-motion machine who ruled his expanding empire with an iron fist. No detail was too small to escape his attention. Nothing was done without his knowledge and approval. During my two and a half years at CBN, I grew accustomed to seeing talented executives have their hands tied by Pat Robertson's ruthless and intrusive management style. (During his presidential campaign Pat tried to minimize his role as a minister by passing himself off as a businessman. What a joke. His success had very little to do with the business acumen that turns small-business entrepreneurs into masters of major conglomerates. His success in building his empire can be more accurately attributed to a burning passion to save souls and a tremendous ability to ignite a similar passion in the hearts of men and women who would, in turn, give generously of their time, talents, and money to help materialize his vision.) Pat's empire is based not on sound business practices but on convincing the sick that they could be healed and on taking advantage of the viewers' willingness to part with their money and to accept dubious shortcuts to prosperity and salvation. (The scam would be far more diabolical and cynical if

Robertson didn't believe it himself.)

Neither before nor since have I seen anyone cram so much strenuous activity into twenty-four hours; and Pat kept up that frantic pace day in and day out, year after year. Beyond handling the pressure and strain of hosting a live ninety-minute broadcast every day, Robertson managed a mountain of administrative details, attended an endless stream of meetings, recorded audiotapes expressly produced for his contributors, orchestrated massive fund-raising drives, made public-speaking appearances, authored numerous books, hosted a weekly half-hour television show called "The Lesson," on which he taught supposedly biblical principles for living, wrote a monthly newsletter to his supporters, studied the Bible, traveled extensively throughout the Middle East, and, in the time that was left, tended to the duties of husband and father. (Interestingly enough, Pat never attended church.) Fatigue was a word without meaning to this man on a holy mission. And it all paid off. By 1980, Pat was the Pope of the video Vatican, and he ruled supreme. Yet something was missing; he wanted more, and he allowed himself to believe that God had still more for him.

Despite his frenetic pace, his intimate involvement with the minor details of the daily operation, the occasional financial crisis sparked by his overambitious building program, and the additional burden of being the chancellor of his own university, Pat, by 1980, was bored. The job, even with its complexity, scope, and challenge, was becoming tedious for this man of immense ability and brilliance. I could see the impatience and the utter frustration in his eyes. He was tired not of the work but of the routine. He became irritated by people who could not rise to the challenges he threw their way. Staff members feared his vitriolic outbursts; yet, because they thought of him as God's prophet, they tolerated his temper.

Pat's spirit wanted to soar, but the miracle he had wrought began to weigh him down. There were no more challenges. He needed new horizons, but what could they be? After all, he already had climbed to the top of the mountain. What was left to conquer. Politics would be the obvious answer, but that possibility, although I know he daydreamed about it, had not seriously entered his mind. Even for this pompous preacher, that would be a tremendous risk. So Pat was content to stand on the political sidelines. But he began to lend his powerful support to issues and politicians he favored by sharing his television platform with them. Slowly, a political message was being woven into the religious fabric of the "700 Club." Piety and politics were the wave of the future for the show, and a temporary diversion for its host.

At last, Pat spotted an unconquered peak on the horizon. It was the liberal-controlled television news. The thought of presenting the news from a conservative Christian point of view actually made him salivate. As I mentioned in Chapter 2, CBN was no longer content with spreading the Good News; it now wanted to gather the world news. But "CBN News" never lived up to Robertson's vision of a full-fledged nightly news show that could go head to head with CBS News. It never even came close. The CBN nightly newscast had more problems than it had viewers and was quickly canceled. It was one of Pat Robertson's few failures, a dream too big to come true. Contrary to what Robertson thought, apparently God didn't want His prophet to be in the news-gathering business—so Pat *made* the news instead.

Add to Pat's discontent, or rather his dissatisfaction with the daily grind of his job, the fact that his prophecy of the eagerly awaited return of Jesus by 1982 did not come to pass, and you get a man ripe for change—a drastic change. Pat was smart enough to realize that the daily operation of CBN could run smoothly without his constant vigilance. The key executives had been around long enough to know exactly how Pat would handle just about every hurdle they might encounter. More important, like every other evangelist, Pat had a son standing in the wings who had been hand-groomed to take over the reins of leadership— especially now that the leader wanted to explore a new path, develop a new plan, and implement an old plot. The path was politics; the plan was the presidency; and the plot was Armageddon. This shift of power inside CBN and the shift in the outlook of its founder did not happen overnight. It was a gradual process of testing and exploration. In religion, impetuousness is a blessing; in politics, it's a curse.

The big question for Pat was whether he could translate his spiritual-superstar status into political punch. Some would think him nuts for even asking the question; but for Pat nothing is impossible if God is on your side—and for him there was no question about that. So shortly after 1982—when all hell didn't break loose—Robertson put his toe gently into the political waters. He became more and more politically outspoken and less and less visible on the "700 Club," because he was traveling around the country speaking to groups that were receptive to his moral message for America. The transformation from prophet to politician was slow and calculated, and it did not meet with instant approval from his faithful followers.

While the thought of having a person who "speaks in tongues" sitting in the Oval Office was enticing to members of the Pentecostal flock, they realized that politics, by its very nature, speaks the language of compromise—and for them compromise is the language of the devil. They were the sole possessors of the revealed Truth, and that Truth could not be watered down or compromised. It's important to mention again that this attitude gave birth to an unbending rigidity and intolerance that rendered these fundamentalist Christians incapable of living harmoniously within a pluralistic society. In fact, for some, pluralism itself was seen as a concept that came straight from the pit of hell. The evil enemy was anyone who disagreed with their prophetic vision and their understanding of God. To them dissenters were nothing more than devils who needed to be saved or, even worse, exorcised from society.

On more than one occasion, I was mortified to hear the death penalty advocated for homosexuals. But harboring a death wish for the wicked is not unusual in fundamentalist circles. One fundamentalist Baptist minister called Supreme Court Justice William Brennan a "baby killer" and exhorted his congregation to pray for the jurist's death so that he could be replaced by a judge opposed to abortion.

During the early days of his unofficial campaign, Robertson expressed that same sentiment not only for Justice Brennan but for two other members of the Supreme Court as well—but he wisely expressed it in a lighter tone: "We have so many social concerns in this country. Most of those social concerns would be solved if Justice Marshall, Justice Brennan, and Justice Stevens were to be either retired or promoted to that great courtroom in the sky." The Pentecostals are not satisfied to have their beliefs coexist with other schools of thought; they want theirs to rule supreme. Despite the narrowness of their religious point of view, they were smart enough to realize that a political platform built on their Truth would not be acceptable to most of the country. To win, the Reverend Pat Robertson would have to reach out and embrace people—heathens, homosexuals, humanists, feminists, liberals, and the numerous special interest groups that stand in opposition to their understanding of the Bible. The question for them was simple: How can Brother Pat mount a successful presidential campaign without tarnishing either the Gospel or himself?

Beyond assuaging this basic concern of the Pentecostals, Pat Robertson had an even bigger obstacle to overcome. The entire family of fundamentalists and Pentecostals would not fall in line behind him, because there were deep divisions within the camp. Yes, there was infighting among the faithful. I was surprised the first time I heard Robertson, in private, bad-mouth Jerry Falwell. To the untrained observer, these two preachers look as though they were cut from the same dark cloth; however, there are tremendous differences in their spiritual understanding and practices. For example, Jerry Falwell does not believe in praying in tongues, while Robertson is fully convinced that it is a normal part of the practice of Christian prayer—left unsaid, of course, is that if you don't pray in tongues you are not, according to Pat Robertson's beliefs, a genuine Christian. Theological squabbles abound in this dark backwater of Christianity. I doubt that you could get any two television hucksters of holiness to agree on very much, yet Pat had to get as many of them as possible to agree on his candidacy—or, at the very least, to agree not to sabotage it.

With that difficult objective in mind, Pat Robertson, on September 9, 1986, made a pilgrimage to Baton Rouge and the headquarters of the worldwide outreach of The Reverend Jimmy Swaggart—a $30-million complex of white concrete-columned buildings spread over one hundred acres. Brother Jimmy, to my mind, is the most dangerous and divisive of all the television preachers, and he was initially opposed to Pat's presidential plans. Hate and intolerance are the fruit of Swaggart's faith, and to his way of thinking the compromising nature of politics would ultimately defile any minister of God—no matter how pure his intentions—who tried to play its dirty game.

During a ninety-minute meeting with Swaggart, Pat must have mustered every ounce of his persuasive powers to get the mordacious minister to open his normally closed mind, because later that night Swaggart made the following statement to his congregation: "I believe the tide is running today in a way that mankind has never known before. It will affect the entire planet. And in a few months a hand is going to be laid on a Bible and take an oath of office for the highest position in mankind. And for the first time in human history the possibility definitely exists that the hand that lays on that Bible to take the oath of the highest office in the land will be joined to a shoulder and a hand and a heart that's saved by the blood of Jesus and baptized in the Holy Spirit."

Thus Pat had one reluctant vote of confidence in his pocket. But it was a very important one, because Swaggart had the power to influence many other votes. Perhaps it was not that Pat had convinced Swaggart of the viability of his political amibitions, but that the two men simply agreed it would be detrimental to the Pentecostal movement for two such high-profile ministers to throw mud at each other in public. (Oddly enough, within a year Swaggart, a high-school dropout, would dump truckloads of mud on a fellow Pentecostal preacher, Bible-school dropout Jim Bakker.)

A more cynical speculation on what caused Swaggart to endorse the Robertson candidacy would take into account the importance of the CBN cable system to Brother Jimmy. The only other evangelical big gun to publicly support Pat Robertson is Charles Stanley. Both Swaggart's and Stanley's television shows are carried on the CBN cable network, and without that boost in viewers their ministries would be crippled. That may be how Swaggart was induced to change his mind. Pat does play hardball. For a noncharismatic like the Reverend Stanley to be willing to have anything at all to do with Robertson invites cynicism, and perhaps disbelief. Profit can make principles bend, even in religion.

In February 1986, shortly after I had delivered the manuscript of *Salvation for Sale* to my publisher, the Reverend Robertson landed on the cover of *Time* magazine. That publicity plum came on the heels of a number of published reports that the television evangelist—who had suddenly found that label distasteful and now preferred to be known as a professional broadcaster—was contemplating entering the race for the 1988 Republican presidential nomination. I must admit that I didn't take these early reports seriously and figured that Pat didn't have a snowball's chance in hell of winning; yet I harbored a hope that his dream would stay alive at least until September 1986 and that the glare of his publicity would deflect some light onto the publication of this book's first edition. I did, however, have an occasional nightmare from which I awoke in a cold sweat with the realization that a peanut farmer and an actor both had made it to the White House. Why not a preacher? Interestingly enough, you couldn't detect in the tone of those early reports the slightest trace of a giggle. I don't think the press knew how to handle Pat Robertson, nor did they have any idea about how to unravel the complexity of his beliefs; And no member of the fourth estate seemed anxious to walk into the minefield of Christianity and risk the chance of igniting the wrath of a very vocal portion of the public. Perhaps the press just thought that Pat would simply fade from the political scene without causing much of a disturbance.

What bothered me the most about the press coverage of Pat Robertson was that he was never asked the tough questions; nor were the implications of his radical religious views examined in reference to his execution of presidential duties. During my radio interviews, I shocked listeners by expressing my projections of where a Pat Robertson presidency would take America; yet it was not *my* words that they found alarming, but the words of Pat Robertson that I quoted as a basis for my conjectures. But mine was a lone voice. Even when I was interviewed by the print media, the published piece was inevitably sugar-coated. Why? Judge Robert H. Bork certainly didn't escape being held accountable for his past ideas and statements and, more important, how they would impact on his future court decisions. Pat Robertson received no such treatment; instead, he was handled with kid gloves—even during the summer of 1987, when television preachers were in the headlines almost daily. Even with the craziness of Oral Roberts's terrorist fund-raising tactics and the rape, blackmail, homosexuality, and financial scandals surrounding and sinking Jim Bakker and the ensuing holy wars over PTL, Robertson turned out to be the teflon preacher—nothing stuck to him. Many people, however, thought Pearlygate dealt a severe blow to whatever slim chance Pat may have had in the political arena. But it did not harm him personally. In fact, Robertson stunned the press and political professionals when he beat both Bush and Dole in a September 1987 Iowa straw poll by amassing nearly 34 percent of the votes. The polls and the press learned an important lesson: Never underestimate the multi-talented Pat Robertson.

In sum, I believe Robertson's presidential aspirations grew out of the failure of his predictions for the future to materialize, his boredom with the routine of running CBN, his sense that there was little left for him to achieve, and his belief, based on a fourteen-year-old "message" from Heaven that God had chosen him to play a key role in the Armageddon scenario—a role that could be better performed from the stage of the White House. Oh yes, there were two more vital ingredients: first, Robertson had reached such a deluded state that he had begun to confuse his own thoughts, desires, and emotions with the so-called "inspiration of the Holy Spirit"; and, second, his enormous ego—about the size of Pittsburgh—which led him to believe that he could actually win, even if the stakes were the largest and most successful television ministry in history. Gradually, in less than four years, Brother Pat cleverly made the transition from prophet to politician. With the realignment of his executive staff and the help of his son—who oddly enough became a campaign issue when it was revealed that he was conceived out of wedlock—who was crowned king of the CBN hill, Pat Robertson needed only to shed his religious collar before putting on his political running shoes and officially entering the race for the presidency.

On September 28, 1987, the Reverend Pat Robertson, by simply writing a letter to the Freemason Street Baptist Church in Norfolk, Virginia, became Mr. Pat Robertson. Twenty-six years after his ordination, Pat had reluctantly resigned as a Southern Baptist minister and severed all "official" ties with CBN. Political reality, not God's voice, told Robertson that he had no other choice. He was in a bind, and he knew it. His ministry was both his biggest asset and his chief liability. Religious fervor gave Robertson a base of power, a platform, financial support, upset caucus victories in Michigan and South Carolina, and a win in a straw poll in Iowa. But, if he was to go any further, the "religious stuff" would have to be drastically toned down, because public opinion polls clearly indicated broad resistance to the election of a minister. In his letter to the church, Pat wrote: "I am keenly aware of the deeply held belief in this nation that there should not be an established religion in the United States of America, nor should the Government prohibit the free exercise of religion by any of the people." He doesn't say he supports that belief, however; but he added: "For this reason, I recognize that although the overwhelming majority of the American people desire leaders with strong religious faith, to many of our citizens the election of an ordained clergyman of any faith—Protestant, Catholic or Jewish—to as high a public office as the Presidency would, in their opinion, be tantamount to a preference of one religious denomination over all others."

So, poof! Pat's not a minister. Well, maybe not officially, but can he really drop from his life something that has been such an integral part of his being for more than a quarter of a century? Long after they are out of office, former governors, senators, and presidents are still addressed by those titles. Mr. Pat Robertson is still the Reverend Pat Robertson, even though it was time for him to vacate his religious office. Just as he had been "unofficially" running for the presidency, isn't he now "unofficially" a minister?

On October 1, 1987, just two days after his resignation, with an all-black jazz combo playing the theme from "Rocky," Pat Robertson stood on the steps of a ghetto tenement in the Bedford-Stuyvesant section of Brooklyn, where he had lived while preparing for the ministry. Before a small gathering of friendly supporters and a vocal band of protestors waving placards with such unfriendly messages as "Hitler in 1939; Robertson in 1988," he officially declared that he was a candidate for the 1988 Republican presidential nomination. Amid the jeers and shouts of "Bigot," "Extremist," and "Go home, Pat"—which forced him to abandon his prepared text—and without ever mentioning God (except for the perfunctory "God bless you" at the conclusion of his rambling rhetoric on family values), Mr. Pat Robertson was off and running— just hours after his swan song appearance on the "700 Club," when he had been surrounded by executives who laid hands on him and prayed for God's blessing on his campaign. The stark contrast between the utter frustration of the Brooklyn greeting and the hope of the Virginia Beach farewell mirrored the dichotomy within the man himself. Pat's official announcement came on the same day that a 6.1 earthquake had Los Angeles rocking and rolling, and I'm sure that the prophet in political skin saw that disaster as God's rumbling approval of his official candidacy, while at the same time it was his punishment of an evil city.

What follows is my scenario of what could very well happen to America's foreign and domestic policies should we the people wake up one morning and find President M. G. (Pat) Robertson sitting in the Oval Office. I believe the exercise of painting a picture of a Robertson presidency is valuable regardless of his chances at capturing the office, because the wave of fundamentalism that carried Reverend Pat to the point of becoming a declared candidate is too powerful to be ignored. The organizational skills and fund-raising ability of fundamentalists have established a strong beachhead on the political waterfront of many southern and western states. Their fervor will not die out, and, moreover, it may be only a matter of time before they push one of their own to the forefront of national politics—a true religious conservative who will not be saddled with the excess baggage of having been a TV evangelist, a burden that will ultimately bring down Pat Robertson. This theoretical candidate will not claim either to hear voices or to be a prophet of God; therefore, he won't be so easily dismissed as a religious fanatic whose sanity is called into question. Whoever the new champion of the religious right will be, you can count on the fact that beneath his— it will *never* be *her*—reasoned exterior will be the burning flame of fundamentalism, and if he is elected, that flame will ignite virtually the same wrath that a Pat Robertson presidency would.

To set the stage for a look at foreign and domestic policy under

President Pat, it may be useful to present some of Robertson's thoughts on government that appear in his book *Answers to 200 of Life's Most Probing Questions.* He writes:

> Government was instituted by God to bring His laws to people and to carry out His will and purposes.

The doctrine of separation of church and state doesn't fit into Pat's understanding of government, where apparently the elected leader gets to decide what the "will and purposes" of God are. In his book, Pat rambles on about how God used to deal directly with the people by speaking to the heads of tribes and families. No other government was necessary. But the people grew rebellious, and according to Pat "clear direction from God was lacking." So God gave the people a judge and a prophet, namely Samuel. Later, God gave the people a king and monarchy, which did a great job of governing up until the reigns of David and his son Solomon. After that, things started slipping. They slipped so badly that a perfect government will not be possible until Jesus returns and sets one up to rule during the coming Millennium. Pat claims that "perfect government comes from God and is controlled by God." Or perhaps from people who are controlled by God, as in the good old days of the Old Testament.

In the same book, Pat Robertson writes:

> We do not owe the government the allegiance we owe God. To God we owe our worship and our loyalty. We must remember that the government exists only as long as God gives it the ability and the power. When any civil government steps outside the mandate authorized by God Almighty, then that government does not have any further claim over its citizens.

That sounds as if it were a quotation from an Iranian ayatollah. Here is more vintage Robertson from *Answers:*

> Christians are supposed to pray for those in authority over them, so that they might live a quiet and godly life. This is so that the Word of God might go forth freely to the end that all should come to the knowledge of the truth.

Notice how one of the roles of the leader is to facilitate the spreading of the "Word of God." And more:

> On the international scene, given the sin of mankind, there must be armed forces. . . . It is necessary for the family of nations to raise up an international police force to restrain evil.

And more:

> The state is attempting to assert control over the life of children. Humanist values are being taught in the schools through such methods as "values clarification." All of these things constitute an attempt to wean children away from biblical Christianity.

And more:

> State social welfare agencies have been known to attempt to prohibit Christian parents from disciplining their children in accordance with biblical precepts.

And more:

> Unless America repents and regains a proper respect for God's law and God's moral order, the time will come when God will punish us.

With Pat Robertson in the White House, the possibility exists that he, Pat not God, will punish decent Americans for what he considers their violation of God's will and their unrepentant attitude.

I'm not an alarmist, but I don't think that the fear of Pat's private religious beliefs' influencing his public political actions is unfounded. Robertson tried to defuse such worries by comparing himself to President John F. Kennedy, who during his presidential campaign encountered similar concerns from people who thought his Catholicism would influence his politics. Protestants feared that the pope would be pulling the presidential strings. However, just because their fears never materialized is not a reason to dismiss the possibility of Robertson being overly influenced by his religious beliefs, because the two men are as different as church and state. Kennedy's Catholic faith certainly did not appear to have a strong influence on his private or public life. Robertson's fundamentalist faith, on the other hand, is the core of his being and is reflected in every action of his private and public life. Once in office,

JFK put on his Catholic piety every Sunday for public display; running for office, Pat hides his Pentecostalism from the public. God did not tell the politically ambitious Jack Kennedy to run for the presidency; nor did Kennedy have to claim to have turned away a hurricane in order to prove he could lead the nation.

In a nutshell, foreign policy under President Robertson would be far to the right of President Reagan's. A quote from Pat Robertson that appeared in the March 23, 1981, edition of the *Washington Post* will give you a good idea of what Pat thinks of the chances for world peace:

> I think a war with the Soviet Union is inevitable, if I read Bible prophecy properly. The chances are that the U.S. will come in as a defender of Israel. It looks like everything is shaping up.

I think it is reasonable to wonder whether such a belief on Pat Robertson's part could become a self-fulfilling prophecy if he were in the White House. For Pat, the issue is simple and clear-cut: "Communists are the enemies of Christianity." On the campaign trail in the fall of 1987, Pat vehemently opposed the proposed Soviet-American nuclear arms reduction agreement, which Reagan vigorously pushed for in hopes that it would be the bright spot of his presidency. I personally find it odd that a minister of the Gospel of Jesus Christ could take a position that exhorts a race for nuclear superiority to ensure peace. It is diametrically opposed to the teachings of Jesus. The author of the best-selling *The Road Less Traveled*, M. Scott Peck, wrote in his book *The Different Drummer* that "the arms race is against everything that Christianity supposedly stands for. It stands for nationalism; Jesus practiced internationalism. The arms race stands for hatred and enmity; Jesus preached forgiveness." Pat's all-consuming passion for the elimination of evil has obliterated from his mind the more peaceful message of Jesus.

To Pat Robertson, the Soviet Union is more than an "evil empire." (Ronald Reagan put forth this view early in his presidency to appeal to the fundamentalists whose support he sought. Now, to the horror of the far right, Reagan is willing to deal with the Russians.) Pat sees communists as the atheistic enemies of God who must be crushed. On March 14, 1987, while campaigning in New Hampshire, Pat urged that the Republican party establish as long-range national policy "the ultimate elimination of communist tyranny from every part of the globe, including the Soviet Union." Along with legions of others, I also deplore the aggressive spread of communism throughout the world and share Robertson's wish to thwart it. But how can you eliminate communism in the Soviet Union without an invasion? That goal is not only extreme, it is utterly ridiculous. Nuclear arms reduction is a sin to Pat Robertson. After all, without nuclear arms, how can you have a nuclear war—which is a vital part of the fundamentalists' twisted understanding of God's plan for the salvation of mankind. Their fear of communism could bring about more dangerous actions than might be caused by communism itself.

When he was on the campaign trail in California, I heard Robertson suggest that the Contras seize a piece of territory from the Sandinistas, erect a fence around it, hoist a flag, and declare themselves the legal government-in-exile, at which point the United States government should supply them with all the money and equipment they would need to attack and eliminate the atheistic enemies of the Lord. This man of God is willing to use force to enlighten people, eliminate evil, and establish peace.

In his *Answers to 200 of Life's Most Probing Questions*, Pat writes:

A lasting peace will never be built upon man's efforts, because man is sinful, vicious, and wicked. Until men are changed and Satan's power is removed, there will not be peace on earth.

It was not surprising to discover *Time* magazine quoting Pat's view that "pacifism is not biblical." Contrast that opinion to what that gentle giant of science and reason, Albert Einstein, had to say about the ethics of war: "To my mind, to kill in war is not a whit better than ordinary murder." The underlying message of Jesus' teachings was that the Kingdom of God could not be established by violence and that only love could manifest it. Einstein, sounding more like a preacher than Pat, also said: "Peace cannot be kept by force. It can only be achieved by understanding."

President Pat Robertson is not likely to be interested in understanding and reconciliation; he is more likely to be interested in elimination and destruction. Pat's strong urge to purge from society those on his list of the evil enemies of his righteous God—which would include communists, liberals, homosexuals, adulterers, feminists, and humanists—can be reduced to a bumper sticker slogan proudly proclaiming "Genocide for

Jesus." I'm not being flippant, the Reverend Dr. Pat Robertson fully supports the concept of genocide. Edmund D. Cohen, author of a comprehensive and insightful book on fundamentalism entitled *The Mind of the Bible-Believer,* first alerted me to Pat's views on the mass elimination of a group of sinful people when, after reading my book, Dr. Cohen sent me a transcript of the May 6, 1985, "700 Club" broadcast. I was horrified as I read Pat Robertson's claim that God sometimes instructs His people to "kill them all." Furthermore, according to Pat, God orders the extermination out of kindness and love, because the unrepentant would only give birth to countless generations of people bound for Hell unless they are stopped from procreating: Destruction today will mercifully reduce the number of people going to Hell tomorrow. As Ed Cohen, who is both a psychologist and a lawyer, pointed out in a letter to me:

> In other words, God uses His people to accomplish planned parenthood in Hell! Since Pat Robertson claims to receive remarkable personal marching orders from God in the same manner as Moses did, this stands as an ominous hint as to what President Robertson might undertake. Note what a favorable construction it puts on the Holocaust, at least where the extermination of conversion-resistant Jews was concerned! The statement necessarily implies that whenever evangelization efforts meet with chronic resistance, extermination should follow.

To capture the full flavor and impact of Robertson's extreme ideas what follows is the exact text from the "700 Club" transcript. Keep in mind that this is not some opinion Pat Robertson held a couple of decades ago and that he could recant today as a product of the faulty thinking of his youth; the date is May 6, 1985, and Pat is well down the road toward his bid for the presidency. (The March 1985 edition of the *Saturday Evening Post,* published by Pat's friend Mrs. Corrie SerVaas, not only featured the preacher on the cover but also disclosed his presidential aspirations in what was essentially a "puff" piece, designed to introduce Pat the politician to the public.)

> Audience Participant: I've been reading through the Book of Numbers recently, and come across that passage in Chapter 31 about the destruction of the Midianites. How do you explain that apparent travesty of the destruction of that people with a just and holy God?
>
> Pat Robertson: The wars of extermination have given a lot of people trouble, unless they understand fully what was going on. The people

in the land of Palestine were very wicked. They were given over to idolatry. They sacrificed their children. They had all kinds of abominable sex practices. They were having sex apparently with animals. They were having sex men with men and women with women. They were committing adultery, fornication. They were serving idols. As I say, they were offering their children up, and they were forsaking God. Now, you say, "God told the Israelites to kill them all: men, women and children; to destroy them." And that seems like a terrible thing to do. Is it or isn't it? Well, let us assume that there were two thousand of them or ten thousand of them living in the land, or whatever number. I don't have the exact number, but pick a number. And God said, "Kill 'em all." Well, that would seem hard, wouldn't it? But that would be ten thousand people who probably would go to Hell. But if they stayed and reproduced, in thirty or forty or fifty or sixty or a hundred more years, there could conceivably be . . . ten thousand would grow to a hundred [thousand], a hundred thousand conceivably could grow to a million, and there would be a million people who would have to spend enternity in Hell. And it's far more merciful to take away a few than to see in the future a hundred years down the road, and say, "Well, I'll have to take away a million people, that will be forever apart from God because the abomination is there." It's like a contagion. God saw that there was no cure for it. It wasn't going to change. Their hearts weren't going to change, and all they would do would cause trouble for the Israelites and pull the Israelites away from God and prevent the truth of God from reaching the earth. And so God in love— and that was a loving thing—took away a small number that he might not have to take away a large number. Now that's a long answer, but I think that's closer to it. Danuta?

Danuta Soderman [Pat's co-host]: Well, my question would be, Pat, why didn't He just save them all? I mean, why didn't he say, "I forgive you. I save you," and save them that way? Why obliterate them?

Robertson: A righteous God, just like a righteous judge—if a man comes into a court who has committed murder, the judge can't say, "Well, I'm a merciful, kind judge, and the jury has found you guilty of premeditated, first degree murder, but I'm such a ni~~ guy, you can just go ahead and I forgive you." He can't do that . .d uphold the law. They would impeach him. A judge has to keep the law and God has certain laws in the universe which must be upheld. The only way He fulfilled those laws was to die Himself in the person of His son on the cross. And He's not going to force anybody to accept Him. It has to be a free choice. And they had freely chosen to reject Him and it doesn't get any better. Itr gets worse.

Can a healthy mind engage in such rancid reasoning? Pat's "inspired" thinking reflects the Old Testament mentality that it was a religious duty to so completely wipe out the defeated enemies of God that not even their cattle and sheep should be spared. The English philosopher Bertrand Russell wrote: "The reformative effect of punishment is a belief that dies hard, chiefly I think, because it is so satisfying to our sadistic impulses." Pat Robertson, with the persuasive power of television at his disposal, was doing his level best to ensure that the policy of a holy, vindictive punishment did not die. Even Robertson's writing clearly indicates that removing the tumor or evil before it spreads throughout the whole body of mankind is a high priority for him. From Robertson's book *Answers* comes this:

> There is evil, then, because of Satan and because of man's nature—the evil has a tendency to multiply itself. The more evil men there are, the more society as a whole begins to take on an evil nature.

Pat's promoting the lie that a chosen people can be used as agents for the Divine desire for the extermination of evildoers because they will have an adverse effect on the future flies in the face of the New Testament teaching that we should "take no thought for the morrow." It is impossible to know what tomorrow will bring for any of us, even for so-called sinners, who might just see the "light," unless of course the "truth" has turned their lights out for good. Centuries ago, the German monk and theologian Meister Eckhart claimed that "God's ultimate purpose is birth." It would seem that for Robertson the opposite is true. Pat's reasoning is rooted in the sin of pride, which permits him to believe he has discovered the truth. Robertson knows how the universe was created and more important, how it can be better than it is, how pain and sorrow can be eliminated. Pat's piety does not permit him to enjoy the world and its creations. In suppressing joy in life, he produces a hatred of life.

For Pat, all that is wrong with the world can be laid at the devil's doorstep, and everything can be set right by eliminating the satanic influence in the world. In *Answers*, Robertson writes:

> The first thing to be said about suffering is that most of it comes about because of activities of a powerful supernatural being called Satan, or the devil. He delights in hurting man.

Buddha taught that "all life is sorrowful." Robertson's inability to accept the consuming nature of life, to take life as it is, with its ups and downs, with its glory and pain, has turned his life into a divine mission to change the world into something that it is not. Pat Robertson's priority is to change society, not himself; however, the underlying teachings of all religions clearly point out that such a goal will never lead to peace. Pat Robertson, for all his abilities, for all his insight, and for all his charm, is not a happy man and contentment is something I doubt he will soon experience. A happy and contented person has no need for miracles or to have God even the score.

Pat Robertson's statement on the acceptability of the mass extermination of the wicked wasn't a one-time television slip, because, according to Ed Cohen, just two months later he gave substantially the same answer to a similar question, which, according to Cohen, "leads one to infer that nobody pointed its outrageousness out to him." Of course not, they all think the same way at CBN and no one dares doubt the teaching of Guru Robertson, because doubt is a stepping-stone to dissent, and Pat Robertson can't tolerate dissent. Pat Robertson gets his marching orders directly from God, and, therefore, in contrast to Albert Einstein, his need for understanding is a very low priority. We—individually and collectively—have the capacity to shape tomorrow by the thoughts we have today. The thoughts that Pat Robertson has today could make tomorrow a very frightening time for all of us—especially if he had the power of the presidency behind him.

Under President Robertson, foreign policy would stress an arms build-up instead of the more widely endorsed policy of arms reduction, and open dialogue with the Russians would be severely thwarted. Pat's expressed belief that, "Karl Marx was a Satanist priest" is not conducive to a parley with the Russians. The cold war of the past could warm up considerably with "Rambo" Robertson in command. Beyond the obvious detrimental effects of a speeded-up nuclear arms race and the increased tensions in Soviet-American relations, there would be another horrendous possibility under President Pat Robertson. Suppose one day Robertson truly believed that God wanted to start the endgame for humanity and he hears the Almighty whisper in his ear, "My son, push the button. Now!" Outrageous? Ridiculous? Farfetched? Impossible? I think not. During a press conference in Buffalo, New York, I expressed my concern about having a man sitting next to the button who might think he heard God telling him to push it. It made the quote of the day in *USA Today*, I imagine because it was eye-catching copy. But when Charles Gibson confronted Robertson with this quotation on "Good

Morning America," Pat claimed that I was, despite being "a right nice guy," a liar, an adulterer, and someone whose opinion wasn't worth much. (During the next few months Robertson would wrongly accuse me of "multiple adultery" and call me a "mixed-up kid" and a "little flaky.") I guess when you don't have a good response you must resort to name-calling.

However, can we afford not to consider the possibility of Pat's believing that God is telling him to do something most people would consider very unreasonable? The facts of Robertson's life and career certainly seem to justify the question, and it deserves a response rather than a simple denial. For example, in 1966, Pat's father, Democratic Senator A. Willis Robertson of Virginia, asked Pat for help in his tough reelection campaign. Pat's response was an emphatic "No," because God had told him, "You cannot tie my eternal purposes to the success of any political candidate." Hmm. I guess God has changed His mind about Pat getting involved in politics. Of course what really changed was Robertson's mind, which he frequently confuses for God's. The French philosopher Jean-Paul Sartre wrote, "Man is nothing else but that which he makes himself." In 1966, Pat made himself a minister who hated politics; twenty years later, he made himself a politician who loved religion. By the way, Pat's father lost the election by a narrow margin.

Here is another, even more heartless, example of unreasonable orders God dictated to Robertson: Pat's wife, Dede, was nearing the end of her pregnancy with their second child, when Pat informed her that he was headed for the wilderness of Canada to be alone with God. Of course that meant she was left alone during the most crucial time of her pregnancy; and as if that weren't bad enough, she also had to single-handedly look after their toddler son and oversee a scheduled move into a new home. Her desperate pleas for Pat not to leave her at that time fell on deaf ears. Pat Robertson only wanted to hear from God, and he told his wife, "This is God who's commanding me," and it was off to the woods for a pow-wow with the Almighty. In response to letters she wrote begging him to come home, because she "needed him desperately," Pat wrote back, after conferring with his pal the Lord of the Universe, that she would have to get by alone. Nice guy.

People at CBN loved these stories, because they were proof that Pat put God above everything else. Nobody ever questioned whether or not God really told Pat to turn his back on his father's plea for help and to abandon his wife just at the time she needed him the most. These just don't sound to me like things a loving God would order somebody to do, especially when it undercuts the cherished value of the family. Could Pat the prophet have used "divine revelations" to suit his own purposes, like prophets of the past? These unreasonable directives from God received a public airing in an article written by T. R. Reid and published in the September 11, 1987, edition of the *Washington Post*, yet it caused no discernible reaction. Again, nothing seemed to stick to the teflon preacher. But candidate Robertson should not be let off the hook on this issue—the hearing of disembodied voices is a serious problem, with major ramifications for all of us. I'm not alone in expressing fear that Pat's apocalyptic religious beliefs could affect President Robertson's foreign policy. On the December 21, 1987, "NBC Nightly News with Tom Brokaw," the Reverend Donald Dunlop, who is pastor of the church where Pat was ordained and also tendered his resignation from the ministry, said: "In practical terms, it might mean that if the world is going to come to a catstrophic end anyway, what is to prevent me from pushing the button."

The real problem with getting specific instructions from "God" is that they rule out reasonable discussion or debate. God said it, that's it. If God is your ally and confidant, opinions of others don't matter, regardless of how well reasoned or intellectually rich they may be. Direct orders from God preclude compromise and common sense; and, worse, opposition becomes heresy. In the realm of foreign policy, common sense and compromise are essential elements in maintaining peace. If you don't think so, note how overzealous religious fundamentalists have turned the Middle East into a powder keg. That's why the possibility of Pat Robertson's finger being near that button really worries me, and it should worry you, too.

Whether the President of the United States hears voices or not, the threat of a nuclear holocaust looms large on humanity's horizon because of the swelling number of people who believe that God wants it to happen, and they are, quietly and almost unnoticed, taking steps to hurry that happy day along. A 1984 Yankelovich poll indicated that 39 percent of Americans believed that the earth will be destroyed in a nuclear Armageddon. The Armageddon scenario thickens with each passing day, and Pat Robertson is its ringleader. I firmly believe that the distorted way he views the world and the future would have a dramatic impact on the way he would handle foreign affairs. You will not hear about Armageddon in his political speeches, because it will be draped in the more readily acceptable language of political conservatism—such as "peace through strength." Recently, I have found myself becoming increasingly more conservative on many political issues; however, the concept of a nuclear war as a tool of justice and salvation has absolutely nothing to do with a choice between a liberal and a conservative approach to government policy. It is a purely religious speculation that, because so many believe and support it, has the potential to become a reality. In fact, during the 1970s almost 20 million people, including Ronald Reagan, bought a book written by a riverboat captain turned minister titled *The Late Great Planet Earth*, whose message was that God long ago planned that humans would fight a decisive nuclear battle in which the forces of good would eliminate the bad guys. This conflict supposedly can't be avoided because God wants it to happen. The seeds for this understanding are planted in Chapters 38 and 39 of the Book of Ezekiel.

Who was this Ezekiel? He was a priest who was deported from Jerusalem to Babylon in 598 B.C. and preached among the exiles until 570 B.C. By his own account, the people thought of him as a storyteller. He was a visionary, a man whose imagination was constantly on fire. His writings contain four long, violently imaginative visions that evoked the power and magnitude of God, and they earned Ezekiel the title of Father of Apocalyptic Tradition. Following the prophetic traditions, Ezekiel promises God's retribution on Israel for her collective and national sins, but he also goes a step farther by emphasizing individual retribution for personal sins. He preached about an inner conversion, the need for a new heart and a new spirit. Yet it is his apocalyptic allegory of Gog (the leader of the immense army that symbolizes all those who stand against God) and his mob—which Robertson believes represents Russia and the Eastern Bloc Communist nations—that has won Ezekiel a place in the hearts of today's fundamentalist Christians. The story was meant to console the pessimistic exiles by showing them that God was going to utterly destroy the evil forces that threatened their existence. All of the apocalyptic literature employs creative descriptions of the cosmological upheavals that will announce the coming of the "Day of the Lord." The stories are sprinkled with fantastic beasts and angels acting as messengers between God and the prophet. If Ezekiel were living today he would be making horror movies. Yet Pat writes: "When you look at the holy books of other religions, you find fantasy and bizarre supernatural events that do not commend themselves to reasonable people. But the Bible is actually authenticated by history." What has been authenticated is that some of the writings thought to have originated with Ezekiel had actually existed long before his time.

The great battle portrayed in Ezekiel is considered by scholars to be the first piece of genuinely apocalyptic literature. And its point, which was vividly driven home, was to convince the downtrodden exiles that all was not lost. Even though God was using the pagans to punish His people, the pagans were now taking their divine mission a bit too seriously and were actually planning on wiping out the chosen people completely; and by overstepping their divine commission to merely punish, they had become God's enemies and He planned on showing them His anger by destroying them in a blaze of fire from heaven.

The fire-from-heaven stuff still appeals to the moralists of today, who firmly believe that by now God has certainly become fed up with the wicked, and Ezekiel fuels their fantasy for the elimination of all of what they think is wrong with the world and the instantaneous establishment of a heavenly utopia here on earth, ruled by King Jesus and administered by them. Many biblical scholars have wondered about the state of Ezekiel's mind. T. J. Meek, in *Hebrew Origins*, writes: "There is a close relationship between prophecy and insanity. The kind of temperament that lends itself to psychic experience, to automations, may result in genius or it may become psychopathic and lead to melancholy and outright insanity." E. C. Broome, in *Ezekiel's Abnormal Personality*, suggests that Ezekiel exhibits behavioristic abnormalities consistent with paranoid schizophrenia. "A true psychotic," his characteristics include "periods of catatonia," "an influencing machine," "a narcissistic-masochistic conflict, with attendant phantasies of castration and unconscious sexual regression, schizophrenic withdrawal, delusions of persecution and grandeur." Well, that sounds as if Ezekiel ought to know a lot about our future. While he is regarded as a prophet, it is interesting to note that most of his prophecies were not very accurate. In *The Date and Character of Ezekiel's Prophecies*, M. Buttenwieser claims that "the entire first part of the book, that is chapters 1-31, are not real prophecies but are only disguised as such. They are, without exceptions, *vaticinia post eventum*," that is, they are "predictions" of what has already happened. It is like betting on a televised football game that is airing on tape delay, when you had already heard the final score on the radio. Ezekiel is one of the most colorful characters in the Bible. He was a foot-stomping, clenched-fisted preacher who would moan and groan in public in order to catch the attention of the passing exiles—and Robertson fully believes that Ezekiel's vision of the future was an authentic revelation from God that will soon be manifested. "Playtime is over." The family of man has a date with destiny.

> The Day of the Lord will come like a thief, and then with a roar the sky will vanish, the elements will catch fire and fall apart, the earth and all that it contains will be burned up. Since everything is coming to an end like this, you should be living holy and saintly lives while you wait and long for the Day of God to come, when the sky will dissolve in flames and the elements melt in heat. What we are waiting for is what he promised: the new heavens and new earth, the place where righteousness will be at home.

That description of the hot day in store for us comes from the Second Letter of Peter (Chapter 3, verses 10-13). Interestingly enough, historical investigation of the letter reveals that it was written after Peter's death and was possibly the work of one of the Apostle's disciples. Even though scholars have doubts about the authorship, fundamentalist Christians have no doubts about it being the revealed word of God that accurately presents our destiny. "Playtime is over."

The vast majority of evangelical-fundamentalist Christians who dominate radio and television believe that peace is not in the cards because God is dealing humanity a holocaust that will kill nine million Jews in an effort to get them to worship Jesus Christ. Jimmy Swaggart summed it up best in a television sermon delivered on September 22, 1985:

> I wish I could say we will have peace. I believe Armageddon is coming. Armageddon is coming. It is going to be fought in the valley of Megiddo. It's coming. They can sign all the peace treaties they want. They won't do any good. There are dark days coming. The problems of Africa will not be solved. The problems of Central America will not be solved. The problems of Europe will not be solved. It's going to get worse. I'm not planning on going through the hell that is coming. The Lord will descend from Heaven with a shout. My Lord! I'm happy about it! He's coming again! I don't care who it [Armageddon] bothers. I don't care who it troubles. It thrills my soul.

Somehow Brother Jimmy's being thrilled by the prospects of a bloodbath for those who do not bow down to his Lord Jesus doesn't sound very loving or Christian. Robert G. Ingersoll's assessment that "if Christ was good enough to die for me, he certainly will not be bad enough to damn me for honestly failing to believe in his divinity" sounds a lot closer to reality than does Swaggart's rhetoric. Nor does it sound right that the "Prince of Peace" is opposed to peace; yet the volatile television evangelist Jim Robison, who at President Reagan's invitation delivered the opening prayer at the 1984 Republican Convention, preaches just such a claim: "There'll be no peace until Jesus comes. Any preaching of peace prior to this return is heresy; it's against the word of God; it's Antichrist."

For these television preachers, the arms race is good for the human race. In truth, however, more than anything else, it symbolizes each individual's failure at communication, reconciliation, and understanding and stands as an ugly monument to humanity's fear and closed-minded national chauvinism. For those readers wishing to get the full picture of this doomsday belief-system and its impact on U.S. policy in the Middle East, I strongly recommend reading journalist Grace Halsell's short and readable book, *Prophecy and Politics.*

Summing up President Robertson's foreign policy can be reduced to one word: Armageddon. The domestic policy plank for Pat's new G.O.P.—which no longer stands for the Grand Old Party, but now means God's Own Party—proposes to penetrate society with the truth of the Gospel and it will be nailed down by the principle that dissenters are devils.

A strong clue to the way Robertson will act in the future is the way he has acted in the past, although I fully realize that people can change. Many a young liberal grows into an older conservative. Yet, in speculating about how Pat Robertson will perform his duties as president, it is not likely that he will stray very far from previously held positions—because the Truth does not change. Armed with an exceptionally high degree of arrogance and self-assurance, Pat is apparently convinced that he is in full possession of a changeless truth. Of course he will mask his true feelings in the acceptable language of moderation because he realizes that for the sake of political survival he must, which is just what the pentecostals feared.

I had my first glimpse of Pat's public modification of a stated view when he appeared on Phil Donahue's show in the spring of 1987. Phil and Pat were having a pleasant little chat, when Phil coyly asked what he must have known to be a trick question, "Do Jews go to heaven?" It was a clear variation on the "God doesn't hear the prayers of Jews" statement that caught a lot of flap for the head of the Southern Baptists a few years ago.

Pat's entire body began to stiffen—for two reasons: first, I'm sure he wanted the conversation to stick to politics and it irritates him that other "politicians" do not have to discuss their religious beliefs; and, second, he knew the question was asked to trap him. After years of watching Pat close-up in all sorts of different situations, I recognized a mannerism he exhibits when he is uncomfortable with what he is saying: His neck tightens up and it expands and contracts during pauses in his speech. I could see this happening as he hesitantly lurched into his answer to Phil's question. I was stunned by his answer. I suddenly realized that Robertson would go a lot further in his campaign than I ever imagined possible, because he clearly demonstrated a willingness to back off from the truth as he understands it. Compromise was a trait I had never seen in Pat Robertson, but his answer compromised his own beliefs. To remain faithful to the dogma of fundamentalism, Pat's answer would have had to be "No," because in order to make it into Heaven you must renounce your sinfulness and accept Jesus Christ as your Lord and Savior—period, no exceptions, end of story! This is not something that Jewish people are in the habit of doing; and, by refusing to go along with the program, they, along with everyone else who refuses, have sealed their own fiery fate. Now, on national television no less, Robertson claimed that there *is* an exception, because the Jews get a special deal from God. Here is the transcript from the Donahue show:

Phil: Do Jews go to heaven?

Pat: The Jews go to heaven in relation to their own religion. And what does their religion say? It's very clear. They go to heaven if they keep all the commandments of the Jewish law. And if you go back into the Old Testament you see that it was necessary, in case they didn't, to have animal sacrifice. That's what was set up in the Old Testament. And in accordance with keeping all of their laws, they are God's chosen people, no question about it.

Phil: When I get to heaven, which I will be doing some day, there'll be Jews there?

Pat: Abraham, Isaac, and David, Jacob, I think, for starters are some rather eminent Jews who will be there welcoming us all, I hope; the ones of us who are going to go.

Phil: So that you don't have to be a Christian to be good in God's sight, in God's eyes?

Pat: Phil, in order to be right in God's eyes you have to do what the Bible says. I may point out that the Biblical truth—I'm a Christian minister, I'm not backing off my Christian beliefs—if one is a politician or a ruler, if you will, or the servant of all the people, in a political sense, it's totally different. I mean, the tenets of Christianity, the Catholic Church, the Protestant Church, are very clear. The tenets of Judaism are very clear, and we work together as best we can with these various groups. But in the body politic we cannot take Christianity, we cannot take Judaism, we cannot take any other religion and enforce it on everyone. That's totally wrong and totally against the traditions of this nation.

Phil: So you don't have to be bathed necessarily in the blood of our Savior Jesus Christ in order to go to heaven?

Pat: Phil, the position of all the churches is that there is salvation in none other and there is no other name given under heaven whereby we must be saved than in Jesus Christ. That was said by Peter, who is considered by the Catholics, of which you are one, the first Pope. That was his word and that's what we all believe. That's the Nicene Creed, it's the Apostle's Creed. I'm not going to back off of the beliefs of my faith. That's what we believe. Now the Jews have a little different deal. If they want to keep their law, if they want to fulfill the covenant, if they want to have the sacrifices provided in the Book of Leviticus, then that is what's available for them. That's the way it is.

Or is it? Pat seemed to be saying that if the Jews followed faithfully the ceremonial law, or compensate by Temple sacrifice, they could sneak in through the back door of Heaven. But there is a wrinkle in what he said. Perfect lifetime compliance with the law is impossible, and Temple sacrifice has been unavailable since the Second Temple was destroyed in A.D. 70; therefore, the practical result is that no unconverted Jews go to heaven, and the reassurances offered by Pat are illusory. Phil followed up on Pat's claim with:

Phil: Okay, but that sounds like you're saying two different things.

Pat: They are two different people. The Jews are special people; they are the chosen people of God. They've got a unique relationship with God. But Jesus Christ, as you know, came as the Jewish Messiah. He said "I'm the Messiah."

Audience: [No.]

Pat: I'm sorry, but that's what He said He was.

The audience's resounding "No" to Pat's statement that Jesus said He was the Messiah clearly demonstrated that they recognized his theological shallowness, because Jesus never claimed, either directly or indirectly, that He was the Messiah. In fact, Jesus forbade people to proclaim him the Messiah. True, there are a few passages in the Gospels where Jesus *appears* to refer to himself as such; however, serious scholars of the New Testament, including those with conservative outlooks, agree that these passages are written in the words of the evangelists who had come to believe that Jesus was the Messiah. Jesus regards his Messiahship as a satanic temptation that must be rejected. Still, faulty theology aside, Pat Robertson had put on the political mask of moderation, which hid his true face. Once in office, maybe he would feel free to remove the mask—and to remove as well many of the freedoms we Americans now enjoy.

The picture I will now paint of Pat's possible domestic policy is colored only by what he has said regarding the key issues of the day and not what he now says in campaign speeches. This picture is based not only on my first-hand observations over an extended period of time but also on those of former associates with whom I have spoken and other "insiders" who have contacted me, as well as on what I have heard Pat say in private and on my thorough examination of his writings.

One of the dominant impressions Robertson left with me was that he was not content with being a Christian within a secular nation; he wanted the United States to be a Christian nation. CBS News national-affairs correspondent Lesley Stahl questioned Robertson about this on the October 4, 1987, "Face the Nation" broadcast. Here's that exchange:

> Stahl: Do you think the American people are ready to elect an evangelical reverend to be president of the United States? And I ask because the polls have shown that up to now they really haven't been.
> Robertson: Lesley, there's a deep feeling in our country that the church as an institution should be on one side, the government as an institution should be on another, and neither should try to interfere and mix with the two.
> Stahl: So you don't think this should be a Christian nation? Yes or no?
> Robertson: I don't think it's going to be possible. We are not one now—and I don't frankly see it happening any time in the future.
> Stahl: I don't want to belabor this, but I'm intrigued that when I asked you this question, now twice, you won't just say no, and I want to know why that is.
> Robertson: I don't want to say no, and the reason is because if the people want this to be a Christian nation, it's up to the people—but they can't do it through law; it's got to be through their own beliefs.

Before entering politics, Pat's desire for this country to be a Christian nation was so strong that he had no qualms about distorting American history to support his thesis that it has been in fact a Christian nation since its birth.

Using the tools that build successful television ministries—oversimplification and exaggeration—Pat deliberately deceived his audience in order to promulgate his political gospel. Yet in his book *Answers*, Pat says that "exaggerating" is a form of lying. He writes: "Lying is a deliberate attempt to deceive by use of any form of untruth." (Still, on the campaign trail Robertson claimed that he was never an evangelist but a broadcaster and that he never practiced faith-healing but only believed in the power of prayer to heal.) Pat Robertson sets strict standards for others. He instructs his readers not to say the boss is out when he is in his office or to tell someone you enjoyed the meal they cooked if in fact you did not. However, he is much easier on himself, especially when he is pushing his gospel of truth, discrediting his detractors, or covering up his sinful transgressions.

Pat writes that "fornication is sex between two unmarried people." He himself was guilty of that sin, but what is more interesting than his human slip is that it revealed his proclivity for deception. He had no problem with lying in falsifying his actual wedding date in order to cover up the sexual sin—he was protecting his wife. It's strange that he had a problem with my lie, which also was told to protect a woman. Ed Cohen, who has been an "unfaithful" but observant viewer of the "700 Club," pointed out that deception does not appear to be offensive to Robertson. In a letter to me, Cohen said: "A member of the studio audience asked Robertson about the story of Rahab the Harlot (in Joshua), and how God could have blessed her deception in hiding spies. In what followed, Pat Robertson explicitly said that deceiving others with calculated half-truths is commended as moral in the Bible, and he adroitly avoided answering whether or not outright lying to achieve godly purposes is biblically permitted."

Pat is a great half-truth teacher of American history, and his tremendous ability to communicate a sense of absolute certainty made his lessons believable. Professor Pat taught that America was founded on biblical principles and that the doctrine of separation of church and state was not the intention of the Founding Fathers. He backed up these erroneous claims by selectively quoting the historical record; that is, he presented half the truth.

While writing this book, I tried to square Pat Robertson's history lessons with the facts by reading a number of history books that focused on early America. Much to my surprise, I discovered that the Founding Fathers made a conscientious effort to keep God out of the governmental process. True, many early settlers were religious, yet they also feared, with good reason, religious persecution. While Pat Robertson and Jerry Falwell both preach that our government was founded on the word of God, the truth is that neither God nor the Bible are mentioned in the Constitution—which may be the reason that this cherished document has endured for more than two hundred years. In chapter 7, I quote from such great Americans as George Washington, Thomas Jefferson, Roger Williams, Thomas Paine, James Madison, Benjamin Franklin, John Adams, and Abraham Lincoln to show the error in Robertson's theory that this is a Christian nation. In fact, neither Thomas Jefferson, Benjamin Franklin, nor John Adams believed in the divinity of Jesus; and, according to the beliefs of Pat Robertson, their unbelief should have landed those distinguished Americans in Hell for all eternity. Holy cosmic justice! Eternity is a stiff penalty to pay for not believing the unbelievable.

Will one of President Pat Robertson's domestic goals be to bring America back to the Bible and make our nation a Christian nation? It's a question that must be asked, especially in light of the following outrageous exchange between Robertson and his two co-hosts, Ben Kinchlow and Danuta Soderman, which took place on the January 11, 1985, "700 Club" program:

> Robertson: The war that we're fighting is on many fronts right now. Jesus Christ is the commander, and he has said, "I've come to bring life and bring it more abundantly." Well, he's Lord of everything; he's Lord of communications; he's Lord of education. . . . Social welfare is God's service, and government is God's service. It's all God's service.
>
> Soderman: How can you disentangle your beliefs and convictions from the way you are governed? I mean, everything that has occurred around the world today is a political cause or a religious conviction. I mean if you look at the Muslims and the Jihad; you look at the Judeo-Christian ethic that this country was founded on, its all religious conviction entangled into the government of the people. So how can you pull them apart and say they are not one?
>
> Robertson: Danuta, you can't. What the people object to is the institution of the church coming into the institution of government and saying, "Here's how you ought to run things." But you said, "Should Christians get involved?" Individual Christians are the only ones really—and, and Jewish [long pause] people, those who trust the God of Abraham, Isaac

and Jacob—are the only ones that are qualified to have reign, because hopefully they'll be governed by God and submitted to him . . . who would be better to take dominion over the universe than those whom God has taken dominion over first?

Kinchlow: Obviously you're not saying that there are no other people qualified to be in government or whatever if they aren't Christians or Jews. What you are saying is—

Robertson: Yeah, I'm saying that. I just said it. [Soderman laughs nervously.] I think anybody whose mind and heart is not controlled by God Almighty is not qualified in the ultimate sense to be the judge of someone else. . . . So, yes, I did say that. You can quote me.

I just did, and that quotation speaks for itself, saying louder than I ever could that President Robertson would like to make this a Christian nation, run by Christians for Christians, and almost reluctantly, Jews would be tolerated. On the same show, Pat spoke about Christians' "taking dominion over the universe," and also played history professor as he explained how the founding of our country happened spontaneously when the Founding Fathers, all devout Christians, got together for a prayer meeting. Too bad there isn't a law against passing off fantasies for history. In a letter to me, Ed Cohen (who unlike Pat Robertson passed his bar exam) said: "This segment is crucial because it clearly establishes that Robertson could never taken an oath of office in good faith, to uphold Article VI, Section 3, of the United States Constitution: '. . . no religious test shall ever be required as a qualification to any office or public trust under the United States.'"

I mentioned Robertson's "Christian and Jews only" plan for government workers on numerous radio shows and in many interviews with the press. Apple pie on a picnic table would get a bigger response from flies. There simply were no outcries from the press. It was, however, briefly mentioned near the end of a two-page piece on Robertson that appeared in the September 28, 1987, issue of *Time* magazine. Much to my surprise, the article reported that Robertson vehemently denied making any such statement. However, Robertson did mention that nonbelievers would have no place in his administration because "I don't think that atheists have their act together." And apparently neither do Mormons; about them, Pat has this to say in *Answers*: "Their religious beliefs are, to put it simply, wrong," and, "When it comes to spiritual matters, the Mormons are far from the truth." (That book answers such burning questions as: What is God like? How powerful is Satan? Is oral sex okay? Does the Bible allow sex for pleasure? Are interracial dating and marriage all right? Is physical punishment of children allowed in the Bible? Is hypnosis wrong? Can I lose my place in heaven? Are organ transplants permissible? When should a Christian disobey the civil government? and What do you think of long hair for a man? The answers are like a bad movie plot: predictable and an insult to one's intelligence.)

Candidate Pat Robertson does not have to embrace atheists and Mormons because they don't make a very large voting bloc. To my mind, Pat's denying he said something that has been immortalized on videotape indicates a character flaw similar to those that forced a couple of Democratic presidential candidates—Gary Hart and Joe Biden—out of the race. The October 26, 1987, issue of *Time* carried my letter to the editor pointing out the truth. The day that magazine hit the stands, I was a guest on WOR-TV's "People Are Talking" and played the videotape on the air. Even with this proof in existence, it does not stick to the teflon preacher.

I found the most interesting part of the original *Time* story to be an accompanying photograph. It spoke louder than the words by showing a group of Pat's placard-waving supporters, mostly women wearing "Robertson '88" tee-shirts. Among the sea of signs bearing the message "Pat for President" was one proclaiming: "Jesus is coming soon!" Its bearer clearly understood why Pat Robertson was running for president.

Before moving on to other domestic-policy possibilities of a Robertson administration, I'd like to expand briefly on a potentially menacing concept that the aforementioned exchange between Pat, Ben, and Danuta gently touched upon. It is too important to leave unexamined, because it gives us a glimpse of Pat's hidden agenda.

Robertson, in talking about who is qualified to hold public office, doesn't use such words as *lead, govern,* or even *rule*; instead, he uses *reign.* On the surface, that choice isn't such a big deal; however, at the same time he also expresses the notion of taking "dominion over the universe." Words like *reign* and *dominion,* which conjure up images of a medieval kingdom, illustrate Pat's goal of establishing a worldwide kingdom of believers whose sole objective is to help make the invisible kingdom of God become a visible kingdom on earth. Part of the plan for reaching that goal was the establishment of CBN University—a graduate school designed to combat this country's unrestrained pluralism, which Pat claims has led to the decline of Western civilization—to train charismatic Christians how to take dominion over every facet of our society through courses offered in government, media, business, education, and science. I lectured on television in one such course at CBN, and one of the graduates is now working at Fox Broadcasting in Hollywood; another is on the staff of ABC News in Washington.

There is a little known but very radical movement within Christianity that seeks a second reconstruction of American society. Its adherents, known as Reconstructionists, propose the abolition of democracy, the reinstitution of slavery, and capital punishment for adultery, sodomy, Sabbath-breaking, apostasy, witchcraft, blasphemy, and—believe it or not—incorrigibility in children. Fun guys! The movement is headed by Rousas Rushdoony, the author of more than thirty books, all dealing with education, cultural issues, and law. The white-bearded Rushdoony, who is seventy-one years old, thinks that it is blasphemous to try to prove there is a God or that the Bible is true, and that God's universal law is exactly as it was revealed to ancient Israel and that it should serve as a model for modern theocratic nations. Despite some superficial differences, Rushdoony's eschatology is right in line with Robertson's prophecy; he believes that Jesus will rule the earth before the end of time. For Rushdoony, democracy is heresy. He is opposed to pluralism because "in the name of toleration, the believer is asked to associate on a common level of total acceptance with the atheist, the pervert, the criminal, and the adherents of other religions." Those frightening words come from his huge opus—more than 1,600 pages in two volumes— *The Institutes of Biblical Law.* Let's hope Hollywood never turns it into a miniseries.

According to Rushdoony, women can't claim equality with men, and there should be no public education for children. He is also opposed to long-term mortgages, because he considers the practice unbiblical. The reason I mention this extremist is because of the Reconstructionist connection to CBN University. CBNU professor Joseph Kickasola has a long history as a Reconstructionist; and the Dean of the Schools of Law and Public Policy is Herb Titus, another well-known Reconstructionist, who admits that the school uses many of Rushdoony's books as texts. Rousas Rushdoony, it comes as no surprise, has also been Pat Robertson's guest on the "700 Club." Anyone interested in a quick but informative review of this movement should read Rodney Clapp's excellent article in the February 20, 1987, issue of *Christianity Today.*

In one of Robertson's most popular books, *The Secret Kingdom,* he shares eight universal laws that God revealed to him under a full moon on the Virginia Beach waterfront. Robertson claims these "kingdom laws" are immutable and that even God must obey them. The very concept of immutable spiritual laws is considered a heresy throughout most of Christianity, and even some bible-believers consider Pat's teaching of such laws an indication that he is really the Antichrist. The notion that you can tap into some source of spiritual power by following certain rituals and secret formulas is the basis for occultism. David Hunt claims, in his book *The Seduction of Christianity*, that the Robertson teachings closely resemble Rosicrucianism.

How does Pat Robertson intend to make God's invisible kingdom a visible reality on earth? Simple, he'll start by weeding out the crabgrass of evil that is destroying the moral lawn of America. Pat's attitude very much resembles that of the early Christians who expected a literal Kingdom of God with the return of Jesus. As time rolled by, many began to understand that the "kingdom" that Jesus spoke about merely symbolized a state of transformed consciousness and not a new earth ruled by the Messiah. Yet Robertson tenaciously clings to the notion of bringing the Kingdom of God into existence, and he considers that task his mission and his destiny. How far removed his holy ideas are from those of the person he claims to follow; Jesus taught that the kingdom is among us already and all that we need to do to manifest it is to love. For Jesus Christ, understanding was essential; for Pat Robertson, evil-crushing is vital. Once again, if you think this "kingdom" stuff is something from Pat's past, hear what the preacher-turned-politician said after his stunning success in the Michigan caucus in 1986, "The Christians have won! . . . What a breakthrough for the Kingdom" (quoted in *Newsweek*).

A Robertson administration is likely to mean a serious setback for women: In Pat's view, women should be more domestic and less involved in worldly affairs. It would be that simple. No matter what Pat says to the contrary or what evidence he supplies to refute it, I am firmly convinced that Pat considers women evil temptations to be avoided. Dede, his faithful wife, is solely responsible for whatever advances women have made within the organizational structure of CBN, and they are significant. Despite that fact, high-ranking female executives with real power do not exist at CBN. Dede Robertson has also goaded her husband into officially moderating his views on women. However, as one man observing another, it appears that women scare the hell out of Pat Robertson, even though he is fully aware that for the most part it was women—those who sent in their money and those who toiled long and hard for little pay—who created CBN. They find him appealing, and they have tremendous love for him. Yet the bottom line in Robertson's mind is that, because Eve caused the downfall of Adam, women should pay the price for her sin. Again, this is purely the impression I have received from Pat's everyday behavior.

The political reality is that he must now embrace women, even though his deepest wish may be to turn the clock back to the time when women didn't even have the right to vote. The belief that women are second-class citizens is vividly reflected in Pastor Pat's teachings on marriage. His *Answer* book, published in 1984, sheds serious doubt about the author's ability to reason. Robertson writes: "A wife has the ability to make her husband the head of the household by urging him to take his proper role as priest in the home." Also: "The wife who refuses to submit to the husband and fights him all the time will make him apprehensive about following the Lord." And: "The wife should submit to his leadership, even though she may disagree with it." And: "Regretfully, a woman with great abilities sometimes marries a man who does not have much ability. This wife must resist the temptation to dominate her husband. Her husband will sometimes make decisions that the wife feels are wrong. She must either gently persuade her husband that he is wrong, or else pray that God will change her husband's mind. A woman has voluntarily surrendered a portion of her autonomy to her husband when she marries."

According to Pat's teaching, the only time a woman is freed from being submissive to her husband is when he wants her "to become involved in bizarre sex practices" or "to engage in group sex." I don't know which is the worse problem in Pat's mind, sex or women. Maybe they are indistinguishable evils. I do know that if I had been Robertson's campaign manager, the first thing I would have done was to burn every available copy of Pat's *Answers* book. Obviously, on the two main women's issues—ERA and abortion—Mr. Robertson takes a very hard line against both.

Rights. We the people of the United States have certain inalienable rights that are guaranteed by the Constitution. *Inalienable* means that they cannot be taken away. The Fourteenth Amendment, ratified after the Civil War in order to ensure the just treatment of blacks, guarantees due process and equal protection under the law to "any person." The freedoms this ensures are taken almost for granted. Only the occasional threat to these freedoms by racial jurists wake us up to the fact that they could gradually be eroded. The possibility of such an erosion as a result of a Robertson presidency deserves and demands our attention.

Just as God is very real to Pat, so is the Devil. When Pat's wife wrote to him in the Canadian wilderness begging him to come home when she desperately needed him, *Time* reported, Robertson was troubled and recalls wondering, "Was God telling me to go home or was it Satan?" Perhaps Satan tricked Dede into writing Pat, just as he tricked Eve into getting Adam to take a bite of the apple. But Pat, being on better speaking terms with God than Adam was, didn't bite and stayed in the paradise of the Canadian wilderness. Robertson believes that the devil is sly and cunning, with more tricks of deception up his sleeve than the greatest of magicians; so talented, in fact, that he can trick entire cities and nations. In *Answers,* Pat writes about having once come under demonic attack as he was waking up in his room in a hotel near Seattle. He was bombarded by thoughts that everyone was against him, and he was seized by a suicidal depression. Just before completely falling to pieces, he realized what was happening and he cast the devil out of the room. Later he learned that the Seattle-Tacoma area led the nation in suicides and reached the conclusion that the area is under a strong demonic influence that specializes in depression. In his book, Robertson writes:

> Just as the angels have archangels and higher powers, the demons have what are called "principalities and powers." It is possible that a demon prince is in charge of New York, Detroit, St. Louis, or any other city. Particular sins are prevalent in certain cities. One city might have rampant homosexuality, while another might be troubled by excessive lust. In another, it might be witchcraft or spiritism. Nations, as well as cities, can be gripped by demon power. This could explain the willingness of the German people to tolerate the attempt of Adolf Hitler and the Nazi SS to exterminate all of the Jews in Europe.

Pat Robertson specializes in offering simple solutions to complex problems and, worse, claiming that these solutions come from God. Pat believes that Satan is so clever that he has infiltrated the government, and, as president, he would like nothing more than to kick him out. A chord that was strummed again and again while I was working at CBN was that the government, in an unholy partnership with Satan, was tricking people into not trusting God and therefore failing to become what God wanted them to be.

A look at two kinds of people, the alcoholic and the homosexual, provides a picture of how Pat's theological perspective allows him to see clearly that Satan has wormed his way inside our government, causing it to become rotten to its core. An April 1987 Gallup poll indicated that about 87 percent of Americans view alcoholism as a disease; yet Pat Robertson views alcoholism as a sin. From Pat's perspective, alcoholism has nothing to do with chemical imbalances or genetics. Likewise, homosexuality is a sin. It has nothing to do with genetics or choice. Pat writes, in *Answers:*

> Although lust, homosexuality, drunkenness, gluttony, and witchcraft are expressions of sinful flesh, these things can also be expressions of demonic activity in the lives of people.

(Oops, it was the devil that made me eat too much pasta last night, and I thought it was just my wife's good cooking.) On the campaign trail, Robertson has suppressed anti-gay rhetoric, but the substance is still here and was clearly demonstrated in a radio interview with Irv Homer in Philadelphia on October 7, 1987, when Pat claimed that AIDS was the result of homosexuals' breaking universal moral laws, and that additional research money to help find a cure for the disease was useless. By classifying these conditions as sins, there is no need for understanding homosexuality or for having compassion for the alcoholic. Sins have no rights; and, according to Pat, the government has no right to pander to or protect people whose "sinful" behavior can be corrected by simply acknowledging their problem and asking God to fix it for them. But is it that easy? Recent scientific research strongly supports the theory that a susceptibility to alcoholism can be inherited. But categorizing alcoholism as a disease doesn't automatically eliminate the role of volition and environment, and a case can be built for the important role of free will in a person's becoming an alcoholic. When it comes to alcoholism, there are no clear-cut, black-and-white answers to its cause or treatment, and we must for now accept the gray area in which the problem resides.

There are no shades of gray for Robertson. Pat thinks that the government treats deviants as if they were a privileged minority and creates programs that legislate tolerance of their sins, giving sinners an excuse for not accepting personal responsibility for their transgressions against the laws of God. But we the people don't have the opportunity to vote on what is a sin. Robertson and his fellow fundamentalist guardians of the Truth are the only ones qualified to make such a designation, because their minds and hearts are controlled by God Almighty. I think it is fair to conclude that many of the freedoms that we take for granted may be seriously threatened should he ever be in a position to try to legislate his own brand of morality. Strangely enough, even the freedom of religion would be in jeopardy, because as Ed Cohen points out in his book, "It is clear that 'cults' and Jehovah's Witnesses have no rights to exist, as far as he [Robertson] is concerned."

However, the Robertson administration would go to great lengths in order to protect the rights of "true" Christians, that is, his kind of Bible-believing Christians. Evidence for the possibility of special treatment being offered to Pentecostal Christians comes directly from the "700 Club." On the broadcast of September 12, 1984, Danuta Soderman, in her innocent and effervescent way, asked Robertson a question about a case in which the state was prosecuting a couple from Indiana for negligent homicide in the death of their child, who died when the parents withheld necessary medical care because as a test of their faith God "commanded" them not to seek medical help. In the view of the state, they committed what amounted to murder; yet in the minds of these believers, had they provided medical help for the child they would have been guilty of the far greater crime of deficient faith.

While Robertson informed his audience that the husband and wife were members of a heretical sect and therefore guilty as charged by the state, he did say that God could very well command a "true" believer to perform an action that the state might consider illegal. What position would Pat take if a believer found himself in the pickle of obeying a direct command from God and therefore breaking man's law? He would have them appear before a special church tribunal charged with the responsibility of discerning whether or not they received an authentic word from God commanding them to do something illegal. This church tribunal would have the governmental power to insulate a believer from prosecution if they were convinced that the revelation the believer received actually came from God. I'm not sure that this tribunal would actually issue God a subpoena for His or Her appearance in court, but without such an Almighty witness the "evidence" submitted on behalf of the defendant would be inconclusive or inadmissible hearsay. I don't think Pat heard this concept while he was studying law at Yale.

If that judicial mix of church and state isn't weird enough, Ed Cohen points out something even more bizarre in *The Mind of the Bible-Believer*. Cohen writes:

He [Pat] stated that there should be special Christian police, empowered to control crime solely on the basis of telepathic messages from God, without regard for familiar Constitutional protections and without any requirements for the usual kinds of evidence. Purely supernatural evidence has not been part of our law since "spectral evidence" was admitted at the Salem witch trials.

Can you imagine the implications of having Pentecostal cops getting a special word of knowledge from God that could result in your arrest without any tangible evidence or, perhaps worse, the officer detaining or arresting you simply because God told him that you were about to commit a crime. Buying a bottle of wine or an issue of *Playboy* could trigger a message from God to a member of the Robertson goon squad. Cohen adds:

Legal institutions under Robertson would be as different from the ones we know as the Third Reich was from the Federal Republic. It may also be significant that Robertson says that considerations of efficiency ought to outweigh individual rights of privacy considerations in the governmental use of computer data from individuals, and that his own headquarters operates along the lines of a high-security military compound.

I am not the paranoid type, nor do I see conspiracy lurking around every corner. Before I began working on this book, I still had respect for Pat Robertson, and during the beginning stages of writing it I regarded him as misguided, but essentially harmless. However, the deeper I dug and the more I analyzed his beliefs and actions, the more fully convinced I became that he had the potential to be dangerous. The wish not to engage in mud-slinging dictated that the tone of the book not be overly critical of him. I was critical, but careful and restrained. The times have changed. I am no longer naive, and Pat is no longer simply an evangelist. Playtime is over. The tough questions demand to be asked. I'm grateful that men like Ed Cohen take the time and trouble to alert us to the potential dangers that lie in store for us if Robertson, or some less overtly religious clone of him, seizes control of this country. I firmly believe that it is fair for all Americans to examine Pat Robertson's ministry and his beliefs very carefully, because not to do so could be disastrous.

The death penalty and abortion are two social issues that have generated heated debate in America, and they clearly demonstrate the schizophrenic nature of Pat Robertson's beliefs. It is possible for a person to have no moral qualms about abortion and still object to the death penalty; however, I find it impossible to understand how a person who completely rejects abortion on moral grounds can still support capital punishment. If life is sacred, even in its early embryonic stage, then it must at all times be cherished and protected. Yet, Pat Robertson is vehemently opposed to the taking of any unborn child's life and, at the same time, fully supports ending the life of a convicted criminal. For Pat, one is murder and the other is justice; yet for Pat to say that they are different is for him to deny his own belief in the sacredness of life.

Is that tiny piece of flesh, less than two inches long, that is aborted really an "unborn child," or does it simply have the potential for becoming a human being? There are two ways of looking at it, and the difference between what is human and what has the potential of being human is important. Those formless cells could hardly be called human in the true sense of the word, and the theological gibberish about when the soul enters the body is simply that—theological gibberish. The sexist theology of St. Thomas Aquinas stated that "ensoulment" took place during the third month after conception for a male and during the fourth month for a female. Personally, I happen to agree with Andy Rooney, who said during a "60 Minutes" essay: "I'm against abortion, but I like the people who are for it better than those who are against it." Rooney is at home in the shaded areas of life that don't offer clear choices. Abortion is the most divisive issue facing America today, and the proponents of the opposing points of view must learn to listen to each other, which is something Pat Robertson seems incapable of doing.

Pat's propensity for seeing evil everywhere and in everyone who hasn't been saved will have a strong influence on his choice of people to serve in his Cabinet and on whose advice he chooses to follow. He is far too smart to select only born-again advisors, but the real problem is not the faith of the Cabinet members, it is Robertson's inability to accept the advice of a person who does not share his faith. This is not idle speculation, because Pat's own writing provides the seed for doubt regarding his willingness to listen to and respect the thoughts of a person who's mind is not controlled by God. In *Answers*, Robertson writes:

> Unconverted man may try to do better, but he is ultimately doomed to failure.

No one is quick to take advice from a failure, but Pat is more than happy to grab a good idea from a sinner who is a winner. When we were redesigning the "700 Club" in an effort to convert it from a dull, languid talk-show into a fast-paced, upbeat magazine format, Pat had no problem adopting the principles that the satanic secular television people had discovered and successfully used to attract a larger audience. When I informed Pat that his long interviews with guests defied the current wisdom that brevity was best—research showed that the attention of most viewers of news and information programs was no more than seven minutes—he readily changed to a keep-it-moving format that had us quickly changing the subject before the viewer had a chance to get bored and change the dial. We went from dreary to dazzling, and the ratings went from dismal to dandy. Pat believed that God's soldiers had to be as cunning as the devil's troops. We had to be as wise as the world, but not of the world. Pat could pick and choose from what worked in the world, but he remained distrustful of anyone, no matter how clever or successful, who had not surrendered to the will of God: they were inherently failures who could not be trusted.

It is likely that a disproportionate number of Pat Robertson's personal staff of presidential advisors and some members of his Cabinet would be Pentecostal Christians. While I personally think that this would be a problem, the far bigger problem is whether or not Pat would listen to those experts in various fields of government who do not share his understanding of God. I doubt that he would. It is one thing to accept a creative idea from an unbeliever in the trivial field of television; it is quite another to accept advice about the godly job of governing from an ungodly person. The bottom line is that Robertson has only one advisor, the God he has created in his own mind. Ed Cohen, a social psychologist, had this to say in a letter responding to my request for a professional diagnosis of Pat Robertson based on what Cohen had seen of the preacher on television and what he had read of Robertson's writings:

> Quite apart from the religious indoctrination in whose idiom his delusions are expressed, Robertson deludes himself that he is under the control of God, acting out a predetermined sequence of events peculiar to him, and this is the product of his own imagination and not simply lifted from the religious sources. The same capacities that a normal person consciously uses to sort out the world and act upon it are somewhat removed from his conscious volition, and serve instead to manage the delusions and furnish the rationalizations that keep those delusions from obvious collision with

the truth. By surrounding himself with sycophants, he supplies himself with social confirmation of the delusions. He is the same in that regard as Lyndon LaRouche or George Lincoln Rockwell. Because disjointed, absurd, and often sanguinary content are such familiar staples of biblical religion, a Robertson does not seem so obviously crazy to the casual observer as a LaRouche or a Rockwell does.

Talk about hitting the nail on the head!

Pat Robertson has always surrounded himself with a closed circle of trusted aides. CBN was a closed society that had all the qualities of a cult. The people believed they were saved, they felt protected, they thought they were chosen, and they were cut off from the world. After I left CBN and its cultic nature began to dawn on me, I hesitantly expressed these feelings during radio interviews. They were flatly denied by Robertson. However, using a criterion that Robertson himself outlined in *Answers*—in response to the question, How do I recognize a cult?— I am even more convinced that CBN is just that. Pat Robertson wrote that "cults frequently attempt to instill fear into their followers," and I certainly found that to be true of Pat and others at the top of CBN. When donations were down, it was assumed that sin had invaded the company. We had corporate prayer meetings at which attendance was mandatory, to uncover the evil and cleanse our souls. Later, during the height of the PTL scandal that rocked the evangelical community, Robertson believed that it was "urgently necessary" to hold a staff prayer meeting in order to seek and ensure God's continued blessings on CBN. In a May 19, 1987, memo to all the staff, Pat wrote:

> Only 40 people showed up for the prayer meeting prior to the telethon. Attendance at this Friday's meeting will not be optional. I am going to ask that all supervisors take a count of who is there. I want all personnel— and I mean *all*, including paid counselors—to be in attendance.

At CBN, the familiar "Let us pray" became the threatening "You will pray." Unacceptable behavior was met with threats of dismissal. There was tremendous pressure to conform to the spiritual norm, which resulted in the suppression of doubts. The foundation of CBN faith was a fear of God, which fostered an infantile sense of guilt and threatened the fires of hell as a psychological sledgehammer that pounded out fearful submission. Strike one against CBN.

Robertson continued his description of cults:

> Cults often center around a man or woman who is trying to gain power, money, or influence from manipulating people.

No comment needed. Strike two against CBN. Robertson concluded thusly:

> A final mark of a cult is the unwillingness of the leaders to let people grow up.

One of the trademarks of a grownup is the ability to make reasoned and free inquiry into a problem or situation and then make an independent and rational decision. At CBN, we were treated like children; we were given the answers but not allowed to ask any questions. Reading either Thomas Merton, the Christian monk, or Bertrand Russell, the agnostic philosopher, was considered satanic. Strike three against CBN. If Pat Robertson were intellectually honest, he would have to admit that CBN, along with the Catholic church and scores of other religious organizations, are also cults.

Protected, comforted, supported, and encouraged by his small circle of advisors, Pat responds violently when any of them comes under attack or criticism from others within the corporation. In early March 1987, I was contacted—first by letter, then by phone—by a former CBN executive who desperately wanted to talk with me in person. Because of the hostility, even death threats, that I had encountered, I was not initially responsive to meeting with him. But because of his gentleness and his obvious sincerity, and my curiosity about the explosive information he claimed to have about CBN, I agreed to meet him at a popular restaurant in the San Fernando Valley on March 23. He recognized me from the picture on the cover of my book. I spotted him because he was carrying a copy of the book. We felt like a couple of real spies.

First, some facts about X, whose identity I promised not to reveal, but whose authenticity can be documented by a number of journalists from major newspapers with whom he has spoken but to whom he did not provide the information you are about to read. X was trained in the field of personnel development by a major corporation before his services were sought by CBN. At CBN, he was the manager of employee relations and employment. He was fired on August 4, 1986, by Pat Robertson. His sin had been to reveal to Pat a list of irregularities and improper actions of key ministry executives. He still is a Christian, a strict and theologically conservative Christian. His wanting to talk with me had nothing to do with getting back at Robertson; he was hurt, frustrated, and confused and simply wanted to talk. In fact, during our lengthy conversation he would not reveal the specifics of the information he had presented in memo form to Robertson, because he believed that the biblical thing to do when you have a grievance against a brother— and at this point he still considered Pat a brother in the Lord—is to confront him directly with it in private. If this attempt at reconciliation fails, you are then free to discuss your problem in a public forum. He did, however, feel free to talk in generalities that he sprinkled with specific, but less volatile, facts.

As X spoke, I made the following notes:

> The treatment of employees, the policies, and the procedures were medieval in the sense that an employee's challenging an idea or policy or directive or the boss was thwarted. If the boss seems wrong, don't confront him or discuss the problems with others. . . . Your duty is only to pray for the boss. I tried to introduce openness and honesty and I was rebuked and finally fired by Pat. I honestly think Pat was blinded by power, pride, and deceit. CBN was cultlike in the way it legislated morality: one poor woman was actually told that she would be fired if she divorced her husband, even though it was known that she was once beaten so badly by the bum that she wound up in a shelter for battered women. It was sick. Pat is a self-appointed prophet who puts himself above the law.
>
> People were paid off for their promise of silence after they were terminated. The ministry was $20 million behind in accounts payable; it was sinful. The payroll was over $44 million a year.
>
> Psychological tests, designed for convicts, were given to employees, and all they did was manage to create paranoia. Some employees who were laid off were asked to sign a silence clause that stipulated they would not talk to the press or bring a suit against CBN. Staff members who were considered rebellious were isolated and led to believe that they were being influenced by Satan. One shunned, psychologically tormented young man committed suicide three months after he was fired without cause. Deceit, secrecy, and thirst for power . . . lots of posturing for higher positions . . . was common practice among executives—even though such behavior is un-Christ-like.
>
> The center was built to last a millennium, as if CBN were to rule the kingdom after the return of Jesus.

And he wouldn't tell me the bad stuff, at least not at that time.

We continued to exchange letters and phone calls. In one letter X wrote:

> After reading your book cover to cover, I feel like I've gotten to know you fairly well. While I can't endorse or receive the wide range of philosophical/religious beliefs and notions you seem to be moving toward, I certainly appreciate your journey and your pursuit of truth. I also stand by you in so many of your CBN conclusions, and yes, I agree that you were very gentle toward your exposing Pat.

While he and I were miles apart on our understanding of religion, still our friendship grew closer because we listened to each other and respected each other. He once sent me a book on Christianity and in the accompanying note said, "God did not tell me to send you this book. . . . It just happens to be one of my favorite accounts of a guy's thorough investigation of the truth . . . not at all what is 'sold' over the airwaves by so many 'not-for-profit' organizatons." Because our communication was honest and open, we were able to break down the wall of misunderstanding that religious intolerance tried to build between us. X said his home was always open to me should I ever find myself in the city where he lives. After eight months of unemployment, X landed a good job in a major city and is well on his way to recovering from the emotional pain he suffered at the hands of Pat Robertson. He is one of the lucky ones; by being fired, X managed to escape the fires of hate and prejudice that eventually would have consumed him.

In October 1987, X sent me a package of information, for my eyes only, labeled "CBN-gate." It revealed that his repeated efforts to receive an official CBN hearing that would examine the wrongdoing and coverup he discovered, and also review his dismissal, met with no success. Even letters to three members of the CBN board of directors drew no response. In a June 24, 1987, letter to board member Tucker Yates, a soft-spoken, honorable southerner who liked wearing loud plaid pants, X wrote:

> Today, I am asking you to use your influence in helping me present some rather alarming matters to Pat Robertson and the CBN Board of Directors. The issues are far too serious for the Board to continue to ignore, and CBN must take immediate corrective action! Included in my presentation are facts of fraud; abusive employee treatment; irresponsible psychological counseling and testing by unlicensed employees and agents; and heavy-handed tactics that led to the suicide of a former CBN employee/CBNU student (documents and testimony can lead to a "wrongful death" conclusion for which CBN would be held acountable).

In another letter, dated June 19, 1987, to board member Bob Slosser, a white-haired former journalist who ghost writes many of Pat Robertson's books, X wrote:

> Bob, you are personally aware of much of the wrongdoing and coverup I found while performing my duties as CBN's Manager, Employee Relations & Employment. Beyond the results of my assigned Employee Relations investigation into CBN's Telemarketing Department, the conclusions of which were fully substantiated and thoroughly documented, and delivered by certified mail to Pat Robertson's office on 8/12/86, there are other very serious matters that CBN must acknowledge and rectify. Ask CBN's Corporate Chaplain about the extraordinarily large number of "suit happy" employees. Now ask the CBN Board why this is so. Do you have any idea of the amount of money that has for years been given to former CBNers to keep them out of court? You may not have trouble with "hush money" payments . . . You must however, concern yourself with one tragedy involving CBN's "heavy handed" tactics that some feel led to the death of a former employee and student.

In another letter, also dated June 19, 1987, to board member Harald Bredessen, a jovial ordained minister and long-time Robertson friend and confidant, X wrote:

> CBNers, both former and present, who know of the unthinkable wrongdoing that thrives in CBN's secrecy, have the responsibility to speak up after their efforts to influence change have failed. This is beginning to happen today (reference Eph. 5:11 and 1 Tim. 5:20-21). At issue, Harald, are immoral and illegal actions. We're talking about fraud; abusive employee treatment; irresponsible psychological counseling and testing by unlicensed individuals; and the possibility of CBN's negligence in allowing "heavy handed" tactics that led to a former student/employee suicide. Don't you feel a responsibility to hear the whole story?

I guess not.

Because of the possibility of his bringing a suit against CBN, X asked me not to reveal the specifics detailed in two pages of documentation he shared with me. However, he did permit me to disclose the following write-in comments from an opinion survey given to 116 CBN employees during a two-day period in December 1985:

> Immediate supervisors have actually lied to cover up something.

> Second-level supervisor does ungodly things.

Treated like children, watched in chapel, bathroom breaks timed.

You should not be fired because you voice your opinion.

Feeling like a child when I have to go to the bathroom.

Supervisors should not stand outside the chapel door recording names.

Constantly having privileges taken away.

CBN sounds like a great place to work.

The following is the last part of Pat Robertson's August 4, 1986, response to X's letter:

> . . . The personnel function at CBN has to do with employee screening, orientation, orderly processing of records, and career pathing of employees.
>
> Our Board of Directors never intended any Assistant Personnel Manager to be named the Grand Inquisitor to bring broad accusations across our organization of "pride, power, and deceit" then to demand retribution on these individuals.
>
> Jesus said, "Judge not that you be judged. For the measure you mete shall be meted out to you."
>
> There is no room at CBN for those who level broadside accusations at key members of our team, then demand accountability for inner motives which only God Himself can judge.
>
> We cannot tolerate such attitudes and method of operation in our Personnel Department lest our organization seethe with discord and suspicion.
>
> Upon receipt of this memorandum, you are hereby discharged from employment at CBN effective immediately.
>
> Please vacate your office today and turn over all records, keys, and credit cards to your Department Head.
>
> I am
>
> > Sincerely yours,
> > Signed: Pat

Remember, Pat Robertson took time out from running for the presidency of the United States to write that memo. The head of Human Resources at CBN read this letter to his staff as an example of what happens to whistleblowers who go over his head.

Although he was an executive with an important job at CBN, X was not part of the inner circle that surrounded Pat, so his honest criticism got him canned. Pat Robertson was no more receptive to bad news about his key executives when it came from one of their wives. Pat couldn't fire them, he simply ignored their pleas for help. One night in May 1987, a woman from Boston left a frantic but cryptic message on my phone-answering machine. I returned the call. She was the ex-wife of a former CBN vice-president of finance. I knew him; he held that job during my time at CBN. She told me that she read and enjoyed my book and felt she just had to talk with me.

My initial puzzlement over her call turned to shock as she revealed the horrors she endured while her husband worked at CBN. Her husband was a wife-beater, and she silently endured the battering for years. Then he began abusing their teenage daughter, which pushed his wife's endurance to the limit. She went to Pat and told him the gruesome details of her marriage. Pat's response: zip. She was stunned by Pastor Pat's complete lack of compassion. Robertson appears really not to care about people but only about advancing the social and political agenda of his gospel. The woman's husband was an important part of the team and Pat wasn't about to confront him with his domestic problem. Pat needed his financial expertise and what the jerk did at home didn't matter.

The woman was in tears as she told me that her teenage daughter ran away from home to get away from her father. Then one day this godly CBN executive just walked out on the distraught woman, moved to another city, and married a younger woman. Her struggles did not end with his departure, because he failed to provide her with any financial assistance, and therefore, on top of everything else, she was now also broke. Tearfully, she told me that she had reason to believe her daughter was working as a prostitute in Los Angeles, and she desperately wanted me to help her find the girl. What little admiration I still had left for Robertson completely dissolved with that phone call. Pat's concern for family values appears to be little more than empty rhetoric designed to attract votes from morally righteous citizens.

Pat Robertson's inner circle at the White House is not likely to be very different from what it was at CBN: composed of yes-men who can do no wrong and will keep the truth from reaching the boss. I believe that Robertson would turn the Oval Office into a bully pulpit that would pound out a domestic policy indistinguishable from the moral message of the Christian right. It could probably be summed up as "self-proclaimed moral righteousness."

This quality was clearly demonstrated during the summer of 1987 at a campaign rally at the Blackhawk Hotel in Davenport, Iowa. Before Robertson entered the room and took the podium, heads were bowed under white straw hats encircled with red-white-and-blue banners emblazoned with "Robertson '88," as an elderly, balding man led the gathering in prayer. With eyes closed and hands raised, his free-form prayer proclaimed that "righteousness exalts a nation" and asked God to forgive the moral sins of America and once again pour out His blessings on the nation. The long-winded prayer ended with:

> And Father, as we look to your Word, we see, too, that wherever there were righteous leaders, you blessed that nation and we want this nation to be blessed of God. And so Father, we ask you now to raise up righteous leaders, men full of your wisdom, men full of your knowledge, and leaders full of your will and your purpose and your understanding. And we ask you to give us the discernment to recognize those leaders as you raise them up and that we would know to stand with them. Father, we think that Pat Robertson is one of those leaders that you have raised up; a man that we look upon as being righteous before you, and a man that is full of wisdom, and knowledge and understanding, a man that has a heart for the people and a heart for God—and we ask your blessing upon him.

The prayer was soon followed by pandemonium, as a smiling, waving Robertson made a dramatic entrance before the standing, clapping, cheering crowd. His anti-communist, pro-family speech was high on rhetoric, low on substance, and frequently punctuated with long periods of applause. In the typical Robertson fashion, the speech was riddled with Bible quotations and statistics. For example: "Thirty percent of all the divorces in America are the result of welfare laws," and "Eighty-five percent of the high-school graduates in one suburb of Philadelphia cannot read and write." The line that drew the loudest applause and the most amens was: "Ladies and gentlemen, as I think about America, and the America that you and I want, we must look for an America where husbands and wives love each other." Claiming that "the greatness of America is going to be restored through moral strength," Robertson suggested that "united in the holy cause of liberty and freedom" nothing will be impossible. "The future is ours."

H. L. Mencken wrote: "The worst government is the most moral. One composed of cynics is often very tolerant and humane. But when fanatics are on top there is no limit to oppression." I give my amen to that. I firmly believe that Pat Robertson wants to recast the country in his own image and change the moral climate by getting everybody down on their knees. With Pat in the White House, religion and politics will wed, and the marriage will form a powerful bond of intolerance, whose offspring will be hate and oppression. Americans believe that every citizen has the right to believe what he wants, but with fundamentalist Christians in power what we believe had better conform to their Truth. I believe that this intolerant attitude on the part of the fundamentalists betrays their own lack of faith in God. If God exists, then he is certainly big enough to take care of himself and to protect the truth of the Bible without any skull-crushing help from his faithful supporters. The God of the fundamentalists apparently needs their help to get the rest of us to believe.

Near the end of the aforementioned 1980 New Year's Day prayer meeting, Pat said over and over again, "The slain of the Lord will be many. Playtime is over." The words are still haunting me. They were delivered in a tone of voice that suggested Pat looked forward with relish to the coming Day of the Lord that would once and for all destroy everyone that he believes is evil. When I first heard those words eight years ago, I was in the psychological grip of a cult. Physically moving away from CBN did not automatically free me from those chains. The only way I could become free was to learn independent, objective thinking. The fact that years after my ouster I still maintained a degree of respect for Pat Robertson indicates that I hadn't progressed very far in the field of free thought. The repressive religious training of my youth bears part of the responsibility not only for making me an easy prey for easy praying but also for my slow recovery.

On October 9, 1987, at the end of a phone interview on WMAQ-Radio in Chicago, Drew Hayes, the host, said, "You've been on with me a few times during the past year; we've talked about Tammy Faye, Jimmy, and Pat. But now I detect a sense of mission in your voice." He was right. As my recovery became more complete, I was able for the first time to feel a sense of anger at all the lies I was told in the name of God. Finally, after years of painful introspection and investigation, I was starting to think for myself, and Robertson was becoming more terrifying to me with each passing day. Playtime was over. I had to speak out more vigorously. I had to protest, sometimes facetiously. A radio interviewer said, "Pat Robertson claims that *Salvation for Sale* is filled with lies. Is it?" Without hesitation, I replied, "Oh no. There are no lies in *Salvation for Sale*. Pat must be confusing my book with his resumé, which apparently has a number of inaccuracies and exaggerations—like graduate study at the University of London being in reality an art class." Playtime is over.

And so is this "Update"—that is, after a brief personal perspective on faith.

"Life is like playing a violin solo in public and learning the instrument as one goes on," wrote the later Samuel Butler. I feel like a street-corner musician, with my battered violin case open beside me on the ground, as if crying out for the attention of uninterested passers-by. Few really listen, yet I play on, driven by a need to get better. I fight off the constant rejection, even from family, by taking strength from the occasional smile of approval, even if only for my dedication and not my actual playing.

For me, life is like the old gag about a guy who, simply wanting directions to Carnegie Hall, asks: "How do I get to Carnegie Hall?" The response he receives is "Practice." Great advice; directions seem useless, the person giving them is usually lost anyway. Everyone, from Pat to the Pope to Shirley MacLaine, seems to be pointing the way to salvation, but does anyone really know where or what it is? Whatever it is, it is hard to find because it's so *close*. It's right inside you. How do you get there? You don't start by asking someone else the way, because there is no yellow-brick road to salvation, and salvation is not for sale. It is nothing more than self-discovery and self-improvement. Practice is the way.

I've been groping along the highway of religion for forty years, and for most of that time I've been hopelessly lost, because I followed the directions given to me by people who seemed to really know where they were going. As it turns out, each was heading down a different deadend street. I'm weary from all the U-turns I had to make. First, I followed the Pope of Rome, whose directions were far from infallible. Then, I followed the Reverend Pat Robertson down the darkened street of fundamentalism—a horrifying journey that left me almost brain dead. Zen a few gurus gently led me down the path of Eastern mysticism, which turned out to be much to do about nothing. With them, instead of being born again, you come back again . . . and again. Now, I no longer practice religion, which I find a hopeless task that defies the maxim that practice makes perfect; instead, I now practice living. I've gotten off the highway of religion. I still explore lots of theological sidestreets, backroads, and even some occasional deadends, but the difference is that I'm doing the driving instead of being taken for a ride. I am also extremely leery of easy answers, and I admire these words of Albert

Einstein: "As for the search for truth, I know from my own painful searching, with its many blind alleys, how hard it is to take a reliable step, be it ever so small, towards the understanding of that which is truly significant."

In retrospect, I realize that I was fooled by Robertson's sincerity. Our emotions are stimulated by sincerity, and the more emotional we normally are, the more stimulated we become when we encounter sincerity, whether or not it is genuine or manufactured. When we think that a person is sincere, we more readily believe that they are telling the truth. For the most part, we prefer a person who seems to be real—that is the root of sincerity—to a person we perceive to be a phony, even if they happen to be right or we agree with what they say. Communications experts teach "sincerity" to those who are going to appear on television.

Charlie Chaplin once said, "Life is a tragedy when seen in close-up, but a comedy in a long shot." We like comedy, but we respond to tragedy. This is why televangelists are successful. Giving the audience what they like is not their objective; getting the audience to respond is. The cameras are zoomed into a close-up shot as they examine the tragedy and pain of life, and the audience can see the raw emotion and can feel the sincerity. The result is that the viewer has been stimulated. Like actors who are skilled at playing to the camera, the video vicars ooze sincerity, which is why candidate Robertson increased his base of support more than any other Republican presidential hopeful as a result of the "Firing Line" debate. On top of the sincerity advantage, just being on television gives evangelists an edge. The person who appears on television seems especially believable, and—maybe even more important—an authority on the subject being discussed. Television exaggerates and makes the preachers bigger than life—almost bigger than God. Once the prayers have hooked their prey, the camera pulls back to a long-shot and reveals the television preacher's emotional beliefs and his narrow solutions, and the viewer suddenly finds them acceptable. Religious beliefs are emotional, and the electronic church knows how to push, with great sincerity, all the emotional buttons.

I like to think that most television preachers begin with some level of genuine sincerity; however, the drive for souls, the demand for dollars to fuel their ministries, and the need to maintain their superstar status causes them to manufacture even more sincerity. They can cry and beg on cue. I hope that well-intentioned, honestly religious people in America will realize that genuine spirituality is more than emotion, more than sincerity, more than a theory on salvation or reincarnation, and a whole lot more than what is offered on television. We need to question and examine our beliefs, but it is a painful and time-consuming task that, sadly, few are inclined to undertake.

William James said: "Faith means belief in something concerning which doubt is theoretically possible." Can anyone really know what they believe? Sure, most of us can make a general list of our spiritual beliefs, often dogmatic certainties; still, that doesn't mean we really know what we believe. For most people, with the exception of extreme religious fanatics whose beliefs are memorized and kept locked up in a prison of fear, it is very difficult to articulate what they believe. I think that for the vast majority of us, no matter what our profession, economic status, or level of education, beliefs are fuzzy, a bit blurred around the edges and bathed in emotionalism. Our faith has been colored and shaped by our lives, influenced by the place of our birth and the beliefs of our parents, as well as by our friends. Facts, on the other hand, are clear, bright, and cold; moreover, they are not subject to debate. It is a fact that the Twins won the World Series in 1987, but whether or not they are the best team in baseball is arguable. Facts are backed up by evidence. Faith is supported by emotion. Unless your beliefs have gone unquestioned and unexamined, or have hardened into ritualistic dogma, it is their nature to change, as you change or as your circumstances change. Preaching to a person in need, whether that need is emotional, physical, material, or even only imagined, will be more successful than preaching to a contented mind. Those near death frequently try to get nearer to God. Newspaper columnist Jimmy Breslin summed it up best in Peter Occhiogrosso's *Once a Catholic,* a collection of twenty-five interviews with current and former Catholics, when he wrote: "Let a guy have one chest pain, one twinge in the chest, and he goes flying back to things he was taught in the third or fourth grade."

Our initial beliefs are built upon suppositions that have been handed to us and which we have accepted, usually without a great deal of critical analysis—especially if we were children when we acquired them. Now, a little more than a year after the first publication of this book, I am even more convinced of the importance of searching for your own truth and to look on doubt as a good friend. No one has all the answers, and with the wide range of divergence in the human family, there is bound to be a wide range of beliefs. Hating another because of their beliefs is a sign of weakness, both personal and spiritual. Yet there is no sign that religious bitterness will end any time soon. It has always been with us, and it looks as if it shall continue to be—no matter how mindless it appears. Thomas Jefferson wrote: "On the dogmas of religion, as distinguished from principles, all mankind, from the beginning of the world to this day, have been quarreling, fighting, burning and torturing one another, for abstractions unintelligible to themselves and to all others, and absolutely beyond the comprehension of the human mind." Yet, in the name of justice, it must stop soon or we will blow ourselves to pieces. While I can no longer consider myself a Christian, I firmly believe, after much thought, that the truth of Christ and the truth of humanism and reason are harmonious.

Woody Allen wrote: "The chief problem about death is the fear that there may be no afterlife—a depressing thought, particularly to those who have bothered to shave." Woody cleverly juxtaposes deep philosophical questions with everyday absurdities. For example: "Not only is there no God, try getting a plumber on the weekend." "The universe is merely a fleeting idea in God's mind—a pretty uncomfortable thought, particularly if you've just made a down payment on a house." In his movie *Love and Death*, Woody explores his two pet themes. Young Boris, a fictional youthful Russian version of Woody Allen, lapses into mystical musings while walking in the forest. He contemplates Christ: "If He was a carpenter, how much did he charge for bookshelves?" Boris then unexpectedly bumps into Death, whom he presses for details about the afterlife: "One key question: Are there girls?" Boris didn't get any good answers.

If Woody Allen had read Robertson's *Answers* he would have found out that: "Not only is there life after death, but God is going to give us new bodies, better than the ones we have now. We are not going to be disembodied spirits." Maybe I'll have more hair! With only a little less certainty, Pat continued, "Perhaps people will be assigned to watch over a planet or two. We do not know for certain what tasks we will be performing in heaven, but there will obviously be an ongoing, functioning universe." Unfortunately, Pat Robertson isn't joking. If I repent, maybe I'll get to watch over the planet Pluto!

It is finished. Again.

December 1987
Los Angeles, California